Why Millions of Moms, Dads, and Doctors Love *What to Expect*® *When You're Expecting*

"What every mother can't do without!"
—NIRA COLYN, MD

◆ ◆ ◆

"*What to Expect* is an incredible pregnancy resource. . . .
The book is very user-friendly and has an excellent index. . . .
Any topic you can think of can be looked up right away."
—BRENDA SMALLEGAN, RN, BSN

◆ ◆ ◆

"This book quite literally has it all. I have never found a more
complete yet completely enjoyable guide to a healthy,
happy pregnancy."
—SUSAN KANE, EDITOR-IN-CHIEF, *BABYTALK* MAGAZINE

◆ ◆ ◆

"*What to Expect When You're Expecting* is a lifesaver.
¡Muchisimas Gracias!"
—MIGUEL A. CANO, MD, FACOG

◆ ◆ ◆

"As a mother this book was my survival guide to getting
through the day."
—BALA MUNIPALLI, MD

◆ ◆ ◆

"A fabulous bible for new moms! I would have been 20 lbs. heavier
and a little less sane without *What to Expect When You're Expecting*!"
—CATHERINE SKOBE, MOTHER

"I love these books! They're full of useful information."
—SUZY A. THOMPSON, MD

♦ ♦ ♦

"I started reading *What to Expect When You're Expecting* the moment I found out I was pregnant. [It] provided me with a road map to a stress-free pregnancy."
—CAROLINE GOLDSTEIN, MOTHER

♦ ♦ ♦

"Excellent to allay patients' fears and provide information. . . . I recommend it highly."
—DONNICA L. MOORE, MD

♦ ♦ ♦

"This book revolutionized prenatal care in America."
—JAMES FAHERTY, MD

♦ ♦ ♦

"I read them faithfully for my two pregnancies and as a pediatrician find them to be right on."
—SUSAN WALTER MANGIAMELI, MD

♦ ♦ ♦

"This is the only book I recommend to my patients!"
—ELIZABETH DOYLE, MD

♦ ♦ ♦

"This is the 'must have' book for any expectant mother, whether it's your first baby or your fifth!"
—SOFIA GARCIA, MOTHER

♦ ♦ ♦

"As a maternity designer and as a mother myself, I know that there is no other book that means so much to so many pregnant women everywhere."
—LIZ LANGE
MOTHER, FOUNDER AND CEO, LIZ LANGE MATERNITY

WHAT TO EXPECT®

WHEN YOU'RE EXPECTING

FOURTH EDITION

by Heidi Murkoff
and Sharon Mazel

Foreword by Charles J. Lockwood, MD

*The Anita O'Keefe Young Professor of Women's Health
and Chair, Department of Obstetrics, Gynecology and
Reproductive Sciences, Yale University School of Medicine*

WORKMAN PUBLISHING • NEW YORK

To Emma and Wyatt, my greatest expectations
To Erik, my everything
To Arlene, with so much love, always and forever
To all the moms, dads, and babies everywhere

Copyright © 1984, 1988, 1991, 1996, 2002, 2008 by What to Expect LLC
Design copyright © by Workman Publishing

WHAT TO EXPECT is a registered trademark of What to Expect LLC
WHAT TO EXPECT When You're Expecting and the series were conceived by
Heidi Murkoff, Arlene Eisenberg, and Sandee Hathaway.

Library of Congress Cataloging-in-Publication Data
Murkoff, Heidi Eisenberg.
What to expect when you're expecting / by Heidi Murkoff and Sharon Mazel;
foreword by Charles J. Lockwood—4th ed.
p. cm.
Includes index
ISBN 978-0-7611-4857-9 (alk. paper)—ISBN 978-0-7611-5079-4 (hardcover)
1. Pregnancy. 2. Childbirth. 3. Postnatal care. I. Mazel, Sharon. II. Title.
RG525.M87 2008
618.2—dc22   2008052796

Book design: Lisa Hollander
Cover design: John Seeger Gilman
Cover illustrations: Tim O'Brien
Cover quilt: Lynette Parmentier, Quilt Creations
Cover photography: Davies + Starr
Interior illustrations: Karen Kuchar

Workman books are available at special discounts when purchased in bulk for premiums
and sales promotions as well as for fund-raising or educational use. Special editions or book
excerpts can also be created to specification. For details, contact the Special Sales Director at
the address below or send an email to specialmarkets@workman.com.

Workman Publishing Company, Inc.
225 Varick Street
New York, NY 10014-4381
workman.com

WORKMAN is a registered trademark of Workman Publishing Co., Inc.

Printed in the United States of America
First printing March 2008
35

MORE THAN I CAN SAY, TO ARLENE EISENBERG, MY FIRST PARTNER
IN WHAT TO EXPECT AND MY MOST IMPORTANT ONE.
YOUR LEGACY OF CARING, COMPASSION, AND INTEGRITY LIVES ON FOREVER;
YOU'LL ALWAYS BE LOVED AND ALWAYS BE REMEMBERED.

Thanks A Lot (More)

I F I'VE LEARNED TWO THINGS OVER the last 23 years, it's that kids don't raise themselves—and books don't write themselves (no matter how long you look at a blank screen).

Fortunately, I haven't had to take either job on by myself. For the kid raising (officially finished, though, let's face it—does it really ever end?), I've had the best partner-in-parenting out there, my husband, Erik—who also happens to be my partner in What to Expect. For the book writing, I've had dozens of colleagues and friends pitch in—contributing support, insight, and ideas in the creation (and re-creation . . . and re-creation . . . and re-creation) of four editions of *What to Expect® When You're Expecting*.

Some of those helpers have come and gone—but others have stood by since day one, and edition one. Thanks a lot to:

Sandee Hathaway, for all your valuable contributions to What to Expect. You're a great sister and an even greater friend.

Suzanne Rafer, editor and friend, who has faithfully guided What to Expect from conception through delivery four times over—dotting every "i," crossing every "t," deleting every misguided pun (and pair of parens). What's in a name? When it comes to What to Expect, a lot—and we have Suzanne to thank for the memorable moniker that helped launch not only 29 million copies, but hundreds of headlines, cartoons, and parodies.

Peter Workman, a publisher of uncommon integrity and uncompromising commitment—who believed in our book when bookstores didn't, who let What to Expect's grass roots take their slow and steady time sprouting, who never gave up on the little series that could, and did.

Everyone else at Workman who's helped with our latest delivery: David Matt, for believing in evolution (of Cover Mom), taking artistic chances, and overseeing our very challenging—and very successful—Extreme Makeover. John Gilman, for your extreme patience in this extreme makeover—and for making illustration magic happen. Lisa Hollander, for always being my favorite designing woman, as well as to Weiheng Tang. Tim O'Brien for bringing to life Cover Mom, The Next Generation—and for finally getting her off her rocker. Lynette Parmentier for re-creating as an actual quilt our iconic illustrated quilt. Karen Kuchar for inking our hot mamas (almost makes me want to run out and get pregnant again!) and Tom Newsom for our fabulous fetuses. Irene Demchyshyn for going with the flow and keeping the flow going. And my other phenomenal friends at Workman, including Suz2 (Suzie Bolotin), Helen Rosner, Beth Doty, Walter Weintz, Jenny Mandel, Kim Small, and Amy Corley. My other partner, Sharon Mazel. You're my mini-me, my other (better) half, my BFF—and I love you. To the beautiful Daniella, Arianne, Kira, and Sophia, for sharing your amazing mom with me (and for getting sick and breaking bones only when absolutely necessary). And to the doctor in the house, Jay, for his great biology lessons and his good nature—but mostly, for letting me be the other woman in Sharon's life.

Dr. Charles Lockwood, our remarkable medical advisor, for your concise and precise advice, your meticulous attention to detail (medical and otherwise), and your obvious compassion for moms and babies. It's truly incredible how much you know, how much you do (I get exhausted just reading your CV), and how much you care.

Steven Petrow (MG), Mike Keriakos, Ben Wolin, Jim Curtis (CSOB), Sarah Hutter, and all my wonderful friends and partners at Waterfront Media, for making our vision of whattoexpect.com and My What to Expect a reality. Thanks, also, to the amazing community of moms—not only for making our site the special place that it is, but for sharing your bellies, babies, and toddlers with me every day.

The two other guys in my life (a girl could get spoiled): Marc Chamlin, for your keen legal eagle eye, your business smarts, your unflagging friendship and support; and Alan Nevins, for your masterful management, phenomenal finessing, endless patience, persistence, and hand-holding.

Jennifer Geddes and Fran Kritz, for helping us get our facts straight (check . . .

check . . . check!). Dr. Jessica Wu, for your impeccable pregnancy skin care counsel, and Dr. Howie Mandel, for being such a good sport about the What to Expect questions I'm always sneaking in at my annuals. And always, to always-inspiring Lisa Bernstein, Executive Director of the What to Expect Foundation, for making miracles happen (plump, full-term miracles), and to Zoe, Oh-That-Teddy, and Dan Dubno.

To Erik, my partner in everything I do, always and forever, for all the reasons listed above, and more than I can list. There's no one I'd rather mix business and pleasure with, and I love you forever. And speaking of love, to my pride and joy (I'm not saying who's who), Emma (the baby who started it all) and Wyatt (the baby who followed). I love you guys—you've made me one lucky mama.

The adorable Howard Eisenberg, father and friend (not necessarily in that order); Victor Shargai (and John Aniello) for your love and support; and to the world's best (and newly trimmest) in-laws, Abby and Norman Murkoff. And to Rachel, Ethan, and Liz, Sandee's fantastic three, and to Tim, her Numero Uno.

To ACOG, for being advocates for women and babies, and to all of the doctors, midwives, nurses, and nurse practitioners who work every day to make pregnancy safer and happier for expectant families. Most of all, to all the expectant, new, and old moms (and dads) who've helped make each edition of What to Expect better than the last. I've said it before, and I'll say it again, parents are my most invaluable resource—so keep those cards, letters, and e-mails coming!

Thanks again, and again, everybody . . . and may all your greatest expectations come true!

Contents

Foreword to the Fourth Edition, by Charles J. Lockwood, MD xx
Introduction: Why This Book Was Born Again, Again xxii

Part 1: First Things First

Chapter 1: Before You Conceive 2

Preconception Prep for Moms 2

Putting It All Together • *It Takes Two, Baby* • *Pinpointing Ovulation* • *Conception Misconceptions*

Preconception Prep for Dads 12

Chapter 2: Are You Pregnant? 14

What You May Be Wondering About 14

Early Pregnancy Signs • Diagnosing Pregnancy • A Faint Line • *Testing for the Irregular* • No Longer Positive • *If You're Not Pregnant* • A Negative Result • *Testing Smart* • Making the First Appointment • Your Due Date

ALL ABOUT

Choosing and Working with Your Practitioner 21

Obstetrician? Family Practitioner? Midwife? • *Birthing Choices* • Types of Practice • Finding a Candidate • *Division of Labor* • Making Your Selection • *Pregnant and Uncovered* • Making the Most of the Patient-Practitioner Partnership • *So You Won't Forget*

Chapter 3: Your Pregnancy Profile 32

Your Gynecological History 33

This Book's for You • Birth Control During Pregnancy • Fibroids • Endometriosis • Colposcopy • HPV (Human Papillomavirus) • *Other STDs and Pregnancy* • Herpes • *Signs and Symptoms of Genital Herpes*

Your Obstetrical History 38
In Vitro Fertilization (IVF) • The Second Time Around • Your Obstetrical History Repeating Itself • Back-to-Back Pregnancies • Having a Big Family • Previous Abortions • *Do Tell* • Preterm Birth • Incompetent Cervix • *Your Pregnancy Profile and Preterm Birth* • Rh Incompatibility

Your Medical History 49
Rubella Antibody Levels • *Immunizations in Pregnancy* • Obesity • *Pregnancy After Gastric Bypass* • Underweight • An Eating Disorder • Having a Baby After 35 • *Is 35 the Magic Number?* • The Father's Age • *Uninsured, Mama?* • Genetic Counseling • *Pregnancy and the Single Mother*

ALL ABOUT
Prenatal Diagnosis...58

First Trimester...59
First-Trimester Ultrasound • First-Trimester Combined Screening • Chorionic Villus Sampling • *It's a . . . Surprise!*

First and Second Trimester....................................63
Integrated Screening

Second Trimester 63
Quad Screening • Amniocentesis • *A False Screen* • *How to Freak Out a Pregnant Woman* • Second-Trimester Ultrasound • *If a Problem Is Found*

Chapter 4: Your Pregnancy Lifestyle 68

What You May Be Wondering About 68
Sports and Exercise • Caffeine • *Caffeine Counter* • Drinking • Smoking • *(Don't) Put That in Your Pipe* • *An Early Baby Present* • Breaking the Smoking Habit • Secondhand Smoke • Marijuana Use • Cocaine and Other Drug Use • Cell Phones • Microwaves • Hot Tubs and Saunas • The Family Cat • *Is Hot Stuff Not So Hot?* • Household Hazards • *The Green Solution* • Air Pollution • *Domestic Violence*

ALL ABOUT
Complementary and Alternative Medicine......................85

Chapter 5: Nine Months of Eating Well 88

Have It Your Way • *Try These Instead* • Nine Basic Principles for Nine Months of Healthy Eating • *The Six-Meal Solution* • *No More Guilt* • The Pregnancy Daily Dozen • *Count 'Em Once, Count 'Em Twice* • *Vegetarian Proteins* • *Can't Find Your Favorite?* • *White Whole Wheat* • *A Little Fat Goes a Long Way* • *The Good Fat Facts* • *What's in a Pill?*

What You May Be Wondering About 104

Milk-Free Mom • *Pasteurized, Please* • A Red-Meat-Free Diet • A Vegetarian Diet • Low-Carb Diets • Cholesterol Concerns • Junk Food Junkie • *Shortcuts to Healthy Eating* • Eating Out • Reading Labels • *You Can't Tell a Fruit by Its Cover* • Sushi Safety • Hot Stuff • Spoiled Food • Sugar Substitutes • Herbal Tea • Chemicals in Foods • *Something's Cooking* • Pick and Choose Organic • *Eating Safe for Two*

Part 2: Nine Months & Counting:
From Conception to Delivery

Chapter 6: The First Month
Approximately 1 to 4 Weeks 120

Your Baby This Month 120

Making the Pregnancy Connection • Pregnancy Timetable

What You May Be Feeling 122

Symptoms? Starting Soon • A Look Inside

What You Can Expect at Your First Prenatal Visit 124

The Wholly Healthy Pregnancy

What You May Be Wondering About 126

Breaking the News • *For the Other Pregnant Half* • Vitamin Supplements • Fatigue • Morning Sickness • *Your Nose Knows* • Excess Saliva • Metallic Taste • Frequent Urination • Breast Changes • Lower Abdominal Pressure • Spotting • *When to Call Your Practitioner* • *No Worries* • HCG Levels • *HCG Levels* • Stress • Relaxation Made Easy • *Expect the Best*

ALL ABOUT

Your Pampered Pregnancy 144

Your Hair • Your Face • Your Teeth • Your Body • *A Day at the Spa* • Your Hands and Feet • *Making Up for Pregnancy*

Chapter 7: The Second Month

Approximately 5 to 8 Weeks 150

Your Baby This Month 150

What You May Be Feeling 151

A Look Inside

What You Can Expect at This Month's Checkup 152

What You May Be Wondering About 153

Heartburn and Indigestion • *Bringing Up Reflux* • *Heartburn Today, Hair Tomorrow?* • Food Aversions and Cravings • Visible Veins • Spider Veins • Varicose Veins • An Achy, Swollen Pelvis • Breakouts • Dry Skin • Eczema • *Belly Piercings* • Come and Go Belly • Losing Your Shape • Measuring Small • Measuring Big • Difficulty Urinating • Mood Swings • Depression • *Panic Attacks*

ALL ABOUT

Weight Gain During Pregnancy 166

How Much Should You Gain? • At What Rate Should You Gain? • *Why More (or Less) Weight Gain Isn't More* • Breakdown of Your Weight Gain • Weight Gain Red Flags

Chapter 8: The Third Month

Approximately 9 to 13 Weeks 170

Your Baby This Month 170

What You May Be Feeling 172

A Look Inside

What You Can Expect at This Month's Checkup 173

What You May Be Wondering About 173

Constipation • *Another Reason for Being Tired, Moody, and Constipated* • Lack of Constipation • Diarrhea • Gas • Headaches • *What's a Corpus Luteum Cyst?* • Stretch Marks • *Body Art for Two?* • First-Trimester Weight Gain • *Boys Will Be Boys* • Showing Early • Carrying Multiples? • Baby's Heartbeat • At-Home Dopplers • *The Heart of the Matter* • Sexual Desire • Cramp after Orgasm

ALL ABOUT

Pregnant on the Job.. 186

When to Tell the Boss • *The Pregnant Worker's Rights* • Making the Announcement • *The Juggling Act* • Staying Comfortable on the Job • *Carpal Tunnel Syndrome* • Staying Safe on the Job • *Quiet, Please* • *Getting All the Facts* • Staying on the Job • Changing Jobs • *Unfair Treatment at Work*

Chapter 9: The Fourth Month

Approximately 14 to 17 Weeks 198

Your Baby This Month 198

More Baby

What You May Be Feeling 200

A Look Inside

What You Can Expect at This Month's Checkup 201

What You May Be Wondering About 201

Dental Problems • *A Gum Alert* • *Pearly White Wisdom* • Breathlessness • *Expecting X-Rays?* • Nasal Stuffiness and Nosebleeds • Snoring • *Snooze or Lose?* • Allergies • *No Peanuts for Your Little Peanut?* • Vaginal Discharge • Elevated Blood Pressure • Sugar in the Urine • *Get Your Flu Shots* • Anemia • *Symptoms of Anemia* • Fetal Movement • Body Image • *A Pregnant Pose* • Maternity Clothes • *Looking Slim When You're Bulking Up* • Pre-Baby Jitters • Unwanted Advice • Unwanted Belly Touching • Forgetfulness

ALL ABOUT

Exercise During Pregnancy..................................... 215

The Benefits of Exercise • *Working in Workouts* • *Can You Kegel?* • *Exercise Smarts* • Exercising the Right Way When You're Expecting • *Thirty Minutes Plus?* • *Shoulder and Leg Stretches* • *Dromedary Droop* • *Neck Relaxer* • Choosing the Right Pregnancy Exercise • *Pelvic Tilt* • *Biceps Curl* • *Leg Lifts* • *Tailor Stretch* • *Hip Flexors* • *Squats* • *Waist Twists* • *Exercise in Bed* • If You Don't Exercise • *Chest Stretches*

Chapter 10: The Fifth Month
Approximately 18 to 22 Weeks 232

Your Baby This Month 232

What You May Be Feeling 234
A Look Inside

What You Can Expect at This Month's Checkup 235

What You May Be Wondering About 235
Heating Up • Dizziness • *When Too Much Is Too Much* • Backache • Abdominal Aches • *The New Skin You're In* • Foot Growth • Fast-Growing Hair and Nails • Vision • Fetal Movement Patterns • Second-Trimester Ultrasound • *A Picture That Lasts a Lifetime* • *Baby's First Mall Portrait* • Placenta Position • Sleeping Position • *Carrying Baby, Fifth Month* • Class Womb? • Carrying Older Children • Approaching Parenthood • Wearing a Seat Belt • Travel • *Jettisoning Jet Lag* • Pregnant at a High Altitude • *Pregnant Women Are Delicious*

ALL ABOUT
Sex and the Pregnant Woman 255
Sex Through the Trimesters • What's Turning You On (or Off)? • *The Ins and Outs of Sex During Pregnancy* • Sexercise • When Sex May Be Limited • *Getting Comfortable* • Enjoying It More, Even If You're Doing It Less

Chapter 11: The Sixth Month
Approximately 23 to 27 Weeks 262

Your Baby This Month 262

What You May Be Feeling 264
A Look Inside

What You Can Expect at This Month's Checkup 265

What You May Be Wondering About 265
Trouble Sleeping • *Save Time (in a Capsule)* • Protruding Navel • Baby Kicking • Itchy Belly • Clumsiness • Numbness in the Hands • Leg Cramps • *Stretching Away Leg Cramps* • *When Something Just Doesn't Feel Right* • Hemorrhoids • Breast Lump • Childbirth Pain • *Bleeding in Mid- or Late Pregnancy* • *Diagnosing Preeclampsia* • Labor Inhibitions • Calling the Labor Shots • Hospital Tours

ALL ABOUT

Childbirth Education 276

Benefits of Taking a Childbirth Class • Choosing a Childbirth Class • *Back to School* • *For Information on Pregnancy/Childbirth Classes* • Childbirth Education Options • *Classes for Second Timers*

Chapter 12: The Seventh Month
Approximately 28 to 31 Weeks 282

Your Baby This Month 282
Baby Brain Food

What You May Be Feeling 284
A Look Inside

What You Can Expect at This Month's Checkup 285

What You May Be Wondering About 285

Fatigue Revisited • Swelling • *Take Them Off, While You Can* • Strange Skin Bumps • Lower Back and Leg Pain (Sciatica) • Restless Leg Syndrome • *Count Your Kicks* • Fetal Hiccups • Accidental Falls • Orgasm and Baby's Kicking • Dreams and Fantasies • *Preparing Fido and Whiskers* • Handling It All • A Birth Plan • *Some Cookies with That Birth Plan?* • *Your Main Squeeze* • *Don't Hold It In* • *Lifesaving Screenings for Newborns* • Glucose Screening Test • *Doulas: Best Medicine for Labor?* • A Low-Birthweight Baby • *Signs of Preterm Labor*

ALL ABOUT

Easing Labor Pain 301

Managing Your Pain with Medications • *Pushing Without the Pain* • Managing Your Pain with CAM • *Just Breathe* • Making the Decision

Chapter 13: The Eighth Month
Approximately 32 to 35 Weeks 308

Your Baby This Month 308

What You May Be Feeling 309
A Look Inside

What You Can Expect at This Month's Checkup 311

What You May Be Wondering About 311
Braxton Hicks Contractions • Not-So-Funny Rib Tickling • Shortness of Breath
• *Choosing a Pediatrician* • Lack of Bladder Control • How You're Carrying •
Carrying Baby, Eighth Month • Your Size and Your Delivery • Your Weight Gain and
the Baby's Size • Baby's Position • Breech Baby • *Turn, Baby, Turn* • *Face Forward*
• *How Does Your Baby Lie?* • Other Unusual Presentations • Cesarean Delivery
• *Be in the Know* • Elective Cesareans • *Scheduled Classes for Scheduled C's* •
Repeat Cesareans • Vaginal Birth After Cesarean (VBAC) • Group B Strep • *Eat
Up* • Taking Baths Now • Driving Now • Traveling Now • Making Love Now • Your
Twosome • *Considering Cord Blood Banking*

ALL ABOUT
Breastfeeding 331
Why Breast Is Best • *Prepping for Breastfeeding* • *The Breast: Sexual or Practical?*
• Why Some Opt for the Bottle • Making the Choice to Breastfeed • *Nursing After
Breast Surgery* • *Got Pierced?* • Mixing Breast and Bottle • When You Can't or
Shouldn't Breastfeed • *When Father Knows Breast*

Chapter 14: The Ninth Month

Approximately 36 to 40 Weeks 338

Your Baby This Month 338

What You May Be Feeling 340
A Look Inside

What You Can Expect at This Month's Checkup 342

What You May Be Wondering About 342
Urinary Frequency—Again • Leaky Breasts • Spotting Now • Water Breaking in
Public • *Baby's Crying Already?* • Baby Dropping • Changes in Baby's Movements
• *Going Down?* • Nesting Instinct • *Getting Ready* • How Is Baby Doing? • When
You Will Deliver • *Do-It-Yourself Labor Induction?* • The Overdue Baby • *Massage
It, Mama* • Inviting Others to the Birth • *Foods to Bring It On?* • *Sounds Like a
Plan* • Another Long Labor? • Mothering • *What to Take to the Hospital or Birthing
Center* • *Fill 'Er Up*

ALL ABOUT
Prelabor, False Labor, Real Labor 358
Prelabor Symptoms • False Labor Symptoms • Real Labor Symptoms • When to
Call the Practitioner • *Ready or Not*

Chapter 15: Labor and Delivery 362

What You May Be Wondering About 362

Mucous Plug • Bloody Show • Your Water Breaking • Darkened Amniotic Fluid • Low Amniotic Fluid During Labor • Irregular Contractions • Calling Your Practitioner During Labor • Not Getting to the Hospital in Time • *Emergency Delivery if You're Alone* • Having a Short Labor • Back Labor • Labor Induction • Eating and Drinking During Labor • *Emergency Delivery: Tips for the Coach* • Routine IV • Fetal Monitoring • Artificial Rupture of Membranes • An Episiotomy • Forceps • Vacuum Extraction • *Vacuum Extractor* • Labor Positions • *Labor Positions* • Being Stretched by Childbirth • *Apgar Score* • The Sight of Blood

ALL ABOUT

Childbirth 380

Stages and Phases of Childbirth

Stage One: Labor 381

Phase 1: Early Labor • *For the Record* • *Call Your Practitioner If . . .* • Phase 2: Active Labor • On to the Hospital or Birthing Center • *Are Things Slowing Down?* • *Don't Hyperventilate* • Phase 3: Transitional Labor

Stage Two: Pushing and Delivery 391

A Baby Is Born • *A First Look at Baby*

Stage Three: Delivery of the Placenta 396

Cesarean Delivery 398

Part 3: Twins, Triplets & More:
When You're Expecting Multiples

Chapter 16: Expecting More Than One 402

What You May Be Wondering About 403

Seeing Double—Everywhere? • Detecting a Multiple Pregnancy • *Fraternal or Identical?* • Choosing a Practitioner • Pregnancy Symptoms • Eating Well with Multiples • Weight Gain • *What to Gain When You're Gaining for Two or More* • *Multiple Time Line* • Exercise • Mixed Feelings • Insensitive Comments • *Multiple Connections* • Safety in Numbers • *Multiple Benefits* • Bed Rest • Vanishing Twin Syndrome

ALL ABOUT

Multiple Childbirth 414
Laboring with Twins or More • *Twin Timing* • *Position, Position, Position* •
Delivering Twins • *Recovering from a Multiple Delivery* • *Breastfeeding for Two
Is Good for Mom, Too* • Delivering Triplets

Part 4: After the Baby Is Born

Chapter 17: Postpartum: The First Week 420

What You May Be Feeling 420

What You May Be Wondering About 421
Bleeding • Afterpains • Perineal Pain • *When to Call Your Practitioner Postpartum*
• Delivery Bruises • Difficulty Urinating • That First Bowel Movement • Excessive
Sweating • Fever • Engorged Breasts • Engorgement if You're Not Breastfeeding
• Where's the Breast Milk? • *Should I Stay or Should I Go Now?* • Bonding •
Rooming-In • Recovery from a Cesarean Delivery • Coming Home with Baby

ALL ABOUT

Getting Started Breastfeeding 435
Nursing and the NICU Baby • Breastfeeding Basics • *Keeping Track* •
Engorgement: When the Milk Comes In • *Next Stop: Easy Street* • The
Breastfeeding Diet • Leaking Milk • *Medication and Lactation* • Sore Nipples •
When Breastfeeding Gets Bumpy • Breastfeeding After a Cesarean Delivery •
Breastfeeding Multiples • *Bottle Baby* • *Tandem Nursing* • *Give It Time*

Chapter 18: Postpartum: The First 6 Weeks 450

What You May Be Feeling 450

What You Can Expect at Your Postpartum Checkup 451

What You May Be Wondering About 452
Exhaustion • Hair Loss • Postpartum Urinary Incontinence • Fecal Incontinence
• *Help for Leaks That Won't Let Up* • Postpartum Backache • Baby Blues •
Postpartum Depression • *Getting Help for Postpartum Depression* • *Thyroiditis
Got You Down?* • Losing Weight Postpartum • Long-Term C-Section Recovery •
Resuming Sex • *Craving More?* • Becoming Pregnant Again

ALL ABOUT

Getting Back into Shape 465

Basic Position • Pelvic Tilt • Leg Slides • Head/Shoulder Lift • Workout Rules for
the First Six Weeks

Phase 1: Twenty-Four Hours After Delivery 468

Phase 2: Three Days After Delivery 469

Close the Gap

Phase 3: After Your Postpartum Checkup 469

Milk It

Part 5: For Dads

Chapter 19: Fathers Are Expectant, Too 472

What You May Be Wondering About 473

Get Ready, Get Set . . . Then Go • Dealing with Her Symptoms • A Partner in
Parenting by Any Name • Sympathy Symptoms • Feeling Left Out • Resources for
Dads • Sex • Expectant Sex Explained • Pregnancy Dreams • It's Your Hormones
(Really) • Surviving Her Mood Swings • Your Pregnancy Mood Swings • Labor and
Delivery Worries • Anxiety Over Life Changes • Being There • Fathering Fears •
Breastfeeding • Your Baby Blues • Bonding • Keep an Eye on Her Mood • Feeling
Unsexy After Delivery • Postpartum Sex?

Part 6: Staying Healthy When You're Expecting

Chapter 20: If You Get Sick 494

What You May Be Wondering About 494

The Common Cold • Is It the Flu or a Cold? • Sinusitis • Flu Season • Flu Shot for
Two • Fever • Strep Throat • Urinary Tract Infection • Yeast Infection • Bacterial
Vaginosis • Stomach Bugs • Listeriosis • Toxoplasmosis • Cytomegalovirus • Fifth
Disease • Measles • Mumps • Staying Well • Rubella • Chicken Pox (Varicella) •
Lyme Disease • Hepatitis A • Hepatitis B • Hepatitis C • Bell's Palsy

ALL ABOUT

Medications During Pregnancy...............................509
Common Medications • *Keeping Current* • If You Need Medication During
Pregnancy • *Herbal Cures*

Chapter 21: If You Have a Chronic Condition.............514

What You May Be Wondering About.........................514
Asthma • *Cancer in Pregnancy* • Cystic Fibrosis • Depression • Diabetes • Epilepsy
• *Helping Others with Epilepsy* • Fibromyalgia • *Making the Most of Your Meds* •
Chronic Fatigue Syndrome • Hypertension • Irritable Bowel Syndrome • Lupus
• Multiple Sclerosis • Phenylketonuria • Physical Disability • Rheumatoid Arthritis
• Scoliosis • Sickle Cell Anemia • Thyroid Disease

ALL ABOUT

Getting the Support You Need...............................532

Part 7: The Complicated Pregnancy

Chapter 22: Managing a Complicated Pregnancy........536

Pregnancy Complications...................................536
Early Miscarriage • *Types of Miscarriage* • *You'll Want to Know . . .* • *If You've
Had a Miscarriage* • *Management of a Miscarriage* • Late Miscarriage • *Repeat
Miscarriages* • Ectopic Pregnancy • *You'll Want to Know . . .* • Subchorionic Bleed
• *You'll Want to Know . . .* • Hyperemesis Gravidarum • *You'll Want to Know . . .*
• Gestational Diabetes • *You'll Want to Know . . .* • Preeclampsia • *The Reasons
Behind Preeclampsia* • *You'll Want to Know . . .* • HELLP Syndrome • Intrauterine
Growth Restriction • *You'll Want to Know . . .* • Placenta Previa • *You'll Want to
Know . . .* • Placental Abruption • Chorioamnionitis • *You'll Want to Know . . .* •
Oligohydramnios • Hydramnios • Preterm Premature Rupture of the Membranes
(PPROM) • *You'll Want to Know . . .* • Preterm or Premature Labor • *You'll Want to
Know . . .* • *Predicting Preterm Labor* • Symphysis Pubis Dysfunction (SPD) • Cord
Knots and Tangles • Two-Vessel Cord

Uncommon Pregnancy Complications..........................560
Molar Pregnancy • *You'll Want to Know* . . . • Choriocarcinoma • *You'll Want to Know* . . . • Eclampsia • *You'll Want to Know* . . . • Cholestasis • Deep Venous Thrombosis • Placenta Accreta • Vasa Previa

Childbirth and Postpartum Complications....................565
Fetal Distress • Cord Prolapse • Shoulder Dystocia • Serious Perineal Tears • Uterine Rupture • Uterine Inversion • Postpartum Hemorrhage • Postpartum Infection

ALL ABOUT
If You're Put on Bed Rest...571
Types of Bed Rest • *Moms Helping Moms*

Chapter 23: Coping with Pregnancy Loss 576
Miscarriage • *A Personal Process* • *Coping with Repeat Miscarriages* • Loss in the Uterus • Loss During or After Birth • *Postpartum Depression and Pregnancy Loss* • *Lactation Suppression When a Baby Dies* • Loss of One Twin • *Why?* • *Pregnancy Reduction* • *Stages of Grief* • *Trying Again*

Index 587

Foreword to the Fourth Edition

By Charles J. Lockwood, MD

*The Anita O'Keefe Young Professor of Women's Health
and Chair, Department of Obstetrics, Gynecology and
Reproductive Sciences, Yale University School of Medicine*

THE OTHER DAY I RECEIVED A wonderful, heartfelt thank-you letter from a patient. Enclosed was a picture of a strapping college hockey player—whom I had delivered 19 years before! I have the best job on earth. I get to share in the most joyful, exciting, and wondrous moment that human beings will ever experience— the birth of their child—only I get to experience it over and over and over. Sure, being an obstetrician has its share of tough moments—some very tiring ones at 3 A.M., and some very frustrating ones, when the pace of a patient's labor appears to be glacial. There is the occasional adrenaline rush, the patient with the challenging symptom, and the inevitable flood of complex emotions, but mostly it's just plain fun.

In a way, my job is a lot like your pregnancy will probably be—every day will bring a little adventure, but most of them will be fun. *What to Expect When You're Expecting* is like having a personal obstetrician to guide you through that adventure. I have been recommending this book for years and thoroughly enjoyed reading the fourth edition— because the best just got better. All new, it's packed with information and useful advice, the kind you would hear from your favorite doctor or midwife—one who is wise but funny, thorough but practical, experienced but enthusiastic, organized but empathetic.

The book starts you off before conception with solid recommendations on what to—and what not to—do before you are expecting. It then gently guides you through conception to your first visit to a provider. It explains what changes you'll need to make in your lifestyle, job, and diet. One of the book's best features is a month-by-month—in fact a week-by-week—guide to how your baby is developing and what she or he is doing in your uterus. This is accompanied by a description of how *you* are developing—and not just your belly but everywhere, from your hair to your toes—and what you should be feeling. It tells you what your provider will do at each visit, and reviews what tests will be ordered and why. Toward the end, it prepares you for the big day, however you might be delivering—vaginally or by cesarean. You'll learn about birthing plans, how to recognize real labor from false labor, and which laboring positions work. Your questions about back labor, fetal monitoring, episiotomy, pain relief, and anesthesia will be answered, even if you didn't know to ask. Then *What to*

Expect guides you through all aspects of the incredible process of birth.

The book also covers the postpartum period, providing tips for differentiating the "blues" from depression. In an important chapter, it covers complications that you can read about if they occur, or skip over if they don't. It covers pregnancy in women with common medical conditions, such as asthma, high blood pressure, and diabetes—and how to maximize your chances of a normal pregnancy. It also covers what to do if you experience a pregnancy loss, and does it with a wonderful mix of compassion and practicality. Partners are not forgotten: The book provides a very practical guide to being a great coach. And parents-to-be of multiples are included, too. An entire chapter is devoted to their undoubtedly doubled questions and concerns.

As a maternal-fetal medicine specialist, I am impressed by just how much is covered in this book. As an editor, I am impressed by the clear, cogent, and concise writing. As a husband and father, I am impressed that the authors know just what moms-to-be and their partners need to know. The best judges of this book, however, have been the hundreds of patients who have raved about it to me, my staff, and other patients in the waiting room.

If you are reading these words, it's likely you are either newly pregnant or about to become so. Congratulations! My advice to you is lie back, get comfortable, and read on—you are about to embark on the adventure of a lifetime.

xxii

Why This Book Was Born Again, Again

TWENTY-FOUR YEARS AGO, I DELIV-ered a daughter and conceived a book within a few hours of each other (it was a busy day). Nurturing both those babies, Emma Bing and *What to Expect When You're Expecting* (as well as the next baby, my son, Wyatt—and the other *What to Expect* offspring) as they've grown and evolved over the years has been at once exhilarating and exhausting, fulfilling and frustrating, heartwarming and nerve-racking. And like any parent, I wouldn't trade a day of it. (Though there was that week when Emma was thirteen . . . okay, make that a year. Maybe two.)

And now I'm thrilled to announce yet another delivery. A brand-new book that I couldn't be prouder to start showing off and sharing: The fourth edition of *What to Expect When You're Expecting.* A cover-to-cover, front-to-back revision that's been completely rewritten from start to finish—a new book for a new generation of expectant parents (you!), featuring a fresh look, a fresh perspective, and a friendlier-than-ever voice.

What's new in the new *What to Expect?* So much that I'm excited about. Week-by-week updates on your little one's transformation from microscopic bundle of cells to cuddly newborn—the incredible development of your baby-to-be that will make all that heartburn, all those trips to the bathroom, all that gas, all those pains, and all the sleep deprivation more than worth it. And (speaking of heartburn and gas), more symptoms and more solutions than ever before—and more of your questions answered (even the ones you didn't know you had yet). There's an expanded section on working during pregnancy (as if being pregnant weren't hard enough work!). And going from the practical to the pampered, a brand-new section on expectant beauty: how to love—or at least cope with—the expectant skin you're in, even when it's blotchy, pimply, rashy, itchy, too oily, and too dry; which skin, hair, nail, and cosmetic regimens you can stick with and which you'll have to ditch until delivery. Lots on your pregnant lifestyle (from sex to travel to exercise to fashion), your pregnancy profile (how your obstetrical, medical, and gynecological backstory may—or may not—affect your pregnancy), your relationships, your emotions. A more realistic than ever chapter on expectant eating that responds to every eating style—from at-the-desk to on-the-run, from vegan to low-carb, caffeine-addicted to junk-food dependent. An expanded section on preconception, a new chapter for all you many moms of multiples. Lots more for that very important (but too often neglected) partner in parenting, the dad-to-be. And, of course, the very latest on all things pregnancy (news you can use, on everything from prenatal diagnosis to labor and delivery and beyond).

And because a cover-to-cover revision wouldn't be complete without a new cover, there's one of those, too. Introducing our new cover mom—off her rocker (okay . . . out of that rocking chair, finally), she's embracing her belly and celebrating one of life's most magical experiences (and the fact that pregnant women now get to wear cute clothes). She's thoroughly enjoying her expectant self—and I, for one, couldn't be happier for her. Almost makes me want to run out and get pregnant again (I said almost).

As always, just as important as what's different in this fourth edition is what's the same. When *What to Expect When You're Expecting* was first con-

ceived, it was with a single mission in mind: to help parents-to-be worry less and enjoy their pregnancies more. That mission has grown, but it hasn't changed. Like the first three editions, this fourth one was written to answer your questions, reassure you, relate to you, empathize with you, and help you get a better night's sleep (at least as good a night's sleep as you can get when you're busy running to the bathroom or fighting off leg cramps and backaches).

I hope you enjoy my new baby as much as I enjoyed creating it—and that it helps you as you go about creating that new baby of yours. Wishing you the healthiest of pregnancies and a lifetime of happy parenting. May all your greatest expectations come true!

Heidi

About The What to Expect Foundation

Every parent should know what to expect. That's why we created The What to Expect Foundation, a non-profit organization that provides vital prenatal health and literacy support to moms in need—so they, too, can expect healthier pregnancies, safer deliveries, and healthy, happy babies. For more information and to find out ways you can help, please visit our website at whattoexpect.org.

PART 1

First Things First

Before You Conceive

S O YOU'VE MADE THE DECISION TO start a family (or to grow that family you've already started). That's a great—and exciting—first step. But before sperm meets egg to create the baby of your dreams, take this preconception opportunity to prepare for the healthiest pregnancy—and baby—possible. The next steps outlined in this chapter will help you (and dad-to-be) get into tip-top baby-making shape, give you a leg up on conception, and get you to the pregnancy starting gate with all systems go.

If you don't get pregnant right away, relax and keep trying (and don't forget to keep having fun while you're trying!). If you're already pregnant—and didn't have a chance to follow these steps before you conceived—not to worry. Conception often sneaks up on a couple, cutting out that preconception period altogether and making those preconception pointers pointless. If your pregnancy test has already given you the good news, simply start this book at Chapter 2, and make the very best of every day of pregnancy you have ahead of you.

Preconception Prep for Moms

R eady to board that cute little passenger on the mother ship? Here are some preconception steps you can take to make sure that ship is in shape.

Get a preconception checkup. You don't have to choose a prenatal practitioner yet (though this is a great time to do so; see facing page), but it would be a good idea to see your regular gynecologist or internist for a thorough physi-

cal. An exam will pick up any medical problems that need to be corrected beforehand or that will need to be monitored during pregnancy. Plus, your doctor will be able to steer you away from medications that are pregnancy (or preconception) no-no's, make sure your immunizations are up to date, and talk to you about your weight, your diet, your drinking and other lifestyle habits, and similar preconception issues.

Start looking for a prenatal practitioner. It's easier to start looking for an obstetrician or midwife now, when the pregnancy meter's not already running, than when that first prenatal checkup is hanging over your head. If you're going to stick with your regular ob-gyn, then you've got a head start. Otherwise, ask around, scout around, and take your time in picking the practitioner who's right for you (see page 21 for tips on choosing one). Then schedule an interview and a prepregnancy exam.

Smile for the dentist. A visit to the dentist before you get pregnant is almost as important as a visit to the doctor. That's because your future pregnancy can affect your mouth—and your mouth can possibly affect your future pregnancy. Pregnancy hormones can actually aggravate gum and tooth problems, making a mess of a mouth that's not well taken care of to begin with. What's more, research shows that gum disease may be associated with some pregnancy complications. So before you get busy making a baby, get busy getting your mouth into shape. Be sure, too, to have any necessary work, including X-rays, fillings, and dental surgery, completed now so that it won't have to be done during pregnancy.

Check your family tree. Get the scoop on the health history on both sides of the family tree (yours and your spouse's). It's especially important to find out if there's a history of any medical issues and genetic or chromosomal disorders such as Down syndrome, Tay-Sachs disease, sickle cell anemia, thalassemia, hemophilia, cystic fibrosis, muscular dystrophy, or fragile X syndrome.

Take a look at your pregnancy history. If you've had a previous pregnancy with any complications or one that ended with a premature delivery or late preg-

Putting It All Together

Does looking at this list of to-do's make you realize there's a lot to do even before sperm meets egg? Having a hard time knowing where to start? For a list of questions to ask when choosing a prenatal practitioner, a complete personal medical and obstetrical health history, a family health history chart, and plenty of other helpful information to help you get organized for your baby-making journey, see *The What to Expect Pregnancy Journal and Organizer* and whattoexpect.com.

nancy loss, or if you've had multiple miscarriages, talk to your practitioner about any measures that can be taken to head off a repeat.

Seek genetic screening, if necessary. Also ask your practitioner about being tested for any genetic disease common to your ethnic background: cystic fibrosis if either of you is Caucasian; Tay-Sachs disease if either of you is of Jewish-European (Ashkenazi), French Canadian, or Louisiana Cajun descent; sickle cell trait if you are of African descent; one of the thalassemias if you are of Greek, Italian, Southeast Asian, or Filipino origin.

Previous obstetrical difficulties (such as two or more miscarriages, a stillbirth, a long period of infertility, or a child with a birth defect) or being married to a cousin or other blood relative are also reasons to seek genetic counseling.

Get tested. While you're seeing all your doctors and checking out all your histories, ask if you can get a head start on some of the tests and health workups every pregnant woman receives. Most are as easy as getting a blood test to look for:

- Hemoglobin or hematocrit, to test for anemia.

- Rh factor, to see if you are positive or negative. If you are negative, your partner should be tested to see if he is positive. (If you're both negative, there is no need to give Rh another thought.)

- Rubella titer, to check for immunity to rubella.

- Varicella titer, to check for immunity to varicella (chicken pox).

- Tuberculosis (if you live in a high-incidence area).

- Hepatitis B (if you're in a high-risk category, such as health-care worker, and have not been immunized).

- Cytomegalovirus (CMV) antibodies, to determine whether or not you are immune to CMV (see page 503). If you have been diagnosed with CMV, it's generally recommended you wait six months before trying to conceive.

- Toxoplasmosis titer, if you have an outdoor cat, regularly eat raw or rare meat, or garden without gloves. If you turn out to be immune, you don't have to worry about toxoplasmosis now or ever. If you're not, start taking the precautions on page 80 now.

- Thyroid function. Thyroid function can affect pregnancy. So if you have or ever had thyroid problems, or if you have a family history of thyroid disease, or if you have symptoms of a thyroid condition (see pages 174 and 531), this is an important test to have.

- Sexually transmitted diseases (STDs). All pregnant women are routinely tested for all STDs, including syphilis, gonorrhea, chlamydia, herpes, human papilloma virus (HPV), and HIV. Having these tests before conception is even better (or in the case of HPV, getting the vaccine; see next page). Even if you're sure you couldn't have an STD, ask to be tested, just to be on the safe side.

Get treated. If any test turns up a condition that requires treatment, make sure you take care of it before trying to conceive. Also consider attending to minor elective surgery and anything else medical—major or minor—that you've been putting off. Now is the time, too, to be treated for any gynecological conditions that might interfere with fertility or pregnancy, including:

- Uterine polyps, fibroids, cysts, or benign tumors.

- Endometriosis (when the cells that ordinarily line the uterus spread elsewhere in the body).

- Pelvic inflammatory disease.

- Recurrent urinary tract infections or other infections, such as bacterial vaginosis.

- An STD.

Update your immunizations. If you haven't had a tetanus-diphtheria-pertussis booster in the past 10 years, have one now. If you know you've never had rubella or been immunized against it, or if testing showed you are not immune to it, get vaccinated now with the measles, mumps, and rubella (MMR) vaccine, and then wait one month before attempting to conceive (but don't worry if you accidentally conceive earlier). If testing shows you've never had chicken pox or are at high risk for hepatitis B, immunization for these diseases is also recommended now, before conception.

If you're under 26, also consider getting vaccinated against HPV, but you'd need to get the full series of three before trying to conceive, so plan accordingly.

Get chronic illnesses under control. If you have diabetes, asthma, a heart condition, epilepsy, or any other chronic illness, be sure you have your doctor's okay to become pregnant, your condition is under control before you conceive, and you start taking optimum care of yourself now (if you aren't already). If you were born with phenylketonuria (PKU), begin a strict phenylalanine-free diet before conceiving and continue it through pregnancy. As unappealing as it is, it's essential to your baby-to-be's well-being.

If you need allergy shots, take care of them now. (If you start allergy desensitization now, you will probably be able to continue once you conceive.) Because depression can interfere with conception—and with a happy, healthy pregnancy—it should also be treated before you begin your big adventure.

Get ready to toss your birth control. Ditch that last package of condoms and throw out your diaphragm (you'll have to be refitted after pregnancy anyway). If you're using birth control pills, the vaginal ring, or the patch, talk your game plan over with your practitioner. Some recommend holding off on baby-making efforts for several months after quitting hormonal birth control, if possible, to allow your reproductive system to go through at least two normal cycles (use condoms while you're waiting). Others say it's okay to start trying as soon as you want. Be aware, though, that it may take a few months or even longer for your cycles to become normal and for you to begin ovulating again.

If you use an IUD, have it removed before you begin trying. Wait three to six months after stopping Depo-Provera shots to try to conceive (many women aren't fertile for an average of 10 months after stopping Depo, so time accordingly).

Improve your diet. You may not be eating for two yet, but it's never too early to start eating well for the baby you're planning to make. Most important is to make sure you're getting your folic acid. Not only does getting enough folic acid appear to boost fertility, but studies show that adequate intake of this vitamin in a woman's diet before she conceives and early in her pregnancy can dramatically reduce the risk of neural tube defects (such as spina bifida) and preterm birth. Folic acid is found naturally in whole grains and green leafy vegetables, and by law it is also added to most refined grains. But taking a prenatal supplement containing at least 400 mcg of folic acid is also recommended (see page 103).

It's also a good idea to start cutting back on junk food and high-fat foods and begin increasing whole grains, fruits, vegetables, and low-fat dairy products (important for bone strength). You can use the Pregnancy Diet (Chapter 5) as a good basic, balanced food plan, but you'll need only two protein servings, three calcium servings, and no more than six whole-grain servings daily until you conceive—plus you won't have to start adding those extra calories (and if you need to lose some weight preconception, you might need to cut some calories out).

Start modifying your fish consumption according to the guidelines for expectant moms (see page 114). But don't cut out fish, because it's a great source of baby-growing nutrients.

If you have any dietary habits that wouldn't be healthy during pregnancy (such as periodic fasting), suffer or

It Takes Two, Baby

Sure, you're closer than ever physically now that you're trying to make a baby (that's something baby-making efforts just about guarantee)—but what about your love connection? As you strive to form that perfect union (of sperm and egg), are you neglecting the other significant union in your lives (the two of you)?

When expanding your twosome becomes your number one priority, when sex becomes functional instead of recreational, when it's less about getting it on than getting it done (and when foreplay consists of running to the bathroom to check your cervical mucus), relationships can sometimes show the strain. But yours definitely doesn't have to—in fact, you can keep it healthier than ever. To stay emotionally connected while you're trying to conceive:

- **Get out.** Been-there, done-that moms will tell you that *now's* the time for you and your spouse to get out of town—or at least out of the house. Once baby's on board, your days (and nights) of picking up and taking off will be numbered. (Maternity leave? More like maternity *stay!*) So take that mini vacation you've been saving up for—or that second honeymoon (you can call it a baby-to-be-moon). No time for a vacation? Try something new on the weekends—preferably something that you won't be able to do once conception cramps your lifestyle (horseback riding or white-water rafting, anyone?). Need something more tame as a twosome? Slip off to a museum on a weekend afternoon, catch a late-night movie (or two) at the multiplex, or just linger over dinner at your favorite restaurant (no babysitters necessary).

- **Rev up the romance.** Pee-on-a-stick ovulation tests and the pressure to

perform (now!) can make sex seem too much like hard work. So bring fun back into the bedroom. Turn up the heat—and not just your basal temperature—with a sexy little nightie, a steamy movie, a sex toy or two, a round of strip poker or nude twister, a new position (kama sutra will be considerably trickier once that belly gets in the way), a new location (serve yourself up on the dining table), or a new tactic (hot fudge on each other instead of on ice cream). Adventurous isn't in your comfort zone? Ratchet up the romance with a moonlight stroll, dinner by candlelight, cuddling in front of the fireplace.

- **Stay on the same page.** Worried that your spouse is more interested in charting the stock market than helping you chart your basal body temperature? Get the feeling that he's blasé about baby making? Go easy on him. Just because he might not be obsessing over ovulation or going ga-ga every time he passes a baby boutique doesn't mean he's not as eager as you are to get the baby show on the road. Maybe he's just being a guy (laid-back, instead of worked up). Maybe he's just keeping his tension about conception to himself (so he doesn't stress you out, too). Maybe he's focusing on the business end of baby making (he's working longer hours because he's concerned about providing a nest egg for the nestling you'll be creating). Either way, remember that taking the plunge into parenthood is a huge step for both of you—but that you're taking it as a team. To stay on the same page (even if you're using different words), communicate as you try to procreate. You'll both feel better knowing you're in this together—even if you're approaching it a little differently.

have suffered from an eating disorder (such as anorexia nervosa or bulimia), or are on a special diet (vegan, macrobiotic, diabetic, or any other), tell your practitioner.

Take a prenatal vitamin. Even if you're eating plenty of foods high in folic acid, it's still recommended that you take a pregnancy supplement containing 400 mcg of the vitamin, preferably beginning two months before you try to conceive. Another good reason to start taking a prenatal supplement preconception: Research indicates that women who take a daily multivitamin containing at least 10 mg of vitamin B_6 before becoming pregnant or during the first weeks of pregnancy experience fewer episodes of vomiting and nausea during pregnancy. The supplement should also contain 15 mg of zinc, which may improve fertility. Stop taking other nutritional supplements before conceiving, however, since excesses of certain nutrients can be hazardous.

Get your weight in check. Being overweight or very underweight not only reduces the chances of conception, but, if you do conceive, weight problems can increase the risk of pregnancy complications. So add or cut calories in the preconception period as needed. If you're trying to lose weight, be sure to do so slowly and sensibly, even if it means putting off conception for another couple of months. Strenuous or nutritionally unbalanced dieting (including low-carbohydrate, high-protein diets) can make conception elusive and can result in a nutritional deficit, which probably isn't the best way to start your pregnancy. If you've been extreme dieting recently, start eating normally and give your body a few months to get back into balance before you try to conceive.

Shape up, but keep cool. A good exercise program can put you on the right track for conception, plus it will tone and strengthen your muscles in preparation for the challenging tasks of carrying and delivering your baby-to-be. It will also help you take off excess weight. Don't overdo that good thing, though, because excessive exercise (especially if it leads to an extremely lean body) can interfere with ovulation—and if you don't ovulate, you can't conceive. And keep your cool during workouts: Prolonged increases in body temperature can interfere with conception. (Avoid hot tubs, saunas, and direct exposure to heating pads and electric blankets for the same reason.)

Check your medicine cabinet. Some—though far from all—medications are considered unsafe for use during pregnancy. If you're taking any medications now (regularly or once in a while, prescription or over-the-counter), ask your practitioner about their safety during preconception and pregnancy. If you need to switch a regular medication that isn't safe to a substitute that is, now's the time to do it.

Herbal or other alternative medications shouldn't necessarily move front and center in your medicine cabinet, either. Herbs are natural, but natural doesn't automatically signal safe. What's more, some popular herbs—such as echinacea, ginkgo biloba, or St. John's wort—can interfere with conception. Do not take any such products or supplements without the approval of a doctor familiar with herbals and alternative medicines and their potential effect on conception and pregnancy.

Cut back on caffeine. There's no need to drop that latte (or switch to decaf) if you're planning on becoming pregnant

Pinpointing Ovulation

Knowing when the Big O (ovulation) occurs is key when doing the Baby Dance (aka trying to conceive). Here are a few ways to help you pin down the big day—and pin each other down for baby-making activities.

Watch the calendar. Ovulation most often occurs halfway through your menstrual cycle. The average cycle lasts 28 days, counting from the first day of one period (day 1) to the first day of the next period. But as with everything pregnancy related, there's a wide range of normal when it comes to menstrual cycles (they can run anywhere from 23 days to 35 days), and your own cycle may vary slightly from month to month. By keeping a menstrual calendar for a few months, you can get an idea of what's normal for you. (And when you become pregnant, this calendar will help give you a better estimate of your baby's due date.) If your periods are irregular, you'll need to be more alert for other signs of ovulation (see below).

Take your temperature. Keeping track of your basal body temperature, or BBT (you'll need a special basal body thermometer to do this), can help you pinpoint ovulation. Your BBT is the baseline reading you get first thing in the morning, after at least three to five hours of sleep and before you get out of bed, talk, or even sit up. Your BBT changes throughout your cycle, reaching its lowest point at ovulation and then rising dramatically (about half a

degree) within a day or so after ovulation occurs. Keep in mind that charting your BBT will not enable you to predict the day you ovulate, but rather it gives you evidence of ovulation two to three days after it has occurred. Over a few months, it will help you to see a pattern to your cycles, enabling you to predict when ovulation will occur in future cycles.

Check your underwear. Another sign you can be alert for is the appearance, increase in quantity, and change in consistency of cervical mucus (the stuff that gets your underwear all sticky). After your period ends, don't expect much, if any, cervical mucus. As the cycle proceeds, you'll notice an increase in the amount of mucus with an often white or cloudy appearance—and if you try to stretch it between your fingers, it'll break apart. As you get closer to ovulation, this mucus becomes even more copious, but now it's thinner, clearer, and has a slippery consistency similar to an egg white. If you try to stretch it between your fingers, you'll be able to pull it into a string a few inches long before it breaks (how's that for fun in the bathroom?). This is yet another sign of impending ovulation, as well as a sign that it's time to get out of the bathroom and get busy in the bedroom. Once ovulation occurs, you may either become dry again or develop a thicker discharge. Combined with cervical position (see below) and BBT on a

or even once you become pregnant. Most experts believe that up to two cups of caffeinated coffee (or the equivalent in other caffeinated beverages) a day is fine. If your habit involves more than that, though, it would be smart to

start moderating. Some studies have linked downing too much of the stuff to lowered fertility.

Cut down on alcohol. Start thinking before drinking. Although a daily drink single chart, cervical mucus can be an extremely useful (if slightly messy) tool in pinpointing the day on which you are most likely to ovulate—and it does so in plenty of time for you to do something about it.

Get to know your cervix. As your body senses the hormone shifts that indicate an egg is about to be released from the ovary, it begins to ready itself for incoming hordes of sperm to give the egg its best chance of getting fertilized. One detectable sign of oncoming ovulation is the position of the cervix itself. During the beginning of a cycle, your cervix—that necklike passage between your vagina and uterus that has to stretch during birth to accommodate your baby's head—is low, hard, and closed. But as ovulation approaches, it pulls back up, softens a bit, and opens just a little to let the sperm through on their way to their target. Some women can easily feel these changes, others have a tougher time. If you're game to try, check your cervix daily, using one or two fingers, and keep a chart of your observations.

Stay tuned in. If you're like 20 percent of women, your body will let you know when ovulation is taking place by sending a bulletin in the form of a twinge of pain or a series of cramps in your lower abdominal area (usually localized to one side, the side where you're ovulating). Called mittelschmerz—German for "middle pain"—this monthly reminder of fertility is thought to be the result of the maturation or release of an egg from an ovary.

Pee on a stick. Ovulation predictor kits (OPKs) are able to pinpoint your date of ovulation 12 to 24 hours in advance by measuring levels of luteinizing hormone, or LH, which is the last of the hormones to hit its peak before ovulation actually occurs. All you have to do is pee on a stick and wait for the indicator to tell you whether you're about to ovulate (talk about easy).

Watch your watch. Another option in the ovulation test arsenal is a device you wear on your wrist that detects the numerous salts (chloride, sodium, potassium) in your sweat, which differ during different times of the month. Called the chloride ion surge, this shift happens even before the estrogen and the LH surge, so these chloride ion tests give a woman a four-day window of when she may be ovulating, versus the 12 to 24-hour window that the standard pee-on-a-stick OPKs provide. The key to success in using this latest technology is to make sure to get an accurate baseline of your ion levels (which means you'll need to wear the device on your wrist for at least six continuous hours to get a proper baseline).

Spit a little. Another ovulation predictor is a saliva test, which tests the levels of estrogen in your saliva as ovulation nears. When you're ovulating, a look at your saliva under the test's eyepiece will reveal a microscopic pattern that resembles the leaves of a fern plant or frost on a windowpane. Not all women get a good "fern," but this test, which is reusable, can be cheaper than those pee-on sticks.

will not be harmful in your pregnancy-preparation phase, heavy alcohol consumption can interfere with fertility by disrupting your menstrual cycle. Plus, once you're actively trying to conceive, there's always the possibility that you'll

have succeeded—and drinking during pregnancy isn't recommended.

Quit smoking. Did you know that smoking can not only interfere with fertility but also cause your eggs to age?

Conception Misconceptions

You've heard plenty of old wives'— and new Internet—tales about how best to make a baby. Here are a few that are ready to be taken off the circuit:

Myth: Having sex every day will decrease sperm count, making conception more elusive.

Fact: Though this was once believed to be true, more recent research has shown that having sex every day around the time of ovulation is slightly more likely to end in pregnancy than having sex every other day. More, apparently, is more.

Myth: Wearing boxer shorts will increase fertility.

Fact: Scientists have yet to rule definitively on the boxers versus briefs debate, but most experts seem to think that the underwear a man favors has little effect on the baby race. Though there is something to be said for keeping the testicles cool and giving them a little breathing room (see page 13).

Myth: Missionary position intercourse is the best way for sperm to reach their target.

Fact: The cervical mucus that turns thin and stretchy around the time of ovulation is the perfect medium for sperm, helping those boys swim up the vaginal tract, through the cervix, past the uterus, and up the fallopian tubes to the awaiting egg. Unless sperm have a motility problem, they'll reach their target no matter what position you're in while you're doing it. It doesn't hurt, however, to lie down for a while after intercourse so the sperm don't run out of the vagina before they even get a running start.

Myth: Lubricant will help the sperm hitch a ride to Egg Central.

Fact: Actually, the opposite is true. Lubricants can change the pH balance in the vagina, creating an inhospitable environment for the sperm. So lay off the Astroglide until after your conception mission is accomplished.

Myth: Daytime sex helps you conceive faster.

Fact: Sperm levels do seem to be higher in the morning, but no clinical evidence supports that making hay while the sun shines will increase your chances of conception. (But don't let that stop you if you'd like to grab a quickie before you grab your lunchbreak sandwich!)

That's right—a 30-year-old smoker's eggs act more like 40-year-old eggs, making conception more difficult and miscarriage more likely. Kicking the habit now is not only the best gift you can give your baby-to-be (before and after birth), but it can make it more likely that you'll conceive that baby-to-be. For some practical tips to help you quit, check out pages 74–75.

Just say no to illegal drugs. Marijuana, cocaine, crack, heroin, and other illicit drugs can be dangerous to your pregnancy. To varying degrees they can prevent your conceiving, and then, if you do succeed, they may be potentially harmful to the fetus and also may increase the risks of miscarriage, prematurity, and stillbirths. If you use drugs, casually or regularly, stop all use immediately. If you can't stop, seek help before trying to conceive.

Avoid unnecessary exposure to radiation. If X-rays are necessary for medical reasons, be sure your reproductive organs are protected (unless they are being targeted) and the lowest radiation doses possible are used. Once you start trying to conceive, inform any technicians taking X-rays that you could be pregnant, and ask them to take all necessary precautions.

Avoid environmental hazards. Some chemicals—though far from all and usually only in very large doses—are potentially harmful to your eggs before conception and, later, to a developing embryo or fetus. Though the risk in most cases is slight or even just hypothetical, play it safe by avoiding potentially hazardous exposure on the job. Take special care in certain fields (medicine and dentistry, art, photography, transportation, farming and landscaping, construction, hairdressing and cosmetology, dry cleaning, and some factory work). Contact the Occupational Safety and Health Administration (OSHA) for the latest information on job safety and pregnancy; also see page 194. In some cases, it may be wise to ask for a transfer to another position, change jobs, or take special precautions, if possible, before trying to conceive.

Because elevated lead levels when you conceive could pose problems for your baby, get tested if you have been exposed to lead in the workplace or elsewhere, such as in your water supply or your home (see page 81). Avoid, too, excessive exposure to other household toxins.

Get fiscally fit. Having a baby can be pricey. So, together with your spouse, reevaluate your budget and begin creating a sound financial plan. As part of your plan, find out if your health insurance pays for the cost of prenatal care, birth, and well-baby care. If coverage will not start until a certain date, consider delaying your pregnancy until then. Or if you plan to switch policies, do so before you become pregnant, since some policies consider pregnancy a preexisting condition. And if you don't have a will yet, now is the time to draw one up.

Work out those work issues. Find out everything you can about your work rights when pregnant (see page 187). If you're planning a job switch, you might want to consider finding that perfect family-friendly job now so you won't have to interview with a belly.

Start keeping track. Become familiar with your monthly cycle and learn the signs of ovulation so you can time intercourse right (see box, page 8). Keeping track of when you have sex will also help you pinpoint conception later on, which will make calculating an estimated date of delivery easier.

Give it time. Keep in mind that it takes an average of six months for a normal, healthy 25-year-old woman to conceive, and longer for women who are older. It may also take longer if your partner is older. So don't stress if baby magic doesn't happen right away. Just keep on having fun trying, and give yourselves at least six months before consulting your practitioner and, if needed, a fertility specialist. If you're over 35, you may want to check in with your practitioner after three months of trying.

Relax. This is perhaps the most important step of all. Of course, you're excited about getting pregnant—and, more than likely, at least a little stressed about it, too. But getting tense and uptight about conception could prevent you from conceiving. Learn to do relaxation exercises, to meditate, and to cut down as much as possible on stress in your daily life.

Preconception Prep for Dads

As a dad-to-be, you won't be providing immediate room and board for your future offspring—but you will be making a vital contribution to the baby-making process (mom can't do it without you). These preconception steps can help you make conception as healthy as possible.

See your doctor. Though you won't be the one carrying the baby—at least not until after delivery—you'll still need a checkup of your own before you begin baby making. After all, making a healthy baby takes the participation of two healthy bodies. A thorough physical can detect any medical conditions (such as undescended testicles or testicular cysts or tumors) that might interfere with conception or a healthy pregnancy for your partner, as well as ensure that any chronic conditions, such as depression, that might interfere with fertility are under control. While you're at the doctor's office, ask about the sexual side effects of any prescription, over-the-counter, or herbal drugs you are taking. Some can cause erectile dysfunction and lower sperm counts—two things you definitely don't want going on when you're in baby-making mode.

Get a genetic screening, if needed. If your spouse is going in for genetic testing, consider tagging along, especially if you have a family history of a genetic problem or other indication.

Improve your diet. The better your nutrition, the healthier your sperm and the more likely you'll conceive. Your diet should be a balanced, healthy one that includes plenty of fresh fruits and vegetables, whole grains, and lean protein. To be sure you get adequate amounts of the most important nutrients (especially vitamin C, vitamin E, vitamin D, zinc, and calcium, all of which appear to affect fertility or the health of sperm), take a vitamin-mineral supplement while you are attempting to conceive. The supplement should contain folic acid; a low intake of this nutrient in fathers-to-be has been linked to decreased fertility as well as to birth defects.

Look at your lifestyle. All the answers are not yet in, but research is beginning to show that the use of drugs—including excessive amounts of alcohol—by the male partner prior to conception could prevent pregnancy or lead to a poor pregnancy outcome. The mechanisms aren't clear, but drug use and daily heavy drinking can apparently damage sperm as well as reduce their number and can alter testicular function and reduce testosterone levels (not a good scenario when you're trying to conceive). Heavy drinking (equivalent to two drinks a day or five on any one day) during the month before conception could also affect your baby's birthweight. Keep in mind, too, that if you cut down on or cut out alcohol, it will be much easier for your partner to do likewise. If you are unable to quit drugs or reduce your alcohol intake, seek help now.

Get your weight on track. Men with a very high BMI (or body mass index, a measure of body fat based on height and weight) are more likely to be infertile than normal-weight men. Even a 20-pound increase in your weight may increase the chance of infertility by 10 percent, according to researchers. So get your weight in check before trying to conceive.

Stop smoking. No ifs, ands, or butts: Smoking reduces the number of sperm and makes conceiving more difficult. In addition, quitting now will improve the health of everyone in your family, since secondhand smoke is nearly as dangerous to them as firsthand smoke is to you. In fact, it can increase your baby-to-be's risk of dying of SIDS (sudden infant death syndrome).

Don't get zapped. High lead levels, as well as some organic solvents (such as those found in paints, glues, varnishes, and metal degreasers), pesticides, or other chemicals can interfere with a male's fertility, so avoid these or limit your exposure as much as possible in preparation for conception.

Keep 'em cool. Sperm production is impaired when the testicles become overheated. In fact, they prefer to be a couple of degrees cooler than the rest of you, which is why they hang away from your body. So avoid hot tubs and hot baths, saunas, electric blankets, and snug clothing, such as tight jeans. Also avoid synthetic pants and underwear, which can overheat you in hot weather. And keep your laptop off your lap, since the heat from the device can raise your scrotal temperature and reduce your sperm count. Until you conceive, treat it like a desktop.

Keep 'em safe. If you play any rough sports (including football, soccer, basketball, hockey, baseball, or horseback riding), wear protective gear to prevent injury to the genitals, which can damage fertility. Even too much bicycling has the potential to cause problems. According to some experts, the constant pressure on the genitals by a bicycle seat may interfere with conception by damaging arteries and nerves. If you experience genital numbness and/or tingling, and changing seats or lifting yourself off the seat periodically as you ride doesn't help, it would be a good idea to cut down on bicycling during the conception-attempting period. Numb genitals don't perform as well as they should. If the numbness (and/or tingling) doesn't go away, see your doctor.

Relax. Sure, you've got a lot on your mind as you contemplate bringing a baby into your lives—and yes, now you have a preconception to-do list to get busy on before you actually get busy on making baby. But don't forget to take the time to relax, too. Stress doesn't just affect your libido and performance, it also affects your testosterone levels and your sperm production. The less you worry, the more easily you'll conceive. So relax and enjoy trying!

Are You Pregnant?

AYBE YOUR PERIOD'S JUST A day overdue. Or maybe it's going on three weeks late. Or maybe your period isn't even slated to arrive yet, but you've got a gut feeling (literally, in your gut) that something's cooking—like a brand-new bun in your oven! Maybe the only heads-up your body's given you so far is that missed period. Or maybe you've already developed every conceivable symptom of conception. Maybe you've been giving baby making everything you've got for six months or longer. Or maybe that hot night two weeks ago was your very first contraceptive-free encounter. Or maybe you haven't been actively trying at all. No matter what the circumstances are that have brought you to this book, you're bound to be wondering: Am I pregnant? Well, read on to find out.

What You May Be Wondering About

Early Pregnancy Signs

"A friend of mine said she knew she was pregnant even before she took a pregnancy test. Is there any way to figure out whether or not I'm pregnant that early on?"

The only way to be positively positive that you're pregnant—at least this early on—is to produce that positive pregnancy test. But that doesn't mean your body is staying mum on whether you're about to become a mom. In fact, it may be offering up plenty of conception clues. Though many women never feel any early pregnancy symptoms at all (or don't feel them until weeks into pregnancy), others get lots of hints that there's a baby in the making. Experiencing any of these symptoms or noticing any of these signs may be just the excuse you need to run to the store for a home pregnancy test:

Tender breasts and nipples. You know that tender, achy feeling you get in your breasts before your period arrives? That's nothing compared to the breast tenderness you might be feeling post-conception. Tender, full, swollen, tingly, sensitive, and even painful-to-the-touch breasts are some of the first signs many (but not all) women notice after sperm meets egg. Such tenderness can begin as early as a few days after conception (though it often doesn't kick in until weeks later), and as your pregnancy progresses, it could get even more pronounced. Make that a lot more pronounced.

Darkening areolas. Not only might your breasts be tender, but your areolas (the circles around your nipples) may be changing colors. It's perfectly normal for the areola to darken in hue during pregnancy and even to increase in diameter somewhat in the weeks after conception. You can thank the pregnancy hormones already surging through your body for these and other skin color changes (much more about those hormones in the coming months).

Goose bumps? Well, not really, but early in pregnancy you may notice an increase and enlargement in the tiny bumps on the areola (called Montgomery's tubercles)—bumps you may have never noticed before. They'll resemble goose bumps but are actually glands that produce oils to lubricate your nipples and areolas—lubrication that'll certainly be welcome when your baby starts sucking on your nipples if you're nursing. Another sign your body is planning ahead.

Spotting. Some (but certainly not all) women experience spotting when the embryo implants in the uterus. Such so-called implantation bleeding will likely arrive earlier than your expected monthly flow (usually around five to ten days after conception) and will probably appear light to medium pink in color (rarely red, like a period).

Urinary frequency. Has the toilet become your seat of choice lately? Appearing on the pregnancy scene fairly early (usually about two to three weeks after conception) may be the need to pee with frightening frequency. Curious why? See page 135 for all the reasons.

Fatigue. Extreme fatigue. Make that exhaustion. Complete lack of energy. Super sluggishness. Whatever you call it, it's a drag—literally. And as your body starts cranking up that baby-making machine, it'll only get more draining. See page 127 for reasons why.

Nausea. Here's another reason why you might want to consider moving into the bathroom, at least until the first trimester is finished. Nausea and vomiting—aka morning sickness (if only it were limited to the morning)—can strike a newly pregnant woman fairly soon after conception, though it's more likely to begin around week 6. For a host of reasons why, see page 130.

Smell sensitivity. Since a heightened sense of smell is one of the first changes some newly pregnant women report, pregnancy might be in the air if your sniffer's suddenly more sensitive—and easily offended.

Bloating. Feeling like a walking flotation device? That bloated feeling can creep up (and out) on you very early in a pregnancy—though it may be difficult to differentiate between a preperiod bloat and a pregnancy bloat. It's too soon to attribute any swelling to your baby's growth, but you can chalk it up to those hormones again.

Rising temperature. Basal body temperature, that is. If you've been tracking your first morning temperature with a special basal body thermometer, you might notice that your basal body temperature rises around one degree when you conceive and continues to stay elevated throughout your pregnancy. Though not a foolproof sign (there are other reasons why you may notice a rise in temperature), it could give you advance notice of big—though still very little—news.

Missed period. It might be stating the obvious, but if you've missed a period (especially if your periods generally run like clockwork), you may already be suspecting pregnancy—even before a pregnancy test confirms it.

Diagnosing Pregnancy

"How can I find out for sure whether I'm pregnant or not?"

Aside from that most remarkable of diagnostic tools, a woman's intuition (some women "feel" they're pregnant within moments of conception), modern medical science is still your best bet when it comes to diagnosing a pregnancy accurately. Luckily, these days there are many ways to find out for sure that you've got a baby on board:

The home pregnancy test. It's as easy as one-two-pee, and you can do it all in the privacy and comfort of your own bathroom. Home pregnancy tests (HPTs) are not only quick and accurate, but you can even start using some brands before you've missed your period (though accuracy will get better as you get closer to P-day).

All HPTs measure urinary levels of human chorionic gonadotropin (hCG), a (developing) placenta-produced hormone of pregnancy. HCG finds its way into your bloodstream and urine almost immediately after an embryo begins implanting in the uterus, between 6 and 12 days after fertilization. As soon as hCG can be detected in your urine, you can (theoretically) get a positive reading. But there is a limit to how soon these HPTs can work—they're sensitive, but not always that sensitive. One week after conception there's hCG in your urine, but it's not enough for the HPT to pick up—which means that if you test seven days before your expected period, you're likely to get a false negative even if you're pregnant.

Just can't wait to pee on that stick? Some tests promise 60 percent accuracy four days before your expected period. Not a betting woman? Wait until the day your period is expected, and you'll have about a 90 percent chance of netting the correct result. Test a week later, and the accuracy rate jumps to 97 percent. Whenever you decide to take the testing plunge, the good news is that false positives are much less common than false negatives—which means that if your test is positive, you can be, too. The other good news: Because HPTs provide a very accurate diagnosis very early in pregnancy—earlier than you would probably consider consulting a physician or midwife—they can give you the opportunity to start taking optimum care of yourself within days of conception. Still, medical follow-up to the test is essential. If the result is positive, have it confirmed by a blood test and a complete prenatal checkup.

The blood test. The more sophisticated blood pregnancy test can detect pregnancy with virtually 100 percent accuracy as early as one week after conception (barring lab error), using just a few drops of blood. It can also help date the pregnancy by measuring the exact amount of hCG in the blood, since hCG values change as pregnancy progresses (see page 140 for more on hCG levels).

Many practitioners order both a urine and a blood test to be doubly certain of the diagnosis.

The medical exam. Though a medical exam can be performed to confirm the diagnosis of a pregnancy, with today's accurate HPTs and blood tests, the medical exam—which looks for physical signs of pregnancy such as enlargement of the uterus, color changes in the vagina and cervix, and a change in the texture of the cervix—is almost beside the point. Still, getting that first exam and beginning regular prenatal care isn't (see page 19).

A Faint Line

"When I took a home pregnancy test, it showed a really faint line. Am I pregnant?"

The only way a pregnancy test can give you a positive result is if your body has a detectable level of hCG running through it (or in this case, through your urine). And the only way that your body can have hCG running through it is if you're pregnant. Which means that if your test is showing a line, no matter how faint it is—you're pregnant.

Just why you're getting a faint line instead of that loud-and-clear line you were hoping for has a lot to do with the type of test you've used (some are much more sensitive than others) and how far along you are in your pregnancy (levels of hCG rise each day, so if you test early, there's only a little hCG to tap into).

To figure out just how sensitive your pregnancy test is, check out the packaging. Look for the milli-international units per liter (mIU/L) measurement, which will tell you the sensitivity of the test. The lower the number, the better (20 mIU/L will tell you you're pregnant sooner than a test with a 50 mIU/L sensitivity). Not surprisingly, the more

Testing for the Irregular

So your cycles don't exactly run on schedule? That'll make scheduling your testing date a lot trickier. After all, how can you test on the day that your period's expected if you're never sure when that day will come? Your best testing strategy if your periods are irregular is to wait the number of days equal to the longest cycle you've had in the last six months—and then test. If the result is negative and you still haven't gotten your period, repeat the test after a week (or after a few days if you just can't wait).

expensive tests usually have greater sensitivity.

Keep in mind, too, that the further along in your pregnancy you are, the higher your levels of hCG. If you're testing very early on in your pregnancy (as in a few days before your expected period or even a few days after your expected period), there might not be enough hCG in your system yet to generate a no-doubt-about-it line. Give it a couple of days, test again, and you'll be sure to see a line that'll erase your doubts once and for all.

No Longer Positive

"My first pregnancy test came back positive, but a few days later I took another one and it came back negative. And then I got my period. What's going on?"

It sounds like you may have experienced a chemical pregnancy, a pregnancy that ends practically before it even begins. In a chemical pregnancy, the egg is fertilized and begins to implant in the uterus, but for some reason it never completes implantation. Instead of turning into a viable pregnancy, it ends in a period. Though experts estimate that up to 70 percent of all conceptions are chemical, the vast majority of women who experience one don't even realize they've conceived (certainly in the days before home pregnancy tests, women didn't have a clue they were pregnant until much later). Often, a very early positive pregnancy test and then a late period (a few days to a week late) are the only signs of a chemical pregnancy, so if there's a downside to early home pregnancy testing, you've definitely experienced it.

Medically, a chemical pregnancy is more like a cycle in which a pregnancy never occurred than a true miscarriage. Emotionally, for women like you who tested early and got a positive result, it can be a very different story. Though it's not technically a pregnancy loss, the loss of the promise of a pregnancy can also be upsetting for both you and your spouse. Reading the information on coping with a pregnancy loss on page 576 can help you with your emotions.

If You're Not Pregnant...

If your pregnancy test is negative this time, but you'd very much like to become pregnant soon, start making the most of the preconception period by taking the steps outlined in Chapter 1. Good preconception preparation will help ensure the best possible pregnancy outcome when you do conceive.

And keep in mind the fact that conception did occur once for you means that it'll more than likely occur again soon, and with the happier end result of a healthy pregnancy.

A Negative Result

"I feel as if I'm pregnant, but the three tests I took came back negative. What should I do?"

If you're experiencing the symptoms of early pregnancy and feel, test or no test—or even three tests—that you're pregnant, act as though you are (by taking prenatal vitamins, avoiding alcoholic beverages, quitting smoking, eating well, and so on) until you find out definitely otherwise. Pregnancy tests aren't infallible, especially when they're taken very early. You may well know your own body better than a pee-on-a-stick test does. To find out if your hunch is more accurate than the tests, wait a week and then try again—your pregnancy might just be too early to call. Or ask your practitioner for a blood test, which is more sensitive to hCG than a urine test is.

It is possible, of course, to experience all of the signs and symptoms of early pregnancy and not be pregnant. After all, none of them alone—or even in combination—is absolute proof positive of pregnancy. If the tests continue to be negative but you still haven't gotten your period, be sure to check with your practitioner to rule out other biological causes of your symptoms. If those are ruled out as well, it's possible that your symptoms may have emotional roots. Sometimes, the mind can have a surprisingly powerful influence on the body, even generating pregnancy symptoms when there's no pregnancy, just a strong yearning for one (or fear of one).

Testing Smart

The home pregnancy test is probably the simplest test you'll ever take (you won't have to study for it—but you should read the package directions and follow them to get the most accurate results). The following tips may seem obvious, but in the excitement of the moment (Will I be? Won't I be?), you might forget a couple of things:

- Depending on the brand, you'll either hold the test stick in your stream of urine for a few seconds or collect your urine in a cup and then dip the stick into it. Most tests prefer you use midstream urine because there's less chance of contamination that way: Urinate for a second or two, stop, hold it, and then put either the stick or the cup in position to catch the rest of the stream.

- If you'll need to wait for the results, place the sample on a flat surface away from heat and in a place where it won't be disturbed. Read the test after the recommended waiting period; not waiting long enough—or waiting too long—can affect the result.

- It isn't necessary to use your first-morning urine, but if you're testing early (i.e., before your period is due), you're more likely to get an accurate result if you haven't peed in the past four hours (because your urine will contain more concentrated levels of hCG).

- Watch for the control indicator (ranging from a horizontal or vertical line to a filled-in circle, or a flashing control symbol in the digital tests) to let you know that the test is working.

- Look carefully—and before you leap to any conclusions. Any line you see (pink or blue, positive sign, or digital readout), no matter how faint it is (or no matter how faint you feel), means there's hCG in your system—and a baby likely in your future. Congratulations—you're pregnant! If the result isn't positive, and your period still hasn't arrived, consider waiting a few days and testing again. It may have just been too soon to call.

Making the First Appointment

"The home pregnancy test I just took came back positive. When should I schedule the first visit with my doctor?"

Good prenatal care is one of the most important ingredients in making a healthy baby. So don't delay. As soon as you suspect you might be pregnant or have a positive home pregnancy test result, call your practitioner to schedule an appointment. Just how soon you'll be able to come in for that appointment may depend on office traffic and policy. Some practitioners will be able to fit you in right away, while some very busy offices may not be able to accommodate you for several weeks or even longer. At certain practitioners' offices, it's actually routine procedure to wait until a woman is six to eight weeks pregnant for that first official prenatal visit, though some offer a "pre-OB" visit to confirm a pregnancy as soon as you suspect you're expecting (or have the positive HPT results to prove it).

But even if your official prenatal care has to be postponed until midway through the first trimester, that doesn't mean you should put off taking care of yourself and your baby. Regardless of when you get in to see your practitioner, start acting pregnant as soon as you see that positive readout on the HPT. You're probably familiar with many of the basics (take your prenatal vitamins, cut out alcohol and smoking, eat well, and so on), but don't hesitate to call your practitioner's office if you have specific questions about how best to get with the pregnancy program. You may even be able to pick up a pregnancy packet ahead of time (many offices provide one, with advice on everything from diet do's and don'ts to prenatal vitamin recommendations to a list of medications you can safely take) to help fill in some of the blanks.

In a low-risk pregnancy, having the first prenatal visit early on isn't considered medically necessary, though the wait can be hard to take. If the waiting's making you unreasonably anxious, or if you feel you may be a high-risk case (because of a history of miscarriages or ectopic pregnancies, for instance), check with the office to see if you can come in earlier. (For more on what to expect from your first prenatal visit, see page 124.)

Your Due Date

"My practitioner has told me my due date, but how accurate is it?"

Life would be a lot simpler if you could be certain that your due date is actually the day you will deliver, but life isn't that simple very often. According to most studies, only 1 in 20 babies is actually born on his or her due date. Because a normal full-term pregnancy can last anywhere from 38 to 42 weeks, most are born within two weeks either way of that date—which

keeps most parents guessing right up to delivery day.

That's why the medical term for "due date" is EDD, or *estimated* date of delivery. The date your practitioner gives you is only an educated estimate. It is usually calculated this way: Subtract three months from the first day of your last menstrual period (LMP), then add seven days—that's your due date. For example, say your last period began on April 11. Count backward three months, which gets you to January, and then add seven days. Your due date would be January 18.

This dating system works well for women who have a fairly regular menstrual cycle. But if your cycle is irregular, the system may not work for you at all. Say you typically get your period every six to seven weeks and you haven't had one in three months. On testing, you find out you're pregnant. When did you conceive? Because a reliable EDD is important, you and your practitioner will have to try to come up with one. Even if you can't pinpoint conception or aren't sure when you last ovulated, there are clues that can help.

The very first clue is the size of your uterus, which will be noted when your initial internal pregnancy examination is performed. It should conform to your suspected stage of pregnancy. The second clue will be an early ultrasound that can more accurately date the pregnancy. (Note that not all women get an early ultrasound. Some practitioners perform them routinely, but others will only recommend one if your periods are irregular, if you have a history of miscarriages or pregnancy complications, or if the estimated due date can't be determined based on your LMP and physical exam). Later on, there are other milestones that will confirm your date: the first time the fetal heartbeat is heard (at about 9 to 12 weeks with a Doppler), when the first flutter of life is felt (at about 16 to 22 weeks), and the height of the fundus (the top of the uterus) at each visit (for example, it will reach the navel at about week 20). These clues will be helpful but still not definitive. Only your baby knows for sure when his or her birth date will be . . . and baby's not telling.

Choosing and Working with Your Practitioner

We all know it takes two to conceive a baby, but it takes a minimum of three—mother, father, and at least one health-care professional—to make that transition from fertilized egg to delivered infant a safe and successful one. Assuming you and your spouse have already taken care of conception, the next challenge you both face is selecting that third member of your pregnancy team and making sure it's a selection you can live with—and labor with. (Of course, you can make this selection even before you conceive.)

Obstetrician? Family Practitioner? Midwife?

Where to begin your search for the perfect practitioner to help guide you through your pregnancy and beyond? First, you'll have to give some thought to what kind of medical credentials would best meet your needs.

The obstetrician. Are you looking for a practitioner who is trained to handle every conceivable medical aspect of pregnancy, labor, delivery, and the postpartum period—from the most obvious question to the most obscure complication? Then you'll want to look to an obstetrician-gynecologist. Ob-gyns not only provide complete obstetrical care, they can also take care of all your nonpregnancy female health needs (Pap smears, contraception, breast exams, and so on). Some also offer general medical care and thus can act as your primary physician as well.

If yours is a high-risk pregnancy, you will very likely need and want to seek out an ob-gyn. You may even want to find a specialist's specialist, an obstetrician who specializes in high-risk pregnancies and is certified in maternal-fetal medicine. Even if your pregnancy looks pretty routine, you may still want to select an obstetrician for your care—more than 90 percent of women do. If you've been seeing an ob-gyn you like, respect, and feel comfortable with for your gynecological care, there may be no reason to switch now that you're pregnant. If you haven't been seeing an ob-gyn, or you're not sure the one you've been seeing is the practitioner you want to spend your pregnancy with, it's time to start shopping around.

The family physician. Like the general practitioner of years ago, today's family physician (FP) provides one-stop medical service. Unlike the obstetrician, who has had postmedical school training in women's reproductive and general health only, the FP has had training in primary care, maternal care, and pediatric care after receiving an MD.

Birthing Choices

From start (when to conceive) to finish (how to deliver), pregnancy these days is full of personal choices. When it comes to birthing that baby, the array of options is dizzying, even in a hospital setting. Leave the hospital and there's yet more to select from.

Though your delivery preferences shouldn't be your only criteria in picking a practitioner, they should certainly be on the table. The following are among those birthing options that you can consider these days. Ask your potential candidates about their feelings on any of these—or any others—that appeal to you (keeping in mind that no firm birthing decisions can be made until further into your pregnancy, and many can't be finalized until the delivery itself):

Birthing rooms. The availability of birthing rooms in most hospitals makes it possible for you to stay in the same bed from labor through recovery (instead of laboring in one room and then being wheeled into a delivery room when you're ready to push), sometimes even for your entire hospital stay, and for your baby to remain at your side from birth on. Best of all, birthing rooms are cozy and comfy.

Some birthing rooms are used just for labor, delivery, and recovery (LDRs). If you're in an LDR, you (and your baby, if he or she is rooming in) will be moved from the birthing room to a postpartum room after an hour or so of largely uninterrupted family togetherness. If you're lucky enough to be in a hospital that offers LDRP (labor, delivery, recovery, postpartum) rooms, you won't have to do any moving at all. You and baby—and in some cases, dad and even siblings—will be able to stay put from check-in to check-out.

Most birthing rooms boast an "at-home-in-the-hospital" look, with soft lighting, rocking chairs, pretty wallpaper, soothing pictures on the wall, curtains on the windows, and beds that look more as if they came out of a showroom than a hospital supply catalog. Though the rooms are thoroughly equipped for low-risk births and even unexpected emergencies, medical equipment is usually stowed out of sight behind the doors of armoires and other bedroom-type cabinetry. The back of the birthing bed can be raised to support the mom in a squatting or semi-squatting position (a squatting bar can often be attached if desired), and the foot of the bed snaps off to make way for the birthing attendants. After delivery, a change of linens, a few flipped switches, and presto, you're back in bed. Many hospitals and birthing centers also offer showers and/or whirlpool tubs in or adjacent to the birthing rooms, both of which can offer hydrotherapy relief during labor. Tubs for water birth are also available in some birthing centers and hospitals. (See page 24 for more on water birth.) Many birthing rooms have sofas for your support team and/or other guests to hang out on—and sometimes even a pullout for your coach to spend the night on.

Birthing rooms at some hospitals are available only for women who are at low risk for childbirth complications; if you don't fit that profile, you may have no choice but to go to a traditional labor and delivery room, where more technology is readily at hand. And a C-section (cesarean delivery) is always performed in an all-business operating room (no homey look there). Fortunately, though, with the increasing availability of birthing rooms for most women, odds are great that you'll be able to experience unrushed, family-friendly, noninterventionist labor and delivery within a traditional hospital setting.

Birthing centers. Birthing centers, usually freestanding facilities (although they may be attached to—or even located in—a hospital), offer a homey, low-tech, and personalized place for childbirth. You'll be able to get all your prenatal care at a freestanding center—from practitioner visits to childbirth education and breastfeeding classes (in-hospital centers are usually only for childbirth itself). In general, most birthing centers offer the most comfortable childbirth amenities—from nicely decorated private rooms with soft lighting to showers and whirlpool tubs. A kitchen may also be available for family members to use. Birthing centers are usually staffed by midwives, but many have on-call obstetricians; others are located just minutes from a hospital in case any emergencies arise. And though birthing centers generally do not use interventions such as fetal monitoring, they do have medical equipment on hand, including IVs, oxygen for the mother and the infant, and infant resuscitators so emergency care can be initiated (if required) while you're waiting for a transfer to the nearby hospital. Still, only women with low-risk pregnancies are good candidates for delivery in birthing centers. Something else to consider: Unmedicated childbirth is the focus in a birthing center, and though mild narcotic medications are available, epidurals aren't. If you end up wanting an epidural, you'll have to be taken to the hospital.

Leboyer (or gentle) births. When the French obstetrician Frederick Leboyer first offered up his theory of childbirth without violence, the medical community was skeptical. Today, many of the procedures he proposed, aimed at making a newborn's arrival in the world more tranquil, are routine. Babies are often delivered in birthing rooms without the bright lights once deemed necessary, on the theory that gentle lighting can make the transition from the dark uterus to the bright outside world more gradual and less jolting. Upending and slapping the newborn is no longer routine anywhere; less aggressive procedures are preferred for establishing breathing when it doesn't start on its own. In some hospitals, the umbilical cord isn't cut immediately; instead, this last physical bond between mother and baby remains intact while they get to know each other for the first time (and until it stops pulsing). And though the warm bath Leboyer recommended for soothing the new arrival and smoothing the transition from a watery home to a dry one isn't common, being put immediately into mommy's arms is.

In spite of the growing acceptance of many Leboyer theories, a full-on Leboyer birth—with soft music, soft lights, and a warm bath for baby—isn't widely available. If you're interested in one, though, ask about it when you're interviewing practitioners.

Home birth. For some women, the idea of being hospitalized when they aren't sick just isn't the ticket. If that sounds like you—or if you just believe that life should begin at home—you might want to consider a home birth. The upside is obvious: Your newborn arrives amid family and friends in a warm and loving atmosphere, and you're able to labor and deliver in the comfort and privacy of your own home, without hospital protocols and personnel getting in the way. The downside is that if something unexpectedly goes wrong, the facilities for an emergency cesarean or resuscitation of the newborn will not be close at hand.

According to the American College of Nurse-Midwives, if you are considering a home birth, you should meet these guidelines:

(continued on next page)

(continued from previous page)

- Be in a low-risk category—no hypertension, diabetes, or other chronic medical problems, and no history of a previous difficult labor and/or delivery.

- Be attended by a physician or a CNM. If you're using a CNM, a consulting physician should be available, preferably one who has seen you during pregnancy and who has worked with the nurse-midwife before.

- Have transportation available and live within 30 miles of a hospital, if the roads are good and traffic's not an issue, or 10 miles if these standards aren't met.

Water birth. The concept of delivering underwater to simulate the environment of the womb is not widely used in the medical community, but it is more accepted among midwives. In a water birth, the baby is eased from the warm, wet womb into another warm, wet environment, offering familiar comfort after the stresses of delivery. The baby is pulled out of the water and placed in the mother's arms immediately after birth.

And since breathing doesn't begin until the baby is exposed to the air, there is virtually no risk of drowning. Water births can be done at home, in birthing centers, and in some hospitals. Many spouses join the mother in the tub or portable pool, often holding her from behind to provide support.

Most women with low-risk pregnancies can choose a water birth, as long as they can find a willing practitioner and hospital (birthing centers may be more likely to offer the option). If you're in a high-risk category, however, it's probably not a wise option, and it's unlikely you'll find even a midwife who will allow you to try a water birth.

Even if you don't find the idea of a water birth inviting—or don't have the option of one open to you—you might welcome the opportunity to labor in a whirlpool tub or regular bath. Most women find that the water not only provides relaxation, pain relief, and freedom from gravity's pull, but it even facilitates the progression of labor. Some hospitals and most birthing centers offer tubs in the birthing rooms. For more information on water births, go to gentlebirthchoices.org or waterbirth.org.

If you decide on an FP, he or she can serve as your internist, obstetrician-gynecologist, and, when the time comes, pediatrician. Ideally, an FP will become familiar with the dynamics of your family and will be interested in all aspects of your health, not just your obstetric ones. If complications occur, an FP may send you to an obstetrician but remain involved in your care for comforting continuity.

The certified nurse-midwife. If you're looking for a practitioner whose emphasis is on you the person rather than you the patient, who will take extra time to talk to you not only about your physical condition but also your emotional well-being, who will be more likely to offer you nutritional advice and breastfeeding support, and who will be oriented toward the "natural" in childbirth, then a certified nurse-midwife (CNM) may be right for you (though, of course, many physicians fit that profile, too). A CNM is a medical professional, a registered nurse who has completed graduate-level programs in midwifery and is certified by the American College of Nurse-Midwives. A CNM is thoroughly trained to care for women with low-risk pregnancies and to deliver uncomplicated births. In some cases, a CNM may provide continuing routine gynecological care and, sometimes, newborn care. Most midwives work in hospital settings, others deliver at birthing centers and/or do home births. Though CNMs have the right in most states to offer epidurals and other forms of pain relief, as well as to prescribe labor-inducing medications, a birth attended by a CNM is less likely to include such interventions. On average, midwives have much lower cesarean delivery rates than physicians, as well as higher rates of VBAC (vaginal birth after cesarean) success—but that may be due in part to the fact that they only care for women with low-risk pregnancies, which are less likely to take a turn for the complicated or result in surgical births. Studies show that for low-risk pregnancies, deliveries by CNMs are as safe as those by physicians. Something else to keep in mind: The cost of prenatal care with a CNM is usually less than that of an ob-gyn.

If you choose a certified nurse-midwife (about 8 percent of expectant mothers do), be sure to select one who is both certified and licensed (all 50 states license nurse-midwives). Most CNMs use a physician as a backup in case of complications; many practice with one or with a group that includes several. For more information about CNMs, look online at midwife.org.

Direct-entry midwives. These midwives are trained without first becoming nurses, though they may hold degrees in other health care areas. Direct-entry midwives are more likely than CNMs to do home births, though some also deliver babies in birthing centers. Those who are evaluated and certified through the North American Registry of Midwives (NARM) are called certified professional midwives (CPMs); other direct-entry

midwives are not certified. Licensing for direct-entry midwives is also currently offered in certain states; in some of those states, the services of a CPM are reimbursable through Medicaid and private health plans. In other states, direct-entry midwives cannot practice legally. For more information, call the Midwives Alliance of North America at (888) 923-6262 or check their website at mana.org.

Types of Practice

You've settled on an obstetrician, a family practitioner, or a nurse-midwife. Next you've got to decide which kind of medical practice you would be most comfortable with. Here are the most common kinds of practices and their possible advantages and disadvantages:

Solo medical practice. In such a practice, a doctor works alone, using another doctor to cover when he or she is away or otherwise unavailable. An obstetrician or a family practitioner might be in solo practice; a nurse-midwife, in almost all states, must work in a collaborative practice with a physician. The major advantage of a solo practice is that you see the same practitioner at each visit. This way, you get to know and, ideally, feel more comfortable with this person before delivery. The major disadvantage is that if your practitioner is not available, a backup you don't know may deliver your baby (although arranging to meet the covering physician or midwife in advance helps remedy this potential drawback). A solo practice may also be a problem if, midway in the pregnancy, you find you're not really crazy about the practitioner. If that happens and you decide to switch practitioners, you'll have to start from scratch again searching for one who suits your needs.

Partnership or group medical practice. In this type of practice, two or more doctors in the same specialty care jointly for patients, often seeing them on a rotating basis (though you usually get to stick with your favorite through most of your pregnancy and only start rotating toward the end of your pregnancy, when you're going to the office weekly). Again, you can find both obstetricians and family doctors in this type of practice. The advantage of a group practice is that by seeing a different doctor each time, you'll get to know them all—which means that when those labor pains are coming strong and fast, there's sure to be a familiar face in the room with you. The disadvantage is that you may not like all of the doctors in the practice equally, and you usually won't be able to choose the one who attends your child's birth. Also, hearing different points of view from the various partners may be an advantage or a disadvantage, depending on whether you find it reassuring or unsettling.

Combination practice. A group practice that includes one or more obstetricians and one or more nurse-midwives is considered a combination practice. The advantages and disadvantages are similar to those of any group practice. There is the added advantage of having at some of your visits the extra time and attention a midwife may offer and at others the extra medical know-how of a physician's extensive training and expertise. You may have the option of a midwife-coached delivery, plus assurance that if a problem develops, a physician you know is in the wings.

Maternity center– or birthing center–based practice. In these practices, certified nurse-midwives provide the bulk of the care, and physicians are on call as needed. Some maternity centers are based in hospitals with special birthing rooms, and others are separate facilities. All maternity centers provide care for low-risk patients only.

The advantage of this type of practice is obviously great for those women who prefer certified midwives as their primary practitioners. A potential disadvantage is that if a complication arises during pregnancy, you may have to switch to a physician and start developing a relationship all over again. Or, if a complication arises during labor or delivery, you may need to be delivered by the doctor on call, who may be a complete stranger. And finally, if you are delivering at a freestanding maternity center and complications arise, you may have to be transported to the nearest hospital for emergency care. A big advantage is likely to be the bottom line: CNMs and birthing centers usually charge less than physicians and hospitals.

Independent certified nurse-midwife practice. In the states in which they are permitted to practice independently, CNMs offer women with low-risk pregnancies the advantage of personalized pregnancy care and a low-tech natural delivery (sometimes at home, but more often in birthing centers or hospitals). An independent CNM should have a physician available for consultation as needed and on call in case of emergency—during pregnancy, childbirth, and postpartum. Care by an independent CNM is covered by most health plans, though only some insurers cover midwife-attended home births or births in a facility other than a hospital.

Finding a Candidate

When you have a good idea of the kind of practitioner you want and the type of practice you prefer, where can you find some likely candidates? The following are all good sources:

Division of Labor

Though not yet common practice nationwide, there's a trend that might be coming to a hospital (and an ob practice) near you. Some obstetricians, tired of running from long office hours to long overnights in the hospital delivering babies—and concerned that fatigue can affect the quality of care they provide—are looking for a better way. Enter the ob hospitalists, also known as laborists—obs who work exclusively in the hospital, only attending labors and delivering babies. These laborists don't have an office and don't follow patients through pregnancy.

If your practitioner tells you there's going to be a laborist at your birth, don't worry. But do take some steps to make sure you're comfortable with the arrangement. First, ask your practitioner if he or she and the hospital laborists have worked closely together in the past (and make sure their philosophies and protocols are similar).

You might also want to call the hospital to ask if you can meet the staff docs before labor, so that you're not being attended by a complete stranger during childbirth. Make sure, too, that you arrive at the hospital with extra copies of your birth plan (if you have one) to hand out, so whoever is attending you is familiar with your wishes even if he or she isn't familiar with you.

If you're uncomfortable with the whole arrangement, think about switching practices sooner rather than later. Remember, though, that if you're with a multiple-doc practice already, there's a good chance your "regular" ob won't be on call the day you go into labor anyway. Keep in mind, too, that because hospitalists focus solely on deliveries, they're extra-prepared to give the best possible care during labor. And extra-rested, also, because they work on shifts instead of around the clock.

- Your gynecologist or family practitioner (if he or she doesn't do deliveries) or your internist, assuming you're happy with his or her style of practice. (Doctors tend to recommend others with philosophies similar to their own.)

- Friends or coworkers who have had babies recently and whose personalities and childbearing philosophies are similar to yours.

- An obstetrical nurse who practices locally.

- The local medical society, which can give you a list of names of physicians who deliver babies, along with information on their medical training,

specialties, special interests, type of practice, and board certification.

- The American Medical Association (ama-assn.org) can help you search for a doctor in your area.

- The American College of Obstetricians and Gynecologists Physician Directory has the names of obstetrician-gynecologists and maternal-fetal specialists. Go to acog.org, or call 202-638-5577.

- The American College of Nurse-Midwives if you're looking for a CNM. Go to acnm.org or mybirthteam.com, or call 240-485-1800.

- The local La Leche League, especially if you're strongly interested in breastfeeding.

- A nearby hospital with facilities that are important to you—for example, birthing rooms with whirlpool tubs, rooming-in for both baby and dad, or a neonatal intensive care unit— or a local maternity or birthing center. Ask them for the names of attending physicians.

- If all else fails, check Yellow Book online or the phone book, under "Physicians." Look for the headings "Obstetrics and Gynecology," "Maternal-Fetal Medicine," or "Family Practice."

If your health insurance company hands you a list of practitioners, try to check them out with friends, acquaintances, or another physician to find the one in the bunch that seems right for you. If that's not possible, visit and meet with several of the candidates personally. In most cases, you should be able to find someone who is compatible. If not, finances permitting, you may want to see if you can switch plans.

Making Your Selection

Once you've secured a prospective practitioner's name, call to make an appointment for a consult. Go prepared with questions that will enable you to sense if your philosophies are in sync and if your personalities mesh comfortably. Don't expect that you'll agree on everything—that doesn't happen even in the most productive of partnerships. Be observant, too, and try to read between the lines at the interview (is the doctor or midwife a good listener? A patient explainer? Does he or she seem to take your emotional concerns as seriously as your physical ones?). Now's the time to find out this candidate's positions on issues that you feel strongly about: unmedicated child-

birth versus pain relief as needed in childbirth, breastfeeding, induction of labor, use of fetal monitoring or routine IVs, cesarean deliveries, or anything else that's important to you. Knowledge is power—and knowing how your practitioner practices will help ensure there won't be unpleasant surprises later.

Almost as important as what the interview reveals about your potential practitioner is what you reveal about yourself. Speak up and let your true patient persona shine through. You'll be able to judge from the practitioner's response whether he or she will be comfortable with—and responsive to—you, the patient.

You will also want to know something about the hospital or birthing center the practitioner is affiliated with. Does it provide features that are important to you—for example, plenty of LDR or LDRP rooms, breastfeeding support, a tub to labor in, the latest fetal monitoring equipment, a neonatal intensive care unit? Is there flexibility about procedures that concern you (say, routine IVs)? Are siblings allowed in the birthing rooms? Is extended family allowed during a surgical delivery?

Before you make a final decision, think about whether your potential

Pregnant and Uncovered

If you're expecting and uninsured, you're probably more concerned with figuring out how you're going to be able to afford prenatal care than you are with who's going to provide it. For tips that can help you get the care you and your baby need, see page 56.

practitioner inspires trust. Pregnancy is one of the most important journeys you'll ever make; you'll want a copilot in whom you have complete faith.

Making the Most of the Patient-Practitioner Partnership

Choosing the right practitioner is only the first step. The next step is nurturing a good working partnership. Here's how:

- Tell the whole truth, and nothing but the truth. Give your practitioner an accurate and complete general, gynecological, and obstetrical medical history. Fess up about an eating disorder you've battled or eating habits that are otherwise unhealthy. Speak up about any drugs—prescription or over-the-counter (including herbal), legal or illegal, medicinal or recreational, including alcohol and tobacco—that you are currently taking or have taken recently, as well as about any past or present illnesses or surgeries. Remember, what you tell your doctor is confidential; no one else will know.

- When a question or concern that doesn't require an immediate call comes up between visits, write it down and take it to your next appointment. (It may help to keep your cell phone or tablet handy or to keep notepads in convenient places—your purse, your desk at work, your bedside table—so that you'll always be within jotting distance of one.) That way you can be sure that you won't forget to ask all your questions and report all your symptoms (you will if you don't write them down; as you'll soon discover, pregnant women are notoriously forgetful). Along with

your list of questions, bring a pen and pad (or your cell phone, tablet, or the *What to Expect Pregnancy Journal and Organizer*) to each office visit so you can record your practitioner's recommendations. If your practitioner doesn't offer up all the information you'll need (side effects of treatments, when to stop taking a medication if one's prescribed, when to check back about a problem situation), ask for it before you leave so there's no confusion once you get home. If possible, quickly review your notes with the practitioner to be sure you've written down just what the doctor (or midwife) ordered.

- When in doubt, call. A symptom has you freaked? A medication or treatment seems to have triggered an adverse reaction? Don't just sit there worrying. Pick up the phone and call your practitioner (or e-mail, if your practitioner prefers to answer nonemergency questions online). Though you won't want to call or e-mail at every pelvic twinge, never hesitate to check in about questions that can't be answered in a book such as this one, and that you feel can't wait until the next visit. Don't be afraid that your concerns will sound silly—if it has you worried, it's not silly. Besides, doctors and midwives expect expectant moms to ask lots of questions, especially if they're first timers. When you do pick up the phone or compose that e-mail, be prepared to be very specific about your symptoms. If you're experiencing pain, be precise about its location, duration, quality (is it sharp, dull, crampy?), and severity. If possible, explain what makes it worse or better—changing positions, for example. If you have a vaginal discharge, describe its color (bright red, dark red, brownish, pinkish, yellow-ish), when it started, and how heavy it is. Also report accompanying symptoms, such as fever, nausea, vomiting, chills, or diarrhea. (See When to Call Your Practitioner, page 138.)

- Keep up to date. Read those parenting magazines and visit those pregnancy websites, by all means. But also realize that you can't believe everything you read, especially since the media often report medical advances before they are proven safe and effective through controlled studies—or report worrisome pregnancy warnings based on preliminary data that's yet to be backed up. When you read (or hear) about something new in obstetrics, ask your practitioner—usually your best information resource—for his or her take on it.

- When you hear or read something that doesn't correspond to what your practitioner has told you, don't keep it to yourself. Ask for an opinion on what you've heard—not in a challenging way, just so you can get your facts straight.

- If you suspect that your practitioner may be mistaken about something (for example, okaying intercourse when you have a history of incompetent cervix), speak up. You can't assume that he or she, even with your chart in hand, will always remember every aspect of your medical and personal history. As a partner in your own health care, and one who knows your body like the back of your hand (and then some), you share the responsibility of making sure mistakes aren't made.

- Ask for explanations. Find out what the potential side effects of a prescribed medication are, and whether there's a nondrug alternative. Be

So You Won't Forget

Because there'll be times when you'll want to do a little writing with your reading, jot down a symptom so you can share it with your doctor, make a note of this week's weight so you can compare it to next week's, record what needs recording so you'll remember what needs remembering—you'll find plenty of space in the *The What to Expect Pregnancy Journal and Organizer* for all your note taking.

sure you know why a test is ordered, what it will involve, what its risks are, and how and when you'll learn the results.

- Put it in writing. If you find your practitioner doesn't seem to have time to respond to all your questions or concerns, try providing a written list. If it isn't possible for you to get a complete response at the visit, ask if you can get the answers you need through a follow-up phone call or e-mail or a longer visit next time.

- Follow your practitioner's recommendations on appointment schedules, weight gain, bed rest, exercise, medication, vitamins, and so on, unless you have a good reason why you feel you shouldn't or can't (in which case, talk it over with your practitioner before you follow your instincts instead).

- Remember that good self-care is a vital component in good prenatal care. So take the best care of yourself that you can, getting enough rest and exercise, eating well, and steering clear of alcohol, tobacco, and other nonprescribed drugs and medications once you find out you're pregnant, or better still, once you start trying to conceive.

- If you have a gripe about anything—from regularly being kept waiting too long to not getting answers to your questions—speak up, in as nice a way as possible. Letting a problem fester can get in the way of a productive practitioner-patient relationship.

- Insurance companies often serve as mediators between patient and practitioner when there is a conflict or complaint. If you have a problem with your practitioner that good com-munication isn't solving, contact your health organization for help.

If you feel you can't follow your practitioner's instructions or go along with a recommended course of treatment, it might be because you're just not on board with the person you've chosen to care for you and your baby during your pregnancy, labor, and delivery. In such a case—or if, for some other reason, your relationship with your practitioner just isn't working—consider looking for a replacement (assuming that's financially feasible and your medical plan permits it).

CHAPTER 3

Your Pregnancy Profile

THE TEST RESULTS ARE BACK; the news has (sort of) sunk in: You're having a baby! Excitement is growing (along with that uterus of yours), and so is your list of questions. Many, no doubt, have to do with those wild and crazy symptoms you might already be experiencing (more on those later). But many others may have to do with your personal pregnancy profile. What's a pregnancy profile? It's a compilation of your gynecological, general medical, and obstetrical (if you're not a first timer) histories—in other words, your pregnancy backstory. You'll be discussing this backstory (which can actually have a lot of impact on the pregnancy story that's about to unfold) with your practitioner at your first prenatal visit. In the meantime, this chapter can help you take stock of your pregnancy profile and figure out how it may affect—or may not affect—your nine months of baby making.

This Book's for You

As you read *What to Expect When You're Expecting*, you'll notice many references to traditional family relationships—to "wives," "husbands," "spouses." These references are not meant to exclude expectant mothers (and their families) who may be somewhat "untraditional"—for example, those who are single, who have same-sex partners, or who have chosen not to marry their live-in partners. Rather, these terms are a way of avoiding phrases (for instance, "your husband or significant other") that are more inclusive but also a mouthful to read. Please mentally edit out any phrase that doesn't fit and replace it with one that's right for you and your situation.

Keep in mind that much of this chapter may not apply to you—that's because your pregnancy profile (like the baby you're expecting) is unique. Read what fits your profile and skip what doesn't.

Your Gynecological History

Birth Control During Pregnancy

"I got pregnant while using birth control pills. I kept taking them for over a month because I had no idea I was pregnant. Will this affect my baby?"

Ideally, once you stop using oral contraceptives, you'd have at least one normally occurring menstrual cycle before you tried to become pregnant. But conception doesn't always wait for ideal conditions, and occasionally a woman becomes pregnant while taking the Pill. In spite of warnings you've probably read on the package insert, there's no reason for concern. There's just no good evidence of an increased risk to a baby when mom has conceived while on oral contraceptives. Need more reassurance? Talk the situation over with your practitioner—you're sure to find it.

"I conceived while using a condom with spermicides and kept using spermicides before I knew I was pregnant. Should I be worried about birth defects?"

No need to worry if you got pregnant while using a condom or diaphragm with spermicides, a spermicide-coated condom, or just plain spermicides. The reassuring news is that no known link exists between spermicides and birth defects. In fact, the most recent and most convincing studies have found no increase in the incidence of problems even with the repeated use of spermicides in early pregnancy. So relax and enjoy your pregnancy, even if it did come a little unexpectedly.

"I've been using an IUD as birth control and just discovered that I'm pregnant. Will I be able to have a healthy pregnancy?"

Getting pregnant while using birth control is always a little unsettling (wasn't that why you were using birth control in the first place?), but it definitely happens. The odds of its happening with an IUD are pretty low—about 1 in 1,000, depending on the type of device used, how long it's been in place, and whether or not it has been properly inserted.

Having beaten the odds and managed conception with an IUD in place leaves you with two options, which you should talk over with your practitioner as soon as possible: leaving the IUD in place or having it taken out. Which of these options is best in your situation will depend on whether or not your practitioner can—on examination—see the removal cord protruding from your cervix. If the cord isn't visible, the pregnancy has a very good chance of proceeding uneventfully with the IUD in place. It will simply be pushed up against the wall of the uterus by the expanding amniotic sac surrounding the baby and, during childbirth, it will usually deliver with the placenta. If, however, the IUD string is visible early in pregnancy, the risk of infection developing is increased. In that case, chances of a safe and successful pregnancy are greater if the IUD is removed as soon as feasible, once conception is confirmed. If it isn't removed, there is a significant chance that the fetus will spontaneously miscarry; the risk drops to only 20 percent when it is removed. If that doesn't sound reassuring, keep in mind that the rate of miscarriage in all known pregnancies is estimated to be about 15 to 20 percent.

If the IUD is left in during the first trimester, be especially alert for bleeding, cramping, or fever because having an IUD in place puts you at higher risk for early pregnancy complications. Notify your practitioner of such symptoms right away.

Fibroids

"I've had fibroids for several years, and they've never caused me any problems. Will they, now that I'm pregnant?"

Chances are your fibroids won't stand between you and an uncomplicated pregnancy. In fact, most often these small nonmalignant growths on the inner walls of the uterus don't affect a pregnancy at all.

Sometimes, a woman with fibroids notices abdominal pressure or pain. If you do, report it to your practitioner, though it usually isn't anything to worry about. Bed rest for four or five days along with the use of safe pain relievers (ask your practitioner to recommend one) usually brings relief.

Very occasionally, fibroids can slightly increase the risk of such complications as abruption (separation) of the placenta, preterm birth, and breech birth, but these minimal risks can be reduced even further with the right precautions. Discuss the fibroids with your physician so you can find out more about the condition in general and the risks, if any, in your particular case. If your practitioner suspects that the fibroids could interfere with a safe vaginal delivery, he or she may opt to deliver by C-section. In most cases, however, even a large fibroid will move out of the baby's way as the uterus expands during pregnancy.

"I had a couple of fibroids removed a few years ago. Will that affect my pregnancy?"

In most cases, surgery for the removal of small uterine fibroid tumors (particularly if the surgery was performed laparoscopically) doesn't affect a subsequent pregnancy. Extensive surgery for large fibroids could, however, weaken the uterus enough so that it wouldn't be able to handle labor. If, after reviewing your surgical records, your practitioner decides this might be true of your uterus, a C-section will be planned. Become familiar with the signs of early labor in case contractions begin before the planned surgery (see page 358), and have a plan in place for getting to the hospital quickly if you do go into labor.

Endometriosis

"After years of suffering with endometriosis, I'm finally pregnant. Will I have problems with my pregnancy?"

Endometriosis is typically associated with two challenges: difficulty in conceiving and pain. Becoming pregnant means that you've overcome the first of those challenges (congratulations!). And the good news gets even better. Being pregnant may actually help with the second challenge.

The symptoms of endometriosis, including pain, do improve during pregnancy. This seems to be due to hormonal changes. When ovulation takes a hiatus, the endometrial implants generally become smaller and less tender. Improvement is greater in some women than in others. Many women are symptom free during the entire pregnancy; others may feel increasing discomfort as the fetus grows and begins packing a stronger punch, particularly if those punches and kicks reach tender areas. Fortunately, however, having endometriosis doesn't seem to raise any risks during pregnancy or childbirth (though if you've had uterine surgery, your practitioner will probably opt to deliver via C-section).

The less happy news is that pregnancy only provides a respite from the symptoms of endometriosis, not a cure. After pregnancy and nursing (and sometimes earlier), the symptoms usually return.

Colposcopy

"A year before I got pregnant, I had a colposcopy and cervical biopsy performed. Is my pregnancy at risk?"

A colposcopy is usually performed only after a routine Pap smear shows some irregular cervical cells. The simple procedure involves the use of a special microscope to better visualize the vagina and cervix. If abnormal cells are noticed on a Pap smear, as they probably were in your case, your physician performs a cervical, or cone, biopsy (in which tissue samples are taken from the suspicious area of the cervix and sent to the lab for further evaluation), cryosurgery (during which the abnormal cells are frozen), or a loop electrocautery excision procedure (LEEP, during which the affected cervical tissue is cut away using a painless electrical current). The good news is that the vast majority of women who have had such procedures are able to go on to have normal pregnancies. Some women, however, depending on how much tissue was removed during the procedure, may be at increased risk for some pregnancy complications, such as incompetent cervix and preterm delivery. Be sure your prenatal practitioner is aware of your cervical history so that your pregnancy can be more closely monitored.

If abnormal cells are noted during your first prenatal visit, your practitioner may opt to perform a colposcopy, but biopsies or further procedures are usually delayed until after the baby is born.

HPV (Human Papillomavirus)

"Can having genital HPV affect my pregnancy?"

Genital HPV is the most common sexually transmitted virus in the United States, affecting more than 75 percent of sexually active people, yet most of those who become infected with it never know. That's because most of the time, HPV causes no obvious symptoms and usually resolves on its own within six to ten months.

There are some times, however, when HPV does cause symptoms. Some strains cause cervical cell irregularities (detected on a Pap smear); other strains can cause genital warts (in appearance they can vary from a barely visible lesion to a soft, velvety "flat" bump or a cauliflower-like growth; colors range from pale to dark pink) that will show up in and on the vagina, vulva, and rectum. Though usually painless, genital warts may occasionally burn, itch, or even bleed. In most cases, the warts clear on their own within a couple of months.

Other STDs and Pregnancy

Not surprisingly, most STDs can affect pregnancy. Fortunately, most are easily diagnosed and treated safely, even during pregnancy. But because women are often unaware of being infected, the Centers for Disease Control and Prevention (CDC) recommends that all pregnant women be tested early in pregnancy for at least the following STDs: chlamydia, gonorrhea, trichomoniasis, hepatitis B, HIV, and syphilis.

Keep in mind that STDs don't happen just to one group of people or only at a certain economic level. They can occur in women (and men) in every age group, of every race and ethnic background, at every income level, and among those living in small towns as well as in big cities. The major STDs include:

Gonorrhea. Gonorrhea has long been known to cause conjunctivitis, blindness, and serious generalized infection in a fetus delivered through an infected birth canal. For this reason, pregnant women are routinely tested for the disease, usually at their first prenatal visit. Sometimes, particularly in women at high risk for STDs, the test is repeated late in pregnancy. If infection with gonorrhea is found, it is treated immediately with antibiotics. Treatment is followed by another culture, to be sure the woman is infection free. As an added precaution, an antibiotic ointment is squeezed into the eyes of every newborn at birth. (This treatment can be delayed for as long as an hour—but no longer—if you want to have some unblurry eye-to-eye contact with your baby first.)

Syphilis. Because this disease can cause a variety of birth defects as well as stillbirth, testing is also routine at the first prenatal visit. Antibiotic treatment of infected pregnant women before the fourth month, when the infection usually begins to cross the placental barrier, almost always prevents harm to the fetus. The very good news is that mother-to-baby transmission of syphilis is down in recent years.

Chlamydia. There are more cases of chlamydia in this country than gonorrhea or syphilis, with the disease affecting sexually active women under 26 years old most often. Chlamydia is the most common infection passed from mother to fetus, and it is considered a potential risk to the fetus and a possible risk to mothers. Which is why chlamydia screening in pregnancy is a good idea, particularly if you have had multiple sexual partners in the past, increasing your chance of infection. Because about half the women with chlamydial infection experience no symptoms, it often goes undiagnosed if it's not tested for.

How does genital HPV affect a pregnancy? Luckily, it's unlikely to affect it at all. Some women, however, will find that pregnancy will affect their HPV, causing the warts to become more active. If that's the case with you, and if the warts don't seem to be clearing on their own, your practitioner may recommend treatment during pregnancy. The warts can be safely removed by freezing, electrical heat, or laser therapy, although in some cases, this treatment may be delayed until after delivery.

If you do have HPV, your practitioner will also want to check your cervix to make sure there are no cervical cell

Prompt treatment of chlamydia prior to or during pregnancy can prevent chlamydial infections (pneumonia, which fortunately is most often mild, and eye infection, which is occasionally severe) from being transmitted by the mother to the baby during delivery. Though the best time for treatment is prior to conception, administering antibiotics (usually azithromycin) to the pregnant infected mother can also be effective in preventing infant infection. The antibiotic ointment routinely used at birth protects the newborn from chlamydial, as well as gonorrheal, eye infection.

Trichomoniasis. The symptoms of this parasite-caused STD (also referred to as trichomonas infection, or "trich") are a greenish, frothy vaginal discharge with an unpleasant fishy smell and, often, itching. About half of those affected have no symptoms at all. Though the disease does not usually cause serious illness or pregnancy problems (or affect a baby whose mom is infected), the symptoms can be irritating. Generally, women are treated during pregnancy only if they're having symptoms.

HIV infection. It is becoming increasingly routine for pregnant women to be tested for HIV (human immunodeficiency virus), whether or not they have a prior history of high-risk behavior. Many states actually require doctors to offer HIV counseling and testing to pregnant women, and ACOG recommends that all pregnant women, regardless of risk, be tested. Infection in pregnancy by the HIV virus, which causes AIDS, is a threat not just to the expectant mother but to her baby as well. About 25 percent of babies born to untreated mothers will develop the infection (testing will confirm it in the first six months of life). Luckily, there is plenty of hope with the treatments that are now available. But before taking any action, anyone who tests HIV positive may want to consider a second test (tests are highly accurate but can sometimes be positive in someone who does not have the virus). If a second test is positive, then formal counseling about AIDS and the treatment options is absolutely imperative. Treating an HIV-positive mother with AZT (also known as zidovudine—ZDV—or Retrovir) or other antiretroviral drugs can dramatically reduce the risk of her passing the infection on to her child, apparently without any damaging side effects. Delivering by elective C-section (before contractions begin and before membranes rupture) can reduce the risk of transmission further.

If you suspect that you may have been infected with any STD, check with your practitioner to see if you've been tested; if you haven't, ask to be. If a test turns out to be positive, be sure that you—and your partner, if necessary—are treated. Treatment will protect not only your health but that of your baby.

irregularities. If abnormalities are found, any necessary cervical biopsies to remove the abnormal cells will likely be postponed until after your baby is delivered.

Because HPV is highly contagious, practicing safe sex and sticking with one partner is the best way to prevent reoccurrence. Though there is a vaccine available now to prevent HPV in women under 26, it's not recommended for use during pregnancy. If you started the vaccine course (it's given in a three-dose series) and then became pregnant before completing the series, you'll need to hold off on the remaining doses until after your baby is born.

Herpes

"I have genital herpes. Can my baby catch it from me?"

Having genital herpes during pregnancy is cause for caution but definitely not for alarm. In fact, the chances are excellent that your baby will arrive safe, sound, and completely unaffected by herpes, particularly if you and your practitioner take protective steps during pregnancy and delivery. Here's what you need to know.

First of all, infection in a newborn is quite rare. A baby has only a less than 1 percent chance of contracting the condition if the mother has a recurrent infection during pregnancy (that is, she's had herpes before). Second, though a primary infection (one that appears for the first time) early in pregnancy increases the risk of miscarriage and premature delivery, such infection is uncommon. Even for babies at greatest risk—those whose mothers have their first herpes outbreak as delivery nears (which in itself is rare because it's tested for routinely)—there is an up to 50 percent chance that they will escape infection. Finally, the disease, though still serious, seems to be somewhat milder in newborns these days than it was in the past.

So if you picked up your herpes infection before pregnancy, which is most likely, the risk to your baby is very low. And with good medical care it can be lowered still further.

To protect their babies, women who have a history of herpes and have recurrent herpes during pregnancy are usually given antiviral medications. Those who have active lesions at the onset of labor are usually delivered by cesarean. In the unlikely event a baby is infected, he or she will be treated with an antiviral drug.

After delivery, the right precautions can allow you to care for—and breastfeed—your baby without transmitting the virus, even during an active infection.

Signs and Symptoms of Genital Herpes

It is during a primary, or first, episode that genital herpes is most likely to be passed on to the fetus, so call your practitioner if you experience the following symptoms of infection: fever, headache, malaise, and achiness for two or more days, accompanied by genital pain, itching, pain when urinating, vaginal and urethral discharge, and tenderness in the groin, as well as lesions that blister and then crust over. Healing of the lesions generally takes place within two to three weeks, during which time the disease can still be transmitted.

Your Obstetrical History

In Vitro Fertilization (IVF)

"I conceived my baby through in vitro fertilization. How different will my pregnancy be?"

Some well-deserved congratulations on your IVF success! With all you've been through to get to this point, you've earned some smooth sailing—and happily, you're likely to get it. The fact that you conceived in a laboratory rather than in bed shouldn't affect your pregnancy all that much, at least once the first trimester is over. Early on, however, there will be some differences in your pregnancy and your care. Because a positive test doesn't necessarily mean that a pregnancy will be sustained, because trying again can be so emotionally and financially draining, and because it's not known right off how many of the transferred embryos are going to develop into fetuses, the first six weeks of an IVF pregnancy are usually more nerve-wracking than most. In addition, if you've miscarried in previous tries, intercourse and other physical activities may be restricted. As an added precaution, the hormone progesterone will likely be prescribed to help support your developing pregnancy during the first two months.

But once this period is past, you can expect that your pregnancy will be pretty much like everyone else's—unless it turns out that you're carrying more than one fetus, as over 30 percent of IVF mothers do. If you are, see Chapter 16.

The Second Time Around

"This is my second pregnancy. How will it be different from the first?"

Since no two pregnancies are exactly alike, there's no predicting how different (or how similar) these nine months will be from the last. There are some generalities, however, about second and subsequent pregnancies that hold true at least some of the time (like all generalities, none will hold true all of the time):

- You'll probably "feel" pregnant sooner. Most second timers are more attuned to the early symptoms of pregnancy and more apt to recognize them. The symptoms themselves may vary

from last time—you may have more or less morning sickness, indigestion, and other tummy troubles; you may be more tired (especially likely if you were able to nap in your first pregnancy but now barely have the chance to sit down) or less tired (perhaps because you're too busy to notice how tired you really are or because you're so used to being tired); you may have more urinary frequency or less (though it's likely to appear sooner).

Some symptoms that are typically less pronounced in second and subsequent pregnancies include food cravings and aversions, breast enlargement and sensitivity, and worry (since you've already been there, done that, and lived to tell about it, pregnancy is less likely to induce panic).

- You'll "look" pregnant sooner. Thanks to abdominal and uterine muscles that are more lax (there's no gentler way to put that), you're likely to "pop" much sooner than you did the first time. You may notice, too, that you'll carry differently than you did with baby number one. Baby number two (or three or four) is liable to be larger than your firstborn, so you may have more to carry around. Another potential result of those "loosened-up" abdominals: Backache and other pregnancy pains may be exacerbated.

- You'll probably feel movement sooner. Something else to thank those looser muscles for—chances are you'll be able to feel baby kicking much sooner this time around, possibly as early as 16 weeks (maybe sooner, maybe later). You're also more likely to know it when you feel it, having felt it before. Of course, if the last pregnancy left you with lots of extra abdominal padding that you haven't been able to shed, those first kicks might not be so easy to feel.

- You may not feel as excited. That's not to say you aren't thrilled to be expecting again. But you may notice that the excitement level (and that compulsion to tell everyone you pass in the street the good news) isn't quite as high. This is a completely normal reaction (again, you've been here before) and in no way reflects on your love for this baby. Keep in mind, too, that you're preoccupied (physically and emotionally) with the child who's already here.

- You will probably have an easier labor and a faster delivery. Here's the really good part about those laxer muscles. All that loosening up (particularly in the areas involved in childbirth), combined with the prior experience of your body, may help ensure a speedier exit for baby number two. Every phase of labor and delivery is likely to be shorter, with pushing time significantly reduced.

You may wonder how to tell baby number one about the new baby who's on the way. Realistic, empathetic, and age-appropriate preparation for your firstborn to make the life-changing transition from only child to older child should begin during pregnancy. For tips, see *What to Expect the First Year* and *What to Expect the Second Year.* Reading picture books such as *What to Expect When Mommy's Having a Baby* and *What to Expect When the New Baby Comes Home* to your child will also help with older sib preparations.

"I had a perfect first baby. Now that I'm pregnant again, I can't shake the fear that I won't be so lucky this time."

Your chances of hitting the baby jackpot once again are excellent—in fact, better still for already having a successful pregnancy under your reexpanding belt. Also, with each pregnancy you get the chance to up the odds even more, by accentuating all those pregnancy positives (good medical care, diet, exercise, and lifestyle choices).

Your Obstetrical History Repeating Itself

"My first pregnancy was very uncomfortable—I must have had every symptom in the book. Will I be that unlucky again?"

In general, your first pregnancy is a pretty good predictor of future pregnancies, all things being equal. So you are a little less likely to breeze comfortably through pregnancy than someone who already has. Still, there's always the hope that your luck will change for the better. All pregnancies, like all babies, are different. If, for example, morning sickness or food cravings had you down in your first pregnancy, they may be barely noticeable in the second (or vice versa). Though luck, genetic predisposition, and the fact that you've experienced certain symptoms before have a lot to do with how comfortable or uncomfortable this pregnancy will be, other factors—including some that are within your control—can alter the prognosis to some extent. The factors include:

General health. Being in good all-around physical condition gives you a better shot at having a comfortable pregnancy.

Weight gain. Gaining weight at a steady rate and keeping the gain within the recommended guidelines (see page 166) can improve your chances of escaping or minimizing such pregnancy miseries as hemorrhoids, varicose veins, stretch marks, backache, fatigue, indigestion, and shortness of breath.

Diet. It can't offer any guarantees, but eating well (see Chapter 5 to find out how) improves every pregnant woman's chances of having a healthier and more comfortable pregnancy. Not only can it up your odds of avoiding or minimizing the miseries of morning sickness and indigestion, it can help you fight excessive fatigue, combat constipation and hemorrhoids, and prevent urinary tract infections and iron-deficiency anemia—even head off headaches. And if your pregnancy turns out to be uncomfortable anyway, by eating well you'll have bestowed on your baby the best chances of being born healthy.

Fitness. Getting enough and the right kind of exercise (see page 215 for guidelines) can help improve your general well-being. Exercise is especially important in second and subsequent pregnancies because abdominal muscles tend to be more lax, making you more susceptible to a variety of aches and pains, most notably backache.

Lifestyle pace. Leading a harried and frenetic life (and who doesn't these days?) can aggravate or sometimes even trigger one of the most uncomfortable of pregnancy symptoms—morning sickness—and exacerbate others, such as fatigue, headache, backache, and indigestion. Getting some help around the house, taking more breaks away from whatever fries your nerves, cutting back at work, letting low-priority tasks go undone for the time being, or practicing relaxation techniques or yoga can help you chill out—and feel better.

Other children. Some pregnant women with other children at home find that keeping up with their offspring keeps them so busy that they barely have time to notice pregnancy discomforts, major or minor. For others, all the running around that comes with running after kids tends to aggravate pregnancy symptoms. For example, morning sickness can increase during times of stress (the getting-to-school or the getting-dinner-on-the-table rush, for instance); fatigue can be heightened because there doesn't seem to be any time to rest; backaches can be an extra pain if you're doing a lot of child toting; even constipation becomes more likely if you never have a chance to use the bathroom when the urge strikes. You are also more likely to come down with colds and other illnesses, courtesy of older germ-spreading kids. (See Chapter 20 for preventing and dealing with such illnesses.)

It's not realistic to always put your pregnant body first when you've got other kids clamoring for care (the days of pampered pregnancy ended with your first delivery). But taking more time to take care of yourself—putting your feet up while you read that story, napping (instead of vacuuming) while your toddler naps, getting into the healthy snack habit even when there's no time for sit-down meals, and taking advantage of help whenever it's available—can help lighten the load your body's carrying, minimizing those pregnancy miseries.

"I had some complications with my first pregnancy. Will this one be just as rough?"

One complicated pregnancy definitely doesn't predict another one. While some pregnancy complications can repeat, many don't repeat routinely. Others may have been triggered by a onetime event, such as an infection or accident, which means they're extremely unlikely to strike twice. Your complications won't recur, either, if they were caused by lifestyle habits that you've now changed (like smoking, drinking, or using drugs), an exposure to an environmental hazard (such as lead) to which you are no longer exposed, or by not getting medical care early in pregnancy (assuming you've sought care early on this time). If the cause was a chronic health problem, such as diabetes or high blood pressure, correcting or controlling the condition prior to conception or very early in pregnancy can greatly reduce the risk of repeat complications. Also keep this in mind: Even if the complications you faced last time have a chance of reoccurrence, earlier detection and treatment (because you and your practitioner will be on the lookout for a repeat) can make a big difference.

Discuss with your practitioner the complications you had last time and what can be done to prevent them from being repeated. No matter what the problems or their causes (even if no cause was ever pinpointed), the tips in the response to the previous question can help make your pregnancy more comfortable, and safer for both you and your baby.

Back-to-Back Pregnancies

"I became pregnant unexpectedly just 10 weeks after I delivered my first child. What effect will this have on my health and on the baby I'm now carrying?"

Expanding your family (and your belly) again a little sooner than expected? Starting another pregnancy before you've fully recovered from the last one can be hard enough without adding stress to the mix. So first of all, relax. Though two closely spaced pregnancies can take their physical toll on a mom-to-be who just became a mom, there are lots of things you can do to help your body better handle the challenge of back-to-back baby making, including:

- Getting the best prenatal care, starting as soon as you think you're pregnant.

- Eating as well as you can (see Chapter 5). It's possible your body has not had a chance to rebuild its stores of vitamins and nutrients, and that can put you at a nutritional disadvantage, particularly if you're still nursing. You may need to overcompensate nutritionally to be sure both you and the baby you are carrying don't get short-changed. Pay particular attention to protein and iron (ask your practitioner whether you should take a supplement) and be sure to continue taking your prenatal vitamins. Try not to let lack of time or energy (you'll have little of both, that's for sure) keep you from eating enough. Healthy grazing may help you fit those nutrients into your busy schedule.

- Gaining enough weight. Your new fetus doesn't care whether or not you've had time to shed the extra pounds his or her sibling put on you. The two of you need the same weight gain this pregnancy, too, unless your practitioner prescribes otherwise. So shelve any weight loss plans for now. A carefully monitored gradual weight gain will be relatively easy to take off afterward, particularly if it was gained on a high-quality diet, and especially once you have a young toddler and an infant to keep up with. Watch your weight gain carefully, and if the numbers don't start climbing as they should, monitor your calorie intake more closely and follow the tips for increasing weight gain on page 180.

- Fair-share feeding. If you're breastfeeding your older baby, you can continue as long as you feel up to it. If you are completely exhausted, you may want to supplement with formula or consider weaning altogether. Discuss the options with your practitioner. If you decide to continue breastfeeding, be sure to get enough extra calories to feed both your baby and your fetus (ask your practitioner what to aim for). You will also need plenty of rest.

■ Resting up. You need more than may be humanly (and new-motherly) possible. Getting it will require not only your own determination but help from your spouse and others as well—who should take over as much of the cooking, housework, and baby care as possible. Set priorities: Let less important chores or work go undone, and force yourself to lie down when your baby is napping. If you're not breastfeeding, let daddy take over nighttime feedings; if you are, at least have him do the baby fetching at 2 A.M.

■ Exercising. But just enough to energize you, not enough to exhaust you. If you can't seem to find the time for a regular pregnancy exercise routine, build physical activity into your day with your baby. Take him or her for a brisk walk in the stroller. Or enroll in a pregnancy exercise class or swim at a club or community center that offers baby-sitting services.

■ Eliminating or minimizing all other pregnancy risk factors that apply to you, such as smoking and drinking. Your body and your baby-to-be don't need any extra stress.

Having a Big Family

"I'm pregnant for the sixth time. Does this pose any additional risk for my baby or for me?"

On your way to testing out that cheaper-by-the-dozen theory? Happily—for you and for your large brood—women receiving good prenatal care have an excellent chance of having healthy, normal babies in sixth (and later) pregnancies. In fact, beyond a small jump in the incidence of multiple births (twins, triplets, and so on—which could mean that your large brood could potentially grow even larger still), these more-the-merrier pregnancies are almost as likely to be uncomplicated as any first or second.

So enjoy your pregnancy and your large family. But while you're at it:

■ Get rest—all the rest you can get. Sure, you could probably do pregnancy in your sleep by now, but that doesn't mean you should try. Every pregnant woman needs her rest, but pregnant women who are also caring for a houseful of other children (plus the house they're filling) need even more.

■ Get help—all the help you can get. This will make getting that rest you need possible (or, at least, somewhat possible). Start with your spouse, who should be shouldering what he can in terms of child and house care, but don't stop there. If you haven't already, teach your older children to be more self-sufficient and assign them age-appropriate chores. Any nonessential chores you can't pass off to someone else, skip for now.

■ Feed yourself. Moms with many mouths to feed often neglect to feed their own. Not only does meal skipping or junk-food-grabbing shortchange you these days (leaving you with even less energy than you already have), but it shortchanges the baby you have on board. So take the time to eat well. Making healthy snacking a habit can help a lot (and finishing off PB&J scraps and half-eaten chicken fingers doesn't necessarily count).

■ Watch your weight. It's not uncommon for women who've had several pregnancies to put on a few extra pounds with each baby. If that's been the case with you, be particularly careful to eat efficiently and keep your gain on target (a target that should be determined by your practitioner). On the flip side, make sure you're not so busy you don't eat enough to gain adequate weight.

Previous Abortions

"I've had two abortions. Will they affect this pregnancy?"

Multiple first-trimester abortions aren't likely to have an effect on future pregnancies. So if your abortions were performed before the 14th week, chances are there's no cause for concern. Multiple second-trimester abortions (performed between 14 and 27 weeks),

however, may slightly increase the risk of premature delivery. In either case, be sure your practitioner knows about the abortions. The more familiar he or she is with your complete obstetrical and gynecological history, the better care you will receive.

Preterm Birth

"I had a preterm delivery in my first pregnancy. I've eliminated all my risk factors, but I'm still worried about having a repeat preterm labor."

Congratulations on doing everything you can to make sure your pregnancy is as healthy as possible this time around—and to give your baby the very best chances of staying on board until term. That's a great first step. Together with your practitioner, there are probably even more steps you can take to minimize the chances for a repeat preterm labor.

First, ask your practitioner about the latest research into preventing preterm labor. Researchers have found that the hormone progesterone—given as shots or a gel during weeks 16 through 36—reduces the risk for preterm birth in women with a prior history of one. If you've had a previous preterm birth, ask your practitioner if you're a good candidate for progesterone.

Second, ask your practitioner if one of the two screening tests available for predicting whether you're at risk for preterm birth would be right for you. Usually, these tests are only recommended for high-risk women since positive test results aren't an accurate predictor of early delivery, but negative results can help avoid unnecessary interventions—and needless anxiety. The fetal fibronectin (fFN) screening test detects a protein in the vagina only present if there has been a separation of

---

Do Tell

Whatever gynecological or obstetrical history is in your past, now's not the time to try to put it behind you. Telling your practitioner everything about your history is more important (and relevant) than you might think. Previous pregnancies, miscarriages, abortions, surgeries, or infections may or may not have an impact on what happens in this pregnancy, but any information you have about them—or any aspect of your obstetrical and gynecological history—should be passed on to your practitioner (all will be handled with confidentiality). The more he or she knows about you, the better care you'll get.

the amniotic sac from the uterine wall (an early indicator of labor). If you have a negative fFN test, it's unlikely you'll go into preterm labor within the next few weeks after the test (so you can breathe easy). If it's positive, your risk of going into preterm labor is significantly higher, and your practitioner may take steps to prolong your pregnancy and prepare your baby's lungs for an early delivery.

The second screening test is for cervical length. The length of your cervix is measured via ultrasound, and if there are any signs that the cervix is shortening or opening, your practitioner may take some steps to reduce your risk of early delivery, such as putting you on bed rest or perhaps stitching your cervix closed (if you're before 22 weeks).

Knowledge is always power—but in this case, knowledge can also help prevent your second baby from being born too soon. And that's a very good thing.

Incompetent Cervix

"I had a miscarriage in the fifth month of my first pregnancy. The doctor said it was caused by an incompetent cervix. I just had a positive home pregnancy test, and I'm worried that I'll have the same problem again."

The good news (and there *is* good news here) is that it doesn't have to happen again. Now that your incompetent cervix has been diagnosed as the cause of your first pregnancy loss, your obstetrician should be able to take steps to prevent it from causing another loss. With proper treatment and careful watching, the odds of your having a healthy pregnancy and a safe delivery this time around are greatly in your favor. (If you have a different practitioner now, make sure you share your history of incompetent cervix so you can receive the best care possible.)

An incompetent cervix, one that opens prematurely under the pressure of the growing uterus and fetus, is estimated to occur in 1 or 2 of every 100 pregnancies; it is believed responsible for 10 to 20 percent of all second-trimester miscarriages. It can be the result of genetic weakness of the cervix, extreme stretching of or severe lacerations to the cervix during one or more previous deliveries, an extensive "cone" biopsy done for precancerous cervical cells, or cervical surgery or laser therapy. Carrying more than one fetus can also lead to incompetent cervix, but if it does, the problem will not usually recur in subsequent single-fetus pregnancies.

Incompetent cervix is usually diagnosed when a woman miscarries in the second trimester after experiencing progressive painless effacement (shortening and thinning) and dilation of the cervix without apparent uterine contractions or vaginal bleeding.

To help protect this pregnancy, your ob may perform cerclage (a procedure during which the opening of the cervix is stitched closed) when you're in your second trimester (anywhere from 12 to 22 weeks). Although recent research has seriously questioned the effectiveness of cerclage (more study needs to be done), many practitioners still perform it routinely. More often, however, doctors will only do cerclage when an ultrasound or a vaginal exam shows that the cervix is shortening or opening. The simple procedure is performed through the vagina under local anesthesia. Twelve hours after surgery, you'll be able to resume normal activities, though sexual intercourse may be prohibited for the rest of your pregnancy, and you may need frequent medical exams. When the sutures will be removed depends partly on the doctor's preference and partly on the situation. Usually they're removed a few weeks before your estimated due date.

Your Pregnancy Profile and Preterm Birth

Here's the good news: It's far more likely your baby will be arriving late (as in overdue) than early. Just about 12 percent of labors and births are considered premature, or preterm—that is, occurring before the 37th week of pregnancy. And around half of these occur in women who are known to be at high risk for premature delivery, including the ever-multiplying percentage of moms-to-be of multiples.

Is there anything you can do to help prevent preterm birth if your pregnancy profile puts you at higher risk for it? In some cases, there isn't—even when a risk factor is identified (and it won't always be), it can't necessarily be controlled. But in other cases, the risk factor or factors that might lead to an early birth can be controlled or at least minimized. Eliminate any that apply to you, and you may up the chances that your baby will stay put contentedly until term. Here are some known risk factors for premature labor that can be controlled:

Too little or too much weight gain. Gaining too little weight can increase the chances your baby will be born early, but so can packing on too many pounds. Gaining just the right number of pounds for your pregnancy profile can give your baby a healthier uterine environment and, ideally, a better chance of staying there until term.

Inadequate nutrition. Giving your baby the healthiest start in life isn't just about gaining the right number of pounds—it's about gaining them on the right types of foods. A diet that lacks necessary nutrients (especially folate) increases your risk for premature delivery; a diet that's nutrition packed decreases that risk. In fact, some evidence indicates that eating well regularly can lower the risk of early delivery.

Lots of standing or heavy physical labor. Check with your practitioner to see if you should cut back on the time you spend on your feet, especially later on in pregnancy. Long periods of being on your feet—especially when it involves *heavy* physical labor and lifting—has been linked to preterm labor in some studies.

Extreme emotional stress. Some studies have shown a link between extreme emotional stress (not your everyday "I've got too much to do and not enough time to do it" stress) and premature labor. Sometimes the cause of such excessive stress can be eliminated or minimized (by quitting or cutting back at an unhealthily high-pressure job, for example); sometimes it's unavoidable (as when you lose your job or there's been illness or death in the family). Still, many kinds of stress can be reduced with relaxation techniques, good nutrition, a balance of exercise and rest, and by talking the problem out with your spouse or friends, your practitioner, or a therapist.

Alcohol and drug use. Expectant moms who use alcohol and illegal drugs boost their risk of having a premature delivery.

Smoking. Smoking during pregnancy may be linked to an increased risk of premature delivery. Quitting before conception or as early as possible in pregnancy is best, but quitting at any time in pregnancy is definitely better than not quitting at all.

Gum infection. Some studies show that gum disease is associated with preterm delivery. Some researchers suspect that the bacteria that cause inflammation in the gums can actually get into the bloodstream, reach the fetus, and initiate early delivery. Other researchers propose another possibility: The bacteria that cause inflammation in the gums can also trigger the immune system to produce inflammation in the cervix and uterus, triggering early labor. Practicing good oral hygiene and getting regular dental care can prevent the bacterial infection and possibly lower your risk for an early labor. Treatment for existing infections prior to pregnancy—though not necessarily during pregnancy—may also help lower the risk for a variety of complications, including preterm labor.

Incompetent cervix. The risk of premature delivery as a result of an incompetent cervix—in which a weak cervix opens early (and, unfortunately, can be suspected only after a woman has experienced a late miscarriage or premature labor once before)—can possibly be reduced by suturing the cervix closed and/or by closely monitoring the length of the cervix via ultrasound (see page 45 for more information).

History of premature deliveries. Your chances of premature delivery are higher if you've had one in the past. If you've had a prior preterm labor and delivery, your practitioner may prescribe progesterone during the second and third trimesters of this pregnancy to avoid a repeat preterm birth.

The following risk factors aren't controllable, but in some cases they can be somewhat modified. In others, knowing they exist can help you and your practitioner best manage the risks, as well as greatly improve the outcome if an early birth becomes inevitable.

Multiples. Women carrying more than one fetus deliver an average of three weeks early (though it has been suggested that full term for twins is actually 37 weeks, which might mean that three weeks early isn't early at all). Good prenatal care, optimal nutrition, and the elimination of other risk factors, along with more time spent resting and restriction of activity as needed in the last trimester, may help prevent a too-early birth. See Chapter 16 for more information.

Premature cervical effacement and dilation. In some women, for reasons unknown and apparently unrelated to an incompetent cervix, the cervix begins to thin out and open up early. Recent research suggests that at least some of this early effacement and dilation may be related to a shorter-than-normal cervix. A routine ultrasound of the cervix midpregnancy uncovers which women are at high risk.

Pregnancy complications. Such complications as gestational diabetes, preeclampsia, and excessive amniotic fluid, as well as problems with the placenta, such as placenta previa or placental abruption, can make an early delivery more likely. Managing these conditions as best as possible may prolong pregnancy until term.

Chronic maternal illness. Chronic conditions, such as high blood pressure; heart, liver, or kidney disease; or diabetes may raise the risk for preterm delivery, but good medical management and self-care may reduce it.

General infections. Certain infections (some sexually transmitted diseases; urinary, cervical, vaginal, kidney, and amniotic fluid infections) can put a mother-to-be at high risk for preterm labor. When the infection is one that could prove harmful to the fetus, early labor may be the body's way of attempting to rescue the baby from a dangerous environment. Preventing the infection or promptly treating it may effectively prevent a too-soon birth.

Under age 17. Teen moms-to-be are often at a higher risk for preterm delivery. Good nutrition and prenatal care can reduce risk by helping to compensate for the fact that both mother and baby are still growing.

In some cases, they may not be removed until labor begins, unless there is infection, bleeding, or premature rupture of the membranes.

You'll have to be alert for signs of an impending problem in the second or early third trimester: pressure in the lower abdomen, bloody discharge, unusual urinary frequency, or the sensation of a lump in the vagina. If you experience any of these, call your doctor right away.

Rh Incompatibility

"My doctor said my blood tests show I am Rh negative. What does that mean for my baby?"

Fortunately, it doesn't mean much, at least now that both you and your doctor know about it. With this knowledge, simple steps can be taken that will effectively—and completely—protect your baby from Rh incompatibility.

What exactly is Rh incompatibility, and why does your baby need protection from it? A little biology lesson can help clear that up quickly. Each cell in the body has numerous antigens, or antenna-like structures, on its surface. One such antigen is the Rh factor. Everyone inherits blood cells that either have the Rh factor (which makes the person Rh positive) or lack the factor (which makes them Rh negative). In a pregnancy, if the mother's blood cells do not have the Rh factor (she's Rh negative) while the fetus's blood cells—inherited from dad—do have it (making the fetus Rh positive), the mother's immune system may view the fetus (and its Rh-positive blood cells) as a "foreigner." In a normal immune response, her system will generate armies of antibodies to attack this foreigner. This is known as Rh incompatibility.

All pregnant women are tested for the Rh factor early in pregnancy, usually at the first prenatal visit. If a woman turns out to be Rh positive, as 85 percent are, the issue of compatibility is moot because whether the fetus is Rh positive or Rh negative, there are no foreign antigens on the fetus's blood cells to cause the mother's immune system to mobilize.

When the mother is Rh negative, as you are, the baby's father is tested to determine whether he is Rh positive or negative. If your spouse turns out to be Rh negative, your fetus will be Rh negative, too (since two "negative" parents can't make a "positive" baby), which means that your body will not consider it "foreign." But if your spouse is Rh positive, there's a significant possibility that your fetus will inherit the Rh factor from him, creating an incompatibility between you and the baby.

This incompatibility is usually not a problem in a first pregnancy. Trouble starts to brew if some of the baby's blood enters the mother's circulation during her first pregnancy or delivery (or abortion or miscarriage). The mother's body, in that natural protective immune response, produces antibodies against the Rh factor. The antibodies themselves are harmless—until she becomes pregnant again with another Rh-positive baby. During the subsequent pregnancy, these new antibodies could potentially cross the placenta into the baby's circulation and attack the fetal red blood cells, causing very mild (if maternal antibody levels are low) to very serious (if they are high) anemia in the fetus. Only very rarely do these antibodies form in first pregnancies, in reaction to fetal blood leaking back through the placenta into the mother's circulatory system.

Prevention of the development of antibodies is the key to protecting the fetus when there is Rh incompatibility. Most practitioners use a two-pronged attack. At 28 weeks, an Rh-negative expectant mom is given a vaccine-like injection of Rh-immune globulin, known as RhoGAM, to prevent the development of antibodies. Another dose is administered within 72 hours after delivery if blood tests show her baby is Rh positive. If the baby is Rh negative, no treatment is required. RhoGAM is also administered after a miscarriage, an ectopic pregnancy, an abortion, chorionic villus sampling (CVS), amniocentesis, vaginal bleeding, or trauma during pregnancy. Giving RhoGAM as needed at these times can head off problems in future pregnancies.

If an Rh-negative woman was not given RhoGAM during her previous pregnancy and tests reveal that she has developed Rh antibodies capable of attacking an Rh-positive fetus, amniocentesis can be used to check the blood type of the fetus. If it is Rh negative, mother and baby have compatible blood types and there's no cause for concern or treatment. If it is Rh positive, and thus incompatible with the mother's blood type, the maternal antibody levels are monitored regularly. If the levels become dangerously high, ultrasound tests are done to assess the condition of the fetus. If at any point the safety of the fetus is threatened because hemolytic or Rh disease has developed, a transfusion of Rh-negative blood to the fetus may be necessary.

The use of RhoGAM has greatly reduced the need for transfusions in Rh-incompatible pregnancies to less than 1 percent, and in the future may make this lifesaving procedure a medical miracle of the past.

A similar incompatibility can arise with other factors in the blood, such as the Kell antigen, though these are less common than Rh incompatibility. If the father has the antigen and the mother does not, there is again potential for problems. A standard screening, part of the first routine blood test, looks for the presence of circulating antibodies in the mother's blood. If these antibodies are found, the father of the baby is tested to see if he is positive, in which case the management is the same as with Rh incompatibility.

Your Medical History

Rubella Antibody Levels

"I was vaccinated against rubella as a child, but my prenatal blood test shows my rubella antibody levels are low. Should I be concerned?"

There's not much cause for concern when it comes to rubella these days, at least in the United States. Not because the illness isn't still harmful to the unborn (it still can be, particularly in the first trimester; see page 506), but because it's next to impossible to catch it. The CDC considers rubella to be eradicated in the United States, and since most children and adults have been—and will continue to be—vaccinated against rubella, the chances of being exposed to the illness are virtually nil.

Though you won't be immunized during pregnancy, you will be given a new rubella vaccine right after you deliver, before you even leave the hospital. It's safe then, even if you're breastfeeding.

Immunizations in Pregnancy

Since infections of various sorts can cause pregnancy problems, it's a good idea to take care of all necessary immunizations before conceiving. Most immunizations using live viruses are not recommended during pregnancy, including the MMR (measles, mumps, and rubella) and varicella (chicken pox) vaccines. Other vaccines, according to the CDC, shouldn't be given routinely but can be given if they're needed. These include hepatitis A and pneumococcal vaccine. You also can be immunized safely against tetanus, diphtheria, pertussis, and hepatitis B with vaccines containing dead, or nonactive, viruses. In the must-have department: The CDC recommends that every woman who is pregnant during flu season (generally October through April) receive a flu shot.

For more information about which vaccines are safe during pregnancy and which, if any, you may need (particularly if you'll be traveling to exotic destinations), check with your practitioner.

Obesity

"I'm about 60 pounds overweight. Does this put me and my baby at higher risk during pregnancy?"

Most overweight—and even obese (defined as someone whose weight is 20 percent or more over her ideal weight)—mothers have completely safe pregnancies and completely healthy babies. Still, obesity always poses extra health risks, and that's the case during pregnancy, too. Carrying a lot of extra weight while you're carrying a baby increases the possibility of certain pregnancy complications, including high blood pressure and gestational diabetes. Being overweight poses some practical pregnancy problems, too. It may be tougher to date your pregnancy accurately without an early ultrasound, both because ovulation is often erratic in obese women and because some of the yardsticks practitioners traditionally use to estimate a due date (the height of the fundus, or top of the uterus, the size of the uterus, hearing the heartbeat) may be difficult to read through layers of fat. The padding may also make it impossible for the practitioner to determine a fetus's size and position (as well as make it harder for you to feel those first kicks). Finally, delivery difficulties can result if the fetus is much larger than average, which is often the case with obese mothers (even among those who don't overeat during pregnancy, and particularly with those who are diabetic). And if a cesarean delivery is necessary, the overample abdomen can complicate both the surgery and recovery from it.

Then there's the issue of pregnancy comfort, or rather discomfort—and unfortunately, as the pounds multiply, so do those uncomfortable pregnancy symptoms. Extra pounds (whether they're pounds you already had or pounds you added during pregnancy) can spell extra backache, varicose veins, swelling, heartburn, and more.

Daunted? Don't be. There's plenty you and your practitioner can do to minimize the risks to you and your baby and the discomfort for you—it'll just take some extra effort. On the medical care side, you will probably undergo more testing than the typical low-risk pregnant woman: ultrasound early on to date your pregnancy more accurately, and later to determine the baby's size and position; at least one glucose toler-

Pregnancy After Gastric Bypass

Double congratulations—you've lost a whole lot of weight, and you're expecting! But as you pat yourself on the back (or the belly), you may also be wondering how having had gastric bypass or lap band surgery will affect your pregnancy. Happily, not that much. Chances are you were advised not to become pregnant for at least the first 12 to 18 months after your surgery—the time of the most drastic weight loss and potential for malnutrition. But once you've passed that benchmark, your chances of having a healthy pregnancy and healthy pregnancy outcome are actually even better than they would have been if you hadn't had the surgery and lost the weight. Still, as you probably know, you'll have to work extra hard to ensure the healthiest outcome:

- Put your weight loss surgeon on your prenatal team. He or she will be best able to advise your ob-gyn or midwife on some of the specific needs of a post–gastric bypass patient.

- You'll need to keep up with your recommended vitamin supplementation while you're expecting (this is not the time to be at a nutritional disadvantage). A prenatal vitamin is a good start, but you may need more

iron, calcium, folic acid, vitamin B_{12}, and vitamin A because of certain malabsorption issues. Be sure to speak to both your prenatal practitioner and your surgeon about your particular supplement needs.

- Watch your weight closely (with your practitioner, of course). You're used to watching it go down, but now it will have to start going up. If you don't gain enough weight during pregnancy, your baby may not be able to grow to its potential. Make sure you know what your target weight gain is (it may be different than for the average expectant mom), and make sure you have an eating plan in place that will help you reach your weight gain goal.

- Watch what you eat, too. As a gastric bypass patient, the quantity of food you can eat is limited, so you'll need to focus on quality (not a bad concept when you're expecting, anyway). Try not to waste calories, and instead try to choose foods that efficiently pack the most nutrients into the smallest volume.

- If at any time you experience abdominal pain and excessive bloating, call your doctor right away.

ance test or screening to determine if you are showing any signs of developing gestational diabetes; and, toward the end of your pregnancy, nonstress and other diagnostic tests to monitor your baby's condition.

As for your part, good self-care will make a big difference. Eliminating all pregnancy risks that are within your control—such as drinking and smoking —will be particularly important for you. Keeping your weight gain on target will

be, too—and it's likely that your target will be smaller than the average expectant mom's and monitored by your doctor more closely. ACOG recommends that overweight women gain 15 to 20 pounds and obese women gain no more than 15 pounds, though your practitioner's recommendations may differ.

Even with a scaled-down bottom line to stick to, your daily diet will have to contain adequate calories and be packed with foods that are concentrated sources of vitamins, minerals, and protein (see the Pregnancy Diet in Chapter 5). Focusing on quality over quantity and making every bite matter will help you make those calories count—and will help your baby get the most nutritional bang for the calories you consume. Taking your prenatal vitamin faithfully will provide extra insurance. (But keep over-the-counter appetite suppressants that you might have been taking prepregnancy off the menu; they can be dangerous during pregnancy. The same goes for beverages that claim to suppress your appetite.) Getting regular exercise, within the guidelines recommended by your doctor, will allow you to eat more of the healthy foods you and your baby need—without packing on too many pounds.

For your next pregnancy, if you are planning on one, try to get as close as possible to your ideal weight before you conceive. It will make everything about pregnancy a lot easier—and less complicated.

Underweight

"I've always been skinny. How will my pregnancy be affected by my being underweight?"

Pregnancy's definitely a time for eating well and gaining weight—for both the skinny and the not-so-skinny. But if you've come into pregnancy on the super-skinny side (with a BMI of 18.5 or less; see page 166 for how to calculate yours), you'll have to be filling up your plate even more. That's because there are some potential risks (such as having a small-for-date baby) associated with being pregnant and extremely underweight, particularly if you're also undernourished. But any added risk can be virtually eliminated with a good diet (one that includes not only extra calories but also fresh fruit and vegetables, which

provide the vitamins and minerals thin people are sometimes short on); prenatal vitamins; and adequate weight gain. Depending on where you started out on the scale, your practitioner may advise you to gain a little extra—possibly 28 to 40 pounds, instead of the 25 to 35 pounds recommended for the average-weight woman. If you've been blessed with a speedy metabolism that makes putting on pounds tricky, see page 181 for some tips. As long as your weight gain stays on track, though, your pregnancy shouldn't encounter any other bumps (besides that belly bump).

An Eating Disorder

"I've been fighting bulimia for the last 10 years. I thought I'd be able to stop the bingeing-purging cycle now that I'm pregnant, but I can't seem to. Will it hurt my baby?"

Not if you get the right kind of help right away. The fact that you've been bulimic (or anorexic) for a number of years means your nutritional reserves are probably low, putting your baby and your body at a disadvantage right off the bat. Fortunately, early in pregnancy the need for nourishment is less than it will be later on, so you have the chance to make up for your body's nutritional shortfall before it can hurt your baby.

Very little research has been done in the area of eating disorders and pregnancy, partly because these disorders cause disrupted menstrual cycles, reducing the number of women who suffer with these problems from becoming pregnant in the first place. But the studies that have been done suggest the following:

- If you get your eating disorder under control, you're just as likely to have a healthy baby as anyone else, all other things being equal.

- It's critical that the practitioner who is caring for your pregnancy know about your eating disorder (so speak up, even if your condition is in the past).

- Counseling from a professional who is experienced in treating eating disorders is advisable for anyone who suffers from such a problem, but it is essential when you're pregnant. You may also find support groups helpful (check online, or ask your practitioner or therapist for a recommendation).

- Continuing to take laxatives, diuretics, and other drugs favored by bulimics and anorexics can harm your developing baby. They draw off nutrients and fluids from your body before they can be utilized to nourish your baby (and later to produce milk), and they may lead to fetal abnormality if used regularly. These medications, like all others, should not be used by any pregnant woman unless prescribed by a physician who is aware of the pregnancy.

- Bingeing and purging during pregnancy (in other words, active bulimia) seems to increase the risk of miscarriage, premature birth, and postpartum depression. Putting those unhealthy habits behind you now will allow you to nourish your baby and yourself well. If you're having trouble doing so, make sure you get the help you need.

- Not gaining enough weight during pregnancy can lead to a number of problems, including preterm delivery and a baby who is small for his or her gestational age.

Just being committed to conquering your eating disorder, so that you can start nurturing that beautiful little baby of yours, is a first and most important step. You'll also need to understand the dynamics of weight gain in pregnancy.

Keep in mind:

- The pregnant shape is universally viewed as healthy and beautiful. Its roundness is normal, a sign that you're growing a baby. Celebrate those curves! Embrace your pregnant self!

- You're supposed to gain weight during pregnancy. The right amount of pregnancy weight gain is vital to your baby's growth and well-being as well as to your own health.

- Weight gained at the right rate, on the right foods, will go to the right places (your baby and those essential baby by-products). If you stay within the recommended guidelines (which are higher for those who begin pregnancy significantly underweight), the weight won't be that difficult to shed once the baby arrives. This strategy (a moderate amount of weight gained steadily on nutritious foods) will help ensure a speedier return to your prepregnancy shape postpartum and help ensure a healthier baby.

- When you starve yourself, you starve your baby. Your baby depends on you for a steady shipment of nutrients. If you don't eat, neither does your baby. If the nutrients you take in are purged (by vomiting, taking laxatives, or taking diuretics), your baby won't have enough left to grow on.

- Exercise can help you keep your weight gain reasonable, while guiding those extra pounds to the right places. But any exercise program you choose should be pregnancy appropriate (check it out with your practitioner first), and strenuous exercise (or too much exercise, which can burn too many calories or raise your temperature excessively) should be avoided.

- All of the weight gain of pregnancy won't drop off in the first few days after delivery. With sensible eating, the average woman returns to close to—but does not hit—her prepregnancy weight about six weeks after delivery. Getting all the weight off and getting back into shape (which requires exercise) can take much longer. For this reason, many women with eating disorders find that negative feelings about their body image cause them to slip back into bingeing and purging or starving during the postpartum period. Because these unhealthy habits could interfere with your ability to recover from childbirth, to parent effectively, and to produce milk if you choose to breastfeed, it's important that you continue professional counseling postpartum with someone experienced in the treatment of eating disorders.

The most important thing to keep in mind: Your baby's well-being depends on your well-being during pregnancy. If you're not well nourished, your baby won't be, either. Positive reinforcement can definitely help, so try putting pictures of cute chubby babies on the fridge, in your office and car, anywhere you might need a reminder of the healthy eating you should be doing. Visualize the food you eat making its way to your baby (and your baby happily gobbling up the meals).

If you can't seem to stop bingeing, vomiting, using diuretics or laxatives, or practicing semistarvation during pregnancy, discuss with your physician the possibility of hospitalization until you get your disorder under control.

Having a Baby After 35

"I'm 38 and pregnant with my first baby. I've read so much about the risks of pregnancy after 35 and wonder whether I should worry."

Becoming pregnant after 35 puts you in good—and growing—company. While the pregnancy rate among women in their 20s has dropped slightly in recent decades, it has increased nearly 40 percent among women over 35. And though the number of babies born to women in their 40s remains relatively small, their ranks have also increased by a third in recent years.

If you've lived for more than 35 years, you're probably aware that nothing in life is completely risk free. These days, pregnancy risks are very small to begin with, but they do increase slightly and gradually as you get older. However, the many benefits of starting a family at the time that's right for you can far outweigh any small risks (all of which can be reduced anyway, thanks to medical advancements).

The major reproductive risk faced by a woman in your age group is that she might not become pregnant at all because of decreased fertility. Once you've overcome that and become pregnant (congratulations!), you also face a somewhat greater chance of having a baby with Down syndrome. The inci-

Is 35 the Magic Number?

Just because you've already clocked in 35 years doesn't mean you'll necessarily need more or different testing than your younger pregnant pals. In fact, screening tests are recommended for all women, regardless of how many birthdays they've celebrated—and only those whose screens show a possible elevated risk need to consider more invasive prenatal diagnosis.

dence increases with mom's age: 1 in 1,250 for 25-year-old mothers, about 3 in 1,000 for 30-year-old mothers, 1 in about 300 for 35-year-old mothers, and 1 in 35 for 45-year-old mothers (you'll notice the risk gradually increases with age—it doesn't just spike at 35). It's speculated that this and other chromosomal abnormalities, though still relatively rare, are more common in older women because their eggs are older, too (every woman is born with a lifetime supply of eggs that age along with her), and have had more exposure to X-rays, drugs, infections, and so on. (It is now known, however, that the egg is not always responsible for such chromosomal abnormalities. An estimated minimum 25 percent of Down syndrome cases can be linked to a defect in an older father's sperm.)

A handful of other risks increase slightly with age. Being older, particularly over 40, means you might be more likely to develop high blood pressure (particularly if you're overweight), diabetes, or cardiovascular disease during pregnancy—but all of these conditions are more common in older groups in general, and all are usually controllable. Older mothers-to-be are also more subject to miscarriage (because of their older eggs), preeclampsia, and preterm labor. Labor and delivery, on average, are longer and slightly more likely to be complicated, with C-section and other forms of assisted delivery (such as vacuum extraction) more common. In some older women, a decrease in muscle tone and joint flexibility may make labor a little tougher—but for many others, especially those who are in excellent physical shape thanks to regular exercise routines and healthy eating, this isn't the case.

But in spite of these slightly increased risks, there's lots of good news for expectant moms over 35, too. Today's older mothers have more going for them than ever before. Though Down syndrome isn't preventable, it can be identified in utero through a variety of screening and diagnostic tests. Even better news: Today's essentially noninvasive first-trimester screenings (see page 59), which are recommended to all pregnant women regardless of age, are much more accurate than in the past, which means they screen out moms who don't necessarily need to proceed to a more invasive diagnostic test (even moms-to-be over 35)—saving money and stress. Chronic conditions that are more common in older moms can be well controlled. Drugs and close medical supervision can sometimes forestall preterm labor. And medical breakthroughs continue to decrease risks in the birthing room.

But as much as medical science can do to help you have a safe pregnancy and a healthy baby, it's nothing compared to what you can do yourself through exercise, diet, and quality prenatal care. Just being older doesn't necessarily put you in a high-risk category, but an accumulation of many individual risks can. Eliminate or minimize as many risk factors as you can, and you'll be able to take years off your pregnancy profile—making your chances of delivering a healthy baby virtually as good as those of a younger mother. Maybe even better.

So relax, enjoy your pregnancy, and be reassured. There's never been a better time to be over 35 and expecting a baby.

The Father's Age

"I'm only 31, but my husband is over 50. Could his age affect our baby?"

Throughout most of history, it was believed that a father's responsibility in the reproductive process was limited to fertilization. Only during the twentieth century (too late to help those

Uninsured, Mama?

Having a baby these days can definitely be an expensive proposition—and that's before you even purchase onesie number one. Still, no expectant mother needs to go through pregnancy and childbirth without the prenatal care she and her baby need, even if she's uninsured. If you can't afford to pick up health insurance now, here are some other ways to find that care at a price you can afford:

- Search online or in the phone book under "Clinics" or "Health Care Centers." Planned Parenthood and other health organizations can provide services, sometimes for free or on a sliding pay-what-you-can basis.

- Turn to the government. If your income is low enough, you may qualify for Medicaid. Through this program, you'll be entitled to prenatal care. If you don't qualify for Medicaid, there are low-cost health insurance programs (that will cover your pregnancy as well as your child's health care after delivery) offered through the government. Ask at any

clinic or call (877) KIDS-NOW or (877) 543-7669. You can also contact the foundation for Health Coverage Education at (800) 234-1317 or coverageforall.org to see if you qualify for state or federal programs. If affording nutritious food is an issue—or will be once you're feeding another mouth—contact WIC (Women, Infants, and Children), a government program that provides pregnant and nursing mothers with food and nutrition counseling. For information, contact WIC, www.fns .usda.gov/wic; (703) 305-2746.

- Call your local hospital. Some hospitals provide a certain amount of free or low-cost obstetrical care to women who need it. Childbirth classes may also be available at little or no cost to women who can't afford to pay full price for them.

- As a very last resort, try the ER. If you experience a pregnancy problem or go into labor before you can secure a practitioner, head to the ER of the nearest hospital immediately.

queens who lost their heads for failing to produce a male heir) was it discovered that a father's sperm holds the deciding genetic vote in determining his child's gender. And only in the last few decades have researchers begun to suspect that an older father's sperm might contribute to an increased risk of miscarriage or birth defects. Like the older mother's eggs, the older father's spermatocytes (undeveloped sperm) have had longer exposure to environmental hazards and might conceivably contain altered or damaged genes or chromosomes. In fact, researchers found that regardless of the mother's age, a couple's risk of

miscarriage increases as the dad's age increases. It also appears that there is an increase in the incidence of Down syndrome when the father is over 50 or 55 (regardless of how old the mother is), though the association is weaker than in the case of maternal age.

Still, the evidence remains inconclusive, mostly because the research involving older dads is still in its infancy. Despite what seems to be a small yet growing body of evidence to implicate paternal age as a factor in birth defects and miscarriages, genetic counselors do not recommend amniocentesis on the basis of a father's age alone. The screening tests that are now offered routinely to every mother-to-be, regardless of her age, should put your mind at ease. If your screening tests turn out normal, you can relax about your husband's age without having to go through amniocentesis.

Genetic Counseling

"I keep wondering if I might have a genetic problem and not know it. Should I get genetic counseling?"

Just about everyone carries at least one gene for a genetic disorder. But fortunately, because most disorders require a matched pair of genes, one from mom and one from dad, they're not likely to show up in their children. One or both parents can be tested for some of these disorders before or during pregnancy—but such testing usually makes sense only if there is a better-than-average possibility that both parents are carriers of a particular disorder. The clue is often ethnic or geographic. For example, testing for cystic fibrosis is offered for all couples but it is especially important for Caucasians of European descent, because about 1 in 25 are carriers of the condition. Jewish couples whose ancestors came from Eastern Europe should be tested for Tay-Sachs, Canavan disease, and possibly for other disorders. Tay-Sachs has also been noted in other ethnic groups, including Louisiana Cajuns and French Canadians, so getting tested is something to consider if your family has these roots. Similarly, black couples should be tested for the sickle cell anemia trait, and those of Mediterranean and Asian descent for thalassemia (a hereditary form of anemia). In most cases, testing is recommended for one parent; testing the second parent becomes necessary only if the first tests positive.

Pregnancy and the Single Mother

Are you a single mom-to-be? Just because you don't have a partner doesn't mean you have to go it alone during pregnancy—and you shouldn't try. The kind of support you'll need can come from sources other than a partner. A good friend or a relative you feel close to and comfortable with can step in to hold your hand, emotionally and physically, throughout pregnancy. That person can, in many ways, play the partner role during the nine months and beyond—accompanying you to prenatal visits and childbirth education classes, lending an ear (and a shoulder) when you need to talk about your concerns and fears as well as your excited anticipation, helping you get both your home and life ready for the new arrival, and acting as coach, supporter, and advocate during labor and delivery. And since no one will know better what you're going through than another single mom, you might also consider joining (or starting) a support group for single mothers, or find an online support group (check out the single mom's message board at whattoexpect.com).

Diseases that can be passed on via a single gene from one carrier parent (hemophilia, for example) or by one affected parent (Huntington's disease) have usually turned up in the family before, though it may not be common knowledge. That's why it's important to keep family health history records and to try to dig up as many health details from your parents, grandparents, and other close relatives as you can when you're pregnant (or are trying to conceive).

Most expectant parents, happily, are at such low risk for transmitting genetic problems that they don't need to see a genetic counselor. In many cases, a prenatal practitioner will discuss with a couple the most common genetic issues, referring to a genetic counselor or a maternal-fetal medicine specialist those with a need for more expertise:

- Couples whose blood tests show they are carriers of a genetic disorder that they might pass on to their children.

- Parents who have already had one or more children with genetic birth defects.

- Couples who have experienced three or more consecutive miscarriages.

- Couples who know of a hereditary disorder on any branch of either of their family trees. In some cases (as with cystic fibrosis or certain thalassemias), doing DNA testing of the parents before pregnancy makes interpreting later testing of the fetus much easier.

- Couples in which one partner has a congenital defect (such as congenital heart disease).

- Pregnant women who have had positive screening tests for the presence of a fetal defect.

- Closely related couples; the risk of inherited disease in offspring is greatest when parents are related (for example, 1 in 9 for first cousins).

The best time to see a genetic counselor is before getting pregnant, or in the case of close relatives who intend to start a family, before getting married. A genetic counselor is trained to give couples the odds of their having a healthy child based on their genetic profiles and can guide them in deciding whether or not to have children. But it's not too late even after pregnancy is confirmed. The counselor can suggest appropriate prenatal testing based on the couple's genetic profile, and if testing uncovers a serious defect in the fetus, a genetic counselor can outline for the expectant parents all the options available and help them decide how to proceed. Genetic counseling has helped countless high-risk couples avoid the heartbreak of giving birth to children with serious problems, while helping them realize their dreams of having completely healthy babies.

Prenatal Diagnosis

Is it a boy or a girl? Will it have blond hair or brown? Green eyes or blue? Will it have mom's mouth and dad's dimples? Dad's voice and mom's knack for numbers (or the other way around)? Babies definitely keep their parents guessing (and placing friendly bets) long before they actually arrive—sometimes before they're conceived. But the one

question that expectant parents wonder about the most is also the one they're most hesitant to speculate on or even talk about: "Will my baby be healthy?"

Until recently, that question could be answered only at birth. Today, it can be answered as early as the first trimester, through prenatal screening and diagnostic tests. Most expectant mothers undergo several screening tests during their 40 weeks—even those whose odds of having a baby with a defect are low (because of age, good nutrition, and excellent prenatal care). That's because such screening tests (from the combined and integrated screenings to the ultrasound and the quad screen) pose no risk to mom or baby but can provide a lot of beneficial reassurance.

Going one step further to definitive diagnostic tests (CVS, amnio, or more detailed ultrasound), however, isn't for everyone. Many parents—particularly those whose screening tests come back negative—can continue to play the waiting game, with the happy assurance that the chances are overwhelming that their babies are indeed completely healthy. But for those whose concerns represent more than normal expectant-parent jitters, the benefits of prenatal diagnosis can far outweigh the risks. Women who are good candidates for such testing include those who:

- Are over 35 (though an older mom with reassuring screening results may decide, after consultation with her practitioner, to skip the diagnostic tests).
- Have been exposed since conception to a substance or substances that they

fear might have been harmful to their developing baby. (Consultation with a physician can help determine whether prenatal diagnosis is warranted in a particular case.)

- Have a family history of genetic disease and/or have been shown to be carriers of such a disease.
- Have a genetic disorder themselves (such as cystic fibrosis or congenital heart disease).
- Have been exposed to infection (such as rubella or toxoplasmosis) that could cause a birth defect.
- Have had pregnancy losses previously, or have had babies with birth defects.
- Have tested positive on a prenatal screening test.

Why go through diagnostic tests if there's some risk involved? The best reason for prenatal diagnosis is the reassurance it almost always brings. The vast majority of babies whose possibly-at-risk moms undergo such testing will receive a perfect bill of health—which means that mom and dad can quit worrying and start enjoying their pregnancy.

First Trimester

First-Trimester Ultrasound

What is it? One of the simplest screening tests is the ultrasound. Using sound waves so high they can't be heard by the human ear, sonography allows visualization and "examination" of the fetus without X-rays. Though sonography tends to

be fairly accurate for most uses, in screening for birth defects the test can yield some false negatives (it seems as though everything is fine, but it's not) and some false positives (it looks as though there is a problem, but there really isn't).

A first-trimester ultrasound (usually a basic level 1 ultrasound) is performed in order to:

- Confirm the viability of a pregnancy

- Date a pregnancy

- Determine the number of fetuses

- Determine the cause of bleeding, if any

- Locate an IUD that was in place at the time of conception

- Locate the fetus prior to CVS or amniocentesis

- Assess the risk for chromosomal abnormality as part of a screening test

How is it done? Though ultrasound examination is often performed using a wand or transducer over the abdomen (transabdominal), during the first trimester a transvaginal exam may be preferred, especially early on. The procedures can last from 5 to 30 minutes and are painless, except for the discomfort of the full bladder necessary for the first-trimester transabdominal exam.

During either exam, you'll lie on your back. For the transabdominal, your bare abdomen is spread with a film of gel that will improve the conduction of sound. A transducer is then moved slowly over your belly. For the transvaginal, the transducer is inserted into your vagina. In both procedures, the instruments record echoes of sound waves as they bounce off parts of your baby and translate them into pictures on a viewing screen.

When is it done? Ultrasound is done anytime during the first trimester of pregnancy, depending on the reason for performing one. A gestational sac can be visualized on ultrasound as early as 4½ weeks after your last period; a heartbeat can be detected as early as 5 to 6 weeks (though it might not be detected that early in all cases). For information on second-trimester ultrasound, see page 66.

How safe is it? After many years of clinical use and study, no known risks and a great many benefits have been associated with the use of ultrasound. Many practitioners order ultrasound exams routinely, at least once in a woman's pregnancy. Still, it's generally recommended by most experts that ultrasound be used in pregnancy only when a valid indication exists.

First-Trimester Combined Screening

What is it? First-trimester combined screening involves both an ultrasound and a blood test. First the ultrasound measures a thin layer of fluid that accumulates in the back of the baby's neck, called nuchal translucency (NT). Increased fluid *may* indicate an increased risk of chromosomal abnormalities such as Down syndrome, congenital heart defects, and other genetic disorders.

Then the blood test measures for high levels of PAPP-A (pregnancy-associated plasma protein A) and hCG, two hormones produced by the fetus and passed into the mother's bloodstream. These levels, combined with the NT measurement and the mother's age, can provide a risk assessment for Down syndrome and trisomy 18.

A few medical centers also look for the absence of a nasal bone in the fetus during the ultrasound. Some studies have shown that the lack of a nasal bone during the first trimester may indicate a higher risk of Down syndrome, but other studies haven't backed that up, making this type of assessment somewhat controversial.

Though the first-trimester combined screening test can't give you the definite diagnosis you'd get from more invasive diagnostic tests, it can help you decide whether you want to undergo diagnostic testing. If your screening test shows that your baby may be at an increased risk of having a chromosomal defect, a diagnostic test such as chorionic villus sampling (CVS; see this page) or amniocentesis (see page 64) will be offered. If the screening test doesn't show an increased risk, your practitioner might recommend that you take the quad screen test in the second trimester (see page 63) to rule out neural tube defects. And because increased NT measurements are also associated with fetal heart defects, your practitioner might suggest a fetal echocardiogram at around 20 weeks to screen for heart defects if your levels are high. Increased NT measurements may also be linked to a very slightly higher risk of preterm labor, so you may be monitored for that as well.

When is it done? First-trimester combined screening is performed between 11 and 14 weeks of pregnancy.

How accurate is it? This screening test doesn't directly test for chromosomal problems, nor does it diagnose a specific condition. Rather, the results merely provide you with your baby's statistical likelihood of having a problem. An abnormal result on the combined screening test doesn't mean that your baby has a chromosomal problem, just that he or she has an increased risk of having one. In fact, most women who have an abnormal result on their screening test go on to have a perfectly normal and healthy child. At the same time, a normal result is not a guarantee that your baby is normal, but it does mean that it is very unlikely that your baby has a chromosomal defect.

The first-trimester combined screening can detect approximately 80 percent of Down syndrome and 80 percent of trisomy 18 problems.

How safe is it? Both the ultrasound and the blood test are painless (unless you count the needle prick for the blood test) and carry no risk to you or your baby. But there is one caveat. This type of screening test requires sophisticated ultrasound technology. To assure the best possible accuracy of the results, it should only be done with special equipment (a high-quality ultrasound machine) and by physicians and sonographers with special ongoing training. Keep in mind, too, that a risk of the test is that a false-positive (screen-positive) result may lead to follow-up procedures that present greater risk. Before you consider taking any action on the basis of prenatal screening, be sure an experienced physician or genetic counselor has evaluated the results. Get a second opinion if you have any doubts.

Chorionic Villus Sampling

What is it? Chorionic villus sampling (CVS) is a prenatal diagnostic test that involves taking a small tissue sample from the finger-like projections of the placenta called the chorionic villi and testing the sample to detect chromosomal abnormalities. At present, CVS is used to detect disorders such as Down syndrome, Tay-Sachs, sickle cell anemia, and most types of cystic fibrosis. CVS cannot test for neural tube and other anatomical defects. Testing for specific diseases (other than Down syndrome) is usually done only when there is a family history of the disease or the parents are known to be carriers. It is believed that CVS will eventually be able to detect over 1,000 disorders for which defective genes or chromosomes are responsible.

How is it done? CVS is most often performed in a hospital, though it can

It's a ... Surprise!

Diagnostic testing can determine your baby's gender. But unless it's a necessary part of the diagnosis, you'll have the option of either learning the results when you receive the CVS or amnio results (if you haven't already found out through ultrasound results) or waiting to find out the old-fashioned way, in the birthing room. Just make sure your practitioner knows about your decision ahead of time so your surprise won't be inadvertently spoiled.

also be performed in a doctor's office. Depending on the location of the placenta, the sample of cells is taken via the vagina and cervix (transcervical CVS) or via a needle inserted in the abdominal wall (transabdominal CVS). Neither method is entirely pain free; the discomfort can range from very mild to moderate. Some women experience cramping (similar to to menstrual cramps) when the sample is taken. Both methods take about 30 minutes, start to finish, though the actual withdrawal of cells takes no more than a minute or two.

In the transcervical procedure, while you lie on your back, a long thin tube is inserted through your vagina into your uterus. Guided by ultrasound imaging, the doctor positions the tube between the uterine lining and the chorion, the fetal membrane that will eventually form the fetal side of the placenta. A sample of the chorionic villi is then snipped or suctioned off for diagnostic study.

In the transabdominal procedure, you'll also lie tummy up. Ultrasound is used to determine the location of the placenta and to view the uterine walls. Then, while still under ultrasound guidance, a needle is inserted through your abdomen and the uterine wall to the edge of the placenta, and the cells to be studied are drawn up through the needle.

Because the chorionic villi are of fetal origin, examining them can give a clear picture of the genetic makeup of the developing fetus. Test results are available in one to two weeks.

When is it done? CVS is performed between the 10th and 13th weeks of pregnancy. Its main advantage is the fact that it can be performed in the first trimester and it can give results (and most often, reassurance) earlier in pregnancy than amniocentesis, which is usually performed after the 16th week. The earlier diagnosis is particularly helpful for those who might consider a therapeutic pregnancy termination if something is seriously wrong, since an earlier abortion is less complicated and traumatic.

How accurate is it? CVS is able to accurately detect chromosomal abnormalities 98 percent of the time.

How safe is it? CVS is safe and reliable, carrying a miscarriage rate of about 1 in 370. Choosing a testing center with a good safety record and waiting until right after your 10th week can reduce any risks associated with the procedure.

Some vaginal bleeding can occur after CVS and should not be a cause for concern, though it should be reported. You should also let your doctor know if the bleeding lasts for three days or longer. Since there is a very slight risk of infection with CVS, report any fever that occurs in the first few days following the procedure.

First and Second Trimester

Integrated Screening

What is it? Like the first-trimester combined screening, the integrated screening test involves both an ultrasound and blood test results, but in this case, the ultrasound (to measure NT) and a first blood test (to measure the concentration of PAPP-A) are performed during the first trimester, and a second blood test (to measure the same four markers in the blood as in the quad screen; see below) is performed during the second trimester. All three tests are integrated to give you the results. Like other screening tests, the integrated test doesn't directly test for chromosomal problems, nor does it diagnose a specific condition; rather, the results merely provide you with your baby's statistical likelihood of having a problem. Once you have that information, you can decide, together with your practitioner, whether you want to undergo diagnostic testing.

When is it done? The ultrasound is performed between the 10th and 14th weeks. The first blood test is done on the same day as the ultrasound, and the second blood test is done between 16 and 18 weeks. The results are reported to you after the second blood test.

How accurate is it? A test gathering and integrating information from both the first and second trimester of pregnancy is more effective than one that uses information from the first or second trimesters alone. With the integrated screening test, about 90 percent of Down syndrome cases and 80 to 85 percent of neural tube defects are detected.

How safe is it? Both the ultrasound and the blood tests are painless and carry no risk to the mom or her baby.

Second Trimester

Quad Screening

What is it? Quad screening is a blood test that measures the levels of four substances produced by the fetus and passed into the mother's bloodstream: alpha-fetoprotein (AFP), hCG, estriol, and inhibin-A. (Some doctors test only for three of the substances in a triple screen.) High levels of AFP may suggest the possibility (but by no means the probability) that a baby is at higher risk for a neural tube defect. Low levels of AFP and abnormal levels of the other markers may indicate that the developing baby may be at higher risk for a chromosomal abnormality, such as Down syndrome. The quad screening, like all screening tests, can't diagnose a birth defect; it can only indicate a higher risk. Any abnormal result simply means that further testing is needed.

Interestingly, studies indicate that women who receive abnormal results on their quad screen but receive normal results on follow-up testing such as amniocentesis *may* still be at very slightly increased risk of certain pregnancy complications, such as a small-for-gestational-age fetus, preterm delivery, or preeclampsia. If you receive results like this, ask your practitioner what steps you can take to reduce the chances of any potential complications later on, keeping in mind that the association between abnormal results and such complictions is very small to begin with.

When is it done? Quad screening is performed between weeks 14 and 22.

How accurate is it? The quad screen can detect an increased risk of the defects for approximately 85 percent of neural tube defects, nearly 80 percent of Down syndrome cases, and 80 percent of trisomy 18 problems. The false-positive rate for the independent quad screen is high. Only 1 or 2 out of 50 women with abnormally high readings eventually prove to have an affected fetus. In the other 48 or 49, further testing reveals that the reason the hormone levels are abnormal is that there is more than one fetus, the fetus is either a few weeks older or younger than originally thought, or the results of the test were just wrong. If the woman is carrying only one fetus and the ultrasound shows the dates are correct, an amniocentesis is offered as follow-up.

How safe is it? Because the quad screen requires only a blood sample, it is completely safe. The major risk of the test is that a positive result may lead to follow-up procedures that present greater risk. Before you consider taking any action on the basis of prenatal screening, be sure an experienced physician or genetic counselor has evaluated the results.

Amniocentesis

What is it? The fetal cells, chemicals, and microorganisms in the amniotic fluid surrounding the fetus provide a wide range of information about the growing baby inside you, such as genetic makeup, present condition, and level of maturity. Being able to extract and examine some of the fluid through amniocentesis has been one of the most important advances in prenatal diagnosis. It is offered when:

- Results of a screening test (the combined first-trimester screen, the integrated screen, triple or quad screen, or ultrasound) turn out to be abnormal, and evaluation of the amniotic fluid is necessary to determine whether or not there actually is a fetal abnormality.

- The mother is older (usually over age 35), primarily to determine if the fetus has Down syndrome (though an older mom with reassuring screening results may opt, in consultation with her practitioner, to skip amnio).

- The couple has already had a child with a chromosomal abnormality, such as Down syndrome, a metabolic disorder, or an enzyme deficiency such as cystic fibrosis (CF).

- The mother is a carrier of an X-linked genetic disorder, such as hemophilia (which she has a 50 percent chance of passing on to any son she bears).

- Both parents are carriers of an autosomal recessive inherited disorder, such as Tay-Sachs disease or sickle cell anemia, and thus have a 1 in 4 chance of bearing an affected child.

- Toxoplasmosis, fifth disease, cytomegalovirus, or other fetal infection is suspected.

- It is necessary to assess the maturity of the fetal lungs late in pregnancy (among the last organs ready to function on their own).

How is it done? While you lie on your back, your baby and the placenta are located via ultrasound, so the doctor will be able to steer clear of them during the procedure. It's possible that your abdomen will be numbed with an injection of a local anesthetic, but because this injection is as painful as the procedure itself, most practitioners skip it. A long, hollow needle is inserted through your abdominal wall into your uterus and a small amount of fluid is withdrawn from the sac that surrounds your fetus. (Don't worry—baby will produce more amniotic fluid to replace what's withdrawn.) The slight risk of accidentally pricking the fetus during this part of the procedure is further reduced by the use of simultaneous ultrasound guidance. The entire procedure—including prep time and ultrasound—will usually take about 30 minutes, start to finish (though the actual withdrawal of amniotic fluid takes no more than a minute or two). If you're Rh negative, you'll be given an injection of Rh-immune globulin (RhoGAM) after the amniocentesis to be sure the procedure does not result in Rh problems (see page 48).

When is it done? Diagnostic amniocentesis is usually performed between the 16th and 18th weeks of pregnancy, but occasionally as early as the 13th or 14th or as late as the 23rd or 24th week. Test results are usually back in 10 to 14 days. Some labs offer the FISH—fluorescent in situ hybridization—method, which quickly counts the number of certain chromosomes within cells. It can be used on an amniocentesis sample to get a faster result, often within a day or two (the Flash FISH offers results in just a couple of hours)—but since the result won't be complete, it's always followed by the usual chromosomal test in the lab. Amniocentesis can also be performed in the last trimester to assess the maturity of fetal lungs.

How accurate is it? Amniocentesis is more than 99 percent accurate in diagnosing—or ruling out, which is

A False Screen

You undergo screening tests for the reassurance you hope they'll provide, but unfortunately, what happens so often instead—particularly with the triple or quad screen—is a false positive (it seems things might not be okay when ultimately it turns out they're just fine). There goes the reassurance you were hoping to find—and here comes the needless anxiety and worry you were so hoping to avoid.

That's why it's so important to start off the screening process with an open discussion with your practitioner about the high rate of false positives and what it really means if you get one. What you'll hear is this reassuring news: More than 90 percent of moms who get that positive screen will end up having perfectly normal and healthy babies. Talk about positive!

far more likely—Down syndrome. (A normal FISH test is about 98 percent accurate.)

How safe is it? Amniocentesis is extremely safe; the risk that the procedure will result in a miscarriage is believed to be as low as 1 in 1,600. You may experience a few minutes to no more than a few hours of mild cramping after the procedure. Some doctors recommend resting for the remainder of the day; others don't. Rarely, slight vaginal bleeding or amniotic fluid leakage may be experienced. If you notice either, report it at once. The chances are very good that both the leakage and the spotting will stop after a few days, but bed rest and careful observation are usually recommended until it does.

How to Freak Out a Pregnant Woman

Happily, most ultrasound exams show that all is going (and growing) well with baby. But for some women, a level 2 ultrasound may go something like this: One minute you're starry-eyed as you gaze at the ultrasound screen, marveling at the miraculous image of your baby floating blissfully inside you. The next minute, the technician is calling for the doctor, who knocks you right off cloud nine and into a state of panic with a few frightening words: "We see something—a soft marker—that might indicate a problem."

But before you panic, it's important to gain some reassuring perspective. Though "soft markers" on an ultrasound (detected during 5 to 10 percent of second-trimester ultrasounds, depending on the marker) are subtle characteristics that may indicate an increased risk of a chromosomal problem (most often Down syndrome or trisomy 18), these characteristics are also found in plenty of babies who are perfectly healthy. In fact, very few babies who show these soft markers (such as choroid plexus cyst, echogenic foci, or pyelectasia, to name a few) actually end up having a chromosomal abnormality. Which means that in the majority of cases, these so-called abnormal findings don't indicate anything abnormal at all.

Your practitioner may suggest some more tests (like an amnio) to find out for sure, but in the meantime, take a deep breath and remember that sometimes technology—which can bring so much joy—can also bring unneeded worry.

Second-Trimester Ultrasound

What is it? Even if you had an ultrasound in your first trimester, you'll probably also get an ultrasound in your second trimester. This level 2, or "targeted," ultrasound is a much more detailed scan that focuses closely on fetal anatomy and can be used to check in on the growing fetus for a variety of other reasons as pregnancy progresses. It also can be a lot more fun to look at, because it gives a far clearer picture of your baby-to-be.

These days, as ultrasound images become ever sharper thanks to newer technology including 3-D and 4-D, even nonexperts (like parents) are able to tell a head from a bottom, and much more. During your level 2 ultrasound, and with the help of the technician or doctor, you may be able to spot your baby's beating heart; the curve of the spine; the face, arms, and legs. You may even catch sight of your baby sucking its thumb. Usually, the genitals can be seen and the sex surmised, although with less than 100 percent reliability and depending on baby's cooperation (if you'd like to keep the sex a surprise until delivery, make sure you let the doctor or technician know this in advance). In most cases, you'll be able to bring home or order up a souvenir of your exam—a digital photo or an electronic copy of the ultrasound video to show to friends and family.

When is it done? It is usually performed between 18 and 22 weeks.

How safe is it? No known risks and many benefits have been associated with the use of ultrasound. And many practitioners order ultrasound exams, at least once in a woman's pregnancy, often several times. Still, most experts advise that ultrasound be used in pregnancy only when a valid indication exists.

If a Problem Is Found

In the vast majority of cases, prenatal diagnosis yields the results that parents hope for—that all is well with their baby-to-be. But when the news isn't good—when something does turn out to be wrong with their baby—the information provided by such a heartbreaking diagnosis can still be valuable to parents. Teamed with expert genetic counseling, it can be used to make vital decisions about this and future pregnancies. Possible options include:

Continuing the pregnancy. This option is often chosen when the defect uncovered is one the couple feels that both they and the baby they're expecting can live with, or when the parents are opposed to abortion under any circumstance. Having some idea of what is to come allows parents to make preparations (both emotional and practical) for receiving a child with special needs into the family, or for coping with the inevitable loss of a child. Parents can also begin working through the reactions (denial, resentment, guilt) that can come with discovering their baby has a problem, rather than waiting until after delivery. They can learn about the particular problem in advance and prepare to ensure the best possible life for their child. Joining a support group—even one online—can help make coping somewhat easier.

Terminating the pregnancy. If testing suggests a defect that will be fatal or extremely disabling, and retesting and interpretation by a genetic counselor confirms the diagnosis, some parents opt to terminate the pregnancy. Should you decide to terminate, an autopsy, in which fetal tissue is carefully examined afterward, may be helpful in determining the chances that the abnormality will repeat in future pregnancies. Most couples, armed with this information

and the guidance of a physician or genetic counselor, do try again, with the hope that the tests and the pregnancy will be completely normal next time around. And most often they are.

Prenatal treatment of the fetus. Treatment may consist of blood transfusion (as in Rh disease), shunts or surgery (to drain an obstructed bladder, for instance), or administration of enzymes or medication (such as steroids to speed lung development when a baby must be delivered early). As technology advances, more kinds of prenatal surgery, genetic manipulation, and other treatments may also become common.

Donating the organs. If diagnosis indicates that the fetal defects are not compatible with life, it may be possible to donate one or more healthy organs to an infant in need. Some parents find that this provides some consolation for their own loss. A maternal-fetal specialist or neonatologist may be able to provide helpful information in such a situation.

As far as prenatal diagnosis has come, it's still important to remember that it's far from infallible. Mistakes happen, even in the best labs and facilities, even with the most skilled professionals wielding the most high-tech equipment—with false positives being much more common than false negatives. That's why further testing and/or consultation with additional professionals should always be used to confirm a result that indicates there is something wrong with the fetus.

It's also important to keep in mind that for the vast majority of couples, it will never come to that. Most expectant mothers who undergo prenatal testing receive the diagnosis they're hoping for right from the start: All is well with their baby and their pregnancy.

Your Pregnancy Lifestyle

O
F COURSE YOU'RE EXPECTING TO make some adjustments in your everyday life now that you're expecting (good-bye baby-tees, hello baby-on-board tees). But you might also be wondering just how drastically your lifestyle will have to change now that you're living for two. How about that predinner cocktail—will it have to wait until postdelivery? Those regular dips in the hot tub at the gym—are those washed up, too? Can you wipe your bathroom sink with that smelly (but effective) disinfectant? And what's that you heard about cat litter? Does being pregnant really mean you have to think twice about all those things you've never given a second thought to—from letting your best friend smoke in your living room to zapping your dinner in the microwave? In a few cases, you'll find, the answer is an emphatic yes (as in "no wine for me, thanks"). But in many others, your expectant self will be able to continue doing business—and pleasure—as usual, with maybe just a side of caution ("Honey, it's your turn to change the cat litter—for the next nine months!").

What You May Be Wondering About

Sports and Exercise

"Can I keep up with my regular exercise program now that I'm pregnant?"

I n most cases, pregnancy doesn't mean giving up the sporting life; just remember that while you're carrying a new life, moderation makes sense. Most practitioners not only permit but encourage expectant moms whose pregnancies are progressing normally to continue their accustomed workout routines and athletic pursuits for as long as is practical—but with several caveats. Among the most important: Always check with your practitioner before continuing or beginning an exercise program, and never exercise to the point of fatigue. (See page 215 for more information.)

Caffeine

"I use coffee to keep me going all day. Do I have to give up caffeine while I'm pregnant?"

No need to surrender your Starbucks card entirely—though you may have to start pulling it out a little less often. Most evidence suggests that drinking up to approximately 200 mg of caffeine a day is safe during pregnancy. Depending on how you take your coffee (black or with lots of milk), that could mean limiting yourself to about two cups (give or take) a day. Which means you're good to go (and fuel your get-up-and-go) if you're a light to moderate coffee drinker—but that you'll have to reassess your intake if you've got a more serious java jones (five-shot lattes, twice a day, come to mind?).

Why go so low? Well, for one thing, you share those lattes—like everything you eat and drink when you're expecting—with your baby. Caffeine (found most famously in coffee but also available in other foods and beverages) does cross the placenta—though to what extent (and at what dose) it affects a fetus is not completely clear. The latest information indicates that heavier caffeine intake early in pregnancy slightly increases the risk of miscarriage.

And there's more to the caffeine story. Sure, it has impressive pick-me-up powers, but in large doses, it also may have equally notable diuretic powers,

causing calcium and other key pregnancy nutrients to be washed out of your system before they can be thoroughly absorbed. Another downside to this diuretic effect: more frequent urination, which is the last thing a pregnant woman needs (you'll be peeing plenty on your own now that you're expecting). Need more motivation for cutting down? Caffeine's stimulating effects may exacerbate your mood swings, making them even more volatile and intense than they already are (or than they will be once your hormones rev into action). It can also prevent you from getting the rest your body's craving more than ever, especially if you drink it after noon. Plus excessive caffeine may interfere with the absorption of the iron both you and your baby need.

Different practitioners have different recommendations on caffeine consumption, so check in with yours for a bottom line on your favorite brew. When calculating your daily caffeine intake, keep in mind that it's not necessarily as easy as counting cups. Caffeine isn't just found in coffee—it's also in caffeinated soft drinks (too many Mountain Dews will have to be a Mountain Don't), coffee ice cream, tea, energy bars and drinks, and chocolate (though the amount varies from product to product). You'll need to know, too, that dark brews sold in coffeehouses contain far more caffeine than homemade; likewise, instant coffee contains less than drip does (see box, next page).

How do you cut down on a hefty caffeine habit (or cut it out altogether)? That depends on what's in the caffeine for you. If it's a part of your day (or many parts of your day—an eye-opener when you wake up, a companion on your way to work, a desktop fixture, an afternoon pick-me-up) that you're not anxious to part with, there's no need to. Just make your morning joes regular and your afternoons decaf. Or order your latte with mostly decaf shots instead of

regular—or with less espresso and more milk (you'll get a bigger calcium bonus anyway).

If it's the lift you crave—and that your body has become accustomed to—cutting back will be a taller order (make that a Venti order). As any coffee lover is well aware, it's one thing to be motivated to cut back on or kick caffeine altogether and another thing to do it. Caffeine is addictive (that's where the craving comes in), and quitting—or even cutting

way back on—a heavy habit comes with its own set of withdrawal symptoms, including headache, irritability, fatigue, and lethargy. That's why it's a good idea to ease off heavy consumption gradually. Try cutting back a cup at a time, and give yourself a few days to adjust to the lower dose before cutting back by another cup. Another way to cut back: Take each cup half-caf, gradually going full decaf in more and more cups—until your total caffeine consumption is down to that two-a-day-or-less goal.

No matter what's been driving you to the coffee bar, cutting back on or kicking caffeine will be less of a drag (literally) if you follow these energizing solutions:

- Keep your blood sugar (and thus your energy level) up. You'll get a natural, longer-lasting boost from eating and snacking on healthy foods often, especially complex carbs and protein (a combo that will give you the lift that keeps on lifting).

- Get some pregnancy-appropriate exercise each day. Exercise also raises the energy roof, while releasing those feel-good endorphins. Adding fresh air to the exercise mix will give you an extra energy boost.

- Clock in enough sleep time. Getting the rest your body needs at night (which will probably be easier to do without all that caffeine keeping you wired) will help you feel more refreshed in the morning, even before you've filled your first mug.

Caffeine Counter

How much caffeine do you get per day? It may be more—or less—than you think (and more or less than that approximate target of 200 mg). Check out this handy list, so you can do the math before you belly up to the coffee bar:

- 1 cup brewed coffee (8 ounces) = 135 mg
- 1 cup instant coffee = 95 mg
- 1 cup decaf coffee = 5 mg
- 6 ounces caffe latte or cappuccino = 90 mg
- 1 ounce espresso = 90 mg
- 1 cup tea = 40 to 60 mg (green tea has less caffeine than black tea)
- 1 can of cola (12 ounces) = about 35 mg caffeine
- 1 can of diet cola = 45 mg
- 1 ounce milk chocolate = 6 mg
- 1 ounce dark chocolate = 20 mg
- 1 cup chocolate milk = 5 mg
- 8 ounces coffee ice cream = 40 to 80 mg

Drinking

"I had a couple of drinks at least a couple of times before I knew I was pregnant. Could the alcohol have harmed my baby?"

Wouldn't it be nice to get an instant message from your body alerting you the moment sperm and egg met up? ("Just wanted to let you know we have a baby on board—time to switch to Evian.") But since that biotechnology doesn't exist (not yet, at least), many moms-to-be are oblivious that baby making has begun until several weeks into their pregnancies. And in the meantime, they're apt to have done a thing or two they wouldn't have done if they'd only known. Like having a few, a few times too many. Which is why your concern is one of the most common ones brought to the first prenatal visit.

Fortunately, it's a concern that you can cross off the list. There's no evidence that a couple of drinks on a couple of occasions very early in pregnancy, when you didn't even know you were pregnant, can harm a developing embryo. So you—and all the other moms who didn't get the message right away—can relax.

That said, it's definitely time to change that drink order now. Although you've probably heard of some women who drank lightly during pregnancy—one glass of wine nightly, for instance—and delivered perfectly healthy babies, there's just no research to support that this is a completely safe bet. In fact, the Surgeon General, ACOG, and the American Academy of Pediatrics (AAP) advise that no amount of alcohol is safe for pregnant women. That recommendation—and the research behind it—also leads to this recommendation: Although you shouldn't worry about what you drank before you knew you were pregnant, it would be prudent to take a pass for the rest of your pregnancy. (You can also ask your own practitioner about what he or she recommends.)

Why such a strong edict from the medical community? It's to be on the safe side—always the best side to be on when you have a baby on board. Though nobody knows for sure whether there is a safe limit when it comes to alcohol con-

sumption during pregnancy (or whether that limit would be different in different women), it is known that alcohol enters the fetal bloodstream in about the same concentrations present in the expectant mother's blood. In other words, a pregnant woman never drinks alone—she shares each glass of wine, each beer, each cocktail equally with her baby. Since it takes the fetus twice as long as its mother to eliminate the alcohol from its system, the baby can be at the point of passing out when the mother is just pleasantly buzzed.

Heavier drinking (generally considered to be the consumption of five or six drinks of wine, beer, or liquor a day) throughout pregnancy can result not only in many serious obstetrical complications but also in fetal alcohol syndrome (FAS). Described as "the hangover that lasts a lifetime," this condition produces infants who are born undersized, usually mentally deficient, with multiple deformities (particularly of the head and face, limbs, heart, and central nervous system) and a high mortality rate. Later, those who survive display vision, learning, behavioral, and social problems, and they generally lack the ability to make sound judgments. They are also more likely to end up with a drinking problem of their own by the time they reach 21. The sooner a heavy drinker stops drinking during pregnancy, the less risk to her baby.

The risks of continued drinking are definitely dose related: The more you drink, the more potential danger to your baby. But even moderate consumption (one to two drinks daily or occasional heavy bingeing on five or more drinks), if it occurs throughout pregnancy, is related to a variety of serious problems, including increased risk of miscarriage, labor and delivery complications, low birthweight, stillbirth, abnormal growth, and developmental and low IQ problems in childhood. Such drinking has also been linked to the somewhat more subtle fetal alcohol effect (FAE), characterized by numerous developmental and behavioral problems.

Passing up a drink during pregnancy is as easily done as said for some women, especially those who develop an aversion to alcohol (its taste and its smell) in early pregnancy, which sometimes lingers through delivery. For others, particularly those who are accustomed to unwinding with a Cosmo at the end of the day or to sipping a glass of red with dinner, abstinence may require a concerted effort and may include a lifestyle change. If you drink to relax, for example, try substituting other methods of relaxation: music, warm baths, massage, exercise, or reading. If drinking is part of a daily ritual that you don't want to give up, try a Virgin Mary (a Bloody Mary without the vodka) at brunch, sparkling juice or nonalcoholic beer at dinner, or a juice spritzer (half juice, half sparkling water, with a twist)—served at the usual time, in the usual glasses (unless, of course, these look-alike beverages trigger a yen for the real stuff). If your spouse joins you on the wagon (at least while in your company), the ride will be considerably smoother.

If you're having trouble giving up alcohol, ask your practitioner for help and for a referral to a program that can help you quit.

Smoking

"I've been smoking cigarettes for 10 years. Will this hurt my baby?"

Happily, there's no clear evidence that any smoking you've done prior to pregnancy—even if it's been for 10 or more years—will harm a developing fetus. But it's well documented (as well as plastered on cigarette packs) that smoking during pregnancy, particularly beyond

(Don't) Put That in Your Pipe

Your baby will thank you, also, for not smoking cigars and pipes—and for avoiding situations where they're being smoked. Because they aren't inhaled, cigars and pipes release even more smoke into the air than cigarettes do, which makes them even more potentially harmful to your baby. Want to announce your expected pride and joy with something safe and festive? Pass out chocolate cigars instead.

the third month, isn't just hazardous to your health—but to your baby's, too.

In effect, when you smoke, your fetus is confined in a smoke-filled womb. Its heartbeat speeds and, worst of all, due to insufficient oxygen, it can't grow and thrive as it should.

The results can be devastating. Smoking can increase the risk of a wide variety of pregnancy complications, including (among the more serious of these) ectopic pregnancy, abnormal placental implantation, premature placental detachment, premature rupture of the membranes, and possibly early delivery.

There is also strong evidence that a baby's development in utero is adversely and directly affected by an expectant mother's smoking. The most widespread risks for babies of smokers are low birthweight, shorter length and smaller head circumference, as well as cleft palate or cleft lip and heart defects. And being born too small is the major cause of infant illness and perinatal death (those that occur just before, during, or after birth).

There are other potential risks as well. Babies of smokers are more likely to die from SIDS (sudden infant death syndrome). They are also more prone to apnea (breathing lapses) and, in general, they aren't as healthy at birth as babies of nonsmokers, with three-pack-a-day maternal smoking associated with a quadrupled risk of low Apgar scores (the standard scale used to evaluate an infant's condition at birth). And evidence indicates that, on average, these children will suffer long-term physical and intellectual deficits, especially if parents continue to smoke around them. They are particularly prone to a lowered immune system, respiratory diseases, ear infections, colic, TB, food allergies, asthma, short stature, obesity, and problems in school, including attention deficit hyperactivity disorder (ADHD). Studies also show that pregnant women who smoke are more likely to have children who are abnormally aggressive as toddlers and who continue to have behavioral problems and even psychotic problems into adulthood. Children of mothers who smoked while pregnant are hospitalized more often in their first year of life than children of mothers who did not smoke while pregnant. These children are also more likely to grow up to be smokers themselves.

The effects of tobacco use, like those of alcohol use, are dose related: Tobacco use reduces the birthweight of babies in direct proportion to the number of cigarettes smoked, with a pack-a-day smoker 30 percent more likely to give birth to a low-birthweight child than a nonsmoker. So cutting down on the number of cigarettes you smoke may help some. But cutting down can be misleading because a smoker often compensates by taking more frequent and deeper puffs and smoking more of each cigarette. This can also happen when she tries to reduce the risk by using low-tar or low-nicotine cigarettes.

An Early Baby Present

There are no sure things when it comes to making a baby, but there are plenty of ways of improving your chances of having the best outcome possible: an uncomplicated pregnancy and delivery, and a perfectly healthy, full-term bundle of joy. And giving up smoking and drinking definitely tops the list.

Of course, there's the possibility that you can have that happy outcome even if you smoke or drink your way through pregnancy (or even smoke or drink lightly but regularly)—after all, everybody's heard of women who have done both and delivered healthy babies, right on time. But there's also the chance—and depending on how much smoking or drinking you do, a very significant risk—that you and your baby wouldn't be that lucky. Consider that different mothers and different babies are affected differently by pregnancy smoking and drinking (and there's no way to predict how you and your baby will be affected). Consider, too, that some of the deficits—physical and intellectual—linked to maternal smoking and drinking don't always show up at birth but often years later (a seemingly healthy infant can grow into a child who is often sick, who is hyperactive, or who has trouble learning).

Giving up pregnancy-unfriendly habits like drinking and smoking isn't always easy—and sometimes it's a real struggle. But giving your baby the very best chances of being born healthy is definitely the very best gift you can give.

Breaking the Smoking Habit

Congratulations—you've decided to give your baby a smoke-free environment, in utero and out. Making that commitment is the first and most important step. Realistically, however—as you probably already know if you've tried quitting before—it's not the most difficult step. Actually quitting is. But with a lot of determination and a little help from the following tips, you *can* do it.

Identify your motivations for quitting. When you're pregnant, that's easy. You've never had a more motivating reason.

Choose your method of withdrawal. Do you want to go cold turkey or taper off? Either way, pick a "last day" that isn't far off. Plan a full schedule of fun and distracting activities for that date—those you don't associate with smoking (in places, preferably, that don't allow smoking).

Identify your motivations for smoking. For example, do you smoke for pleasure, stimulation, or relaxation? To reduce tension or frustration? To have something in your hand or mouth? To satisfy a craving? Perhaps you smoke out of habit, lighting up without thinking about it. Once you understand your motivations, it'll help you find substitutes:

- If you smoke mainly to keep your hands busy, try playing with a pencil, beads, or a straw. Knit, play Sudoku on the computer, squeeze a stress ball, catch up on your e-mail, play video games, paint, doodle, do a crossword puzzle—anything that might make you forget to reach for a cigarette.

- If you smoke for oral gratification, try a substitute: a toothpick, gum, raw vegetables, popcorn, a lollipop or hard candy.

- If you smoke for stimulation, try to get your lift from a brisk walk, a workout session at the gym, an absorbing book, a long chat with a friend.

- If you smoke to reduce tension and relax, try exercise instead. Or relaxation techniques. Or listening to soothing music. Or a long walk. Or a massage. Or making love.

- If you smoke for pleasure, seek pleasure in other pursuits, preferably in no-smoke situations. Go to a movie, visit baby boutiques, tour a favorite museum, attend a concert or a play, have dinner with a friend who's a nonsmoker. Or try something more active, like a prenatal fitness class.

But the news isn't all bad. Some studies show that women who quit smoking early in pregnancy—no later than the third month—can eliminate all of the associated risks. For some smoking women, quitting will never be easier than in early pregnancy when they might develop a sudden distaste for cigarettes—probably the warning of an intuitive body. Sooner is better, but quitting even in the last month can help preserve oxygen flow to the baby during delivery.

If you're concerned that quitting will cause you to gain extra weight, keep in mind that although there is no evidence that smoking actually keeps weight down (many smokers are overweight, after all), it is true that some smokers gain weight while in the process of quitting. Interestingly enough, those who gain some

■ If you smoke out of habit, avoid the settings in which you habitually smoke and friends who smoke; frequent places with no-smoking rules instead.

■ If you associate smoking with a particular beverage, food, or meal, avoid the food or beverage, or eat the meal in a different location. (Say you smoke with breakfast but you never smoke in bed. Have breakfast in bed for a few days. You always smoke with your coffee? Have that latte in the coffeehouse, where smoking's not on the menu.)

■ When you feel the urge to smoke, take several deep breaths with a pause between each. Hold the last breath while you strike a match. Exhale slowly, blowing out the match. Pretend it was a cigarette and crush it out.

If you do slip up and have a cigarette, put it behind you. Don't give a second thought to the cigarette you smoked—think instead about all the ones you passed up. Get right back on your program, knowing that every cigarette you don't smoke is going to help your baby.

Try to look at smoking as nonnegotiable. When you were a smoker, you couldn't smoke in theaters, subways, at the mall, in many restaurants, and probably at your workplace. That was that. Now try telling yourself that you can't smoke, period—and that's that.

Let your baby inspire you. Post copies of your baby's ultrasound picture everywhere you might be tempted to smoke (make it your screensaver, frame it on the kitchen table, tape it on your dashboard, carry one in your bag). No ultrasound yet? Post pictures of adorable babies that you've cut out from magazines.

Get some support. There's plenty of help for smokers who want to quit. Look into hypnosis, acupuncture, and relaxation techniques, which have made quitters out of many smokers. If you're comfortable with a group approach to quitting, consider programs run by Nicotine Anonymous (misery often loves company—and support), the American Lung Association, the American Cancer Society, and SmokEnders, which have helped millions of smokers break the habit. Or seek support online from other pregnant women who are trying to call it quits.

If at first you don't succeed, try, try again. Nicotine is a powerful drug, and giving it up isn't easy, but it can be done. Many smokers don't succeed the first time they try quitting, yet they do if they keep trying. So don't beat yourself up when you slip up—pat yourself on the back for your efforts, and then up your efforts. You can do it!

Note: Check with your doctor to find out if using nicotine patches, lozenges, or gums while you're expecting is recommended in your case.

weight while trying to break the smoking habit are more likely to succeed—and they find it fairly easy to drop those few pounds later. Trying to diet while trying to quit usually leads to failure in both arenas. What's more, dieting while growing a baby is never a good idea. So though you should definitely pack away the cigarettes for good, don't worry if you start packing on a few more pounds than you otherwise

would have. There's never been a better reason for both.

Since nicotine is an addictive drug, most people experience withdrawal symptoms when they quit smoking, though the symptoms and their intensity vary from person to person. Besides the obvious craving for tobacco, some of the most common symptoms are irritability, anxiety, restlessness, tingling or numbness in the hands and feet, lightheadedness, fatigue, and sleep and gastrointestinal disturbances. Some people also find that both physical and mental performance are impaired at first. Most find that they initially cough more, rather than less, because their bodies are suddenly better able to bring up all the secretions that have accumulated in the lungs.

To try to slow the release of nicotine and the jitteriness that may result, avoid caffeine, which can add to the jitters. Get plenty of rest (to counter fatigue) and exercise (to replace the kick you used to get from nicotine). Avoid activities that require a lot of focus and concentration if you find you're in something of a fog, but keep busy by doing mindless tasks. Hanging out wherever smoking is prohibited by your state laws may also help. If you experience serious depression as part of withdrawal, talk to your practitioner immediately.

The worst effects of withdrawal will last a few days to a few weeks. The benefits, however, will last a lifetime—for you and your baby. See box, previous page, for more tips on how to quit.

Secondhand Smoke

"I don't smoke, but my husband does. Will this hurt our baby?"

Smoking doesn't affect just the smoker. It affects everyone around him, including a developing fetus whose mother happens to be nearby. So if your spouse (or anyone else you spend time with) smokes, your baby's body is going to pick up nearly as much contamination from tobacco smoke by-products as if you were lighting up.

If your spouse says he can't quit smoking, ask him to at least do all his smoking out of the house, away from you and the baby (but remember that smoke and its by-products will stick to

his clothes and skin, which means you'll still get some exposure to them). Quitting, of course, would be better, not just for his own health, but also for the baby's long-term well-being. Parental smoking—mother's or father's—increases the risk of SIDS in infancy, of respiratory problems at all ages, and of damage to the lungs even into adulthood. And it ups the chances that your children will become smokers one day.

You probably won't be able to get friends and other relatives to kick the habit, but you may be able to get them to curb their smoking around you (otherwise, you'll have to spend less time around them). Keeping smoking coworkers out of your breathing space will be easier to do if there are laws protecting nonsmokers in your workplace (many states have such laws). If the law isn't on your side, try tactful persuasion—show them this section on the dangers of secondhand smoke to a fetus. If that fails, try to get a regulation passed where you work that limits smoking to certain areas, such as a lounge, and prohibits smoking in the vicinity of nonsmokers. If all else fails, try to move your work space for the duration of your pregnancy.

Marijuana Use

"I smoke pot occasionally—basically only socially—and have for years. Could this have caused harm to the baby I'm now carrying? And is smoking pot during pregnancy dangerous?"

You can safely put past pot behind you. While it's usually recommended that couples trying to conceive pass on pot because it can interfere with conception, you're already pregnant—so that won't be a problem for you. And there's no present evidence that the marijuana you've smoked before you conceived will harm your fetus.

But now that you're pregnant, it's time to get off the pot. All the research isn't in yet, and the research that has been done so far isn't the most helpful kind. That's because it's hard to study marijuana use—like many lifestyle choices—in a vacuum. Often those who smoke pot during pregnancy are also drinking alcohol, smoking cigarettes, or using other drugs, making the data inconclusive (is it the pot or the beer or the cigarettes that resulted in a poor fetal outcome?). Other times, pregnant women who smoke marijuana may have less than optimal prenatal care, so it's hard to know whether a bad outcome came from the pot or the lack of pre-natal care. What is known so far about marijuana use during pregnancy is that the drug passes through the placenta, which means that when you smoke pot, you're sharing it with your unborn baby. Some studies show that marijuana use is associated with poor fetal growth and babies born small for gestational age; other studies show no such relationship. Still other studies have shown even more negative effects—from tremors and withdrawal-like crying during the newborn period to attention, learning, and behavioral problems later on in childhood.

With no sure proof that it's safe to smoke pot during pregnancy—and some evidence that suggests it may be quite harmful—it's wise to treat marijuana as you would any other drug during pregnancy: Just say no.

If you have already smoked early in your pregnancy, don't worry. But if you're tempted to continue using it, try some of the suggestions for quitting tobacco (and alcohol)—kicking one addiction is similar to kicking another. Focus especially on healthy forms of relaxation that'll net you that natural high (yoga, meditation, massage, even endorphin-releasing exercise). If you can't seem to stop smoking pot,

speak to your practitioner or seek other professional help as soon as possible.

Cocaine and Other Drug Use

"I did some cocaine a week before I found out I was pregnant. Now I'm worried about what that could have done to my baby."

Don't worry about past cocaine use; just make sure it was your last. On the upside: A single use of cocaine before you found out you were pregnant isn't likely to have had any effect. On the downside: Continuing to use it during pregnancy could be dangerous. How dangerous isn't quite clear. Studies on cocaine use during pregnancy aren't that easy to interpret, mostly because cocaine users are often also smokers—which means that it's difficult to separate the probable negative effects of cocaine use from the documented negative effects of smoking. What numerous studies have shown is that cocaine not only crosses the placenta once it develops, but it can damage it, reducing blood flow to the fetus and restricting fetal growth, particularly that of the baby's head. It is also believed to lead to birth defects, miscarriage, premature labor, low birthweight; jitteriness and withdrawal-like crying in the newborn; as well as numerous long-term problems for a child, including neurological and behavioral problems (such as difficulty with impulse control, with paying attention, and with responding to others), motor development deficits, and possibly lower IQ scores later on in childhood. Certainly, the more often an expectant mother uses cocaine, the greater the risk to her baby.

Tell your practitioner about any cocaine use since you've conceived. As with every aspect of your medical history, the more your doctor or midwife knows, the better care you and your baby will receive. If you have any difficulty giving up cocaine entirely, seek professional help immediately.

Pregnant women who use drugs of any kind—other than those that have been prescribed by a physician who knows they are pregnant—are putting their babies at risk. Every known illicit drug (including heroin, meth, crack, Ecstasy, "ice," LSD, and PCP) and many prescription drugs that are often abused (including narcotics, tranquilizers, sedatives, and diet pills) can, with continued use, cause serious harm to a developing fetus and/or to your pregnancy. Check with your practitioner or another knowledgeable doctor about any drugs you've used during pregnancy. Then, if you are still using drugs, get professional support (from a certified addiction counselor, an addictionologist, or a treatment center) to help you quit now. Enrolling in a drug-free-pregnancy program now can make a tremendous difference in the outcome of your pregnancy.

Mobile Devices

"I spend hours a day on my smartphone. Could this have any effect on my baby?"

Look who's talking, texting, and social networking on the run: practically everyone. And there are plenty of good reasons to keep connected through mobile technology—it can allow you to be available for that call from your doctor or midwife, manage your baby registry, scout pediatricians and scour crib reviews, check in with your message board buddies, and alert your spouse at the first signs of labor when you're nowhere near a landline. A mobile device can also allow you to be more flexible in your workday and in the amount of time spent chained to a desk (which might

result in more time for needed rest and relaxation or baby preparations).

That said, the convenience of cell phones and other mobile devices (including tablets) may not come completely risk free. While long-term effects of mobile technology are still being studied, experts recommend reducing your exposure (and your baby's) to radio-frequency energy by taking precautionary measures, such as going Bluetooth, holding your mobile device away from your belly when texting or using the Internet, and using a landline whenever possible.

A risk that is proven (and illegal in many areas): driving while talking on a cell phone or texting while driving. Even a hands-free phone conversation can be risky if it takes your attention off the road. Play it safe by pulling over to a safe area before making a call or texting.

Microwaves

"I use my microwave practically every day to heat up food or even cook. Is microwave exposure safe during pregnancy?"

A microwave oven can be a mother-to-be's best friend, helping to make healthy eating-on-the-run possible—with a minimum of effort and cooking odor. And happily, all the research indicates that microwaves are completely safe to use during pregnancy (and at all other times). Two sensible precautions: Use only cookware that is specifically manufactured for use in the microwave, and don't let plastic wrap touch foods during microwaving.

Hot Tubs and Saunas

"We have a hot tub. Is it safe for me to use it while I'm pregnant?"

You won't have to switch to cold showers, but it's probably a good idea to stay out of the hot tub. Anything that raises the body temperature over 102°F and keeps it there for a while—whether it's a soak in a hot tub or an extremely hot bath, or an overzealous workout in hot weather—is potentially hazardous to the developing embryo or fetus, particularly in the early months. Some studies have shown that a hot tub doesn't raise a woman's temperature to dangerous levels immediately—it takes at least 10 minutes (longer if the shoulders and arms are not submerged or if the water is 102°F or less). But because individual responses and circumstances vary, play it safe by keeping your belly out of the hot tub. Feel free, however, to soak your feet.

If you've already had some brief dips in the hot tub, there is probably no cause for concern. Most women spontaneously get out of a hot tub before their body temperatures reach 102°F because they become uncomfortable. It's likely you did, too. If you are concerned, however, speak to your practitioner about the possibility of having an ultrasound exam or other prenatal test to help put your mind at ease.

Lengthy stays in the sauna or steam room aren't smart, either. A pregnant woman is at greater risk for dehydration, dizziness, and lower blood pressure in general, and these are all symptoms that may be exacerbated by such extreme heat. And as with a hot tub, pregnant women should avoid anything that might potentially raise their body temperatures.

For more information on the safety of other types of spa treatments (massage, aromatherapy, and so on), see page 147.

The Family Cat

"I have two cats at home. I've heard that cats carry a disease that can harm a fetus. Do I have to get rid of my pets?"

Is Hot Stuff Not So Hot?

Considering cuddling up with an electric blanket when the winter chill sets in? Or easing that achy-breaky back with a heating pad? Too much heat isn't so hot when you're pregnant, since it may raise your body temperature excessively. So cuddle up to your sweetie instead of that electric blanket (or if his tootsies are as icy as yours, invest in a down comforter, push up the thermostat, or heat the bed with an electric blanket and then turn it off before you turn in). Still feeling the chill? Keep in mind that as the months pass, you'll probably be keeping yourself so warm—thanks to a pregnancy-boosted metabolism—that you'll be kicking off all your covers anyway.

As for that heating pad, wrap it in a towel before you apply it to your back, belly, or shoulders to reduce the heat it passes along (an ankle or knee can take the heat), keep it at the lowest setting, limit applications to 15 minutes, and avoid sleeping with it. Already spent some time under that electric blanket or heating pad? Not to worry—there's no proven risk.

Don't send your feline friends packing. Since you've lived with them for a while, the chances are pretty good that you've already contracted the cat-related disease toxoplasmosis and have developed an immunity to it. It's estimated that up to 40 percent of the American population has been exposed, and the rates of exposure are much higher among people who have cats that spend time outdoors, as well as among people who frequently eat raw meat or drink unpasteurized milk, both of which can also harbor and transmit the infection. If you weren't tested prenatally to see if you were immune, it's not likely you will be tested now, unless you show symptoms of the disease (though some practitioners run regular tests on all pregnant women and others test only those who live with cats). If you were tested prenatally and were not immune, or if you're not sure whether you are immune or not, take the following precautions to avoid infection:

- Have your cats tested by a veterinarian to see if they have an active infection. If one or more do, board them at a kennel or ask a friend to care for them for at least six weeks, the period during which the infection is transmissible. If they are free of infection, keep them that way by not allowing them to eat raw meat, roam outdoors, hunt mice or birds (which can transmit toxoplasmosis to cats), or hang out with other cats.

- Have someone else handle the litter box. If you must do it yourself, use disposable gloves and wash your hands when you're finished, as well as after you touch your cats. The litter should be changed daily.

- Wear gloves when gardening. Don't garden in soil in which cats may have deposited feces. If you have children, don't allow them to play in sand that may have been used by cats or other animals.

- Wash fruits and vegetables, especially those grown in home gardens, rinsing very thoroughly, and/or peel or cook them.

- Don't eat raw or undercooked meat or unpasteurized milk. In restaurants, order meat well done.

- Wash your hands thoroughly after handling raw meats.

Some practitioners are urging routine testing before conception or in very early pregnancy for all women, so that those who test positive can relax, knowing they are immune, and those who test negative can take the necessary precautions to prevent infection. However, public health officials believe the financial cost of such testing outweighs the benefit it may provide. Check with your practitioner to see what he or she recommends.

Household Hazards

"How much do I really have to worry about household hazards like cleaning products and bug sprays? And what about tap water—is it safe to drink it while I'm pregnant?"

A little perspective goes a long way when you're expecting. Sure, you've read or heard that cleaning products, insecticides, drinking water, and other substances around the house can be dangerous to live with, especially when you're living for two. But the fact is that your home is probably a very safe place for you and your baby to hang out—especially if you couple a little caution with a lot of common sense. Here's what you need to know about so-called household hazards:

Household cleaning products. Mopping your kitchen floor or polishing your dining room table may be tough on your pregnant back, but it's not tough on your pregnancy. Still, it makes sense to clean with care when you're expecting. Let your nose and the following tips be your guide:

- If the product has a strong odor or fumes, don't breathe it in directly. Use it in an area with plenty of ventilation, or don't use it at all (what better excuse for getting your spouse to scrub the toilet?).

- Never (even when you're not pregnant) mix ammonia with chlorine-based products; the combination produces deadly fumes.

- Try to avoid using products such as oven cleaners and dry-cleaning fluids whose labels are plastered with warnings about toxicity.

- Wear rubber gloves when you're using a really strong product. Not only will this spare your hands a lot of wear and tear, it'll prevent the absorption of chemicals through the skin.

Lead. Exposure to lead isn't just potentially harmful to small children but to pregnant women and their fetuses as well. Fortunately, it's also pretty easy to avoid. Here's how:

- Since drinking water is a common source of lead, be sure yours is lead free (see below).

- Old paint is a major source of lead. If your home dates back to 1955 or earlier and layers of paint are to be removed for any reason, stay away from the house while the work is being done. If you find paint is flaking in an older home, or if you have a piece of old painted furniture that's flaking, see about having the walls or furniture repainted to contain the flaking lead paints, or have the old paint removed—again, stay away while the job is being done.

- Flea market fan? You might want to know that lead can also be leached from older earthenware, pottery, and china. If you have pitchers or dishes that are home-crafted, imported, antique, or just plain old (the FDA did

not set limits on lead in dishes until 1971), don't use them for serving food or beverages, particularly those that are acidic (citrus, vinegar, tomatoes, wine, soft drinks).

Tap water. It's still the best drink in the house—and in most houses, water is completely safe and drinkable straight from the tap. To be sure that when you fill a glass of water you'll be drinking to your—and your baby's—good health, do the following:

- Check with your local Environmental Protection Agency (EPA) or health department about the purity and safety of community drinking water or a well, if that is the source of your tap water (go to epa.gov/safewater/dwinfo/index.html). Or check with the EPA Water Safety Hotline at (800) 426-4791 or online at scorecard.org. If there is a possibility that the quality of your water might differ from the rest of the community's (because of pipe deterioration, because your home borders on a waste disposal area, or because of odd taste or color), arrange to have it tested. Your local EPA or health department can tell you how.

- If your tap water fails the test, invest in a filter (what kind depends on what turns up in your water) or use bottled water for drinking and cooking. Be aware, however, that bottled waters are not automatically free of impurities; some contain more than tap water, and some are bottled directly from the tap (talk about throwing money down the drain). Many bottled waters also don't contain fluoride, an important mineral, especially for growing teeth (your baby's). To check the purity of a particular brand, contact the National Sanitation Foundation at (800) 673-6275 or nsf.org. Avoid distilled waters (from which beneficial minerals have been removed).

- If you suspect lead in your water, or if testing reveals high levels, changing the plumbing would be the ideal solution, but this is not always feasible. To reduce the levels of lead in the water you drink, use only cold water for drinking and cooking (hot leaches more lead from the pipes), and run the cold-water tap for about five minutes in the morning (as well as anytime the water has been off for six hours or more) before using it. You can tell that lead-free fresh water from the street pipes has reached your faucet when the water has gone from cold to warmer to cold again.

- If your water smells and/or tastes like chlorine, boiling it or letting it stand, uncovered, for 24 hours will evaporate much of the chemical.

Pesticides. Can't live with roaches, ants, and other yucky insects? Living with them, of course, often means eliminating them through the use of chemical pesticides. Fortunately, pest control and pregnancy can be completely compatible, with a few precautions. If your neighborhood is being sprayed, avoid hanging around outside for long periods until the chemical odors have dissipated, usually about two to three days. When indoors, keep the windows closed. If spraying for roaches or other insects is necessary in your apartment or house, be sure all closets and kitchen cabinets are tightly closed (so the chemicals don't seep in and settle on dishes and food) and all food-preparation surfaces are covered. Ventilate with open windows until the fumes have dissipated. Once the spray has settled, make sure food-preparation surfaces in or near the sprayed area have been thoroughly wiped down.

Whenever possible, try to take a natural approach to pest control. Pull weeds instead of spraying them. Eliminate some pests from garden and houseplants by spraying with a forceful stream from the garden hose or with a biodegradable insecticidal soap mixture (the procedure may need to be repeated several times to be effective). Invest in an infantry of ladybugs or other beneficial predators (available from some garden supply houses) that like to feed on the bugs that are bugging you.

Inside the house, use "motel" or other types of traps, strategically placed in heavy bug traffic areas, to get rid of roaches and ants; use cedar blocks instead of mothballs in clothes closets; and check an environmentally friendly store or catalog for nontoxic pesticides. If you have young children or pets, keep all traps and pesticide products out of their reach. Even so-called natural pesticides, including boric acid, can be toxic when ingested or inhaled, and they can be irritating to the eyes. For more information on natural pest control, contact your regional Cooperative Extension Service or a local environmental group. You may even have a "green" exterminator in your neighborhood.

Also keep in mind that brief, indirect exposure to insecticides or herbicides isn't likely to be harmful. What does increase the risk is frequent, long-term exposure, the kind that working daily around such chemicals (as in a factory or heavily sprayed field) would involve.

Paint fumes. In the entire animal kingdom, the period before birth (or egg laying) is spent in hectic preparation for the arrival of the new offspring. Birds feather their nests, squirrels line their tree-trunk homes with leaves and twigs, and human mothers and fathers sift madly through online design catalogues. And almost invariably, plans involve painting the

The Green Solution

L ooking for a way to breathe easier about the air you're breathing at home? Go green, filling your living space with living plants. Plants have the ability to absorb assorted pollutants in the air while adding oxygen to the indoor environment. In making your selections, however, be sure to avoid plants that are toxic when ingested, such as philodendron or English ivy. You won't likely be munching on shrubbery, but the same can't necessarily be said for your baby once he or she begins crawling around the house.

Air Pollution

"Can city air pollution hurt my baby?"

T ake a deep breath. Ordinary breathing in the big city is a lot safer than you'd think. After all, millions of women live and breathe in major cities across the nation and give birth to millions of healthy babies. Still, it's always sensible to avoid extraordinarily high doses of most air pollutants. Here's how:

- **Avoid smoke-filled rooms.** Since tobacco smoke is one pollutant that's known to hurt the fetus, ask family, guests in your home, and coworkers not to smoke near you. That goes for cigars and pipes, too, because they release even more smoke into the air than cigarettes do.

- Have the exhaust system on your car checked to be sure there is no leakage of noxious fumes and the exhaust pipe isn't rusting away. Never start your car in the garage with the garage door closed; keep the tailgate on an SUV or minivan closed when the engine is running; keep your car's outside air vent closed when driving in heavy traffic.

- If there is a pollution alert in your area, stay indoors as much as you can, with the windows closed and the air conditioner, if you have one, running. Follow any other instructions given by health officials for residents who are at special risk. If you want to work out, go to the gym or go for a long walk at an indoor mall.

- Don't run, walk, or bicycle along congested highways, no matter what the weather, since you breathe in more air—and pollution—when you're active. Instead, choose a route through a park or a residential area with little traffic and a lot of trees. Trees, like indoor greenery, help to keep the air clean.

baby's room (once you can settle on the color, that is). Fortunately, today's paints don't contain lead or mercury and are safe to use when you're pregnant. Still, there are plenty of good reasons why you should pass the paintbrush to someone else—even if you're trying desperately to keep busy in those last weeks of waiting. The repetitive motion of painting can be a strain on back muscles already under pressure from the extra weight of pregnancy. In addition, balancing on ladder tops is precarious at the least, and paint odors (though not harmful) can offend the pregnant nose and bring on a bout of nausea.

While the painting is being done, try to arrange to be out of the house. Whether you're there or not, keep windows open for ventilation. Avoid exposure to paint removers entirely, because they are highly toxic, and steer clear of the paint-removing process (whether chemicals or sanders are used), particularly if the paint that's being removed is older and might contain mercury or lead.

- Make sure fireplaces, gas stoves, and wood-burning stoves in your home are vented properly. Also, make sure the fireplace flue is open before lighting a fire.

- Try the Green Solution (see previous page). Plants, and the air-purification properties that they provide, can help you breathe easier both inside your home and out.

Domestic Violence

Protecting her baby from harm is every expectant mother's most basic instinct. But sadly, some women can't even protect themselves during pregnancy. That's because they're victims of domestic violence.

Domestic violence can strike at any time, but it's especially common during pregnancy. While having a baby brings out a new (or renewed) tenderness in many relationships, it rocks others, sometimes triggering unexpectedly negative emotions in a woman's partner (from anger to jealousy to a feeling of being trapped), particularly if the pregnancy wasn't planned. In some cases, unfortunately, those emotions play out in the form of violence against both the mother and her unborn baby.

Surprisingly, domestic violence is the leading cause of death among pregnant women, killing more often than pregnancy complications or car crashes. Even without the homicides, the statistics are just as alarming: Nearly 20 percent of women experience violence at the hands of their partners during pregnancy. This means, statistically, that pregnant women are twice as likely to experience physical abuse during their nine months than experience a preterm birth or preeclampsia.

Domestic abuse (emotional and physical) against pregnant women carries more than just the immediate risk of injury to the mother-to-be and her baby (such as uterine rupture or hemorrhaging). Being battered during pregnancy can lead to numerous negative health consequences for the mom-to-be, including poor nutrition, poor prenatal care, substance abuse, and so on. Its effects on the pregnancy can also include stillbirth or miscarriage, preterm labor, premature rupture of the membranes, or low birthweight. And once a baby is born into a physically abusive household, he or she can easily become a victim of direct violence as well.

Abused women come from all backgrounds and socioeconomic areas, every age, every race and ethnicity, and every educational level. If you're the victim of domestic violence, remember that it is not your fault. You have done nothing wrong. If you are in an abusive relationship, don't wait—get help now. Without intervention, the violence will only get worse. Keep in mind that if you're not safe in your relationship, your child won't be safe either.

Talk to your practitioner, tell your trusted friends and family, and call a local domestic violence hotline. Many states have programs that can help you with shelter, clothing, and prenatal care. Check out The Safety Zone, thesafetyzone.org; Violence Against Women, 4woman.gov/violence/index .cfm; Family Violence Prevention Fund, endabuse.org; National Coalition Against Domestic Violence, ncadv.org; or call the National Domestic Violence Hotline at (800) 799-7233.

If you are in immediate danger, call 911.

Complementary and Alternative Medicine

The days when alternative medicine was about as welcome in traditional medical practice as old wives' tales (and regarded with about as much credibility) are over. Today, these seemingly unrelated branches of healing are no longer considered incompatible; in fact, more and more practitioners in both consider them complementary. Which is why complementary and alternative medicine (CAM) is more and more likely to find a place—in some form—in your life and the life of your family.

The practitioners who practice complementary medicine take a broad view of health and well-being, examining and integrating the nutritional, emotional, and spiritual influences, as well as the physical ones. CAM also emphasizes the body's ability to heal itself—with a little help from some natural friends, including herbs, physical manipulation, the spirit, and the mind.

Since pregnancy is not an illness but rather a normal part of life, it would seem that CAM might make a natural addition to traditional obstetrical care. And for an increasing number of women and their health care providers, it has. A variety of CAM practices are currently being used in pregnancy, labor, and delivery, with varying degrees of success, including the following:

Acupuncture. The Chinese have known for thousands of years that acupuncture can be used to relieve a number of pregnancy symptoms—but it's only recently that the traditional obstetrical community has started to catch on. Scientific studies now back up the ancient wisdom; researchers have found that acupuncture triggers the release of several brain chemicals, including endorphins, which block pain signals. How is it done? An acupuncturist inserts dozens of thin needles at prescribed points along invisible paths (or meridians) on the body. According to ancient tradition, the paths are the channels through which chi, the body's life force, flows. Researchers have found that the points correspond to deep-seated nerves, so that when the needles are twirled (or electrically stimulated, in a procedure known as electropuncture), the nerves are activated, leading to the release of endorphins—and relief from back pain, nausea, and other symptoms, including pregnancy depression. Acupuncture may also be used during labor to relieve pain, as well as to help speed progress along. For those finding conception elusive, acupuncture may help with fertility issues.

Acupressure. Acupressure—or shiatsu—works on the same principle as acupuncture, except that instead of getting poked with needles, your practitioner will use thumb or finger pressure, or will apply firm pressure with small beads, to stimulate the points. Pressure on a certain point just above your inner wrist can ease nausea (which is why Sea-Bands can also work; see page 134). Acupressure on the center of the ball of the foot is said to help back labor. There are several acupressure points that are said to induce contractions (such as those in the ankle)—which is why they should be avoided until term (at which point, impatient moms-to-be might want to give them a try—at the hands of a professional, that is).

Biofeedback. Biofeedback is a method that helps patients learn how to control their biological responses to physical pain or emotional stress, and it can be used safely to relieve a variety of pregnancy symptoms, including headache, backache, and other pains, plus insomnia and possibly morning sickness. Biofeedback can also be used to lower blood pressure and combat depression, anxiety, and stress.

Chiropractic medicine. This therapy uses physical manipulation of the spine and other joints to enable nerve impulses to move freely through an aligned body, encouraging the body's natural ability to heal. Chiropractic medicine can help pregnant women battle nausea; back, neck, or joint pain; and sciatica (plus other types of pain), as well as help relieve postpartum pain. Be sure any chiropractic practitioner you see during pregnancy is familiar with caring for expectant women, using tables that adjust for a pregnant woman's body and using techniques that avoid pressure on the abdominal area.

Massage. Massage can help relieve some of pregnancy's discomforts, including heartburn, nausea (but only in some women; others may be more nauseated by massage), headaches, backache, and sciatica, while preparing muscles for childbirth. It can also be used during labor and delivery to relax muscles between contractions and reduce the pain of back labor. What's more, it's a great way to reduce stress and relax. Just make sure you're being massaged by someone who's trained in the art of prenatal massage (not all massage therapists are); see page 147 for more.

Reflexology. Similar to acupressure, reflexology is a therapy in which pressure is applied to specific areas of the feet, hands, and ears to relieve a variety of aches and pains, as well as to stimulate labor and reduce the pain of contrac-

tions. Because applying pressure to certain areas on or near the feet and on the hands can trigger contractions, it's very important that the reflexologist you visit be well trained and aware of your pregnancy, and that he or she avoids these areas before term (afterward, again, they could be just the ticket to bring on a long-awaited labor).

Hydrotherapy. This therapeutic use of warm water (usually in a whirlpool tub) is used in many hospitals and birthing centers to help relax a laboring woman and reduce her discomfort. Some women choose to give birth in water; see page 24.

Aromatherapy. Scented oils are used to heal body, mind, and spirit and are utilized by some practitioners during pregnancy; however, most experts advise caution, since certain aromas (in this concentrated form) may pose a risk to pregnant women; see page 147.

Meditation, visualization, and relaxation techniques. All of these can help a woman safely through a variety of physical and emotional stresses during pregnancy, from the miseries of morning sickness to the pain of labor and delivery. They can work wonders on general expectant mom anxiety, too; see page 142 for a relaxation exercise you can try.

Hypnotherapy. Hypnosis may be useful in relieving pregnancy symptoms (from nausea to headaches), reducing stress and easing insomnia, turning a breech birth (in conjunction with the more traditional external cephalic version), holding off preterm labor, and providing pain management during labor and delivery (hypnobirthing). It works by getting you deeply relaxed—and in the case of pain management, so relaxed that you're unaware of any discomfort. Keep in mind that hypnosis isn't for everyone; about 25 percent of the population is highly resistant to hypnotic suggestion, and many more aren't suggestive enough to use it for effective pain relief. Make sure any hypnotherapist you use is certified and experienced in pregnancy therapies. For more on hypnobirthing, see page 306.

Moxibustion. This alternative medicine technique combines acupuncture with heat (in the form of smoldering mugwort, an herb) to gradually help turn a breech baby. If you're interested in trying moxibustion to turn your breech baby, look for a practitioner who's experienced in the technique (not all acupuncturists are).

Herbal remedies. "Botanicals" have been used since humankind first began looking for relief from ailments, and they are today used by some practitioners to relieve pregnancy symptoms. Most experts, however, do not recommend herbal remedies for pregnant women because adequate studies on safety have not yet been done.

Clearly, CAM is making an impact in obstetrics. Even the most traditional ob-gyns are realizing that it's a holistic force to be reckoned with, and one to begin incorporating into ob-business as usual. But in making CAM a part of your pregnancy, it's wise to proceed with prudence and with these caveats in mind:

- Make sure your traditional ob-gyn or midwife is aware that you're seeking a CAM treatment, so your care is truly complementary. Keeping your entire prenatal team in the know is important for your safety and that of your baby.

- Complementary medications (such as homeopathic and herbal preparations) are not tested or approved by the FDA. Because they haven't been thoroughly tested—as FDA-approved drugs are—their safety hasn't been clinically established. Which is not to say that there aren't complementary medications that are safe to use in pregnancy and possibly very beneficial, just that there is no official system in place to determine those that are and those that aren't. Until more is known, it makes sense to avoid taking any homeopathic, herbal medication, dietary supplement, or aromatherapy treatment unless it has been specifically prescribed by a traditional practitioner who is knowledgeable in CAM and who knows you're pregnant. (This is also true once the baby is born if you are breastfeeding.)

- Complementary procedures that are usually benign—or even beneficial—for the nonpregnant may not be safe during pregnancy. From therapeutic massage to chiropractic maneuvers, special precautions must be observed when a patient is pregnant.

- CAM can still be strong medicine. Depending on how it's used, this potency can be therapeutic or it can be hazardous. Keep in mind that "natural" is not synonymous with "safe" any more than "chemical" is synonymous with "dangerous." Have your practitioner help you navigate through the potential pitfalls and steer you toward CAM practices that can help—not hurt—when you're expecting.

Nine Months of Eating Well

THERE'S A TINY NEW BEING DEVEL-oping inside of you—a baby in the making. Adorable little fingers and toes are sprouting, eyes and ears are forming, brain cells are rapidly growing. And before you know it, the speck of a fetus inside of you will come to resemble the baby of your dreams: fully equipped and suitable for cuddling.

Not surprisingly, a lot goes into making a baby. Happily for babies and the parents who love them, nature's incredibly good at what it does. Which means that the chances that your baby will be born not only perfectly cute, but perfectly healthy, are already excellent. What's more, there's something you can do to help make those excellent chances even better—while helping yourself to a healthier and more comfortable pregnancy. It's something that's relatively easy to do (except maybe when you're feeling queasy)—and something that you probably already do at least three times a day. Yes, you guessed it: eating. But the challenge during pregnancy isn't just to eat (though that may be challenge enough during those early months)—it's to eat as well as you can. Think of it this way. Eating well when you're expecting is one of the first and best gifts you can give to your soon-to-arrive bundle of joy—and it's a gift that can keep on giving, handing out not just a healthier start in life but a healthier lifetime.

The Pregnancy Diet is an eating plan dedicated to baby's good health—and yours. What's in it for your baby? Among many other impressive benefits, a better chance for a bouncing birth weight, improved brain development, reduced risk for certain birth defects—and as a bonus, believe it or not, better eating habits as baby grows to be a potentially picky preschooler (a perk you'll really appreciate when broccoli's on the dinner menu). It may even make it more likely that your child will grow to be a healthier adult.

And your baby's not the only one who's likely to benefit. The Pregnancy Diet can also increase the chances that you'll have a safe pregnancy (some complications, such as anemia, gestational diabetes, and preeclampsia, are less common among women who eat well); a comfortable pregnancy (a sensibly selected diet can minimize morning sickness, fatigue, constipation, and a host of other pregnancy symptoms); a balanced emotional state (good nutrition can help moderate those crazy mood swings); a timely labor and delivery (in general, women who eat regularly and well are less likely to deliver too early); and a speedier postpartum recovery (a well-nourished body can bounce back faster and more easily, and weight that's been gained at a sensible rate can be shed more quickly). For more on the many benefits of a healthy diet during pregnancy, see *What to Expect: Eating Well When You're Expecting.*

Luckily, scoring those benefits is a piece of (carrot) cake, especially if you're already eating pretty well, and even if you're not (you'll just have to be a little more selective before bringing fork to mouth). That's because the Pregnancy Diet isn't all that different from the average healthy diet. While a few modifications have been made for the pregnant set (not surprisingly, baby making requires more calories and more of certain nutrients), the foundation is the same: a good, balanced mix of lean protein and calcium, whole grains, a rainbow of fruits and vegetables, and healthy fats. Sound familiar? It should—after all, it's what sensible folks in the nutrition field have been touting for years.

And here's some more good news. Even if you're coming to your pregnancy (and bellying up to the table) with less than ideal eating habits, changing them to follow the Pregnancy Diet won't be

Have It Your Way

Have your doubts about diets? Not a fan of eating plans? Just don't like being told what to eat—or how much? No problem. The Pregnancy Diet is one way to feed yourself and your baby well, but it definitely isn't the only way. A balanced, healthy diet—one that includes plenty of protein, whole grains, and fruits and vegetables, plus about 300 extra calories a day—will get the job done, too. So if you'd rather not keep track—don't. Eat well, your way!

that tough, especially if you're committed to making the changes. There are healthy alternatives for almost every less healthy food and beverage you've ever brought to your lips (see box, next page), which means there are nourishing ways to have your cake (and cookies and chips and even fast food) and eat it, too. Plus, there are countless ways to sneak crucial vitamins and minerals into recipes and favorite dishes—which means that you can eat well when you're expecting without your taste buds being the wiser.

There is a very important point to keep in mind as you embark on making a diet change for the better: What's presented in this chapter is the ideal, the best possible plan for eating well when you're expecting. Something you should strive for, certainly, but nothing you should stress over (especially early in pregnancy, when your appetite for healthy foods may face a smorgasbord of suppressive symptoms—from nausea to food aversions). Maybe you'll choose to follow the diet closely, at least most of the time. Or you'll follow it loosely, all of the time. But even if your allegiance remains to burgers and fries, you'll still

---

Try These Instead

Looking for healthy alternatives to your not-so-healthy favorite foods? Here are some ideas to get you started:

Instead of . . .	Try . . .
Potato chips	Soy chips
A bag of M&M's	Trail mix (with a few M&M's)
Before-dinner pretzels	Before-dinner edamame
Fried chicken	Grilled chicken
Hot fudge sundae	Frozen yogurt with fruit and granola
Taco chips and cheese sauce	Veggies and cheese sauce
French fries	Roasted sweet potato chips
Anything on white bread	Anything on whole wheat
A soft drink	A fruit smoothie
Sugar cookies	Whole-grain Fig Newtons

---

pick up in the pages that follow at least a few pointers that will help nourish you and your baby better during the next nine months (salad with that burger?).

Nine Basic Principles for Nine Months of Healthy Eating

Bites count. Chew on this: You've got nine months' worth of meals and snacks (and nibbles and noshes) ahead of you—each one of them an opportunity to feed your baby well before he or she is even born. So open wide, but think first. Try to make your pregnancy bites count by choosing them (at least most of the time) with baby in mind. Remember that each bite during the day is an opportunity to feed that growing baby of yours healthy nutrients.

All calories are not created equal. Choose your calories with care, selecting quality over quantity when you can. It may seem obvious—and inherently unfair—but those 200 calories in a doughnut are not equal to the 200 calories in a whole-grain raisin-bran muffin. Nor are the 100 calories in 10 potato chips equal to the 100 calories in a baked potato served in its skin. Your baby will benefit a lot more from 2,000 nutrient-rich calories daily than from 2,000 mostly empty ones. And your body will show the benefits postpartum as well.

Starve yourself, starve your baby. Just as you wouldn't consider starving your baby after it's born, don't consider starving it when it's at home in your uterus. A fetus can't thrive by living off your flesh, no matter how much you're sporting. It needs regular nourishment at regular intervals—and as the sole caterer of your uterine café, only you can provide it. Even if you're not hungry, your baby is. So try not to skip meals. In fact, eating frequently may be the best route to a well-nourished fetus. Research shows that mothers who eat at least five times a day (three meals plus two snacks or six mini meals, for instance) are more likely to carry to term. Of course, that's easier said than done, especially if you've been too busy hugging the toilet to even think about eating. And what if your heartburn has made eating a pain—literally? You'll find plenty of tips on how to eat around these pregnancy inconveniences on pages 130 and 153.

Efficiency is effective. Think it's impossible to fill each of the Daily Dozen requirements (see page 93) each and every day (let's see, six whole-grains means one every four hours . . .)? Worried that even if you do manage to eat it all, you'll end up looking like a pregnant blimp? Think and worry no more. Instead, become an efficiency expert. Get more nutritional bang for your buck by choosing foods that are lightweights when it comes to calories, heavy hitters when it comes to nutrients. Need an example? Eating a cup of pistachio nuts at 715 calories (about 25 percent of your daily allotment) is a considerably less efficient way of netting a 25-gram protein serving than eating a 4-ounce turkey burger, at 250 calories. Another efficiency case in point: Eating a cup and a half of ice cream (about 500 calories; more if you've chosen the really good stuff) is a fun but far less efficient way of scoring a 300-mg calcium serving than eating a cup of nonfat frozen yogurt (still fun, but only about 300 calories). Because fat has more than twice as many calories per gram as either proteins or carbohydrates, opting often for lower-fat foods will step up your nutritional efficiency. Choose lean meats over fatty ones, fat-free or low-fat milk and dairy products over full-fat versions, grilled or broiled foods over fried. Spread butter lightly; use a tablespoon of olive oil for sautéing, not a quarter of a cup. Another trick of the efficient-eating trade: Select foods that are overachievers in more than one Daily Dozen category, thus filling two or more requirements at once.

Efficiency is important, too, if you're having trouble gaining enough weight. To start tipping the scale toward a healthier weight gain, choose foods that are dense in nutrients and calories—avocados, nuts, and dried fruits, for instance—that can fill you and your baby out without filling you up too much.

Carbohydrates are a complex issue. Some women, concerned about gaining too much weight during pregnancy, mistakenly drop carbohydrates from their diets like so many hot potatoes. There's no doubt that refined carbs (like white bread, crackers, and pretzels; white rice; refined cereals, cakes, and cookies) are nutritional slackers. But unrefined (complex) carbohydrates (whole-grain breads and cereals, brown rice, fresh fruits and vegetables, dried beans and peas, and, of course, hot potatoes in their skins) supply essential B vitamins, trace minerals,

The Six-Meal Solution

Too bloated, queasy, heartburned, or constipated (or all four) to contemplate a full meal? No matter what tummy troubles are getting you down (or keeping food from staying down), you'll find it easier to spread your Daily Dozen (see page 93) into five or six mini meals instead of three squares. A grazing approach keeps your blood sugar level, so you'll get an energy boost, too (and who couldn't use that?). And you'll have fewer headaches—and fewer wild mood swings.

protein, and important fiber. They're good not only for your baby, but also for you (they'll help keep nausea and constipation in check). And because they are filling and fiber-rich but not fattening, they'll help keep your weight gain in check, too. Recent research suggests yet another bonus for complex carbohydrate consumers: Eating plenty of fiber may reduce the risk of developing gestational diabetes. Be careful to move from a low-fiber diet to a high-fiber diet slowly to avoid possible stomach upset (too much fiber too fast can pump you up with too much gas).

No More Guilt

Willpower has its place, particularly while you're trying to eat well for two. Still, everyone needs to give in to temptation now and then, without feeling guilty about it. So lose the guilt, hold the deprivation, and allow yourself a treat every once in a while—something that doesn't add appreciably to your nutritional bottom line but makes your taste buds jump for joy: a blueberry muffin that's probably more sugar than blueberries but is also off-the-charts yummy, a double scoop of cookies-and-cream (when frozen yogurt just doesn't cut it), the fast-food burger you've been craving like crazy. And when you say "yes" to that occasional frosted brownie or candy bar, serve it up without a side of remorse.

But when venturing down the path of least nutritious, try to pump it up—add a slice of banana and some nuts to your ice-cream sundae; choose a candy bar that's filled with almonds; order your burger with cheese and tomato (and maybe a side salad). Keeping portions of these foods small is another good strategy: Share that serving of onion rings; take a slender slice of pecan pie instead of a hefty slab. And remember to stop before you get too carried away; otherwise, you might just begin to feel that guilt after all.

Sweet nothings are exactly that. There's no gentle way to put this: Sugar calories, sadly, are empty calories. And though empty calories are fine once in a while—even when you're pregnant—they tend to add up a lot more quickly than you'd think, leaving less room in your diet for nutritionally substantial calories. In addition, researchers are finding that sugar may not only be void of value, but in excessive amounts may potentially be harmful. Studies have suggested that in addition to contributing to obesity, heavy sugar consumption may be linked to tooth decay, diabetes, heart disease, and colon cancer. Perhaps sugar's biggest shortcoming, however, is that large quantities are often found in foods and drinks that are, on the whole, nutritional underachievers (candy and soda come to mind).

Refined sugar goes by many names on the supermarket shelves, including corn syrup and dehydrated cane juice. Honey, an unrefined sugar, has a nutritional edge because it contains disease-fighting antioxidants. Plus, it is more likely to find its way into more nutritious foods—particularly those whole-grain ones you'd find in the health food sections of your market. Try to limit your intake of all forms of sugar, however, since the calories you save can be spent on foods that pack a much more wholesome punch.

For delicious and nutritious sweetness, substitute fruit, dried or freeze-dried fruit, and fruit juice concentrates for sugar when you can. Besides being sweet, they contain vitamins, trace minerals, and valuable phytochemicals (plant chemicals that may help the body defend itself against disease and aging), all absent in sugar. You can also find sweet revenge in the calorie-free sugar substitutes that appear to be safe for pregnancy use (see page 111).

Good foods remember where they came from. Nature knows a thing or two about nutrition. So it's not surprising that the most nutritious foods are often the ones that haven't strayed far from their natural state. Choose fresh vegetables and fruits when they're in season, or nothing-added frozen or canned when fresh are unavailable or you don't have time to prepare them. Freeze-dried is another nutritious (and convenient) way to go. And when it comes to preparation, less is more—more nutrients, that is. Try to eat some raw vegetables and fruit every day, and when you're cooking, opt for steaming or a light stir-fry, so more vitamins and minerals will be retained.

And there's more nutritional knowhow in nature's model. Avoid processed foods; not only have they picked up a lot of chemicals, fat, sugar, and salt on the assembly line, but they're frequently low in nutrition. Choose fresh roasted turkey breast over smoked turkey, macaroni and cheese made with whole-grain macaroni and natural cheese over that bright orange variety, fresh oatmeal made from rolled oats over the lower-fiber and super sugary instant varieties.

Healthy eating begins at home. Let's face it. It isn't easy to nibble on fresh fruit when your darling husband's diving headfirst into a half-gallon of ice cream—right next to you on the sofa. Or to reach for the soy chips when he's filled the cabinets with those orange cheese balls you can't resist. So enlist him—and other family members—in making your home a healthy food zone. Make whole wheat your house bread,

stock your freezer with frozen yogurt, and ban the unhealthy snacks you can't help attacking when they're within reach. And don't stop after delivery. Research associates a good diet not only with a better pregnancy outcome but with a lower risk of many diseases, including adult-onset diabetes and cancer. Which means the family that eats well together is more likely to stay healthy together.

Bad habits can sabotage a good diet. Eating well is only part of the healthy prenatal picture. The best pregnancy diet in the world can be undermined by alcohol, tobacco, and other unsafe drugs. If you haven't done so already, change your other lifestyle habits to match.

The Pregnancy Daily Dozen

Calories. Technically, a pregnant woman is eating for two (rejoice, food lovers). But it's important to remember that one of the two is a tiny developing fetus whose caloric needs are significantly lower than mom's—a mere 300 on average a day, more or less (sorry, food lovers). So, if you're of average weight, you now need only about an average of 300 calories more than you used to eat prepregnancy—the equivalent of two glasses of skim milk and a bowl of oatmeal (not exactly the all-you-can-eat sundae bar you were envisioning). Pretty easy to spend (or overspend), given the extra nutritional requirements of pregnancy. What's more, during the first trimester you probably don't need any extra calories at all (that baby you're growing is only pea size), unless you're trying to compensate for starting out underweight. By the time your metabolism speeds up during the second trimester, you can aim for 300 to 350 extra calories. Later in pregnancy (when your baby is much bigger) you may even need more, or upward of about 500 extra calories a day.

Eating more calories than you and your baby need isn't only unnecessary, it isn't smart—and can lead to excessive weight gain. Eating too few calories, on the other hand, is not only unwise but also potentially dangerous as pregnancy progresses; women who don't take in enough calories during the second and third trimesters can seriously slow the growth of their babies.

There are four exceptions to this basic formula—and if any apply to you, it's even more important to discuss your caloric needs with your practitioner. If you're overweight, you can possibly do with fewer calories, as long as you have the right nutritional guidance. If you're seriously underweight, you'll need more calories so you can catch up weightwise. If you're a teen, you're still growing yourself, which means you have unique nutritional needs. And if you're carrying multiples, you'll have to add about 300 calories for each additional baby.

While calories count during pregnancy, keep in mind that they don't have to be literally counted. Instead of adding them up at every meal, step on a reliable scale every once in a while (once a week if you're really curious, once every two to three weeks if you're more scale-phobic) to check your progress. Weigh yourself at the same time of day, either naked or wearing the same clothing (or clothing that weighs about the same), so that your calculations won't be thrown off by a heavy meal one week or heavy jeans the next. If your weight gain is going according to schedule (an average of about one pound a week in the second and third trimesters), you're getting the right number of calories. If it's less than that, you're getting too few; if it's

---

Count 'Em Once, Count 'Em Twice

Many of your favorite foods fill more than one Daily Dozen requirement in each serving, giving you two for the caloric price of one. Case in point: A slice of cantaloupe nets a Green Leafy and a Vitamin C in one delicious package. One cup of yogurt yields 1 Calcium serving and half a Protein serving. Use such overlappers as often as you can to save yourself calories and stomach space.

---

more than that, you're getting too many. Maintain or adjust your food intake as necessary, but be careful not to cut out nutrients you need along with calories.

Protein foods: 3 servings daily. How does your baby grow? Using, among other nutrients, the amino acids (the building blocks of human cells) from the protein you eat each day. Because your baby's cells are multiplying rapidly, protein is an extremely crucial component of your pregnancy diet. Aim to have about 75 grams of protein every day. If that sounds like a lot, keep in mind that most Americans (including you, most likely) consume at least that much daily without even trying, and those on high-protein diets pack away a lot more. To get your share of protein, all you have to do is eat a total of three servings of Protein foods from the list that follows. When tallying your Protein servings, don't forget to count the protein found in many high-calcium foods: a glass of milk and an ounce of cheese each provide a third of a Protein serving; a cup of yogurt equals half a serving. Whole grains and legumes contribute protein, too.

Every day have three of the following (each is 1 Protein serving, or about 25 grams of protein), or a combination equivalent to three servings. Keep in mind that most of the dairy options also fill calcium requirements, which make them especially efficient choices.

24 ounces (three 8-ounce glasses) of milk or buttermilk

1 cup cottage cheese

2 cups yogurt

3 ounces (¾ cup grated) cheese

4 large whole eggs

7 large egg whites

3½ ounces (drained) canned tuna or sardines

4 ounces (drained) canned salmon

4 ounces cooked shellfish, such as shelled shrimp, lobster, clams, or mussels

4 ounces (before cooking) fresh fish

4 ounces (before cooking) skinless chicken, turkey, duck, or other poultry

4 ounces (before cooking) lean beef, lamb, veal, pork, or buffalo

Calcium foods: 4 servings daily. Back in elementary school, you probably learned that growing children need plenty of calcium for strong bones and teeth. Well, so do growing fetuses on their way to becoming growing children. Calcium is also vital for muscle, heart, and nerve development, blood clotting, and enzyme activity. But it's not only your baby who stands to lose when you don't get enough calcium. If incoming supplies aren't keeping up, your baby-making factory will tap into the calcium in your own bones to help meet its quota, setting you up for osteoporosis later in life. So do your best to get your four servings of calcium-rich foods a day.

Can't stomach the idea—or the taste—of four glasses of milk each day? Luckily, calcium doesn't have to be served in glasses at all. It can be served up as a cup of yogurt or a piece of cheese. It can be enjoyed in smoothies, soups, casseroles, cereals, dips, sauces, desserts, and more.

For those who can't tolerate or don't eat dairy products at all, calcium also comes in nondairy form. A glass of calcium-fortified orange juice, for instance, efficiently provides a serving of Calcium and Vitamin C; 4 ounces of canned salmon with bones provides both a serving of Calcium and Protein; one portion of cooked greens yields not only a Green Leafy and a Vitamin C serving, but a bonus of calcium. For women who are vegans or lactose-intolerant, or who for other reasons cannot be sure they're getting enough calcium in their diets, a calcium supplement (one that includes vitamin D as well) may be recommended.

Aim for four servings of calcium-rich foods each day, or any combination of them that is equivalent to four servings (so don't forget to count that half cup of yogurt, that sprinkle of cheese). Each serving listed below contains about 300 mg of calcium (you need a total of about 1,200 mg a day), and many also fill your protein requirements:

¼ cup grated cheese

1 ounce hard cheese

½ cup pasteurized ricotta cheese

1 cup milk or buttermilk

5 ounces calcium-added milk (shake well before serving)

⅓ cup nonfat dry milk (enough to make 1 cup liquid)

1 cup yogurt

1½ cups frozen yogurt

1 cup calcium-fortified juice (shake well before serving)

4 ounces canned salmon with bones

Vegetarian Proteins

Good news for vegans: You don't have to combine to conquer vegetarian proteins, as long as you have some of each type (legumes, grains, and seeds and nuts) every day. To be sure you are getting a full protein serving at each meal, double or choose two half servings listed below. And keep in mind that many of these foods fulfill the requirements for Whole Grains and Legumes as well as Protein.

The following selections are nutritious foods for all pregnant women—you don't have to be a vegetarian to tap into them and count them in your daily total. In fact, many may be soothing protein alternatives when early-pregnancy queasiness and aversions push meat off the menu.

Legumes (half Protein servings)

¾ cup cooked beans, lentils, split peas, or chickpeas (garbanzos)

½ cup cooked edamame

¾ cup green garden peas

1½ ounces peanuts

3 tablespoons peanut butter

¼ cup miso

4 ounces tofu (bean curd)

3 ounces tempeh

1½ cups soy milk*

3 ounces soy cheese*

½ cup vegetarian "ground beef"*

1 large vegetarian "hot dog" or "burger"*

1 ounce (before cooking) soy or high-protein pasta

Grains (half Protein servings)

3 ounces (before cooking) whole-wheat pasta

⅓ cup wheat germ

¾ cup oat bran

1 cup uncooked (2 cups cooked) oats

2 cups (approximately) whole-grain ready-to-eat cereal*

½ cup uncooked (1½ cups cooked) couscous, bulgur, or buckwheat

½ cup uncooked quinoa

4 slices whole-grain bread

2 whole-wheat pitas or English muffins

Nuts and Seeds (half Protein servings)

3 ounces nuts, such as walnuts, pecans, or almonds

2 ounces sesame, sunflower, or pumpkin seeds

½ cup ground flaxseed

*Protein content varies widely, so check labels for 12 to 15 grams protein per half serving.

3 ounces canned sardines with bones

3 tablespoons ground sesame seeds

1 cup cooked greens, such as collards or turnips

1½ cups cooked Chinese cabbage (bok choy)

1½ cups cooked edamame

1¾ tablespoons blackstrap molasses

You'll also score a calcium bonus by eating cottage cheese, tofu, dried figs, almonds, broccoli, spinach, dried beans, and flaxseed.

Vitamin C foods: 3 servings daily. You and baby both need vitamin C for tissue repair, wound healing, and various other metabolic (nutrient-utilizing) processes. Your baby also needs it for proper growth and for the development of strong bones and teeth. Vitamin C is a nutrient the body can't store, so a fresh supply is needed every day. Lucky for you, vitamin C usually comes from foods that naturally taste good. As you can see from the list of Vitamin C foods below, the old standby orange juice (good as it is) is far from the only, or even the best, source of this essential vitamin.

Aim for at least 3 Vitamin C servings every day. (Fruit fanatic? Help yourself to more.) Your body can't store this vitamin, so try not to skip a day. Keep in mind that many Vitamin C foods also fill the requirement for Green Leafy and Yellow Vegetables and Yellow Fruit.

½ medium-size grapefruit

½ cup grapefruit juice

½ medium-size orange

½ cup orange juice

2 tablespoons juice concentrate

¼ cup lemon juice

½ medium-size mango

¼ medium-size papaya

⅛ small cantaloupe or honeydew (½ cup cubed)

⅓ cup strawberries

⅔ cup blackberries or raspberries

½ medium-size kiwi

½ cup diced fresh pineapple

2 cups diced watermelon

¼ cup freeze-dried mango, strawberries, or other vitamin C-rich fruit

¼ medium-size red, yellow, or orange bell pepper

½ medium-size green bell pepper

½ cup raw or cooked broccoli

1 medium-size tomato

¾ cup tomato juice

½ cup vegetable juice

½ cup raw or cooked cauliflower

½ cup cooked kale

1 packed cup raw spinach, or ½ cup cooked

¾ cup cooked collard, mustard, or turnip greens

2 cups romaine lettuce

¾ cup shredded raw red cabbage

1 sweet potato or baking potato, baked in skin

1 cup cooked edamame

Green Leafy and Yellow Vegetables and Yellow Fruits: 3 to 4 servings daily. These bunny favorites supply the vitamin A, in the form of beta-carotene, that is vital for cell growth (your baby's cells are multiplying at a fantastic rate), healthy skin, bones, and eyes. The green leafies and yellows also deliver doses of other essential carotenoids and vitamins (vitamin E, riboflavin, folic acid, and other B vitamins), numerous minerals (many green leafies provide a good deal of calcium as well as trace minerals), disease-fighting phytochemicals, and constipation-fighting fiber. A bountiful selection of green leafy and yellow vegetables and yellow fruit can be found in the list that follows. Those with an anti-vegetable agenda may be pleasantly surprised to discover that broccoli and

Can't Find Your Favorite?

Is your favorite fruit, grain, or protein food nowhere to be found on these lists? That doesn't mean it doesn't rate nutritionally. For reasons of space, only the more common foods are listed. There are longer food lists in *What to Expect: Eating Well When You're Expecting,* and even longer ones on the USDA National Nutrient Database: nal .usda.gov/fnic/foodcomp/search/.

spinach are not the only sources of vitamin A and that the vitamin comes packaged in some of nature's most tempting
sweet offerings—including apricots,
mangoes, yellow peaches, and cantaloupe. And those who like to drink
their vegetables may be happy to know
that they can count a glass of vegetable
juice, a bowl of carrot soup, or a mango
smoothie toward their daily Green Leafy
and Yellow allowance.

Try to eat at least three to four servings a day. Aim to have some yellow and
some green daily (and eat some raw for
extra fiber). Remember, many of these
foods also fill a Vitamin C requirement.

⅛ cantaloupe (½ cup cubed)

2 large fresh apricots or 6 dried
apricot halves

½ medium-size mango

¼ medium-size papaya

1 large nectarine or yellow peach

1 small persimmon

¼ cup freeze-dried mango or other
yellow fruit

¾ cup pink grapefruit juice

1 pink or ruby red grapefruit

1 clementine

½ carrot (¼ cup grated)

½ cup raw or cooked broccoli pieces

1 cup coleslaw mix

¼ cup cooked collard greens,
Swiss chard, or kale

1 packed cup green leafy lettuce, such
as romaine, arugula, or red or green leaf

1 packed cup raw spinach, or ½ cup
cooked

¼ cup cooked winter squash

½ small sweet potato or yam

2 medium-size tomatoes

½ medium-size red bell pepper

¼ cup chopped parsley

**Other fruits and vegetables: 1 to 2 serv-
ings daily.** In addition to produce rich
in vitamin C and beta-carotene (vitamin
A), aim to eat at least one or two "other"
types of fruit or vegetable daily. While
"Others" were once considered nutritional B-listers, they're now getting a
second look. Turns out they're rich not
only in minerals, such as potassium and
magnesium, that are vital to good pregnancy health, but also in a host of other
trace minerals. Many also have phytochemicals and antioxidants in abun-
dance (particularly those that sport the
colors of the rainbow, so pick produce
that's brightly hued for the biggest nutritional return). From that apple a day to
those headline-making blueberries and
pomegranates, "Others" are definitely
worthy of a spot in your daily diet.

You're sure to find plenty of "Others"
among your favorite fruits and vegetables.
Round out your produce picks with one
to two from this list daily:

1 medium-size apple

½ cup apple juice or applesauce

½ cup pomegranate juice

2 tablespoons apple juice concentrate

1 medium-size banana

½ cup pitted fresh cherries

¼ cup cooked cranberries

1 medium-size white peach

1 medium-size pear or 2 dried halves

½ cup unsweetened pineapple juice

2 small plums

½ cup blueberries

¼ cup freeze-dried "Other" fruit

½ medium-size avocado

½ cup cooked green beans

½ cup fresh raw mushrooms

½ cup cooked okra

½ cup sliced onion

½ cup cooked parsnips

½ cup cooked zucchini

1 small ear cooked sweet corn

1 cup shredded iceberg lettuce

½ cup green garden peas or snow peas

Whole Grains and Legumes: 6 or more servings a day. There are plenty of reasons to go with the grain. Whole grains (whole wheat, oats, rye, barley, corn, rice, millet, wheat berries, buckwheat, bulgur, quinoa, and so on) and legumes (peas, beans, and peanuts) are packed with nutrients, particularly the B vitamins (except for vitamin B_{12}, found only in animal products) that are needed for just about every part of your baby's body. These concentrated complex carbohydrates are also rich in iron and trace minerals, such as zinc, selenium, and magnesium, which are very important in pregnancy. An added plus: Starchy foods may also help reduce morning sickness. Though these selections have many nutrients in common, each has its own strengths. To get the maximum benefit, include a variety of whole grains and legumes in your diet. Be adventurous: Coat your fish or chicken with whole-wheat bread crumbs seasoned with herbs and Parmesan cheese. Try quinoa (a tasty high-protein grain) as a side dish, or add bulgur or wheat berries to a wild-rice pilaf. Use oats in your favorite cookie recipe. Substitute navy beans for limas in your soup. And though you'll likely sometimes eat them, remember that refined grains just don't stack up nutritionally. Even if they're "enriched," they are still lacking in fiber, in protein, and in more than a dozen vitamins and trace minerals that are found in the original whole grain.

Aim for six or more from this list every day. Don't forget that many also contribute toward your protein requirement, often significantly.

White Whole Wheat

Not a whole-hearted fan of whole wheat—or craving the comfort of white during your queasy days? There's a new bread in town that might be just the ticket. "White wheat" breads are made with naturally white wheat, which has a milder, sweeter taste than the red wheat that whole wheat's made from. Is white whole wheat the best thing since sliced bread? Well, maybe not exactly. It's definitely healthier than white, but since it's processed, some nutrients are still lost on the assembly line—which means that whole wheat's still top shelf nutritionally. Still, if your cravings—or queasiness—are sending you reaching for the white, "white wheat" is definitely the best one to reach for. Also, if you're baking, look for it in flour form for less dense results than regular whole wheat.

1 slice whole-wheat, whole-rye, or other whole-grain or soy bread

½ whole-wheat pita, roll, bagel, 12-inch wrap, tortilla, or English muffin

1 cup cooked whole-grain cereal, such as oatmeal or Wheatena

1 cup whole-grain ready-to-eat cereal (serving sizes vary, so check labels)

½ cup granola

2 tablespoons wheat germ

½ cup cooked brown or wild rice

½ cup cooked millet, bulgur, couscous, kasha (buckwheat groats), barley, or quinoa

1 ounce (before cooking) whole-grain or soy pasta

½ cup cooked beans, lentils, split peas, or edamame

2 cups air-popped popcorn

1 ounce whole-grain crackers or soy crisps

¼ cup whole-grain or soy flour

Iron-rich foods: some daily. Since large amounts of iron are essential for the developing blood supply of the fetus and for your own expanding blood supply, you'll need to pump up your iron intake during these nine months. Get as much of your iron as you can from your diet (see the list below). Eating foods rich in vitamin C at the same sitting as Iron-rich foods will increase the absorption of the mineral by your body.

Because it's sometimes difficult to fill the pregnancy iron requirement through diet alone, your practitioner may recommend that you take a daily iron supplement in addition to your prenatal vitamins from the 20th week on, or whenever routine testing shows an iron shortfall. To enhance the absorption of the iron in the supplement, take it between meals with a fruit juice rich in vitamin C (caffeinated beverages, antacids, high-fiber foods, and high-calcium foods can interfere with iron absorption).

Small amounts of iron are found in most of the fruits, vegetables, grains, and meats you eat every day. But try to have some of the following higher-iron-content foods daily, along with your supplement. Again, many Iron-rich foods also fill other requirements at the same time.

Beef, buffalo, duck, turkey

Cooked clams, oysters, mussels, and shrimp

Sardines

Baked potato with skin

Spinach, collard, kale, and turnip greens

Seaweed

Pumpkin seeds

Oat bran

Barley, bulgur, quinoa

Beans and peas

Edamame and soy products

Blackstrap molasses

Dried fruit

Fats and high-fat foods: approximately 4 servings daily (depending on your weight gain). As you're probably all too aware, the requirement for fat is definitely not only the easiest to fill, it's also the easiest to overfill. And though there's no harm—and probably some benefit—in having a couple of extra Green Leafies or Vitamin C foods, excess Fat servings could spell excess pounds. Still, though keeping fat intake moderate is a good idea, eliminating all fat from your diet is a dangerous one. Fat is vital to your developing baby; the essential fatty acids in them are just that—essential. Especially beneficial in the third trimester are omega-3 fatty acids (see facing page).

A Little Fat Goes a Long Way

Trying to keep those calories down by skipping the dressing on your salad or the oil in your stir-fry? You'd be getting an "A" for willpower—but less "vitamin A" in your veggies. Research shows that many of the nutrients found in vegetables aren't well absorbed by the body if not accompanied by a side of fat. So make a point of including a little fat (keep in mind that a little goes a long way) with your veggies: Enjoy oil with your stir-fry, a sprinkle of nuts on your broccoli, and dressing with your salad.

A Grain of Salt?

At one time, the medical establishment prescribed restricting salt during pregnancy because it contributed to water retention and swelling. Now it's believed that some increase in body fluids in pregnancy is necessary and normal, and a moderate amount of sodium is needed to maintain adequate fluid levels. In fact, sodium deprivation can be harmful to the fetus. Still, very large quantities of salt and very salty foods (such as those pickles you can't stop eating, soy sauce by the gallon on your stir-fry, and potato chips by the bagful), especially if they're consumed frequently, aren't good for anyone, pregnant or not. High sodium intake is closely linked to high blood pressure, a condition that can cause complications in pregnancy, labor, and delivery. As a general rule, salt only lightly—or don't salt at all—during cooking; salt your food to taste at the table instead. Have a pickle when you crave it, but try to stop at one or two instead of eating half the jar. And, unless your practitioner recommends otherwise (because you are hyperthyroid, for example), use iodized salt to be sure you meet the increased need for iodine in pregnancy.

Keep track of your fat intake; fill your daily quota but try not to overfill it. And in keeping track, don't forget that the fat used in cooking and preparing foods counts, too. If you've fried your eggs in ½ tablespoon of butter (a half serving) and tossed your cole slaw with a tablespoon of mayonnaise (one serving), include the one and a half servings in your daily tally.

If you're not gaining enough weight, and increasing your intake of other nutritious foods hasn't done the trick, try adding an extra Fat serving each day; the concentrated calories it provides may help you hit your optimum weight gain stride. If you're gaining too quickly, you can cut back by one or two servings.

The foods in this list are comprised completely (or mostly) of fat. They certainly won't be the only source of fat in your diet (foods such as cream sauces, full-fat cheeses and yogurts, and nuts and seeds are all high in fat), but they're the only ones you need to keep track of. If your weight gain is on target, aim for about four full (about 14 grams each) or eight half (about 7 grams each) servings of fat each day. If not, consider adjusting your fat intake up or down.

1 tablespoon oil, such as vegetable, olive, canola, or sesame

1 tablespoon regular butter or margarine

1 tablespoon regular mayonnaise

2 tablespoons regular salad dressing

2 tablespoons heavy or whipping cream

¼ cup half-and-half

¼ cup whipped cream

¼ cup sour cream

2 tablespoons regular cream cheese

2 tablespoons peanut or almond butter

Omega-3 fatty acids. Are you fat phobic (especially since pregnancy put you on the weight gain fast track)? Fear not your fat—just choose the right ones. After all, not all fats are created equal. Some fats are good ones—and they're especially good (make that great) when you're expecting. Omega-3 fatty acids, most notably DHA, are the best addition you can make to your diet when you're eating for two. That's because DHA is essential for proper brain growth and eye development in fetuses and young babies. In fact, researchers have found that toddlers whose moms consumed plenty of DHA during pregnancy had better hand-eye coordination than their peers. Getting enough of this vital baby brain fuel in your diet is especially important during the last three months (when your baby's brain grows at a phenomenal pace) and while you're nursing (the DHA content of a baby's brain triples during the first three months of life).

And what's good for the expected is also good for the expecting. For you, getting enough DHA may mean moderated mood swings and a lowered risk of preterm labor and postpartum depression. Another postpartum perk? Getting enough DHA when you're expecting means you're more likely to have a baby with better sleep habits. Luckily, DHA is found in plenty of foods you probably already eat—and like to eat: salmon (choose wild when you can) and other oily fish, such as sardines; walnuts; DHA-rich eggs (sometimes called omega-3 eggs); arugula; crab and shrimp; flaxseed; and even chicken. You can also ask your practitioner about pregnancy-safe DHA supplements. Some prenatal supplements contain some DHA.

Fluids: at least eight 8-ounce glasses daily. You're not only eating for two, you're drinking for two. Your baby's body, like yours, is composed mostly of fluids. As that little body grows, so does its demand for fluids. Your body needs fluids more than ever, too, since pregnancy pumps up fluid volume significantly. If you've always been one of those people who goes through the day with barely a sip, now's the time to tap into fluids. Water helps keep your skin soft, eases constipation, rids your body of toxins and waste products (and baby's,

too), and reduces excessive swelling and the risk of urinary tract infection and preterm labor. Be sure to get at least 8 glasses a day—more if you're retaining a lot of fluid (paradoxically, a plentiful fluid intake can flush out excess fluids), if you're exercising a lot, or if it's very hot. Try not to do your drinking just before meals, though, or you might end up too full to eat.

Of course, not all your fluids have to come from the tap (or from the water cooler). You can count milk (which is two-thirds water), fruit and vegetable juices, soups, decaffeinated coffee or tea (hot or iced), and bottled plain and sparkling waters. Cutting fruit juice with sparkling water (half and half) will keep you from pouring on too many calories. Fruit and vegetables count, too (five servings of produce net two fluid servings).

Prenatal vitamin supplements: a pregnancy formula taken daily. With all the nutrients already prepacked into the Daily Dozen (or any healthy diet), why would you need to add a prenatal vitamin to the mix? Couldn't you fill all of your requirements by filling yourself with the right foods? Well, you probably could—that is, if you lived in a laboratory where your food was precisely prepared and measured to calculate an adequate daily intake, if you never ate on the run, had to work through lunch, or felt too sick to eat. In the real world—the one you most likely live in—a prenatal supplement provides extra health insurance for you and your baby, covering those nutritional bases when your diet doesn't. And that's why one is recommended daily.

Still, a supplement is just a supplement. No pill, no matter how complete, can replace a good diet. It's best if most of your vitamins and minerals come from foods, because that's the way nutrients can be most effectively utilized. Fresh foods contain not only nutrients that we know about and can be synthesized in a pill, but probably lots of others that are as yet undiscovered. Food also supplies fiber and water (fruits and vegetables are loaded with both) and important calories and protein, none of which comes efficiently packaged in a pill.

But don't think that because a little is good, a lot is better. Vitamins and minerals at high doses act as drugs in the body and should be treated as drugs, especially by expectant moms; a few, such as vitamins A and D, are toxic at levels not much beyond the recommended dietary allowance (RDAs are now called DRIs, dietary reference intakes, or DVs, daily values). Any supplementation beyond the DRI should be taken only under medical supervision. The same goes for herbal and other supplements. As for vitamins and minerals you can get from your diet, you can't overdo the nutrients by piling up your plate at the salad bar—so no need to hold back when the carrots call or the broccoli beckons.

What's in a Pill?

What's in a prenatal pill? That depends on which one you're taking. Since there aren't any standards set for prenatal supplements, formulas vary. Chances are your practitioner will prescribe or recommend a supplement, which will take the guesswork (and homework) out of choosing a formula yourself. If you're facing the pharmacy shelves without a recommendation, get ready to do some reading, and to look for a formula that contains:

- No more than 4,000 IU (800 mcg) of vitamin A; amounts over 10,000 IU could be toxic. Many manufacturers have reduced the amount of vitamin A in their vitamin supplements or have replaced it with beta-carotene, a much safer source of vitamin A.

- At least 400 to 600 mcg of folic acid (folate)

- 250 mg of calcium. If you're not getting enough calcium in your diet, you will need additional supplementation to reach the 1,200 mg needed during pregnancy. Do not take more than 250 mg of calcium at the same time as supplementary iron because these minerals interfere with iron

absorption. Take any larger doses at least two hours before or after your iron supplement.

- 30 mg iron

- 50 to 80 mg vitamin C

- 15 mg zinc

- 2 mg copper

- 2 mg vitamin B$_6$

- At least 400 IU of vitamin D

- Approximately the DRI for vitamin E (15 mg), thiamin (1.4 mg), riboflavin (1.4 mg), niacin (18 mg), and vitamin B$_{12}$ (2.6 mg). Most prenatal supplements contain two to three times the DRI of these. There are no known harmful effects from such doses.

- Some preparations may also contain magnesium, fluoride, biotin, phosphorus, pantothenic acid, extra B$_6$ (to combat queasiness), ginger (ditto), and/or baby brain–boosting DHA.

Also important: Scan for ingredients that shouldn't be in your prenatal supplement, such as herbs. When in doubt, ask your practitioner.

What You May Be Wondering About

Milk-Free Mom

"I can't tolerate milk, and drinking four cups a day would really make me uncomfortable. But don't babies need milk?"

It's not milk your baby needs, it's calcium. Since milk is one of nature's finest and most convenient sources of calcium in the American diet, it's the one most often recommended for filling the greatly increased requirement during pregnancy. But if milk leaves you with more than a sour taste in your mouth and a mustache above your lip (got gas?), you probably think twice before reaching for that glass of the white stuff. Fortunately, you don't have to suffer so your baby can grow healthy teeth and bones. If you're lactose intolerant or just don't have a taste for milk, plenty of substitutes are available that fill the nutritional bill just as well.

Even if milk turns your tummy, you still might be able to tolerate some kinds of dairy products, such as hard cheeses, fully processed yogurts (choose ones with active cultures, which actually help your digestion), and lactose-free milk, in which all of the lactose has been converted to a more easily digested form. Another advantage of using lactose-free milk products: Some are fortified with extra calcium. Check labels and choose one that is. Taking a lactase tablet before ingesting milk or milk products, or adding lactase drops or tablets to your milk, can also minimize or eliminate dairy-induced tummy troubles.

Even if you've been lactose intolerant for years, you may discover that you're able to handle some dairy products during the second and third trimesters, when fetal needs for calcium are the greatest. If that's so, don't overdo it; try to stick primarily to products that are less likely to provoke a reaction.

If you can't handle any dairy products or are allergic to them, you can still get all the calcium your baby requires by drinking calcium-fortified juices and eating the nondairy foods listed under Calcium foods on page 95.

If your problem with milk isn't physiological but just a matter of taste, try some of the dairy or nondairy calcium-

Pasteurized, Please

When it was invented by French scientist Louis Pasteur in the mid-1800s, pasteurization was the greatest thing to happen to dairy products since cows. And it still is, particularly as far as pregnant women are concerned. To protect yourself and your baby from hazardous bacterial infections, such as listeria, make sure all the milk you drink is pasteurized, and all the cheeses and other dairy products you eat are made from pasteurized milk ("raw milk" cheeses are not). Juice, which can contain *E. coli* and other dangerous bacteria when it's raw, should also always be purchased pasteurized. Even eggs now come pasteurized (which eliminates the risk of salmonella without changing taste or nutrition). It's unclear whether flash pasteurization, a fast method, is safe enough when you're expecting, so until more is known, stick to products that have undergone conventional pasteurization.

rich alternatives. There are bound to be plenty that your taste buds can embrace. Or disguise your milk in cereal, soups, and smoothies.

If you can't seem to get enough calcium into your diet, ask your practitioner to recommend a calcium supplement (there are plenty of chewable varieties that are sweet revenge for those who find a pill hard to swallow). You'll also need to be sure that you're getting enough vitamin D (which is added to cow's milk). Many calcium supplements include vitamin D (which actually boosts absorption of calcium), and you'll also be getting some in your prenatal supplement.

A Red-Meat-Free Diet

"I eat chicken and fish but no red meat. Will my baby get all the necessary nutrients without it?"

Your baby won't have a beef with your red-meat-free diet. Fish and lean poultry, in fact, give you more baby-building protein and less fat for your calories than beef, pork, lamb, and organ meats—making them more efficient pregnancy choices. They're also rich sources, like red meat, of many of the B vitamins your baby needs. The only nutrient poultry and fish can't always compete for with meat is iron (duck, turkey, and shellfish are iron-rich exceptions), but there are plenty of other sources of this essential mineral, which is also easy to take in supplement form.

A Vegetarian Diet

"I'm a vegetarian and in perfect health. But everyone says that I have to eat animal products to have a healthy baby. Is this true?"

Vegetarians of every variety can have healthy babies without compromising their dietary principles—they just have to be a little more careful in planning their diets than meat-eating mothers-to-be. When choosing your meat-free menus, make sure you get all of the following:

Enough protein. For the ovo-lacto vegetarian, who eats eggs and milk products, getting enough protein is as easy as getting enough of these dairy-case favorites. If you're a vegan (a vegetarian who eats neither milk nor eggs), you may find you'll need to work a little harder in the protein department, turning to ample quantities of dried beans, peas, lentils, tofu, and other soy products (see page 96 for more vegetarian proteins).

Enough calcium. This is no tall order for the vegetarian who eats dairy products, but it can be trickier for those who don't. Luckily, dairy products are the most obvious but not the only sources of calcium. Calcium-fortified juices offer as much calcium as milk, ounce for ounce (just make sure you shake them before using). Other nondairy dietary sources of calcium include dark leafy green vegetables, sesame seeds, almonds, and many soy products (such as soy milk, soy cheese, tofu, and tempeh). For added insurance, vegans should probably also take a calcium supplement; check with your practitioner for a recommendation.

Vitamin B$_{12}$. Though B$_{12}$ deficiencies are rare, vegetarians, particularly vegans, often don't get enough of this vitamin because it is found only in animal foods. So be certain to take supplemental B$_{12}$, as well as folic acid and iron (ask your practitioner if you need more B$_{12}$ than what's provided in your prenatal vitamin). Other dietary sources include B$_{12}$-fortified soy milk, fortified cereals, nutritional yeast, and fortified meat substitutes.

Vitamin D. Many experts say most women don't get enough of this vital vitamin, a deficiency of which is linked to increased pregnancy risk. While the body produces vitamin D when exposed to sunlight, making enough can be challenging—especially for those who have darker skin, live in less-sunny climates, don't get outdoors enough, or who wear sunscreen. Can you eat (or drink) your D? Not easily, since it isn't found in large amounts in any food. Fortified milk and juices contain some, as do sardines and egg yolks, but not nearly enough to prevent a D deficit. Your best bet: Ask your practitioner about testing your vitamin D levels, and prescribing a supplement as needed.

Low-Carb Diet

"I've been on a low-carb/high-protein diet to lose weight. Can I continue the diet while I'm pregnant?"

Here's the low-down on low-carb: When you're expecting, low isn't the way to go. Going low on any essential nutrient, in fact, isn't smart when you're expecting. Your highest pregnancy priority: getting a balance of all of the best baby-making ingredients, including carbs. As popular as they are, diets that limit carbohydrates (including fruits, vegetables, and grains) limit the nutrients—especially folic acid—that growing fetuses need. And what's bad for baby can also be bad for mom: Skimp on complex carbohydrates and you'll be skimping on constipation-fighting fiber, plus all the B vitamins known to battle morning sickness and pregnancy-unsettled skin.

Another important point: Pregnancy is a time for healthy eating, not for dieting. So shelve those weight-loss books

(at least until after you deliver) and stay well-balanced for a well-fed baby.

Cholesterol Concerns

"My husband and I are very careful about our diets, and we limit the cholesterol we eat. Should I keep doing this while I'm pregnant?"

Tired of hearing about all the things you can't have, shouldn't have, or need to cut back on now that you're pregnant? Then this bulletin should cheer you up: Cholesterol doesn't have to be off the table when you're expecting. Pregnant women, and to a lesser extent nonpregnant women of childbearing age, are protected to a certain degree against the artery-clogging effects of cholesterol—putting them in an enviable position as far as bacon, egg, and burger lovers are concerned. In fact, cholesterol is necessary for fetal development, so much so that the mother's body automatically increases its production, raising blood cholesterol levels by anywhere from 25 to 40 percent. Though you don't have to eat a high-cholesterol diet to help your body step up production, you can feel free to indulge a bit (unless your practitioner advised you otherwise). Scramble some eggs for breakfast (choose omega-3 eggs for the best fat benefits), use cheese to meet your calcium requirement, and bite into that burger, all without guilt.

Junk Food Junkie

"I'm addicted to junk foods like doughnuts, chips, and fast food. I know I should be eating healthier—and I really want to—but I'm not sure I can change my habits."

Ready to junk the junk food? Getting motivated to change your eating habits is the first and most important step—so congratulate yourself on taking it. Actually making the changes will involve some serious effort—but the effort will be seriously worth it. Here are several ways to make your withdrawal from your junk food habit almost as painless as it is worthwhile:

Move your meals. If the coffee crumble calls when you breakfast at your desk, fill up on a better breakfast at home (one that's packed with the blood-sugar stabilizing, stick-with-you combo of complex carbs and protein, like oatmeal, will actually help you fight those junk food cravings when they strike later on). If you know you can't resist the golden fries once you pass through the Golden Arches, don't go there—literally. Order in a healthy sandwich from the local deli—or head to that wrap place that doesn't fry anything.

Plan, plan, and plan some more. Planning for meals and snacks ahead of time (instead of grabbing what's easiest or nearest, like that package of cheese crackers from the vending machine) will keep you eating well throughout your pregnancy. So pack those brown bags. Keep a supply of takeout menus from restaurants that offer healthy options, so a nourishing meal's always just a phone call away (and place your order before hunger strikes). Stock your home, workplace, bag, and car with wholesome but satisfying snacks: fresh, dried, or dehydrated fruit, trail mix, soy chips, whole-grain granola bars and crackers, individual-size yogurts or smoothies, string cheese or wedges. So that the soda won't speak to you next time you get thirsty, keep water at the ready.

Don't test temptation. Keep candy, chips, cookies, and sugar-sweetened soft drinks out of the house so they'll be out of reach (if not out of mind). Step away from the pastry case before

that Danish makes eye contact with you. Drive the long way home from the office if it means you won't drive by the drive-through.

Make substitutions. Crave a Krispy Kreme with your morning coffee? Dunk a bran muffin instead. The midnight munchies have you digging for Doritos? Settle for the baked tortilla chips (that you were smart enough to stock up on at the market last time), dipped in salsa for more flavor and a healthy helping of vitamin C. Is your sweet tooth aching for ice cream? Stop by the juice bar for a thick, creamy, sweet fruit smoothie instead.

Keep baby on your mind. Your baby eats what you eat, but that's sometimes hard to keep in mind (especially when the smell of a cinnamon bun tries to seduce you at the mall). If you find it helps keep baby-feeding front of brain, put pictures of cute, well-fed babies wherever you might need a little inspiration (and a lot of willpower). Keep one on your desk, in your wallet, in your car (so when you're tempted to veer into the drive-through, you'll drive by instead).

Know your limits. Some junk food junkies can handle a once-in-a-while approach to indulging their cravings, others can't (and you know who you are). If enough junk food is never enough for you—if a snack-size candy bar leads to king-size, if a single doughnut leads to a dozen, if you know you'll polish off the whole bag of chips once you tear it open—you might have an easier time quitting your habit cold turkey than trying to moderate it.

Remember that good habits can last a lifetime, too. Once you've put the effort into developing healthier eating habits, you might want to consider keeping them. Continuing to eat well after delivery will give you more of the energy you'll need to fuel your

Shortcuts to Healthy Eating

Healthy food can be fast food, too. Here's how:

- If you're always on the run, remember that it takes no more time to make a roast turkey, cheese, lettuce, and tomato sandwich to take to work (or to order one at the deli) than it does to stand in line for a burger.

- If the prospect of preparing a real dinner every night seems overwhelming, cook enough for two or three dinners at one time and give yourself alternate nights off.

- Keep it simple when you're cooking healthy. For a quick meal, broil a fish fillet and top it with your favorite jarred salsa, a little chopped avocado, and a squeeze of fresh lime juice. Layer tomato sauce and mozzarella cheese on a cooked boneless chicken breast, and then run it under the broiler. Or scramble some eggs and wrap them in a corn tortilla along with shredded cheddar and some microwave-steamed vegetables.

- When you don't have time to start from scratch (when do you ever?), turn to canned beans, soups, frozen or packaged ready-to-prepare healthy entrees, frozen vegetables, or the fresh prewashed veggies sold in supermarket produce sections (the ones you can microwave in the bag are especially convenient).

---

new-mom lifestyle. Plus it'll make it more likely that your baby will grow up with a taste for the healthier things in life.

Eating Out

"I try hard to stay on a healthy diet, but I eat out so often, it seems impossible."

For many pregnant women, it isn't substituting mineral water for martinis that poses a challenge at the restaurant table; it's trying to put together a meal that's baby friendly and doesn't break the calorie bank. With those goals in mind, and the following suggestions, it's easy to take the Pregnancy Diet out to lunch or dinner.

- Look for whole grains before you leap into the bread basket. If there aren't any in the basket, ask if there are any in the kitchen. If not, try not to fill up too much on the white stuff. Go easy, too, on the butter you spread on your bread and rolls, as well as the olive oil you dip them into. There will probably be plenty of other sources of fat in your restaurant meal—dressing on the salad, butter or olive oil on the vegetables—and, as always, fat adds up quickly.

- Go for a green salad as a first course. Other good first-course choices include shrimp cocktail, steamed seafood, grilled vegetables, or soup.

- If soup's on, look to ones with a vegetable base (particularly sweet potato, carrot, winter squash, or tomato). Lentil or bean soups pack a protein punch, too. In fact, a large bowl may eat like a meal, especially if you toss some grated cheese on top. Generally steer clear of cream soups, and take Manhattan-style when it comes to clam chowder.

- Make the most of your main. Get your protein—fish, seafood, chicken breast, or beef—the lean way (good words to look for: grilled, broiled, steamed, and poached). If everything comes heavily sauced, ask for yours on the side. And don't shy away from special requests (chefs are used to them; plus, it's hard to turn down a pregnant woman). Ask if that chicken breast can be broiled plain, instead of breaded and pan-seared or if the snapper can be grilled instead of fried. If you're a vegetarian, scan the menu for tofu, beans and peas, cheeses, and combinations of these. Vegetable lasagna, for example, might be a good choice in an Italian restaurant, bean curd and vegetables in a Chinese one.

- Be selective on the side, scouting for baked white or sweet potatoes, brown or wild rice, legumes (beans and peas), and fresh vegetables.

- Consider a fruity finish to your restaurant meal (fresh berries can be surprisingly satisfying). Fruit alone doesn't cut it (at least not all the time)? Add whipped cream, sorbet, or ice cream. Craving serious sweets? Join the "two spoons" club and share a decadent dessert with others at your table.

Reading Labels

"I'm eager to eat well, but it's difficult to figure out what's in the products I buy. I just can't make sense out of the labels."

Labels aren't designed to help you as much as to sell you. Keep this in mind when filling your shopping cart, and learn to read the small print, especially the ingredients list and the nutrition label (which *is* designed to help you).

The ingredients listing will tell you, in order of predominance (with the first ingredient the most plentiful and the last the least), exactly what's in a product. A quick look will tell you whether the major ingredient in a cereal is a refined grain or a whole grain. It will also tell you when a product is high in sugar, salt, fat, or additives. For example, when sugar is listed near the top of the ingredients list or when it appears in several different forms on a list (corn syrup, honey, and sugar), you know the product is chock-full of sugar.

Checking the grams of sugar on the label will not be useful until the FDA orders that the grams of "added sugar" be separated from the grams of "naturally occurring sugar" (those found in the raisin part of the raisin bran you're considering, for instance). Though the number of grams of sugar on the present label may be the same on a container of orange juice and a container of fruit drink, they aren't equivalent. It's like comparing oranges and corn syrup: The real OJ gets its naturally occurring sugar from fruit; the fruit drink contains added sugar.

Nutrition labels, which appear on most packaged products on your grocer's shelves, can be particularly valuable for a pregnant woman counting her protein and watching her calories, since they provide the grams of the former and the number of the latter in each serving. The listing of percentages of the government's recommended dietary allowance (called DRIs), however, is less useful because the DRI for pregnant women is different than the DRI used on package labels. Still, a food that scores high in a wide variety of nutrients is a good product to drop into your cart.

While it's important to pay attention to the small print, it's sometimes just as important to ignore the large print. When a box of English muffins boasts, "Made with whole wheat, bran, and honey," reading the small print may reveal that the major ingredient (first on the list) is white, not whole wheat, flour, that the muffins contain barely any bran (it's near the bottom of the ingredients

You Can't Tell a Fruit by Its Cover

When it comes to nutrition, the darker the color of most fruits and vegetables, the more vitamins and minerals (especially vitamin A) you'll be able to harvest from them. But keep in mind that it's the color inside—not outside—that signals good nutrition. So while cucumbers (dark on the outside, pale on the inside) are lightweights in that department, cantaloupes (pale on the outside, dark on the inside) are standouts.

list), and that there's a lot more white sugar (it's high on the list) than honey (it's low).

"Enriched" and "fortified" are also banners to be wary of. Adding a few vitamins to a not-so-good food doesn't make it a good food. You'd be much better off with a bowl of oatmeal, which comes by its nutrients naturally, than with a refined cereal that contains 12 grams of added sugar and a few pennies' worth of tossed-in vitamins and minerals.

Sushi Safety

"Sushi is my favorite food, but I heard you're not supposed to eat it while you're pregnant. Is that true?"

Sorry to say, sushi and sashimi will have to go the way of sake (the Japanese wine often served with them) during pregnancy—which is to say, they're off the table. Same holds true for raw oysters and clams, ceviche, fish tartares or carpaccios, and other raw or barely cooked fish and shellfish. That's because when seafood isn't cooked, there's a slight chance that

it can make you sick (something you definitely don't want to be when you're pregnant). But that doesn't mean you have to steer clear of your favorite Japanese restaurants. Plenty of other options exist there, even at the sushi bar. Rolls that contain cooked fish or seafood and/or vegetables are, in fact, healthy options. (But don't worry about any raw fish you've eaten up to this point.)

Hot Stuff

"I love spicy food—the hotter, the better. Is it safe to eat it while I'm pregnant?"

Hot mamas-to-be can continue to challenge their taste buds with four-alarm chilis, salsas, and stir-fries—as long as you can tolerate the almost inevitable heartburn and indigestion that follow. There's no risk from spicy foods during pregnancy, and, in fact, since peppers of all kinds (including hot ones) are packed with vitamin C, many of these foods are extra nutritious. So enjoy—just make sure you save room for Tums.

Spoiled Food

"I ate a container of yogurt this morning without realizing that it had expired a week ago. It didn't taste spoiled, but should I worry?"

No need to cry over spoiled milk . . . or yogurt. Though eating dairy products that have recently "expired" is never a particularly good idea, it's rarely a dangerous one. If you haven't shown any ill effects from your post-date snack (symptoms of food poisoning usually occur within eight hours), there's obviously no harm done. Besides, food poisoning is an unlikely possibility if the yogurt had been refrigerated continuously. In the future, however, check dates more carefully before you buy or eat perishables, and, of course, never eat foods that appear to have developed mold. For more on food safety, see the box on page 116.

"I got food poisoning from something I ate last night, and I've been throwing up. Will that hurt my baby?"

You're much more likely to suffer from the food poisoning than your baby is. The major risk—for you and your baby—is that you'll become dehydrated from vomiting and diarrhea. So make sure you get plenty of fluids (which are more important in the short term than solids) to replace those that you're losing. And contact your practitioner if your diarrhea is severe and/or your stools contain blood or mucus. See page 501 for more on stomach bugs.

Sugar Substitutes

"I'm trying not to gain too much weight, but I love sweets. Can I use sugar substitutes?"

It sounds like a sweet deal, but the truth is that sugar substitutes are a mixed bag for expectant moms. Though most are probably safe, some research is still inconclusive. Here's how sugar substitutes stack up at the moment:

Sucralose (Splenda). Made from sugar, but chemically converted to a form that's not absorbable by the body, sucralose appears right now to be the best bet for pregnant women seeking sweetness with no calories and little aftertaste. You can sweeten your coffee or tea with sucralose, and use it in cooking and baking (unlike other sugar substitutes, it doesn't lose its sweetness when heated), or buy products that have been sweetened with it (including drinks, yogurts, candy, and ice cream). Keep in mind that moder-

ation's probably sm; seems to be safe, the new, and no long-ter to confirm that.

Aspartame (Equal, NutraSweet). Aspartame is used in beverages, yogurt, and frozen desserts but not in baked goods or cooked foods (the sweetness doesn't survive when heated for long periods). The jury is still out on the safety of this widely used sugar substitute. Many practitioners consider it harmless and will okay light or moderate use in pregnancy. Others are less convinced of its safety and suggest that, until more is known, pregnant women be cautious in their use of this sweetener. Check with your practitioner for his or her aspartame bottom line. (Women with PKU must limit their intake of phenylalanine and are advised never to use aspartame.)

Saccharin. Not much research has been done on saccharin use in human pregnancy, but animal studies show an increase in cancer in the offspring of pregnant animals who ingest large quantities of the chemical. Whether a similar risk exists for human offspring is unclear (especially because animal studies don't always correlate well to human reality—after all, you're not pregnant with a baby rat). Still, combined with the fact that the sweetener crosses the placenta in humans and is eliminated very slowly from fetal tissues, most practitioners advise minimizing its use during pregnancy. Don't worry, however, about saccharin you had before finding out that you were pregnant because, again, there are no documented risks.

Acesulfame-K (Sunett). This sweetener, 200 times sweeter than sugar, is approved for use in baked goods, gelatin desserts, chewing gum, and soft drinks. The FDA says it's okay to use in moderation during pregnancy, but since few studies been done to prove its safety, ask your practitioner what he or she thinks before gobbling the stuff up.

Sorbitol. This is a relative of sugar found naturally in many fruits and berries. With half the sweetness of sugar, it is used in a wide range of foods and beverages and is safe for use in pregnancy in moderate amounts. But it does present a problem in large doses: Too much can cause bloating, gas pains, and diarrhea—a trio no pregnant woman needs.

Mannitol. Less sweet than sugar, mannitol is poorly absorbed by the body and thus provides fewer calories than sugar (but more than other sugar substitutes). Like sorbitol, it is safe in modest amounts, but large quantities can cause gastrointestinal unrest.

Xylitol. This sugar alcohol, which is produced as a sugar substitute from plants (but is also naturally occurring in many fruits and vegetables and is even created by the body during normal metabolism), is found in chewing gum, toothpaste, candies, and some foods. One of its benefits is that it can prevent tooth decay (which is why chewing gum made with xylitol can be a very good thing). Xylitol has 40 percent fewer calories than sugar and is considered safe during pregnancy in moderation (so in other words, it's fine to chew one pack of xylitol gum—but you might not want to chew five).

Stevia. Derived from a South American shrub, stevia has not been approved by the FDA as a sweetener (it's considered a dietary supplement). No clear research proves stevia is safe during pregnancy, so before you dip into this sweetener, check with your practitioner for his or her recommendation.

Lactose. This milk sugar is one sixth as sweet as table sugar and adds light sweetening to foods. For those who are

lactose-intolerant, it can cause uncomfortable symptoms; otherwise it's safe.

Honey. Everyone's all abuzz about honey these days because of its high levels of antioxidants (darker varieties, such as buckwheat honey, are the richest in antioxidants). But it's not all sweet news. Though it's a good substitute for sugar, honey is definitely not low-cal. It's got 19 more calories per tablespoon than sugar does. How's that for sticky?

Fruit juice concentrates. Unquestionably nutritious, fruit juice concentrates, such as white grape and apple, are a safe (if not low-calorie) sweetener to turn to during pregnancy. They're surprisingly versatile in the kitchen (you can substitute them for the sugar in many recipes) and they're readily available in frozen form at the supermarket. Look for them in a host of commercial products, too, from jams and jellies to whole-grain cookies, muffins, cereals, and granola bars, to pop-up toaster pastries, yogurt, and sparkling sodas. Unlike most products sweetened with sugar or other sugar substitutes, the majority of fruit-juice-sweetened products are made with nutritious ingredients, such as whole-grain flour and healthy fats. How sweet it is.

Herbal Tea

"I drink a lot of herbal tea. Is it safe to keep drinking it while I'm pregnant?"

Should you take (herbal) tea for two? Unfortunately, since the effect of herbs in pregnancy has not been well researched, there's no definitive answer to that question yet. Some herbal teas are probably safe, some probably not—and some, such as red raspberry leaf, taken in very large amounts (more than four 8-ounce cups a day), are thought to trigger contractions (good if you're 40 weeks and impatient, not good if you haven't reached term). Until more is known, the FDA has urged caution on the use of most herbal teas in pregnancy and during lactation. And though many women have drunk lots of herbal teas throughout pregnancy without a problem, it is probably safest to stay away from, or at least limit, herbal teas while you're expecting—unless they've been specifically recommended or cleared by your practitioner. Check with your practitioner for a list of which herbs he or she believes are safe and which are pregnancy no-no's.

To make sure you're not brewing up trouble (and an herb your practitioner hasn't cleared) with your next cup of tea, read labels carefully; some brews that seem from their names to be fruit based also contain a variety of herbs. Stick to regular (black) tea that comes flavored, or mix up your own by adding any of the following to boiling water or regular tea: orange, apple, pineapple, or other fruit juice; slices of lemon, lime, orange, apple, pear, or other fruit; mint leaves, cinnamon, nutmeg, cloves, or ginger (a great alleviator of the queasies). Chamomile is also considered safe in small amounts during pregnancy and can be soothing to a pregnancy-unsettled tummy. The jury's still out on green tea, which can decrease the effectiveness of folic acid, that vital pregnancy vitamin—so if you're a green tea drinker, drink in moderation. And never brew a homemade tea from a plant growing in your backyard, unless you are absolutely certain what it is and that it's safe for use during pregnancy.

Chemicals in Foods

"With additives in packaged foods, pesticides on vegetables, PCBs and mercury in fish, antibiotics in meat, and nitrates in hot dogs, is there anything I can safely eat during pregnancy?"

Take heart—and take it easy. You don't have to go crazy (or hungry) to protect your baby from food hazards. In spite of anything you might have read and heard, very few substances found in food have been absolutely proven harmful to the unborn.

Still, it's smart to reduce risk whenever you can—particularly when you're reducing risk for two. And it's not that difficult to do, especially these days. To feed yourself and your baby as safely as you can, use the following as a guide to help you decide what to drop into your shopping cart and what to pass up:

- Choose your foods from the Pregnancy Diet. Because it steers away from processed foods, it steers you clear of many questionable and unsafe substances. It also supplies Green Leafies and Yellows, rich in protective beta-carotene, as well as other fruits and vegetables rich in phytochemicals, which may counteract the effects of toxins in food.

- Whenever possible, cook from scratch with fresh ingredients or use frozen or packaged organic ready-to-eat foods. You'll avoid many questionable additives found in processed foods, and your meals will be more nutritious, too.

- Go as natural as you can, when you can. Whenever you have a choice (and you won't always), choose foods that are free of artificial additives (colorings, flavorings, and preservatives). Read labels to screen for foods that are either additive free or use natural additives (a cheddar cheese cracker that gets its orange hue from annatto, instead of red dye #40, and its flavor from real cheese, instead of artificial cheese flavoring). Keep in mind that although some artificial additives are considered safe, others are of questionable safety, and many are used to enhance foods that aren't very nutritious to start with. (For a listing of questionable and safe additives, go to cspinet.org/reports/chemcuisine.htm).

■ Generally avoid foods preserved with nitrates and nitrites (or sodium nitrates), including hot dogs, salami, bologna, and smoked fish and meats. Look for those brands (you'll find plenty in the market these days) that do not include these preservatives.

■ Fish is a great source of lean protein, as well as baby brain–building omega-3 fatty acids, two good reasons to keep it on your pregnancy menu—or even to consider adding it (aversions allowing) if you've never been a fish eater before. And in fact, research has shown brain benefits for babies whose moms eat lots of fish when they're expecting. So go fish, by all means, but fish selectively, sticking to those varieties that are considered safe. According to the EPA and other experts, it's smart to avoid shark, swordfish, king mackerel, tilefish, and tuna steaks. These large fish can contain high levels of methylmercury, a chemical that in large, accumulated doses can possibly be harmful to a fetus's developing nervous system. Don't worry if you've already enjoyed a serving or two of swordfish—any risks would apply to regular consumption—just skip these fish from now on. Also limit your consumption of canned tuna (chunk light tuna contains less mercury

than white) and freshwater fish caught by recreational fishers to an average of 6 ounces (cooked weight) per week; commercially caught fish usually has lower levels of contaminants, so you can safely eat more. Steer clear of fish from waters that are contaminated (with sewage or industrial runoff, for example) or tropical fish, such as grouper, amberjack, and mahimahi (which sometimes contain toxins). Fortunately, that leaves plenty of fish in the sea to enjoy safely and often (an average of 12 ounces of cooked fish per week is considered safe according to government guidelines). Choose from salmon (wild caught is best), sole, flounder, haddock, tilapia, halibut, ocean perch, pollack, cod, and trout, as well as other smaller ocean fish (anchovies, sardines, and herring are not only safe, but also loaded with omega-3) and seafood of all kinds. Remember, all fish and seafood should be well cooked. For the latest information on fish safety, contact the FDA at (888) SAFE-FOOD (723-3366) or cfsan.fda.gov or the EPA at epa.gov/ost/fish.

■ Choose lean cuts of meat and remove visible fat before cooking, since chemicals that livestock ingest tend to concentrate in the fat of the animal. With poultry, remove both the fat and the skin to minimize chemical intake. And don't eat organ meats (such as liver and kidneys) very often, for the same reason.

■ When it's available and your budget permits, buy meat and poultry that has been raised organically (or grass-fed), without hormones or antibiotics (remember, you eat what your dinner ate). Choose organic dairy products and eggs, when possible, for the same reason. Free-range chickens (and eggs) are not only less likely to be contaminated with chemicals, they are also less

Something's Cooking

You can find recipes that put it all together in *What to Expect: Eating Well When You're Expecting.*

likely to carry such infections as salmonella because the birds are not kept in cramped, disease-breeding quarters. And here's a plus when it comes to grass-fed beef: It's likely to be lower in calories and fat, higher in protein, and a rich source of those baby-friendly omega-3 fatty acids.

- Buy organic produce when possible and practical. Produce that is certified organic usually is as close as possible to being free of all chemical residues. Transitional produce may still contain some residues from soil contamination but should be safer than conventionally grown produce. If organic produce is available locally and you can afford the premium price, make it your choice—just keep in mind as you load up your shopping cart that organic produce will have a much shorter shelf life (same goes for organic poultry and meats). If price is an object, pick organic selectively (see box).

- As a precaution, give all vegetables and fruits a bath. Washing produce thoroughly is important no matter what (even organic produce can wear a coating of bacteria), but it's key to removing chemical pesticides your fruits and veggies may have picked up in the field. Water will wash off some, but a dip in or a spray with produce wash will take off much more (rinse thoroughly afterward). Scrub skins when possible and practical to remove surface chemical residues, especially when a vegetable has a waxy coating (as cucumbers and sometimes tomatoes, apples, peppers, and eggplant do). Peel skins that still seem "coated" after washing.

- Favor domestic produce. Imported (and foods made from such produce) often contain higher levels of pesticides than U.S.-grown equivalents because

Pick and Choose Organic

Spending the big bucks on organic produce isn't always worth it. Here's the lowdown on when to spring for the organic and when it's safe to stick with conventional:

Best to buy organic (because even after washing, these foods still carry higher levels of pesticide residue than others): Apples, cherries, grapes, peaches, nectarines, pears, raspberries, strawberries, bell peppers, celery, potatoes, and spinach.

No need to go organic on these foods (because these products generally don't contain pesticide residue on them): Bananas, kiwi, mango, papaya, pineapples, asparagus, avocado, broccoli, cauliflower, corn, onions, and peas.

Consider organic for milk, beef, and poultry because they won't contain antibiotics or hormones, though they will cost more. Don't bother with so-called organic fish. There are no USDA organic certification standards for seafood (which means producers are making their own claims about why it's organic).

pesticide regulation in other countries is often lax or nonexistent.

- Go local. Locally grown produce is likely to contain more nutrients (it's fresh from the field) and possibly sport less pesticide residue. Many of the growers at your local farmers' market may grow without pesticides (or with very little), even if their products aren't marked "organic." That's because certification is too expensive for some small growers to afford.

- Vary your diet. Variety ensures not only a more interesting eating experience

Eating Safe for Two

...he pesticides ...ed up in South ...ble, especially because you're trying to eat safely for two. But what about the sponge you're about to wipe that peach down with (the one that's been hanging around your sink for the last three weeks)? Have you thought about what that might have picked up lately? And the cutting board you were planning to slice your peach on—isn't that the same one you diced that raw chicken on last night before you tossed it into the stir-fry? Here's a food safety reality check: A more immediate—and proven—threat than the chemicals in your food are the little organisms, bacteria and parasites, that can contaminate it. It's not a pretty picture (or one that's visible without the help of a microscope), but these nasty bugs can cause anything from mild stomach upset to severe illness. To make sure that the worst thing you'll pick up from your next meal is a little heartburn (the last thing an expectant mom needs is another reason for gastrointestinal upset), shop, prepare, and eat with care:

- When in doubt, throw it out. Make this your mantra of safe eating. It applies to any food you even suspect might be spoiled. Read and abide by freshness dates on food packages.

- When food shopping, avoid fish, meat, and eggs that are not well refrigerated or kept on ice. Steer clear of jars that are leaky or don't "pop" when you open them and cans that are rusty or seem swollen or

otherwise misshapen. Wash can tops before opening (and wash your can opener frequently in hot soapy water or in the dishwasher).

- Wash your hands before handling food and after touching raw meat, fish, or eggs. If you have a cut on your hand, wear rubber or plastic gloves while you prepare food, and remember, unless they're disposable, the gloves need to be washed as often as your bare hands.

- Keep kitchen counters and sinks clean. Same goes for cutting boards (wash with soap and hot water or in the dishwasher). Wash dishcloths frequently and keep sponges clean (replace them often, wash them in the dishwasher each night, or periodically pop dampened ones into the microwave for a couple of minutes); they can harbor bacteria.

- Serve hot foods hot, cold foods cold. Leftovers should be refrigerated quickly and heated until steaming before reusing. (Toss perishable foods that have been left out for more than two hours.) Don't eat frozen foods that have been thawed and then refrozen.

- Measure the fridge interior temperature with a refrigerator thermometer and be sure it stays at 41°F or less. Ideally, the freezer should be at 0°F, though many freezers are not designed to meet that requirement; don't worry if yours isn't.

and better nutrition but also better chances of avoiding excessive exposure to any one chemical. Switch between broccoli, kale, and carrots,

for instance; melon, peaches, and strawberries; salmon, halibut, and sole; cereals made from whole wheat, corn, and oats.

- Thaw foods in the refrigerator, time permitting. If you're in a rush, thaw food in a watertight plastic bag submerged in cold water (and change it every 30 minutes). Never thaw foods at room temperature.

- Marinate meat, fish, or poultry in the refrigerator, not on the counter. Discard the marinade after use, because it contains potentially hazardous bacteria. If you'd like to use the marinade as a dip or sauce, or to baste with, reserve a portion for that purpose before you add the meat, poultry, or fish. Use a new spoon or brush each time you baste to avoid recontaminating the marinade, or just cook for a few more minutes after the last basting.

- Don't eat raw or undercooked meats, poultry, fish, or shellfish while you're expecting. Always cook meats and fish to medium (to 160°F) and poultry thoroughly (to 165°F). In general, place the thermometer in the thickest part of the food, away from bone, fat, or gristle. In poultry, place it in the dark meat.

- Don't eat eggs that are runny (prefer well-scrambled to sunny-side up), and if you're mixing a batter that contains raw eggs, resist the urge to lick the spoon (or your fingers). The exception to this rule: eggs that are pasteurized, since this process effectively eliminates the risk of salmonella poisoning.

- Wash raw vegetables thoroughly (especially if they won't be cooked before eating). Those fresh blueber-

ries from the farmers' market might have been grown organically—but that doesn't mean they're not sporting a layer of bacteria.

- Avoid alfalfa and other sprouts, which are often contaminated with bacteria.

- Stick to pasteurized dairy products, and make sure those that you use have been refrigerated continuously. Soft cheeses, such as imported feta, Brie, blue cheeses, and soft Mexican-style cheese made from unpasteurized milk, can be contaminated with listeria (see page 501) and should be avoided by pregnant women, unless heated until bubbly. Domestic cheese is almost always pasteurized except for those made from "raw milk."

- Hot dogs, deli meats, and cold-smoked seafood can also be contaminated. As a precaution, even ready-cooked meats or smoked fish should be heated to steaming before eating (use them in casseroles).

- Juice should be fully pasteurized, too. Avoid unpasteurized or flash pasteurized juice or cider, whether it's bought at a health food store or a roadside stand. If you're not sure whether a juice is pasteurized, don't drink it.

- When eating out, avoid establishments that seem to ignore basic sanitation rules. Some signs are pretty obvious: Perishable foods are kept at room temperature, the bathrooms are unclean, it's open season for flies, and so on.

- Drive yourself to the health food market, but don't drive yourself crazy. Though it's smart to try to avoid theoretical hazards in food, making your life stressful in the pursuit of a natural meal isn't necessary. Do the best you can—and then sit back, eat well, and relax.

PART 2

Nine Months & Counting

From Conception to Delivery

The
First
Month

Approximately 1 to 4 Weeks

CONGRATULATIONS, AND WELCOME to your pregnancy! Though you almost certainly don't look pregnant yet, chances are you're already starting to feel it. Whether it's just tender breasts and a little fatigue you're experiencing, or every early pregnancy symptom in the book (and then some), your body is gearing up for the months of baby making to come. As the weeks pass, you'll notice changes in parts of your body you'd expect (like your belly), as well as places you wouldn't expect (your feet and your eyes). You'll also notice changes in the way you live—and look at—life. But try not to think (or read) too far ahead. For now, just sit back, relax, and enjoy the beginning of one of the most exciting and rewarding adventures of your life.

Your Baby This Month

Week 1 The countdown to baby begins this week. Only thing is, there's no baby in sight—or inside. So why call this week 1 of pregnancy if you're not even pregnant? Here's why. It's extremely hard to pinpoint the precise moment when sperm meets egg (sperm from your partner can hang out in your body for several days before your egg comes out to greet it, and your egg can be kept waiting for a day for the sperm to make their appearance).

What isn't hard to pinpoint, however, is the first day of your last menstrual period (LMP, which you're having right now—so mark the calendar), allowing your practitioner to use that as the standard starting line for your 40-week pregnancy. The upshot of this dating system (besides a lot of potential for confusion)? You get to clock in two weeks of your 40 weeks of pregnancy before you even get pregnant (how's that for a head start?).

Week 2 Nope, still no baby yet. But your body isn't taking a break this week. In fact, it's working hard gearing up for the big O—ovulation. The lining of your uterus is thickening (feathering its nest for the arrival of the fertilized egg) and your ovarian follicles are maturing—some faster than others—until one becomes the dominant one, destined for ovulation. And waiting in that dominant follicle is an anxious egg (or two, if you're about to conceive fraternal twins) with your baby's name on it—ready to burst out and begin its journey from single cell to bouncing boy or girl. But first it will have to make a journey down your fallopian tube in search of Mr. Right—the lucky sperm that will seal the deal.

Your Baby, Month 1

Week 3 Congratulations—you've conceived! Which means your soon-to-be baby has started its miraculous transformation from single cell to fully formed baby boy or girl ready for cuddles and kisses. Within hours after sperm meets egg, the fertilized cell (aka zygote) divides, and then continues to divide (and divide). Within days, your baby-to-be has turned into a microscopic ball of cells, around one fifth the size of the period at the end of this sentence. The blastocyst—as it is now known (though you'll almost certainly come up with a cuter name soon)—begins its journey from your fallopian tube to your waiting uterus. Only 8½ more months—give or take—to go!

Week 4 It's implantation time! That ball of cells that you'll soon call baby—though it's now called embryo—has reached your uterus and is snuggling into the uterine lining where it'll stay connected to you until delivery. Once firmly in place, the ball of cells undergoes the great divide—

splitting into two groups. Half will become your son or daughter, while the other half will become the placenta, your baby's lifeline during his or her uterine stay. And even though it's just a ball of cells right now (no bigger than a poppy seed, actually, but a lot sweeter), don't underestimate your little embryo—he or she has already come a long way since those blastocyst days. The amniotic sac—otherwise known as the bag of waters—is forming, as is the yolk sac, which will later be incorporated into your baby's developing digestive tract. Each layer of the embryo—it has three now—is beginning to grow into specialized parts of the body. The inner layer, known as the endoderm, will develop into your baby's digestive system, liver, and lungs. The middle layer, called the mesoderm, will soon be your baby's heart, sex organs, bones, kidneys, and muscles. The outer layer, or ectoderm, will eventually form your baby's nervous system, hair, skin, and eyes.

Make the Pregnancy Connection

Log on to whattoexpect.com—your interactive pregnancy companion. Just fill in your due date, and you'll get weekly reports on your baby's growth and development, plus access to useful tools like the Pregnancy Planner and Baby Name Finder. Connect with other moms on the message boards, create your own blogs and profile pages, and make new friends!

Pregnancy Timetable

Though most women count their pregnancies in months, your doctor or midwife will do the calculations in weeks. And that's where things can get a little tricky. The average pregnancy lasts 40 weeks, but because counting begins from the first day of your last menstrual period (LMP)—and ovulation and conception don't take place until two weeks after that (if your periods are regular)—you actually become pregnant in week 3 of your pregnancy. In other words, you've already clocked two weeks by the time sperm meets egg. This may sound very confusing, but as your pregnancy progresses and you experience preg-

nancy milestones traditionally marked by weeks (baby's heartbeat heard with Doppler around 10 weeks; the top of the uterus reaches your belly button at 20 weeks), you'll start to make sense of the weekly calendar.

Though this book is organized in chapters by month, corresponding weeks are also provided. Weeks 1 to 13 (approximately) make up the first trimester and include months 1 to 3; weeks 14 to 27 (approximately) comprise the second trimester and include months 4 to 6; and weeks 28 to 40 (approximately) are the third trimester and include months 7 to 9.

What You May Be Feeling

While it's true that pregnancy has its share of wonderful moments and experiences to cherish, it also has a boatload (make that a bloatload) of less

Symptoms? Starting Soon

Most early pregnancy symptoms begin making their appearance around week 6, but every woman—and every pregnancy—is different, so many may begin earlier or later for you (or not at all, if you're lucky). If you're experiencing something that's not on this list or in this chapter, look ahead to the next chapters or check it out in the index.

than fabulous symptoms. Some you're probably expecting to have (like that queasy feeling that might already be settling in). Others you'd probably never expect (like drooling—who knew?). Many you'll probably not discuss in public (and will try your best not to do in public, like passing gas), and many you'll probably try to forget (which you might, by the way, since forgetfulness is another pregnancy symptom).

Here are a couple of things to keep in mind about these and other pregnancy symptoms. First, because every woman and every pregnancy is different, few pregnancy symptoms are universal. So while your sister or best friend might have sailed through her pregnancy without a single nauseous moment, you might be spending every morning (and afternoon and evening) hovering over the toilet. Second, the symptoms that follow are a good sampling of what you might expect to experience (though you almost certainly, thankfully, won't experience them all—at least not all at once), but there are plenty more where these came from. Chances are just about every weird and wacky sensation you feel during the next nine months (both the physical ones and the emotional ones) will be normal for pregnancy, and normal for you. But if a symptom ever leaves you with a nagging doubt (can this really be normal?), always check it out with your practitioner, just to be sure.

Though it's unlikely that you'll even know you're expecting this month (at least not until the very end of the month), you might begin noticing something's up—even this early on. Here's what you might experience this month:

Physically

- Possible staining or spotting when the fertilized egg implants in your uterus, around five to ten days after conception (fewer than 30 percent of women experience such so-called implantation bleeding)

- Breast changes (possibly more pronounced if you typically have breast changes before your period, and possibly somewhat less pronounced if you've had babies before): fullness, heaviness, tenderness, tingling, darkening of the areolas (the pigmented area around your nipples)

- Bloating, flatulence

- Fatigue, lack of energy, sleepiness

- More frequent urination than usual

- Beginnings of nausea, with or without vomiting (though most women don't start feeling queasy until around six

A Look Inside

There's definitely no way to tell this book by its cover yet. Though you may recognize a few physical changes in yourself—your breasts may be a little fuller, your tummy a tad rounder (though that's from bloat, not baby)—no one else is likely to have noticed. Make sure you take a good look at your waist: It may be the last time you'll see it for many months to come.

weeks of pregnancy), and/or excess saliva

- Increased sensitivity to smells

Emotionally

- Emotional ups and downs (like amped-up PMS), which may include mood swings, irritability, irrationality, inexplicable weepiness

- Anxiousness while waiting for the right time to take a home pregnancy test

What You Can Expect at Your First Prenatal Visit

Your first prenatal visit probably will be the longest you'll have during your pregnancy—and definitely will be the most comprehensive. Not only will there be more tests, procedures (including several that will be performed only at this visit), and data gathering (in the form of a complete medical history), but there will be more time spent on questions (questions you have for the practitioner, questions he or she will have for you) and answers. There will also be plenty of advice to take in—on everything from what you should be eating (and not eating) to what supplements you should be taking (and not taking) to whether (and how) you should be exercising. So be sure to come equipped with a list of the questions and concerns that have already come up, as well as with a pen and notebook (or *The What to Expect Pregnancy Journal and Organizer*).

One practitioner's routine may vary slightly from another's. In general, the exam will include:

Confirmation of your pregnancy. Your practitioner will check the following: the pregnancy symptoms you are experiencing; the date of your LMP to determine your estimated date of delivery (EDD), or due date (see page 20); your cervix and uterus for signs and approximate age of the pregnancy. A pregnancy test (urine and blood) will most likely be performed. Many practitioners also do an early ultrasound, which is the most accurate way of dating a pregnancy.

A complete history. To give you the best care possible, your practitioner will want to know a lot about you. Come prepared by checking records at home or calling your primary care doctor to refresh your memory on the following: your personal medical history (chronic illness, previous major illness or surgery, known allergies, including drug allergies); nutritional supplements (vitamins, minerals, herbal, and so on) or medications (over-the-counter, prescription) you are presently taking or have taken since conception; your family medical history (genetic disorders, chronic diseases, unusual pregnancy outcomes); your gynecological history (age at first period, usual length of your cycle, duration and regularity of periods); your obstetrical history (past live births, miscarriages, abortions), as well as the course of past pregnancies, labors, and deliveries. Your practitioner will also ask questions about your social history (such as your age and occupation) and about your lifestyle habits (what you typically eat, whether you exercise, drink, smoke, or use recreational drugs) and other factors in your personal life that might affect your pregnancy (information about the baby's father, information on your ethnicity).

A complete physical examination. This may include assessment of your general health through examination of heart, lungs, breasts, abdomen; measurement of your blood pressure to serve as a baseline reading for comparison at future visits; notation of your height and your weight (prepregnancy and present, if they're already different); a look at your arms and legs for varicose veins and swelling to serve as a baseline for comparison at future visits; examination of external genitalia and of your vagina and cervix (with a speculum in place, as when you get a Pap smear); examination

The Wholly Healthy Pregnancy

Not surprisingly, getting regular medical care in the form of prenatal visits makes a big difference in the outcome of your pregnancy. Women who see a practitioner regularly during pregnancy have healthier babies, and they are less likely to deliver prematurely and to have other serious pregnancy-related problems.

But though your health care should begin with your belly when you're expecting, it shouldn't end there. It'll probably be easy to remember to see your prenatal practitioner regularly (it's worth it just to hear the baby's heartbeat!), but will you remember to take care of the rest of you, even the less apparently pregnant parts?

To keep yourself wholly healthy during your whole nine months, stay on top of all your health care maintenance. Pay a visit to your dentist for a cleaning and a checkup; most dental work, particularly the preventive kind, can be done safely during pregnancy and may actually prevent pregnancy complications. Check in with your internist, family physician, or specialist if you have any chronic conditions or other medical problems that will need monitoring (make sure your pregnancy practitioner's in the loop about other care you're receiving). And see your allergist, if necessary. You probably won't begin a course of allergy shots now, but you may need to look into different treatment options now that you're breathing for two.

If new medical problems come up while you're expecting, don't ignore them, even if you're already in over your head with pregnancy-related symptoms. Check any issue out (even ones that seem relatively innocuous— a persistent sore throat or a chronic headache) with an appropriate physician. Your baby needs a wholly healthy mother.

of your pelvic organs bimanually (with one hand in the vagina and one on the abdomen) and also possibly through the rectum and vagina; assessment of the size and shape of the bony pelvis (through which your baby will eventually try to exit).

A battery of tests. Some tests are routine for every pregnant woman; some are routine in some areas of the country, or with some practitioners and not others; some are performed only when circumstances warrant. The most common prenatal tests given at the first visit include:

- Urinalysis to screen for glucose (sugar), protein, white blood cells, blood, and bacteria.

- A blood test to determine blood type and Rh status, hCG levels, and to check for anemia and possibly for vitamin D deficiency.

- Blood screens to determine antibody titer (levels) and immunity to such diseases as rubella.

- Tests to disclose the presence of infections such as syphilis, gonorrhea, hepatitis B, chlamydia, and HIV.

- A Pap smear for the detection of abnormal cervical cells.

Depending on your particular situation, and if appropriate, you may also receive:

- Genetic tests for cystic fibrosis, sickle

cell anemia, Tay-Sachs, or other genetic diseases.

- A blood sugar level test to check for any tendency toward diabetes, especially if you have a family history of diabetes, have high blood pressure, have previously had an excessively large baby or one with birth defects,

or gained excessive weight with an earlier pregnancy. (All women receive a glucose screening test for gestational diabetes at around 28 weeks; see page 297.)

An opportunity for discussion. Here's the time to bring out that list of questions and concerns.

What You May Be Wondering About

Breaking the News

"When should we tell friends and family that we are expecting?"

This is one question only you can answer. Some expectant parents can't wait to tell everyone they know (not to mention a fair number of strangers) the good news. Others tell only selectively at first, starting with those nearest and dearest (close relatives and

friends, perhaps), and waiting until their condition is obvious before making the pregnancy common knowledge. Still others decide they'd rather put off issuing any announcements until the first trimester has been successfully completed or until prenatal testing has been finished up.

So talk it over, and do what feels most comfortable. Just remember: In spreading the good news, don't forget to take the time to savor it as a twosome.

For tips on when to break the news at work, see page 188.

For the Other Pregnant Half

There isn't a page in this book that isn't intended for both expectant mothers and fathers. As a father-to-be, you'll gain plenty of insight into the pregnancy experience (as well as make some sense out of those crazy symptoms your spouse has been complaining about) by reading along with her, month by month. But because you're likely to have some questions and concerns that are uniquely yours, there's a chapter dedicated to you—the other pregnant half. See Chapter 19: Fathers Are Expectant, Too.

Vitamin Supplements

"Should I be taking vitamins?"

Virtually no one gets a nutritionally perfect diet every day, especially early in pregnancy, when round-the-clock morning sickness is a common appetite suppressant, or when the little nutrition some women manage to get down often doesn't stay down (sound familiar?). Though a daily vitamin supplement can't take the place of a good prenatal diet, it can serve as some dietary insurance, guaranteeing that your baby won't be cheated if you don't always hit the nutritional mark you're aiming for, especially during the early months when so much of your baby's most crucial construction occurs.

And there are other good reasons to take your vitamins. For one thing, studies show that women who take a vitamin supplement containing folic acid and vitamin B_{12} during the first months of pregnancy (and even prior to pregnancy) significantly reduce the risk of neural tube defects (such as spina bifida) in their babies, as well as help prevent preterm birth. For another, research has shown that taking a supplement containing at least 10 mg of vitamin B_6 before and during early pregnancy can minimize morning sickness (and who needs a better reason than that?).

Good formulations designed especially for expectant mothers are available by prescription or over-the-counter. (Ask your practitioner for a recommendation and see page 103 for details on what the supplement should contain.) Don't take any kind of dietary supplements other than such a prenatal formula without your practitioner's approval.

Some women find that taking the typical horse-size prenatal supplement increases nausea, especially early in pregnancy. Switching vitamin formulas or pill types may help, as may taking your pill with food (unless you usually throw up after eating) or taking it during the time of day when you're least likely to be nauseous. A coated pill is often easier to tolerate, as well as easier to swallow. If even that bothers you, you might consider a chewable supplement or a slow-release one. If your nausea is particularly bad, look for a formulation that's higher in vitamin B_6 (ginger is another good addition for the queasy set). But be sure any formula you select approximates the requirements for supplements designed for pregnancy and doesn't contain any extras that might not be safe (such as

herbs). If your practitioner prescribed your supplement, check with him or her before switching.

In some women, the iron in a prenatal vitamin causes constipation or diarrhea. Again, switching formulas may bring relief. Taking a pregnancy supplement without iron and a separate iron preparation (your doctor can recommend one that dissolves in the intestines rather than in the more sensitive stomach—or one that is a slow release) may also relieve symptoms.

"I eat a lot of cereals and breads that are enriched. If I'm also taking a prenatal supplement, will I be taking in too many vitamins and minerals?"

You can get too much of a good thing, but not usually this way. Taking a prenatal vitamin along with the average diet, which includes plenty of enriched and fortified products, isn't likely to lead to excessive intake of vitamins and minerals. To take in that many nutrients, you'd have to be adding other supplements beyond the prenatal ones—which an expectant mother should never do unless advised by a physician who knows that she's pregnant. It's wise, however, to be wary of any foods (or drinks) that are fortified with more than the recommended daily allowance of vitamins A, E, and K, because these can be toxic in large amounts. Most other vitamins and minerals are water-soluble, which means any excesses that the body can't use are simply excreted in the urine. Which is, by the way, the reason why supplement-crazy Americans are said to have the most expensive urine in the world.

Fatigue

"Now that I'm pregnant, I'm tired all the time. Sometimes I feel as if I won't even be able to get through the day!"

Can't lift your head off the pillow each morning? Dragging your feet all day? Can't wait to crawl into bed as soon as you arrive home at night? If it seems like your get-up-and-go has left the building—and doesn't plan to be back anytime soon—it's not surprising. After all, you're pregnant. And even though there might not be any evidence on the outside that you're busily building a baby, plenty of exhausting work is going on inside. In some ways, your pregnant body is working harder when you're resting than a nonpregnant body is when running a marathon—only you're not aware of the exertion.

So what exactly is your body up to? For one thing, it's manufacturing your baby's life-support system, the placenta, which won't be completed until the end of the first trimester. For another, your body's hormone levels have increased significantly, you're producing more blood, your heart rate is up, your blood sugar is down, your metabolism is burning energy overtime (even when you're lying down), and you're using up more nutrients and water. And if that's not enough to wear you out, just toss into the enervating equation all the other physical and emotional demands of pregnancy that your body is adjusting to. Add it all up, and it's no wonder you feel as if you're competing in a triathlon each day—and coming in dead last (or at least, dead tired).

Happily, there is some relief headed your way—eventually. Once the herculean task of manufacturing the placenta is complete (around the fourth month) and your body has adjusted to the hormonal and emotional changes pregnancy brings, you'll feel a little peppier.

In the meantime, keep in mind that fatigue is a sensible signal from your body that you need to take it easier these days. So listen up, and get the rest your body needs. You may also be able to recapture some of that get-up-and-go with some of the following tips:

Baby yourself. If you're a first-time expectant mother, enjoy what will probably be your last chance for a long while to focus on taking care of yourself without feeling guilty. If you already have one or more children at home, you will have to divide your focus (see next page). But either way, this is not a time to strive for supermom-to-be status. Getting adequate rest is more important than keeping your house spotless or serving four-star dinners. Let the dishes wait until later, and turn the other way as the dust bunnies breed under your dining table. Order your groceries (and anything else you can think of) online instead of dragging yourself to the stores. Be a regular on the take-out circuit. Don't book activities—or take care of chores—that aren't essential. Never been a slacker? There's never been a better time to try it on for size.

Let others baby you. You're doing enough heavy lifting these days, so make sure your spouse is doing his fair share (right now, that should be more than half) of household chores, including laundry and grocery shopping. Accept your mother-in-law's offer to vacuum and dust the house when she's visiting. Have a pal pick up some essentials for you while she's going on a shopping run anyway. That way, you might actually have enough energy left to drag yourself out for a walk (before you drag yourself into bed).

Chill out more. Exhausted once the day's over? Spend evenings chilling out (preferably with your feet up) instead of stepping out. And don't wait until nightfall to take it easy. If you can squeeze in an afternoon nap, by all means go for it. If you can't sleep, lie down with a good book. If you're a working mom-to-be, a nap at the office may not be an option, of course, unless you have a flexible schedule and access to a comfortable sofa, but putting your feet up at your desk or on the sofa in the ladies' room during breaks and lunch hours may be possible. (If you choose to rest at lunch hour, make sure you make time to eat, too.)

Be a slacker mom. Have other kids? Fatigue may be more pronounced, for obvious reasons (you have less time to rest, more demands on your body). Or it may be less noticeable, since you're already accustomed to exhaustion—or too busy to pay attention to it. Either way, it's not easy babying yourself when you have other babies (and older children) clamoring for your attention. But try. Explain to them that growing a baby is hard work and it's leaving you beat. Ask for their help around the house, and their help in letting you get more rest. Instead of running around playgrounds during the day and chasing children at night, spend more time at quiet pursuits—reading, doing puzzles, being the patient in a game of "hospital" (you'll get to lie down), watching DVDs. Napping when you're mothering full-time may also be difficult, but if you can time your rest with the children's naptime (if they still nap), you may be able to swing it.

Get some more sleep. It may be stating the obvious, but just in case: Getting even an hour more sleep at night can pick you up come morning. Skip the *Late Show* and turn in earlier; ask your spouse to fix breakfast so you can turn out later. But don't overdo. Too many z's can actually leave you feeling even more exhausted.

Eat well. To keep your energy up, you need a steady supply of premium fuel.

Make sure you're getting enough calories each day (which may be easier said than done if morning sickness has you down—but is definitely worth the effort), and focus on long-lasting energy boosters, such as protein, complex carbohydrates, and iron-rich foods. Caffeine or sugar (or both) may seem like the perfect quick fix for an energy slump, but they're not. Though that candy bar or those jolt-in-a-can energy drinks might pick you up briefly, that blood sugar high will be followed by a free-falling crash, leaving you more beat than ever. (Plus, some canned energy drinks may contain dietary supplements that aren't safe for pregnancy use.)

Eat often. Like so many other pregnancy symptoms, fatigue responds well to the Six-Meal Solution (see page 91). Keeping your blood sugar on an even keel will help keep your energy steady, too—so resist meal skipping, and opt for frequent mini meals and snacks (the sustaining kind, comprised of protein and complex carbs).

Take a hike. Or a slow jog. Or a stroll to the grocery store. Or do a pregnancy exercise or yoga routine. Sure, the couch has never looked more inviting—but paradoxically, too much rest and not enough activity can heighten fatigue. Even a little exercise can be more rejuvenating than a sofa break. Just don't overdo it—you want to finish up your workout feeling energized, not enervated—and be sure to follow the guidelines starting on page 218.

Though fatigue will probably ease up by month 4, you can expect it to return in the last trimester (could it be nature's way of preparing you for the long sleepless nights you'll encounter once the baby has arrived?).

Morning Sickness

"I haven't had any morning sickness. Can I still be pregnant?"

Morning sickness, like a craving for pickles and ice cream, is one of those truisms about pregnancy that isn't necessarily true. Studies show that nearly three quarters of all expectant women experience the nausea and vomiting associated with morning sickness, which means that a little more than 25 percent of moms-to-be don't. If you're among those who never have a nauseous moment, or who feel only occasionally or mildly queasy, you can consider yourself not only pregnant but also lucky.

"My morning sickness lasts all day. I'm afraid that I'm not keeping down enough food to nourish my baby."

Welcome to the queasy club—a club that up to 75 percent of pregnant women belong to. Happily, though you and all the other miserable members are definitely feeling the effects of morning sickness—a misnamed malady, as you've already noticed, since it can strike morning, noon, night, or all three—your baby almost definitely isn't. That's because your baby's nutritional needs are minuscule right now, just like your baby (who's not even the size of a pea yet). Even women who have such a hard time keeping food down that they actu-

Your Nose Knows

Have you noticed, now that you're expecting, that you can smell what's on the menu before you even set foot in the restaurant? That heightened sense of smell you're experiencing is actually a very real side effect of pregnancy, caused by hormones (in this case estrogen) that magnify every little scent that wafts your way. What's worse, this bloodhound syndrome can also ramp up morning sickness symptoms. Smell trouble? Here are some strategies you can try to give your poor nose a break:

- If you can't stand the smell, get out of the kitchen. Or the restaurant. Or the perfume aisle of the department store. Or anywhere odors that sicken you hang out.

- Open your windows whenever possible to banish cooking or musty odors. Or run the exhaust fan on the stove.

- Wash your clothes more often than usual, since fibers tend to hold on to odors. Use unscented detergent and softener, though, if the scented ones bother you (same goes for all your cleaning supplies).

- Switch to unscented or lightly scented toiletries.

- Ask those who are regularly within sniffing distance of you (and who you know well enough to ask) to be extra considerate of your sensitive smell status. Get your spouse to wash up, change his clothes, and brush his teeth after stopping for a chili cheeseburger. Request that friends and coworkers go easy on the perfume when they're with you. And, of course, avoid people who are smoking.

- Try to surround yourself with those scents (if there are any) that actually make you feel better. Mint, lemon, ginger, and cinnamon are more likely to be soothing, especially if you're queasy, though some expectant moms suddenly embrace smells that invoke infants, such as baby powder.

ally lose weight during the first trimester aren't hurting their babies, as long as they make up for the lost weight in later months. Which is usually pretty easy to do because the nausea and vomiting of morning sickness don't generally linger much beyond the 12th to 14th week. (An occasional expectant mom continues to experience symptoms into the second trimester, and a very few, particularly those expecting multiples, may suffer some well into the third.)

What causes morning sickness? No one knows for sure, but there's no shortage of theories, among them the high level of the pregnancy hormone hCG in the blood in the first trimester, elevated estrogen levels, gastroesophageal reflux (GER), the relative relaxation of muscle tissue in the digestive tract (which makes digestion less efficient), and the enhanced sense of smell that pregnant women develop.

Not all pregnant women experience morning sickness the same way. Some have only occasional queasy moments, others feel queasy round the clock but never vomit, others vomit once in a while, and still others vomit frequently. There are probably several reasons for these variations:

Hormone levels. Higher-than-average levels (as when a woman is carrying multiple fetuses) can increase morning sickness; lower levels may minimize or eliminate it (though women with normal hormone levels may also experience little or no morning sickness).

Sensitivity. Some brains have a nausea command post that's more sensitive than others, which means they're more likely to respond to hormones and other triggers of pregnancy queasiness. If you have a sensitive command center (you always get carsick or seasick, for instance), you're more likely to have more severe nausea and vomiting

in pregnancy. Never have a queasy day ordinarily? You're less likely to have lots of them when you're expecting.

Stress. It's well known that emotional stress can trigger gastrointestinal upset, so it's not surprising that symptoms of morning sickness tend to worsen when stress strikes.

Fatigue. Physical or mental fatigue can also exacerbate the symptoms of morning sickness (conversely, severe morning sickness can increase fatigue).

First-time pregnancy status. Morning sickness is more common and tends to be more severe in first pregnancies, which supports the idea that both physical and emotional factors may be involved. Physically, the novice pregnant body is less prepared for the onslaught of hormones and other changes it's experiencing than one that's been there, done that. Emotionally, first timers are more likely to be subject to the kinds of anxieties and fears that can turn a stomach—while women in subsequent pregnancies may be distracted from their nausea by the demands of caring for older children. (Generalities never hold true for every expectant mom, though, and some women are queasier in subsequent pregnancies than they were in their first.)

No matter the cause (and does it really matter when you're upchucking for the third time today?), the effect of morning sickness is the same: pure misery. Though there is no sure cure for the queasies but the passing of time, there are ways of minimizing the misery while you're waiting for a less nauseous day to dawn:

- Eat early. Morning sickness doesn't wait for you to get up in the morning. In fact, nausea's most likely to strike when you're running on empty, as you are after a long night's sleep. That's because when you haven't eaten in a while, the acids churning around inside your empty tummy have nothing to digest but your stomach lining—which, not surprisingly, increases queasiness. To head off heaving, don't even consider getting out of bed in the morning without reaching for a nibble (crackers or rice cakes, dry cereal, a handful of trail mix) that you stashed on your nightstand the night before. Keeping nibbles next to the bed also means you don't have to get up for them if you wake up hungry in the middle of the night. It's a good idea to have a bite when you rise for those midnight bathroom runs, too, just so your stomach stays a little bit full all night long.

- Eat late. Eating a light snack high in protein and complex carbs (a muffin and a glass of milk, string cheese and a handful of freeze-dried blueberries) just before you go to sleep will help ensure a happier tummy when you wake up.

- Eat light. A stuffed tummy is just as susceptible to queasiness as an empty one. Overloading—even when you feel hungry—can lead to upchucking.

- Eat often. One of the best ways to keep nausea at bay is to keep your blood sugar at an even keel—and your stomach a little filled—all the time. To head off an attack of the queasies, join the graze craze. Eat small, frequent meals—six mini meals a day is ideal—instead of three large ones. Don't leave home without a stash of snacks that your tummy can handle (dried fruit and nuts, granola bars, dry cereal, crackers, soy chips, or pretzels).

- Eat well. A diet high in protein and complex carbohydrates can help combat queasiness. General good nutrition may help, too, so eat as well as

you can (given the circumstances, that might not always be so easy).

- Eat what you can. So the eating well thing isn't working out so well for you? Right now, getting anything in your tummy—and keeping it there—should be your priority. There will be plenty of time later on in your pregnancy for eating a balanced diet. For the queasy moment, eat whatever gets you through the day (and night), even if it's nothing but ice pops and gingersnaps. If you can manage to make them real fruit ice pops and whole-grain gingersnaps, great. If you can't, that's fine, too.

- Drink up. In the short term, getting enough fluids is more important than getting enough solids—particularly if you're losing lots of liquids through vomiting. If you're finding liquids are easier to get down when you're feeling green, use them to get your nutrients. Drink your vitamins and minerals in soothing smoothies, soups, and juices. If you find fluids make you queasier, eat solids with a high water content, such as fresh fruits and vegetables—particularly lettuce, melons, and citrus fruits. Some women find that drinking and eating at the same sitting puts too much strain on their digestive tract; if this is true for you, try taking your fluids between meals.

- Get chilly. Experiment with temperature, too. Many women find icy cold fluids and foods are easier to get down. Others favor warm ones (melted cheese sandwiches instead of cold ones).

- Switch off. Often, what starts out as a comfort food (it's the only thing you can keep down, so you eat it 24/7) becomes associated with nausea—and actually starts to trigger it. If you're so sick of crackers that they're actually beginning to make you sick, switch off to another comforting carb (maybe it'll be Cheerios or watermelon next).

- If it makes you queasy, don't go there. Period. Don't force yourself to eat foods that don't appeal or, worse, make you sick. Instead, let your taste buds (and your cravings, and your aversions) be your guide. Choose only sweet foods if they're all you can tolerate (get your vitamin A and protein from peaches and yogurt at dinner instead of from broccoli and chicken). Or select only savories if they're your ticket to a less tumultuous tummy (have reheated pizza for breakfast instead of cereal).

- Smell (and see) no evil. Thanks to a much more sensitive sense of smell, pregnant women often find once appetizing aromas suddenly offensive—and offensive ones downright sickening. So stay away from smells that trigger nausea—whether it's the sausage and eggs your spouse likes to make on the weekends or the aftershave of his that used to make you head over heels (but now makes you head for the toilet). Steer clear, too, of foods that you can't stand the sight of (raw chicken is a common culprit).

- Supplement. Take a prenatal vitamin supplement to compensate for nutrients you may not be getting. Afraid you'll have trouble choking the pill down—or keeping it down? Actually, that one-a-day can decrease nausea symptoms (especially if you take a slow-releasing vitamin that's higher in queasy-combating vitamin B_6). But take it at a time of day when you are least likely to chuck it back up, possibly with a substantial bedtime snack. If your symptoms are particularly rough, ask your practitioner about

taking extra vitamin B_6, which can help relieve nausea in some women.

- Tread gingerly. It's true what the old wives (and midwives) have been saying for centuries: Ginger can be good for what ails a queasy pregnant woman. Use ginger in cooking (gingercarrot soup, ginger muffins), steep it into tea, nibble on some ginger biscuits, nosh on some crystallized ginger, or suck on some ginger candy or lollipops. A drink made from real ginger (regular ginger ale isn't) may also be soothing. Even the smell of fresh ginger (cut open a knob and take a whiff) may quell the queasies. Or try another trick of the queasy trade: lemons. Many women find the smell—and taste—of lemons comforting (when life gives you morning sickness, make lemonade?). Sour sucking candies are the ticket to relief for others.

- Rest up. Get some extra sleep and relaxation. Both emotional and physical fatigue can exacerbate nausea.

- Go slow-mo. Don't jump out of bed and dash out the door—rushing tends to aggravate nausea. Instead, linger in bed for a few minutes, nibbling on that bedside snack, then rise slowly to a leisurely breakfast. This may seem impossible if you have other children, but try to wake up before they do so you can sneak in some quiet time, or let your spouse take the dawn shift.

- Minimize stress. Easing the stress can ease the quease. See page 141 for tips on dealing with stress during pregnancy.

- Treat your mouth well. Brush your teeth (with a toothpaste that doesn't increase queasiness) or rinse your mouth after each bout of vomiting, as well as after each meal. (Ask your dentist to recommend a good rinse.) Not only will this help keep your mouth fresh and reduce nausea, it will decrease the risk of damage to teeth or gums that can occur when bacteria feast on regurgitated residue in your mouth.

- Try Sea-Bands. These 1-inch-wide elastic bands, worn on both wrists, put pressure on acupressure points on the inner wrists and often relieve nausea. They cause no side effects and are widely available at drug and health food stores. Or your practitioner may recommend a more sophisticated form of acupressure: a battery-operated wristband that uses electronic stimulation.

- Go CAM crazy. There are a wide variety of complementary medical approaches, such as acupuncture, acupressure, biofeedback, or hypnosis, that can help minimize the symptoms of morning sickness—and they're all worth a try (see page 85). Meditation and visualization can also help.

Though there are medications that may help ease morning sickness (often a combo of doxylamine—an antihistamine found in Unisom Sleep Tabs—and vitamin B_6), they'll usually only be recommended or prescribed when morning sickness is severe. Keep in mind, too, that the antihistamine part of the combo will make you drowsy—a good thing if you're going to sleep, but not such a good thing if you're driving to work. Don't take any medication (traditional or herbal) for morning sickness unless it is prescribed by your practitioner.

In fewer than 5 percent of pregnancies, nausea and vomiting become so severe that medical intervention may be needed. If this seems to be the case with you, see page 545.

Excess Saliva

"My mouth seems to fill up with saliva all the time—and swallowing it makes me queasy. What's going on?"

It may not be cool to drool (especially in public), but for many women in the first trimester, it's an icky fact of life. Overproduction of saliva is a common—and unpleasant—symptom of pregnancy, especially among morning sickness sufferers. And though all that extra saliva pooling in your mouth may add to your queasiness—and lead to a gaggy feeling when you eat—it's completely harmless, and thankfully short-lived, usually disappearing after the first few months.

Spitting mad about all that spit? Brushing your teeth frequently with a minty toothpaste, rinsing with a minty mouthwash, or chewing sugarless gum can help dry things up a bit.

Metallic Taste

"I have a metallic taste in my mouth all the time. Is this pregnancy related—or is it caused by something I ate?"

So your mouth tastes like loose change? Believe it or not, that metal mouth taste is a fairly common—though not often talked about—side effect of pregnancy, and one more you can chalk up to hormones. Your hormones always play a role in controlling your sense of taste. When they go wild (as they do when you have your period—and as they do with a vengeance when you're pregnant), so do your taste buds. Like morning sickness, that icky taste should ease up—or, if you're lucky, disappear altogether—in your second trimester when those hormones begin to settle down.

Until then, you can try fighting metal with acid. Focus on citrus juices, lemonade, sour sucking candy, and—assuming your tummy can handle them—foods marinated in vinegar (some pickles with that ice cream?). Not only will such assertive acidics have the power to break through that metallic taste, they'll also increase saliva production, which will help wash it away (though that could be a bad thing, if your mouth's already flooded with the stuff). Other tricks to try: Brush your tongue each time you brush your teeth, or rinse your mouth with a salt solution (a teaspoon of salt in 8 ounces of water) or a baking soda solution (¼ teaspoon baking soda in 8 ounces of water) a few times a day to neutralize pH levels in your mouth and keep away that flinty flavor. You might also ask your practitioner about changing your prenatal vitamin; some seem to lead to metal mouth more than others.

Frequent Urination

"I'm in the bathroom every half hour. Is it normal to be peeing this often?"

It may not be the best seat in the house, but for most pregnant women, it's the most frequented one. Let's face it, when you gotta go, you gotta go—and these days (and nights) you gotta go all the time. And while nonstop peeing might not always be convenient, it's absolutely normal.

What causes this frequent urination? First, hormones trigger not only an increase in blood flow but in urine flow, too. Second, during pregnancy the efficiency of the kidneys improves, helping your body rid itself of waste products more quickly (including baby's, which means you'll be peeing for two). Finally, your growing uterus is pressing on your bladder now, leaving less storage space in the holding tank for urine and triggering that "gotta go" feeling.

This pressure is often relieved once the uterus rises into the abdominal cavity during the second trimester and doesn't usually return until the third trimester or when the baby's head "drops" back down into the pelvis in the ninth month. But because the arrangement of internal organs varies slightly from woman to woman, the degree of urinary frequency in pregnancy may also vary. Some women barely notice it; others are bothered by it for most of the nine months.

Leaning forward when you urinate will help ensure that you empty your bladder completely, as can making it good to the last drop by double voiding (pee, then when you're done, squeeze out some more). Both tactics may reduce trips to the bathroom, though realistically, not by much.

Don't cut back on liquids thinking it'll keep you out of the bathroom. Your body and your baby need a steady supply of fluids—plus dehydration can lead to urinary tract infection (UTI). But do cut back on caffeine, which increases the need to pee. If you find that you go frequently during the night, try limiting fluids right before bedtime.

If you're always feeling the urge to urinate (even after you've just urinated), talk to your practitioner. He or she might want to run a test to see if you've got a UTI.

"How come I'm not urinating frequently?"

No noticeable increase in the frequency of urination may be perfectly normal for you, especially if you ordinarily pee often. But be sure you're getting enough fluids (at least eight 8-ounce glasses a day—more if you're losing some through vomiting). Not only can too little fluid intake cause infrequent urination, it can lead to dehydration and urinary tract infection.

Breast Changes

"I hardly recognize my breasts anymore—they're so huge. And they're tender, too. Will they stay that way, and will they sag after I give birth?"

Looks like you've discovered the first big thing in pregnancy: your breasts. While bellies don't usually do much growing until the second trimester, breasts often begin their expansion within weeks of conception, gradually working their way through the bra cup alphabet (you may ultimately end up three cups bigger than you started out). Fueling this growth are those surging hormones—the same ones that boost your bust premenstrually but at much greater levels. Fat is building up in your breasts, too, and blood flow to the area is increasing. And there's a swell reason for all this swelling—your breasts are gearing up to feed your baby when he or she arrives.

In addition to their expanding size, you will probably notice other changes to your breasts. The areola (the pigmented area around the nipple) will darken, spread, and may be spotted with even darker areas. This darkening may fade but not disappear entirely after birth. The little bumps you may notice on the areola are lubrication glands, which become more prominent during pregnancy and return to normal afterward. The complex road map of blue veins that traverses the breasts—often vivid on a fair-skinned woman and sometimes not even noticeable on darker women—represents a mother-to-baby delivery system for nutrients and fluids. After delivery—or, if you're breastfeeding, sometime after baby's weaned—the skin's appearance will return to normal.

Fortunately, that cup size gain won't continue to come with pain (or uncomfortable sensitivity). Though your breasts will probably keep growing throughout your nine months, they're not likely to stay tender to the touch past the third or fourth month. Some women find that the tenderness eases well before that. In the achy meantime, find relief in cool or warm compresses (whichever is more soothing).

As for whether or not your breasts will end up sagging, a lot of that's up to genetics (if your mom drooped, you may, too), but some of it's up to you. Sagging results not just from pregnancy itself but from a lack of support during pregnancy. No matter how firm your breasts are now, protect them for the future by wearing a supportive bra (though in that tender first trimester, you may want to avoid restrictive underwires). If your breasts are particularly large or have a tendency to sag, it's a good idea to wear a bra even at night. You'll probably find a cotton sports bra most comfortable for sleeping.

Not all women notice pronounced breast changes early in pregnancy, and some find the expansion takes place so gradually that it's not perceptible. As with all things pregnancy, what's normal is what's normal for your breasts. And don't worry: Though slower growth—or less substantial growth—means you won't have to replace bras so often, it won't have any impact on your ability to breastfeed.

"My breasts became very large in my first pregnancy, but they haven't seemed to change at all in my second. Is that normal?"

Last time your breasts were newbies—this time, they entered pregnancy with previous experience. As a result, they may not need as much preparation—or react as dramatically to those surging hormones—as they did in your first round of baby making. You may find that your breasts will enlarge gradually as your pregnancy progresses—or you may find that their expansion holds off until after delivery, when milk production begins. Either way, this slow growing is completely normal—and an early indication of how very different two pregnancies can be.

Lower Abdominal Pressure

"I've been having a nagging feeling of pressure in my lower abdomen. Should I be worried?"

It sounds like you're very tuned in to your body—which can be a good thing (as when it helps you recognize ovulation) or a not-so-good thing (when it makes you worry about the many innocuous aches and pains of pregnancy).

Don't worry. A feeling of pressure or even mild crampiness without bleeding is very common, especially in first pregnancies—and is usually a sign that everything's going right, not that something's going wrong. Chances are, that sensitive body radar of yours is just picking up some of the many dramatic changes that are taking place in your lower abdomen, where your uterus is currently located. What you're feeling may be the sensation of implantation, increased blood flow, the buildup of the uterine lining, or simply your uterus beginning to grow—in other words, your first growing pains (there will be many more to come). It could also be gas pains or bowel spasms that come with constipation (another common pregnancy side effect).

For further reassurance, ask your practitioner about the feeling (if you're still having it) at your next office visit.

Spotting

"I was using the toilet and noticed a small amount of blood when I wiped. Am I having a miscarriage?"

It's definitely scary to see blood down below when you're pregnant. But what's not definite is that bleeding is a sign that something's wrong with your pregnancy. Many women—about 1 in 5, in fact—experience some bleeding during pregnancy, and a very large majority go on to have a perfectly healthy pregnancy and baby. So if you're only noticing light spotting—similar to what you see at the beginning or end of your period—you can take a deep breath and read on for a probable (and probably reassuring) explanation. Such light spotting is usually caused by one of the following:

Implantation of the embryo into your uterine wall. Affecting 20 to 30 percent of women, such spotting (called "implantation bleeding" in the obstetrical business) will usually occur before (or in some cases around the time) you expected your period, around five to ten days after conception. Scantier than your monthly flow (and lasting anywhere from a few hours to a few days), implantation bleeding is usually light to medium pink or light brown in color and is spotty. It occurs when the little ball of cells you'll one day call your baby burrows its way into the uterine wall. Implantation bleeding is not a sign that something is wrong.

Intercourse or an internal pelvic exam or Pap smear. During pregnancy, your cervix becomes tender and engorged with blood vessels and can occasionally become irritated during intercourse or an internal exam, resulting in some light bleeding. This type of bleeding is common, can occur at any time during your pregnancy, and usually doesn't indicate

When to Call Your Practitioner

It's best to set up a protocol for emergencies with your practitioner before an emergency strikes. If you haven't, and you are experiencing a symptom that requires immediate medical attention, try the following: First call the practitioner's office. If he or she isn't available, leave a message detailing your symptoms. If you don't get a call back within a few minutes, call again or call the nearest emergency room and tell the triage nurse what's going on. If he or she tells you to come in, head to the ER and leave word with your practitioner. Call 911 if no one can take you to the ER.

When you report any of the following to your practitioner or to the triage nurse, be sure to mention any other symptoms you may be experiencing, no matter how unrelated they may seem to the immediate problem. Also be specific, mentioning when you first noticed each symptom, how frequently it recurs, what seems to relieve or exacerbate it, and how severe it is.

Call immediately if you experience:

- Heavy bleeding or bleeding with cramps or severe pain in the lower abdomen.

- Severe lower abdominal pain, in the center or on one or both sides, that doesn't subside, even if it isn't accompanied by bleeding.

- A sudden increase in thirst, accompanied by reduced urination, or no urination at all for an entire day.

- Painful or burning urination accompanied by chills and fever over 101.5°F and/or backache.

- Fever over 101.5°F.

- Very sudden and severe swelling or puffiness of hands, face, and eyes, accompanied by headache, vision difficulties, or sudden significant weight gain not related to overeating.

- Vision disturbances (blurring, dimming, double vision) that persist for more than a few minutes.

---

a problem, but do tell your practitioner about any post-intercourse or -exam spotting for extra reassurance.

Infection of the vagina or cervix. An inflamed or irritated cervix or vagina might cause some spotting (though the spotting should disappear once you're treated for the infection).

Subchorionic bleed. Subchorionic bleeding occurs when there is an accumulation of blood under the chorion (the outer fetal membrane, next to the placenta) or between the uterus and the placenta itself. It can cause light to heavy spotting but doesn't always (sometimes it is only

detected during a routine ultrasound). Most subchorionic bleeds resolve on their own and do not end up being a problem for the pregnancy (see page 545 for more).

Spotting is as variable in a normal pregnancy as it is common. Some women spot on and off for their entire pregnancies. Other women spot for just a day or two—and others for several weeks. Some women notice mucousy brown or pink spotting; others see small amounts of bright red blood. But happily, most women who experience any kind of spotting continue to have com-

- A severe headache or a headache that persists for more than two or three hours.

- Bloody diarrhea.

Call the same day (or the next morning, if it's the middle of the night) if you experience:

- Blood in your urine.

- Swelling or puffiness of your hands, face, eyes.

- Sudden excessive weight gain not related to overeating.

- Painful or burning urination.

- Fainting or dizziness.

- Chills and fever over 100°F in the absence of cold or flu symptoms (start bringing down any fever over 100°F promptly by taking acetaminophen, or Tylenol).

- Severe nausea and vomiting; vomiting more often than two or three times a day in the first trimester; vomiting later in pregnancy when you didn't earlier.

- Itching all over, with or without dark urine, pale stools, or jaundice (yellowing of skin and whites of the eye).

- Frequent (more than three times a day) diarrhea, especially if it's mucousy (if it's bloody, call right away).

Your practitioner may want you to call for different reasons or within different parameters, so be sure to ask him or her what protocol you should follow if you experience any of these symptoms.

Keep in mind, too, that there might be some times when you have none of the symptoms listed here, but you feel unusually exhausted, achy, not quite right. If a good night's sleep and some extra relaxation don't team up to make you feel better in a day or two, check with your practitioner. Chances are what you're feeling is normal—par for the pregnancy course. But it is also possible that you've become anemic or you're fighting an infection of some kind. Certain conditions—UTI, for example—can do their dirty work without causing any clear-cut symptoms. So when in doubt, check it out.

pletely normal and healthy pregnancies and end up delivering perfectly healthy babies. Which means that there's probably nothing for you to worry about (though, realistically, that doesn't mean you'll stop worrying).

For extra reassurance, put in a call to your practitioner (no need to call immediately or during non–office hours unless you're noticing spotting accompanied by cramping or bright red, soak-through-a-pad bleeding), who will likely order an ultrasound. If you're past the sixth week, you'll probably be able to see your baby's heartbeat during the ultrasound, which will reassure you that

your pregnancy is progressing along just fine, even with the spotting.

What if the spotting progresses to heavier bleeding similar to a period? Though such a scenario is more cause for concern (especially if it's accompanied by cramps or pain in your lower abdomen) and does warrant an immediate call to your practitioner, it's not a sign that you're inevitably miscarrying. Some women bleed—even heavily— for unknown reasons throughout their pregnancies and still deliver healthy babies at term.

If it does end up that you're having a miscarriage, see page 536.

No Worries

Some expectant moms (and you know who you are) will always find something to worry about—especially in the first trimester and particularly in first pregnancies. Topping the list of most common concerns, understandably, is a fear of miscarriage.

Fortunately, most expectant worriers end up worrying unnecessarily. Most pregnancies continue uneventfully, and happily, to term. Just about every normal pregnancy includes some cramps, some abdominal aches, or some spotting—and many include all three. While any of these symptoms can be understandably unnerving (and when it comes to a stain on your underwear, downright scary), more often than not, they're completely innocuous—and not a sign that your pregnancy is in trouble. Though you should report them to your practitioner at your next visit (or sooner if you need some professional reassurance), the following are no cause for concern. So don't worry if you have:

- Mild cramps, achiness, or a pulling sensation in the lower abdomen or on one or both sides of the abdomen. This is probably caused by the stretching of ligaments that support the uterus. Unless cramping is severe, constant, or accompanied by significant bleeding, there's no need to worry.

- Slight spotting that isn't accompanied by cramps or lower abdominal

pain. There are plenty of reasons why pregnant women spot, and it often has nothing to do with a miscarriage. See page 137 for more on spotting.

Of course, it's not just symptoms that pregnant women worry about in early pregnancy—it's a lack of symptoms, too. In fact, not "feeling pregnant" is one of the most commonly reported first-trimester concerns. And that's not surprising. It's hard to feel pregnant this early on even if you're experiencing every early pregnancy symptom in the book—and it's far harder still to feel pregnant if you're relatively symptom-free. Without tangible proof yet of that baby-to-be growing inside you (a swelling belly, those first flutters of movement), it's pretty easy to start wondering whether the pregnancy is going well—or whether you're even still pregnant at all.

Once again, not to worry. A lack of symptoms—such as morning sickness or breast tenderness—is not a sign that something's wrong. Consider yourself lucky if you're spared these and other unpleasant early pregnancy symptoms—and also consider that you might be a late bloomer. After all, since every pregnant woman experiences pregnancy symptoms differently and at different times, these and other symptoms may be just around the corner for you.

HCG Levels

"My doctor gave me the results of my blood test and it says that my hCG level is at 412 mIU/L. What does that number mean?"

It means you're definitely pregnant! Human chorionic gonadotropin (hCG) is manufactured by the cells of the newly developing placenta within days after the fertilized egg implants in your uterine lining. HCG is found in your urine (you came face-to-stick with hCG the day that positive readout showed up on your home pregnancy test) and in your blood, which explains why your practitioner ran a blood test to find out your expectant status for sure. When you're very early in the pregnancy game (as you are), the level of hCG in your blood will be quite low (it's just starting to show up in your system, after all). But within days, it'll begin to soar, doubling every 48 hours (give or take). The rapid increase peaks somewhere between 7 and 12 weeks of pregnancy and then starts to decline.

But don't start swapping your numbers with those of your pregnant best friend. Just as no two women's pregnancies are alike, no two pregnant women's hCG levels are alike either. They vary enormously from day to day, person to person, even as early as the first missed day of a period and continuing throughout pregnancy.

What's more important and relevant to you is that your hCG level falls within the very wide normal range (see box, this page) and continues to increase over the coming weeks (in other words, look for a pattern of increasing levels instead of focusing on specific numbers). Even if your readings fall outside these ranges, don't worry. It's still quite likely that everything's fine (your due date might just be off—a very common cause of hCG number confusion—or you might be carrying more than one baby). As long as your pregnancy is progressing normally and your hCG levels are increasing during the first trimester, you don't have to obsess about these numbers or even try to find them out (plus, if your practitioner is happy with your numbers, then you can be, too). Ultrasound findings after five or six weeks of pregnancy are much more predictive of pregnancy outcome than are hCG levels. Of course, as always, if you are concerned, talk with your practitioner about your results.

HCG Levels

Really want to play the hCG numbers game? The following are ranges of "normal" hCG levels based on date. Keep in mind that anywhere in that wide range is normal—your baby doesn't have to be scoring off the charts for your pregnancy to be progressing perfectly—and that a slight miscalculation in your dates can throw the numbers off completely.

Weeks of Pregnancy	Amount of hCG in mIU/L
3 weeks	5 to 50
4 weeks	5 to 426
5 weeks	19 to 7,340
6 weeks	1,080 to 56,500
7 to 8 weeks	7,650 to 229,000
9 to 12 weeks	25,700 to 288,000

Stress

"My job is a high-stress one. I wasn't planning to have a baby now, but I got pregnant. Should I quit work?"

Depending on how you handle and respond to it, stress can be good for you (by sparking you to perform better, to function more effectively) or it can be bad for you (when it gets out of control, overwhelming and debilitating you). Research shows that pregnancy isn't affected by typical stress levels—and if you're able to cope well with your on-the-job stress (even if it's more than most people could take on), then your baby will be able to cope just fine, too. But if the stress makes you anxious,

Relaxation Made Easy

Is your growing bundle of joy making you a quivering bundle of nerves? Now's a great time to learn some soothing relaxation techniques—not just because they can help you cope with pregnancy concerns, but because they'll come in handy in your hectic life as a new mom. Yoga's a fabulous destresser, if you have time to take a prenatal class or practice with a DVD. If you don't, you can try this simple relaxation technique, which is easy to learn and to do anywhere, anytime. If you find it helpful, you can do it when anxiety strikes and/or regularly several times a day to try to ward it off.

Sit with your eyes closed and imagine a beautiful, peaceful scene (a sunset over your favorite beach, waves gently lapping the shore; a serene mountain vista, complete with babbling brook), or even your fantasized baby-to-be, wrapped in your arms on a sunny day in the park. Then, working your way up from your toes to your face, concentrate on relaxing every muscle. Breathe slowly, deeply, through your nose (unless it's stuffed up) and choose a simple word (such as "yes" or "one") to repeat aloud every time you exhale. Ten to 20 minutes should do the trick, though even a minute or two is better than nothing.

Since negative reactions to stress can take a toll, especially if they continue into the second and third trimesters—learning to handle the stress constructively, or cutting back on it, as needed, should become a priority now. The following should help:

Unload it. Allowing your anxieties to surface is the best way of ensuring that they don't get you down. Make sure you have somewhere to vent—and someone to vent to. Maintain open lines of communication with your spouse, spending some time at the end of each day (preferably not too close to bedtime, which should be as stress free as possible) sharing concerns and frustrations. Together you may be able to find some relief, some solutions—and ideally a good laugh or two. Is he too stressed to absorb enough of your stress? Find others who can lend an ear—a friend, another family member, coworkers (who will understand your workplace stress better?), or your practitioner (especially if you're concerned about the physical effects of your stress). Empathy helps, too, so try to find other expectant moms who can relate, either in a pregnancy group or online. If you need more than a friendly ear, consider counseling to help you develop strategies to better deal with your stress.

Do something about it. Identify sources of stress in your life and determine how they can be modified. If you're clearly trying to do too much, cut back in areas that are not high priority (this is something you're going to have to do big time anyway, once you have a bigger priority—a new baby—on the agenda). If you've taken on too many responsibilities at home or at work, decide which can be postponed or delegated. Learn to say no to new projects or activities before you're overloaded (another skill you're wise to cultivate pre-baby).

sleepless, or depressed, if it's causing you to experience physical symptoms (such as headache, backache, or loss of appetite), if it's causing you to turn to unhealthy behaviors (smoking, for instance), or if it is exhausting you, then it could eventually pose a problem.

Sometimes, sitting down with a pad or PDA and making lists of the hundreds of things you need to get done (at home or at work), and the order in which you're planning to do them, can help you feel more in control of the chaos in your life. Cross items off your list as they're taken care of for a satisfying sense of accomplishment.

Sleep it off. Sleep is the ticket to regeneration—for mind and body. Often, feelings of tension and anxiety are prompted by not getting enough shut-eye—and, of course, having too much tension and anxiety can also prevent you from getting enough shut-eye. If you're having trouble sleeping, see the tips on page 265.

Nourish it. Hectic lifestyles can lead to hectic eating styles. Inadequate nutrition during pregnancy can be a double whammy: It can hamper your ability to handle stress, and it can eventually affect your baby's well-being. So be sure to eat well and regularly (six mini meals will best keep you going when the going gets tough). Focus on complex carbs and protein, and steer clear of excesses of caffeine and sugar, two staples of the stressed life that can actually leave you less able to cope.

Wash it away. A warm bath is an excellent way to relieve tension. Try it after a hectic day; it will also help you to sleep better.

Run it off. Or swim it off. Or prenatal yoga it off. You might think that the last thing you need in your life is more activity, but exercise is one of the best stress relievers—and mood boosters. Build some into your busy day.

CAM it. Explore the many complementary and alternative therapies that can promise inner calm from CAM, among them biofeedback, acupuncture, hypnotherapy, massage (ask your spouse

Expect the Best

It's long been speculated that optimistic people live longer, healthier lives. Now it's been suggested that an expectant mother's optimistic outlook can actually improve the outlook for her unborn baby, too. Researchers have found that seeing the bright side reduces the chance of a high-risk woman delivering a preterm or low-birthweight baby.

A lower level of stress in optimistic women definitely plays a part in the lowered risk; high levels of stress, after all, have been implicated in a variety of health problems both in and out of pregnancy. But stress itself apparently doesn't tell the whole story. Women who are optimistic, not surprisingly, are more likely to take better care of themselves—eating well, exercising right, getting regular prenatal care, not smoking, drinking, or using drugs. And these positive behaviors—fueled by the power of positive thinking—can, of course, have a very positive effect on pregnancy and fetal well-being.

Researchers point out that it's never too late to start reaping the benefits of optimism, even if you're already pregnant. Learning how to expect the best—instead of the worst—can actually help make those expectations come true: a good reason to start seeing that glass of milk as half full instead of half empty.

for a back or shoulder rub, or splurge on a professional pregnancy massage). Meditation and visualization can also melt the stress away (just close your eyes and picture a bucolic scene, or keep them open and gaze at a soothing picture or photo placed strategically in your office). Practice relaxation techniques (see box, page 142), not just because they'll come in handy during childbirth, but because they can help drain the strain anytime. See page 85 for more on CAM techniques.

Get away from it. Combat stress with any activity you find relaxing. Lose it in reading; a good movie; listening to music (take your iPod to coffee breaks and lunch, or even use it while you work, if you can); knitting (you can relax while you get a head start on those booties); window-shopping for baby clothes; lunching with a fun friend; keeping a journal (another good way to vent your feelings); browsing baby sites online; scrapbooking. Or walk away

from it (even a quick stroll can be relaxing and rejuvenating).

Cut it back. Maybe what's causing the stress just isn't worth it. If it's your job that's got you too wired, consider taking early maternity leave or cutting back to part-time (if either of these options is financially feasible), or delegating at least part of your workload to reduce stress to a load that doesn't weigh you down. A change of jobs or careers might be impractical to pull off now that you're expecting, but it might be something to consider once your baby arrives.

Remember, your stress quotient is only going to increase once the baby is born; it makes sense to try to find ways of handling it better (or bringing it down to a manageable level) now.

Your Pampered Pregnancy

Talk about extreme makeovers. Pregnancy is a radical full-body transformation that may have you feeling your most beautiful (you glow, girl!), your least attractive (those zits! those chin hairs!), or both (in the same day). But it's also a time when your usual beauty regimen might need a makeover, too. Before you reach into your medicine cabinet for the acne cream you've been using since junior high or head to your favorite spa for a bikini wax and a facial, you'll need to know what's a beauty do—and what's a beauty don't—when you're expecting. Here's the lowdown from tip (highlights) to toes (pedicure) on how you can pamper your pregnant self beautifully—and safely.

Your Hair

When you're expecting, your hair can take a turn for the better (when lackluster hair suddenly sports a brilliant shine) or for the worse (when once-bouncy hair goes limp). One thing's for sure: Thanks to hormones, you'll have more of it than ever before (and sadly, not just on your head). Here's the heads-up on hair treatments:

Coloring. Here's the root of the problem when it comes to hiding your roots during pregnancy. Even though no evidence suggests the small amount of chemicals absorbed through the skin during hair coloring is harmful when you're expecting, some experts still advise waiting out the first trimester before heading back to the salon for retouching. Others maintain that it's safe to dye throughout pregnancy. Check with your practitioner—you'll likely get the green light on color. If you're uncomfortable with a full dye job, consider highlights instead of single-process color. This way the chemicals don't touch your scalp at all, plus highlights tend to last longer than all-over color, enabling you to revisit the salon fewer times during your pregnancy. You can also ask your colorist about less harsh processing (an ammonia-free base or an all-vegetable dye, for instance). Just keep in mind that hormonal changes can make your hair react strangely—so you might not get what you expect, even from your regular formula. Before you do your whole head, try a test strand so you don't wind up with punk purple instead of that ravishing red you were hoping for.

Straightening treatments or relaxers. Thinking about a straightening treatment to calm those curls? Though there's no evidence that hair relaxers are dangerous during pregnancy (the amount of chemicals that enter the body through the scalp is probably minimal), there's no proof they're completely safe, either. So check with your practitioner; you may hear that it's safest to let your hair do what comes naturally, especially during the first trimester. If you do decide to go straight, keep in mind that there's a possibility that your hormone-infused locks may respond oddly to the chemicals (you might end up with a helmet of frizz instead of ramrod-straight tresses). Plus, your hair will grow faster during pregnancy, making those curls reappear at your roots sooner than you'd like. Thermal reconditioning processes that involve different—and often gentler—chemicals to tame your frizz may be a safer option (again, ask first). Or just buy a flat iron of your own, and coax your hair into smooth submission.

Permanents or body waves. So your hair's not as full as your figure's becoming? Ordinarily, a permanent or a body wave might be the answer for hair that's limping, but it probably isn't during pregnancy. Not because it isn't safe (it probably is, though check with your practitioner), but because hair responds unpredictably under the influence of pregnancy hormones. A permanent might not take at all—or might result in frizz instead of waves.

Hair removal. If pregnancy has you looking like a Planet of the Apes resident, stay calm—this hairy situation is only temporary. Your armpits, bikini line, upper lip, even your belly may be fuzzier than usual due to those raging hormones. Rather not wear fur? Your options for hair removal are somewhat limited during pregnancy. Like most cosmetic procedures and products, lasers, electrolysis, depilatories, and bleaching haven't been studied enough in pregnancy to prove safety (or risks). Many practitioners advise moms-to-be to skip them; others give some of them the okay after month three. Which leaves you with either unwanted hair—or reliance on lower-tech options. Those old reliables—shaving, plucking, and waxing—are perfectly safe. Even a full-on Brazilian is fine, but proceed with caution—pregnancy skin can be extra-sensitive and easily irritated. If you're heading to the salon, let the aesthetician know you're expecting so she can be extra gentle.

Eyelash treatments. As for the hair that no one can get enough of—you'll have to make do with the eyelashes you've got for now. The prescription eyelash growing treatment, Latisse, as well as many of the OTC products touted to lengthen lashes, aren't recommended for expectant and breastfeeding moms because (you guessed it) they haven't been studied in pregnancy. It's probably also smart to avoid dying your eyelashes or brows.

Your Face

Your pregnancy may not be showing in your belly yet, but it's almost certainly showing on your face. Here's the good, bad, and the ugly about face care when you're expecting.

Facials. Face facts: Not every mom-to-be is blessed with that expectant radiance you've always read about. If your glow decides not to show, a facial might be just the ticket, working wonders when it comes to clearing pores clogged by extra oil (thanks to extra hormones). Most facials are absolutely safe during pregnancy, though some abrasive treatments (like microdermabrasion or glycolic peels) may do more harm than good, as they might be especially irritating to skin made supersensitive by pregnancy hormones. Facials that use an electrical microcurrent are off limits during pregnancy. Discuss with the esthetician which preparations might be most soothing and least likely to provoke a reaction. If you're unsure about a particular treatment's safety, check with your practitioner before signing up.

Antiwrinkle treatments. A wrinkly baby is cute; a wrinkly mommy, not so much. But before you stop by your dermatologist's office to treat those fine lines (or fill those lips), consider this: The safety of injectable fillers (such as collagen, Restylane, or Juvederm) during pregnancy hasn't been established through studies yet. The same goes for Botox, which means you're better off staying unfilled (and uninjected) for now. As for antiwrinkle creams, it's best to read the fine print (and check with your practitioner). You'll likely be advised to bid a temporary farewell to products that contain vitamin A (in any of its many retinoid forms), vitamin K, or BHA (beta-hydroxy acid or salicylic acid). Check with your practitioner about other ingredients you're unsure about, too. Most practitioners will green-light products containing AHA (alpha-hydroxy acid) or fruit acids, but get the all-clear first. On the bright side, you may find that normal pregnancy fluid retention plumps up your face nicely, leaving your wrinkles less noticeable without the help of cosmetic procedures.

Acne treatments. Got more pimples than a high school marching band? You can blame pregnancy hormones for that. But before you march to the medicine cabinet for your usual zit zappers, check them out with your practitioner. Accutane (which causes serious birth defects) is definitely off-limits. So is Retin-A (ask your practitioner and dermatologist about over-the-counter products that contain retinol). Laser treatments and chemical peels for acne should also probably wait until after the baby is born. Two common topical acne medications, beta-hydroxy acid (BHA) and salicylic acid, have not been studied in pregnant women and may be absorbed through the skin. Ask your practitioner about the safety of products that contain these medications and those that contain benzoyl peroxide, another ingredient that's often not green-lighted. Glycolic acid and exfoliating scrubs, as well as azelaic and topical antibiotics like erythromycin, are probably safe to use (check first), though watch out for irritation. You can also try to tame eruptions naturally by drinking plenty of water, eating well, and keeping your face clean. And no popping or picking.

Your Teeth

You've got plenty to smile about now that you're expecting, but will your teeth be up to the task? Cosmetic dentistry's popular, but not always pregnancy approved.

Whitening products. Eager to flash your pearly whites? While there are no proven risks to tooth whitening during pregnancy, it's a procedure that probably falls into the better-safe-than-sorry category (so you'll be wise to wait a few months to debut that new million-dollar smile). Be sure to keep your teeth clean and well flossed, though. Your pregnancy-sensitive gums will thank you for the attention.

Veneers. Here's one more for the better-safe-than-sorry side, even though there are no proven risks to adding veneers to your teeth during pregnancy. There's another reason why you might consider waiting until you're postpartum before you veneer your teeth: Your gums might be extra-sensitive when you've got a baby on board, making any dental procedure—including veneers and whitening—more uncomfortable than usual.

Your Body

Your body definitely pays for the privilege of pregnancy—in ways you probably never imagined. So more than any body, it deserves some pampering. Here's how to give it what it needs—safely.

Massage. Aching for some relief from that nagging backache—or from that nagging anxiety that's keeping you up at night? There's nothing like a massage to rub away the aches and pains of pregnancy, as well as the stress and strain. But though a massage may be just what the feel-good doctor ordered, you'll need to follow some guidelines to ensure your pregnancy massages are not only relaxing but also safe:

- Get rubbed by the right hands. Make sure your massage therapist is licensed and well versed in the do's and don'ts of prenatal massage.

- Wait for your rub. Avoid massage during the first three months of pregnancy because it may trigger dizziness and add to morning sickness early on. But don't worry if you've already had a massage during your first trimester. There's no danger, just the potential for being uncomfortable.

- Relax in the right position. It's best to avoid spending a lot of time on your back after the fourth month, so ask your massage therapist to use a table that's equipped with a cut-out for your belly, special pillows designed for pregnancy use, or a cushioned foam padding that conforms to your body, or to position you on your side.

- Try some nonscents. Ask for an unscented lotion or oil, not only because your pregnancy-sharpened sniffer might be offended by strong fragrances, but also because some aromatherapy oils can stimulate contractions; see below.

- Rub the right spots (and stay away from the wrong ones). Direct pressure on the area between the anklebone and heel can trigger contractions, so be sure your therapist stays away from there (another good reason to choose a massage therapist with prenatal training). He or she should also probably stay away from the abdomen area for comfort's sake. And if your therapist is working too deeply or if the massage is too intense, speak up. This is about you feeling good, after all.

Aromatherapy. When it comes to scents during pregnancy, it's good to use some common sense. Because the effects of many plant oils in pregnancy are unknown and some may be harmful, approach any kind of aromatherapy with caution. The following essential oils are considered safe for prenatal massage, though experts recommend that the oils be mixed at a concentration that's half the standard usage: rose, lavender, chamomile, jasmine, tangerine, neroli, and ylang-ylang. Pregnant women should particularly avoid the following oils because some of them can trigger uterine contractions: basil, juniper, rosemary, sage, peppermint, pennyroyal, oregano, and thyme. (Midwives often use these oils during labor precisely because they trigger contractions.) If you've had an aromatherapy massage with these oils (or used them in home baths or treatments), don't worry. The absorption of the oil is very low, especially because the skin on your back is pretty thick. Just steer clear of them in future treatments. Scented lotions or beauty products sold at bath and beauty shops (like peppermint foot lotion, for instance) are fine since the scents aren't concentrated.

Body treatments, scrubs, wraps, hydrotherapy. Body scrubs are generally safe, as long as they're gentle (some scrubs can be too vigorous for sensitive pregnant skin). Some herbal wraps can be safe, but most are off-limits because they might raise your body temperature excessively. A short warm bath (no hotter than 100°F) as part of hydrotherapy is safe and relaxing, but stay out of the sauna, steam room, and hot tub.

Tanning beds, sprays, lotions. Looking for a way to go beyond the pale (pale skin, that is) during your pregnancy? Sorry, but tanning beds are out. Not only are they bad for your skin, they up your chances of getting chloasma (the skin discoloration called the "mask of pregnancy"). Worse, tanning beds can raise your body temperature to a level that could be harmful to your developing baby. Still a fan of the tan? Before you fake it with sunless tanning lotions and sprays, talk to your practitioner. And

A Day at the Spa

Ahhh, the spa. No one deserves—and needs—a day of pampering more than an expectant mother. And happily, more and more spas are offering treatments specifically catering to the pregnant set. But before you head off for your day of pampering, check out this chapter and ask your practitioner for any specific caveats for your situation. Then, when you call to make your appointment, tell the receptionist that you're expecting. Discuss any restrictions you may have so the spa can tailor treatments to fit your needs. Also be sure to inform any esthetician or therapist who will be working on you that you're pregnant.

even if you get the go-ahead, consider that your hormones can cause your skin to play games with the color (and take a turn for the terra-cotta). Plus, as your belly expands, applying a sunless tanner evenly might get tricky (especially once you can no longer see your legs, and even if you're getting a spray-on tan).

For information on the safety of tattoos, henna, and piercings during pregnancy, check out pages 160 and 180.

Your Hands and Feet

Yes, even your hands and feet will show the effects of pregnancy (though you won't be able to see the effects on your feet once you reach the third trimester). But even when you're feeling swell—as in fingers and ankles that are puffy with fluids—your hands and feet can still look their best.

Making Up for Pregnancy

Between breakouts, funky skin discolorations, and normal pregnancy swelling, your face will be facing some challenges over the next nine months. Luckily, you'll be able to make up for them with the right makeup:

■ Go under cover. Corrective concealer and foundation can cover a multitude of pregnancy skin issues, including chloasma and other discolorations (see page 240). For those dark spots, look for brands that are designed to cover hyperpigmentation, but make sure all makeup is non-comedogenic and hypoallergenic. Match both to your skin tone, but select a concealer that's a shade lighter than your natural complexion. Apply the concealer only to the dark spots, stippling the edges to blend. Then lightly blend the foundation over the area. Less is definitely more when it comes to heavy coverage products, so use the least you can get away with—you can always top it off. Set with powder.
  Keep coverage lighter when it comes to pregnancy pimples to avoid calling attention to them (they'll likely call enough attention to themselves). Start with foundation, then

apply a concealer—that matches your skin—directly to the zit, blending with your finger. If you're going to prespot before you cover up, use a pregnancy-approved topical that's clear.

■ Play with shadows. Chip away at those chipmunk cheeks you'll likely be growing: After you've applied your all-over foundation, apply a highlighting shade (one shade lighter) to the center of your forehead, under your eyes, on the tops of your cheekbones, and on the tip of your chin. Then brush a contouring shade (one shade darker) down the sides of your face, starting at the temples. Blend, and presto—instant cheekbones!

■ Stop the spread. Sure, you expect your belly to plump up, and maybe even your hips—but your nose? Don't worry—any widening is temporary, the result of pregnancy swelling. Slim a swollen sniffer by applying a highlighting shade (one shade lighter than your overall foundation) down the center of your nose; then contour the vertical edges of the sides of your nose with a darker shade. Make sure you blend well.

Manicure and pedicure. It's perfectly safe to polish while pregnant (and take advantage now because it's likely that your nails are growing faster and stronger than ever). If you get your nails done in a salon, make sure it's a well-ventilated one. Inhaling those strong chemical smells is never a good idea but especially not when you're breathing for two (and at the very least, the fumes might make you queasy). Do be sure the manicurist doesn't massage the area between your anklebone and heel when you're getting your pedicure

(it could theoretically trigger contractions). As for acrylics, there's no proof that the chemicals are harmful, but you might want to err on the cautious side and forgo those tips until post-baby—not only because the application smell can be extremely strong, but because they can become a nail bed for infection, something you might be more prone to while you're pregnant. And remember, you may not need the extra length or strength of acrylics anyway because your nails will be growing at warp speed.

The
Second
Month

Approximately 5 to 8 Weeks

VEN IF YOU'RE NOT TELLING anyone you're expecting yet, and though no one around you could possibly know (unless you've already blabbed the big news), your baby's certainly spilling the beans to you. Not in so many words, but in so many symptoms. Like that nagging nausea that follows you wherever you go, or all that excess saliva pooling in your mouth (am I *drooling*?). Like the gotta-go feeling you're getting all day (and all night), and that 24/7 bloat you just can't seem to deflate.

Even with all this evidence you're pregnant, you're probably still getting used to the idea that a new life is developing inside you (after all, you've just found out for sure you've got a baby—and not a stomach bug—on board). You're also probably just getting used to the demands of pregnancy, from the physical (so that's why I'm tired!) to the logistical (the shortest route to the bathroom is . . .) to the dietary (make my Sea Breeze a virgin). It's a wild ride, and it's only just beginning. Hold on tight!

Your Baby This Month

Week 5 Your little embryo, which at this point resembles a tadpole more than a baby (complete with teeny tail), is growing fast and furious and is now about the size of an orange seed—still

small, but a lot bigger than it's been. This week, the heart is starting to take shape. In fact, the circulatory system, along with the heart, is the first system to be operational. Your baby's heart (about the size of a poppy seed) is made up of two tiny channels called heart tubes—and though it's still far from fully functional, it's already beating—something you might be able to see on an early ultrasound. Also in the works is the neural tube, which will eventually become your baby's brain and spinal cord. Right now the neural tube is open, but it will close by next week.

Your Baby, Month 2

Week 6 Crown (head) to rump (bottom) measurements are used for babies in utero because their tiny, newly forming legs are bent, making it difficult to measure the full length of the body. How's baby measuring up this week? That crown to rump measurement has reached somewhere between a fifth and a quarter of an inch (no bigger than a nail head). This week also sees the beginning of the development of your baby's jaws, cheeks, and chin. Little indentations on both sides of the head will form into ear canals. Small black dots on the face will form the eyes, and a small bump on the front of the head will turn into a button nose in a few weeks' time. Also taking shape this week: your baby's kidneys, liver, and lungs. Your baby's tiny heart is beating 80 times per minute and getting faster each day—a stat that's probably got your heart racing.

Week 7 Here's an amazing fact about your baby right now: He or she is 10,000 times bigger now than at conception—about the size of a blueberry. A lot of that growth is concentrated on the head (new brain cells are being generated at the rate of 100 cells per minute). Your baby's mouth and tongue are forming this week and so are his or her arm and leg buds, which are beginning to sprout into paddle-like appendages and to divide into hand, arm, and shoulder segments—and leg, knee, and foot segments. Also in place now are your baby's kidneys, and they're poised to begin their important work of waste management (i.e., urine production and excretion). At least you don't have to worry about dirty diapers yet!

Week 8 Your baby is growing up a storm, this week measuring about half an inch in length, or about the size of a large raspberry. And that sweet little raspberry of yours is looking less reptilian and more human (happily), as his or her lips, nose, eyelids, legs, and back continue to take shape. And though it's still too early to hear from the outside, your baby's heart is beating at the incredible rate of 150 times per minute (that's twice as fast as your heart beats). Something else new this week: Your baby is making spontaneous movements (twitches of the trunk and limb buds too tiny for you to feel).

What You May Be Feeling

As always, remember that every pregnancy and every woman is different. You may experience all of these symptoms at one time or another, or only one or two. Some may have continued from last month, others may be new. You may also have other, less common, symptoms. Don't be surprised, no matter what your symptoms (or lack thereof), if you don't "feel" pregnant yet. Here's what you might experience this month:

Physically

- Fatigue, lack of energy, sleepiness

- Frequent urination

- Nausea, with or without vomiting

- Excess saliva

- Constipation

- Heartburn, indigestion, flatulence, bloating

- Food aversions and cravings

- Breast changes: fullness, heaviness, tenderness, tingling; darkening of the areolas (the pigmented area around your nipples); lubrication glands in the areolas becoming prominent, like large goose bumps; a network of bluish lines that appear under your skin as the blood supply to your breasts increases

- Slight whitish vaginal discharge

- Occasional headaches

- Occasional faintness or dizziness

- A little rounding of your belly; your clothes feeling a little snugger

Emotionally

- Emotional ups and downs (like amped-up PMS), which may include

mood swings, irritability, irrationality, inexplicable weepiness

- Misgivings, fear, joy, elation—any or all of these

- A sense of unreality about the pregnancy ("Is there really a baby in there?")

A Look Inside

Even though you still won't look like you're pregnant to those around you, you might notice your clothes are getting a little tighter around the waist. You might also need a bigger bra now. By the end of this month, your uterus, usually the size of a fist, has grown to the size of a large grapefruit.

What You Can Expect at This Month's Checkup

If this is your first prenatal visit, see page 124. If this is your second exam, you'll find it will be a much shorter visit. And if those initial tests have already been taken care of, you probably won't be subjected to much poking and prodding this time. You can expect your practitioner to check the following, though there may be variations depending on your particular needs and your practitioner's style of practice.

- Weight and blood pressure

- Urine, for sugar and protein

- Hands and feet for swelling, and legs for varicose veins

- Symptoms you've been experiencing, especially unusual ones

- Questions or problems you want to discuss—have a list ready

What You May Be Wondering About

Heartburn and Indigestion

"I have indigestion and heartburn all the time. Why, and what can I do about it?"

No one does heartburn like a pregnant woman does heartburn. Not only that, but you're likely to keep doing it—and doing it at least as well—throughout your whole pregnancy (unlike many early pregnancy symptoms, this one's a keeper).

So why does it feel like you have a flamethrower stationed in your chest? Early in pregnancy, your body produces large amounts of the hormones progesterone and relaxin, which tend to relax smooth muscle tissue everywhere in the body, including the gastrointestinal (GI) tract. As a result, food sometimes moves more slowly through your system, resulting in indigestion (a feeling of fullness and bloating in the upper abdomen and chest; heartburn is a symptom of indigestion). This may be uncomfortable for you, but it's actually beneficial for your baby. The alimentary slowdown allows better absorption of nutrients into your bloodstream and subsequently through the placenta and into your baby.

Heartburn results when the ring of muscle that separates the esophagus from the stomach relaxes (like all the other smooth muscle in the GI tract), allowing food and harsh digestive juices to back up from the stomach to the esophagus. These stomach acids irritate the sensitive esophageal lining, causing a burning sensation right around where the heart is—thus the term heartburn—though the problem has nothing to do with your heart. During the last two trimesters, the problem can be compounded by your blossoming uterus as it presses up on your stomach.

It's nearly impossible to have an indigestion-free nine months; it's just one of the less pleasant realities of pregnancy. There are, however, some pretty effective ways of avoiding heartburn

Bringing up Reflux

If you have GERD (gastroesophageal reflux disease), heartburn's nothing new, but treating it during pregnancy might be. Now that you're expecting, ask your practitioner about whether the prescription meds you're used to taking are still okay to take. Some are not recommended for use during pregnancy, but most are safe. Many of the tips for fighting heartburn can also help with your reflux.

and indigestion most of the time, and of minimizing the discomfort when it strikes:

- Don't pull the triggers. If a food or drink brings on the burn (or other tummy troubles), take it off the menu for now. The most common offenders (and you're sure to know those that offend you) are spicy and highly seasoned foods, fried or fatty foods, processed meats, chocolate, coffee, carbonated beverages, and mint.

- Take it small. To avoid digestive system overload (and backup of gastric juices), opt for frequent mini meals over three large squares. The Six-Meal Solution is ideal for heartburn and indigestion sufferers (see page 91).

- Take it slow. When you eat too quickly, you tend to swallow air, which can form gas pockets in your belly. And rushing through meals means you're not chewing thoroughly, which makes your stomach work harder digesting your food—and makes heartburn more likely to happen. So even when you're starving or in a hurry, make an effort to eat slowly, taking small bites and chewing well (your mother would be proud).

- Don't drink and eat. Too much fluid mixed with your food distends the stomach, aggravating indigestion. So try to take most of your fluids in between meals.

- Keep it up. It's harder for gastric juices to back up when you're vertical than when you're horizontal. To keep them where they belong (down in your stomach), avoid eating while lying down. Or lying down after eating—or eating a big meal before bed. Sleeping with your head and shoulders elevated about 6 inches can also fight the gastric backup with gravity. Another way: Bend at the knees, not at the waist. Anytime your head dips, you're more likely to experience burn.

- Keep it down. Your weight gain, that is. A gradual and moderate gain will minimize the amount of pressure on your digestive tract.

- Keep it loose. Don't wear clothing that's tight around your belly or waist. A constricted tummy can add to the pressure, and the burn.

- Pop some relief. Always keep a supply of Tums or Rolaids at popping distance (they'll also give you a healthy dose of calcium while they ease the burn), but avoid other heartburn medicines unless they've been cleared by your practitioner. Sick of antacids already? Try one of these burn-banishing folk remedies: a tablespoon of honey in warm milk, a handful of almonds, or some fresh or dried papaya.

- Chew on it. Chewing sugarless gum for a half hour after meals can reduce excess acid (increased saliva can neutralize the acid in your esophagus). Some people find that mint-flavored

Heartburn Today, Hair Tomorrow?

Feeling the burn bad? You may want to stock up on baby shampoo. New research has actually backed up what old wives have maintained for generations: The more heartburn you have during pregnancy, the more likely your baby will be born with a full head of hair. Implausible as it sounds, seems the hormones responsible for heartburn are the same ones that cause fetal hair to sprout. So pass the Tums, and the detangler.

gum exacerbates heartburn; if so, choose a non-minty gum.

- Don't smoke (yet another reason to quit today, if you haven't already).

- Relax for relief. Stress compounds all gastric upset, especially heartburn, so learn to relax (see page 142). Also try some complementary and alternative medical (CAM) approaches, such as meditation, visualization, biofeedback, or hypnosis (see page 85).

Food Aversions and Cravings

"Certain foods that I've always loved taste strange now. Instead, I'm having cravings for foods that I never liked. What's going on?"

The pregnancy cliché of a harried husband running out in the middle of the night, raincoat over his pajamas, for a pint of ice cream and a jar of pickles to satisfy his wife's cravings has definitely played out more often in the heads of old-school sitcom writers than in real life. Not many pregnant women's cravings carry them—or their spouses—that far.

Still, most expectant moms find their tastes in food change somewhat in pregnancy. Most experience a craving for at least one food (most often ice cream, though usually without the pickles), and more than half will have at least one food aversion (poultry ranks right up there, along with vegetables of all varieties). To a certain extent, these suddenly eccentric (and sometimes borderline bizarre) eating habits can be blamed on hormonal havoc, which probably explains why they're most common in the first trimester of first pregnancies, when that havoc is at its height.

Hormones, however, may not tell the whole story. The long-held theory that cravings and aversions are sensible signals from our bodies—that when we develop a distaste for something, it's usually bad for us, and when we lust after something, it's usually something we need—often does seem to stand up. Like when you suddenly can't face the morning coffee you once couldn't face your morning without. Or when a glass of your favorite wine sips like vinegar. Or when you can't gobble down enough grapefruit. On the other hand, when you call "fowl" at the sight of chicken, or your beloved broccoli becomes bitter, or your cravings launch you into a full-fledged fudge frenzy—well, it's hard to credit your body with sending the smartest signals.

The problem is that body signals relating to food are always hard to read when hormones are involved—and may be especially tough to call now that humans have departed so far from the food chain (and now that so many food chains sell fast food). Before candy bars were invented, for instance, a craving for something sweet might have sent a pregnant woman foraging for berries. Now it's more likely to send her foraging for M&M's.

Do you have to ignore your cravings and aversions in the name of healthy pregnancy eating? Even if that were possible (hormone-induced food quirks are a powerful force), it wouldn't be fair. Still, it's possible to respond to them while also paying attention to your baby's nutritional needs. If you crave something healthy—cottage cheese by the crateful or peaches by the pile—don't feel like you have to hold back. Go for the nutritious gusto, even if it means your diet's a little unbalanced for a while (you'll make up for the variety later on in pregnancy when the cravings calm down).

If you crave something that you know you'd probably be better off without, then try to seek a substitute that satisfies the craving (at least somewhat) but also satisfies a nutritional requirement (and doesn't fill you up with too many empty calories): chocolate frozen yogurt instead of a frozen chocolate bar; a bag of trail mix instead of a bag of jelly beans; baked cheese puffs instead of the kind that turn your fingers orange. If substitutes don't fully satisfy, adding sublimation to the mix may be helpful. When MoonPies at the 7-Eleven howl your name, try doing something that takes your mind off them: taking a brisk walk, chatting with friends on a pregnancy message board, checking out maternity jeans online. And, of course, completely giving in to less nutritious cravings is fine (as is enjoying them, so leave that side of guilt off the menu when you indulge), as long as they don't include something risky (such as an alcoholic beverage) and as long as your indulgences don't take the place of nutritious foods in your diet on a regular basis.

Most cravings and aversions disappear or weaken by the fourth month. Cravings that hang in there longer may be triggered by emotional needs—the need for a little extra attention, for example. If both you and your spouse are aware of this need, it should be easy to satisfy. Instead of requesting a middle-of-the-night pint of Chunky Monkey (with or without the sour dills), you might settle for an oatmeal cookie or two and some quiet cuddling or a romantic bath.

Some women find themselves craving, even eating, such peculiar non-food substances as clay, ashes, and paper. Because this habit, known as pica, can be dangerous and may be a sign of nutritional deficiency, particularly of iron, report it to your practitioner. Craving ice may also mean you're iron deficient, so also report any compulsion to chew ice.

Visible Veins

"I have unsightly blue lines all over my breasts and belly. Is that normal?"

Not only are these veins (which can make your entire chest and belly look like a road map) normal and nothing to worry about, they are a sign that your body is doing what it should. They're part of the network of veins that has expanded to carry the increased blood supply of pregnancy, which will be nourishing your baby. They may show up earliest and be much more prominent in very slim or fair-skinned women. In some women, particularly those who are overweight or dark-skinned, the veins may be less visible or not noticeable at all, or they may not become obvious until later in pregnancy.

Spider Veins

"Since I became pregnant I've got awful-looking spidery purplish red lines on my thighs. Are they varicose veins?"

They aren't pretty, but they aren't varicose veins. They are probably spider nevi, commonly dubbed "spider veins," for obvious reasons. There are a few reasons why spider veins might choose to spin their web across your legs. First, the increased volume of blood you're carrying can create significant pressure on blood vessels, causing even tiny veins to swell and become visible. Second, pregnancy hormones can do a number on all your blood vessels, big and small. And third, genetics can predispose you to spider veins (thanks, Mom).

If you're destined to have spider veins, there's not much you can do to avoid them altogether, but there are ways to minimize their spread. Since your veins are as healthy as your diet is, try eating enough vitamin C foods (the body uses it to manufacture collagen and elastin, two important connective tissues that help repair and maintain blood vessels). Exercising regularly (to improve circulation and leg strength) and getting into the habit of not crossing your legs (which restricts blood flow) will also help keep spider veins at bay.

Prevention didn't do the trick? Some, though far from all, spider veins fade and disappear after delivery; if they don't, they can be treated by a dermatologist—either with the injection of saline (sclerotherapy) or glycerin, or with the use of a laser. These treatments destroy the blood vessels, causing them to collapse and eventually disappear—but they aren't recommended during pregnancy. In the meantime, you can try camouflaging your spider veins with flesh-toned concealers specifically designed for that purpose.

Varicose Veins

"My mother and grandmother both had varicose veins during pregnancy. Is there anything I can do to prevent them in my own pregnancy?"

Varicose veins run in families—and they definitely sound like they have legs in yours. But being genetically predisposed to varicose veins doesn't mean you have to be resigned to them, which is why you're wise to be thinking now about bucking your family tradition with prevention.

Varicose veins often surface for the first time during pregnancy, and they tend to worsen in subsequent pregnancies. That's because the extra volume of blood you produce during pregnancy puts extra pressure on your blood vessels, especially the veins in your legs, which have to work against gravity to push all that extra blood back up to your heart. Add to that the pressure your burgeoning uterus puts on your pelvic blood vessels and the vessel-relaxing effects of the extra hormones your body is producing, and you have the perfect recipe for varicose veins.

The symptoms of varicose veins aren't difficult to recognize, but they vary in severity. There may be a mild achiness or severe pain in the legs, or a sensation of heaviness, or swelling, or none of these. A faint outline of bluish veins may be visible, or serpentine veins may bulge from ankle to upper thigh. In severe cases, the skin overlying the veins becomes swollen, dry, and irritated (ask your practitioner about moisturizers that can help). Occasionally, superficial thrombophlebitis (inflammation of a surface vein due to a blood clot) may develop at the site of a varicosity, so always check with your practitioner about varicose vein symptoms.

To give your legs a leg up against varicose veins:

- Keep the blood flowing. Too much sitting or standing can compromise blood flow, so avoid long periods of either when you can—and when you can't, periodically flex your ankles. When sitting, avoid crossing your legs and elevate them if possible. When lying down, raise your legs by placing a pillow under your feet. When resting or sleeping, try to lie on your left side, the best one for optimum circulation (though either side will do).

- Watch your weight. Excess poundage increases the demands on your already overworked circulatory system, so keep your weight gain within the recommended guidelines.

- Avoid heavy lifting, which can make those veins bulge.

- Push gently during bowel movements. Straining can be a strain on those veins. Staying regular (see page 173) will help keep things moving.

- Wear support panty hose (light support hose seem to work well without being uncomfortable) or elastic stockings, putting them on before getting out of bed in the morning (before blood pools in your legs) and taking them off at night before getting into bed. While neither will contribute to your sexiest pregnancy moment, they help by counteracting the downward pressure of your belly and giving the veins in your legs a little extra upward push.

- Stay away from clothes that might restrict your circulation: tight belts or pants, panty hose and socks with elastic tops, and snug shoes. Also skip high heels, favoring flats or medium chunky heels instead.

- Get some exercise, such as a brisk 20- to 30-minute walk or swim every day. But if you're experiencing pain, avoid high-impact aerobics, jogging, cycling, and weight training.

- Be sure your diet includes plenty of foods rich in vitamin C, which helps keep blood vessels healthy and elastic.

Surgical removal of varicose veins isn't recommended during pregnancy, though it can certainly be considered a few months after delivery. In most cases, however, the problem will improve after delivery, usually by the time prepregnancy weight is reached.

An Achy, Swollen Pelvis

"My whole pelvic area feels achy and swollen, and really uncomfortable—and I think I felt an actual bulge in my vulva. What is that all about?"

Legs may have the market share of varicose veins, but they definitely don't have a monopoly. Varicose veins can also appear in the genital area (and in the rectum, where they're called hemorrhoids), for the same reason you might get them in your legs—and it sounds like they've made that appearance in you. Called pelvic congestion syndrome, or PCS, the symptoms (aside from bulging in the vulva) include chronic pelvic pain and/or abdominal pain, an achy, swollen, "full" feeling in the pelvic area and the genitals, and sometimes pain with intercourse. The tips for minimizing varicose veins in the legs will also help you (see previous question), but do be sure to check with your practitioner, both for the diagnosis and for possible treatment options (usually after delivery).

Breakouts

"My skin is breaking out the way it did when I was a teenager."

The glow of pregnancy that some women are lucky enough to radiate isn't just a result of joy, but of the stepped-up secretion of oils brought on by hormonal changes. And so, alas, are the less-than-glowing breakouts of pregnancy that some not-so-lucky expectant women experience (particularly those whose skin ordinarily breaks out like clockwork before their periods). Though such eruptions are hard to eliminate entirely, the following suggestions may help keep them at a minimum—and keep you from resembling your eighth-grade yearbook picture:

- Wash your face two or three times a day with a gentle cleanser. But don't get overaggressive with scrubs—not only because your skin is extra-sensitive during pregnancy, but because overstripped skin is actually more susceptible to breakouts.

- Get the all clear on any acne medications (topical or oral) before you use them. Some are considered safe to slather on; others aren't. Check with your practitioner, and see page 146.

- Use an oil-free moisturizer to keep skin hydrated. Sometimes skin that is overly dried by harsh acne soaps and other products is more pimple prone.

- Choose skin-care products and cosmetics that are oil free and labeled "non-comedogenic," which means they won't clog pores.

- Keep everything that touches your face clean, including those blush brushes at the bottom of your makeup bag.

- Pop (and pick) not. Just like your mother always told you, popping or picking at pimples won't make them go away—and can actually make them stick around longer by pushing bacteria back down into the zit. Plus, when you're pregnant, you're more prone to infections. Poked-at pimples can also leave scars.

- Eat well by following the Pregnancy Diet. It's good for your skin as well as for your baby.

- Don't pass a tap without filling your glass. Drinking water helps keep your skin moist and clear.

- Switch to a nonsoap cleanser such as Cetaphil or Aquanil, and use it no more than once a day (at night if you're taking off makeup). Wash with just water the rest of the time.

- Slather on moisturizer while your skin is still damp (after a bath or shower), and use the moisturizer as often as you can—and certainly before you turn in for the night.

- Cut down on bathing and keep your showers short (5 minutes instead of 15). Too much washing can dry out your skin. Make sure, too, that the water is lukewarm and not hot. Hot water removes natural oil from the skin, making it dry and itchy.

- Add unscented bath oils to your tub, but be careful with the slippery surface you've created. (Remember, as your belly grows, so will your klutz factor.)

- Drink plenty of fluids throughout the day to stay hydrated, and be sure to include good fats in your diet (those omega-3's that are so baby friendly are also skin friendly).

- Keep your rooms well humidified.

- Wear a sunscreen with an SPF of at least 15 (preferably 30) every day.

Dry Skin

"My skin is terribly dry. Is that pregnancy related, too?"

Feeling a tad reptilian these days? You can blame your hormones for your dry, often itchy, skin. Hormonal changes rob your skin of oil and elasticity, leaving you with that oh-so-sexy alligator look. To keep your skin as soft as your baby-to-be's bottom:

Eczema

"I've always been prone to eczema, but now that I'm pregnant, it's gotten much worse. What can I do?"

Unfortunately, pregnancy (or more accurately, its hormones) often exacerbates the symptoms of eczema, and for women who suffer from it, the itching and scaling can become practically unbearable. (Some lucky eczema sufferers find that pregnancy actually causes the eczema to go into remission.)

Belly Piercings

It's cool, it's stylish, it's sexy—and it's one of the cutest ways to show off a flat, toned tummy. But once your belly starts to bulge, will you have to give up on your belly piercing? Nope—not as long as your belly piercing is healed (read: your trip to the Piercing Pavilion wasn't last month) and healthy (in other words, not red, weeping, or inflamed). Remember, your belly button marks where you connected to your own mom in the womb, not where your baby connects to you—which means a piercing won't provide a path for pathogens to reach your baby. You also don't have to worry about a belly ring interfering with birth, or even a cesarean delivery.

Of course, as your pregnancy progresses and your tummy starts to jut out in earnest, you may find that your belly bar or belly ring becomes too uncomfortable to wear, thanks (or no thanks) to your taut, stretched-to-the-limit skin. The belly ring might also start to rub—and even get caught on—your clothing, especially when your belly button "pops" out later in pregnancy. And that rubbing can hurt, big time.

If you do decide to take out the jewelry entirely, just run your belly ring through the hole every few days to keep the piercing from closing up shop (unless you've had it for a number of years, in which case the likelihood that the hole will close is pretty slim). Or consider replacing your bar or ring with a flexible belly bar made of Teflon or PTFE (for polytetrafluoroethylene).

As far as getting your belly (or anywhere else on your body) pierced during pregnancy: better to hold off until after delivery. It's never a good idea to puncture the skin during pregnancy, because it ups the chances of infection.

Fortunately, low-dose hydrocortisone creams and ointments are safe to use during pregnancy in moderate amounts. Ask your practitioner or dermatologist which ones he or she recommends. Antihistamines may also be helpful in coping with the itchiness, but again, be sure to check with your practitioner first. Cyclosporine, long used on severe cases that don't respond to other treatment, is generally off limits during pregnancy. Some topical and systemic antibiotics may not be safe for use during pregnancy either, so check with your practitioner first. The newer nonsteroidals (Protopic and Elidel) aren't recommended because they haven't been studied in pregnancy and can't be ruled safe until more is known.

If you're an eczema sufferer, you know that prevention can go a long way in keeping the itch away. Try the following:

- Use a cold compress—not your fingernails—to curb the itch. Scratching makes the condition worse and can puncture the skin, allowing bacteria to enter and cause an infection. Keep nails short and rounded to decrease the likelihood that you will puncture the skin when you do inevitably scratch.

- Limit contact with potential irritants such as laundry detergents, household cleaners, soaps, bubble bath, perfumes, cosmetics, wool, pet dander, plants, jewelry, and juices from meats and fruits.

- Moisturize early and often (while skin is still damp, if you're just out of the water) to lock in the skin's own moisture and prevent dryness and cracking.

- Don't spend too much time in the water (showers, baths, swimming pools), especially hot water.

- Try not to get too hot or sweaty (two of the most common eczema triggers). Of course that's easier said than done when you're pregnant and already one hot, sweaty mama. Stay cool by wearing loose, cotton clothes and avoiding synthetic fabrics, wool, or any material that feels rough to the touch. Avoid overheating by favoring that layered look—and peeling off layers as you start to warm up.

- Try to keep your cool, too, when it comes to stress—a common eczema trigger. When you feel anxiety creeping in, take some relaxation breaths (see page 230).

Something to keep in mind: Though eczema is hereditary (meaning that your baby has a chance of having it, too), research suggests that breastfeeding may prevent eczema from developing in a child. That's just one more good reason to nurse your baby if you can.

Come and Go Belly

"It's the strangest thing—one day it'll look like I'm showing, and the next day my belly will be completely flat again. What's up with that?"

What's up are your bowels, actually. Bowel distention (the result of constipation and excess gas, two of a newly pregnant woman's constant companions) can make a flat belly round in no time flat. And just as quickly as it appeared, your belly can disappear—once you've had a bowel movement, that is. A little unnerving, yes ("But I looked pregnant just yesterday!"), but completely normal.

Don't worry. Pretty soon you'll have a belly that doesn't come and go—and that's more baby than bowel. In the meantime, see page 173 for tips on fighting constipation.

Losing Your Shape

"Will I ever get my body back after I have a baby?"

Well, that kind of depends—mostly, on you. The 2 to 4 permanent pounds the average woman puts on with each pregnancy, and the flab that often goes with them, aren't inevitable. In fact, if you gain the right amount of weight, at the right rate, on the right foods, your chances of recovering your prepregnancy shape are really very good, particularly if you team your sensible eating efforts with pregnancy-approved exercise, and especially if you keep your regimen up after your baby arrives. Mind you, that recovery won't happen overnight (think three to six months, minimum).

So fear not your pregnancy weight gain. Remember, it's set to accumulate for the very best reason: the nourishment of your baby now, and, if you choose to breastfeed, later.

Measuring Small

"At my last prenatal visit, my midwife told me my uterus is measuring a little small. Does this mean the baby's not growing right?"

Parents rarely wait until their babies are born to begin worrying about their size. But—just as is usually the case after birth—there's rarely anything to worry about before. After all, trying to size up your uterus from the outside isn't an exact science anytime in pregnancy, and especially not this early in the game. Calculating what that size should be isn't easy either (unless you're certain about which day you conceived on), since the date of your pregnancy may be off by as much as several weeks on either side. Chances are your midwife is planning to schedule an ultrasound to pinpoint more precisely the size of your uterus and the date of your pregnancy and to see if there are any discrepancies, which there most likely aren't.

Measuring Big

"I was told my uterus is measuring ten weeks, but according to my dates I'm only eight weeks pregnant. Why is my uterus so large?"

There's a good chance that your uterus is bigger than it's supposed to be because you're further along than you think. It's likely that your dates are off, or that your size was miscalculated, both pretty common scenarios. To check this out, and because there are other, much less likely explanations (for example, that you might be carrying twins—though it's unlikely at this early stage that multiples would make a difference in uterine size), your practitioner will probably order an ultrasound.

Difficulty Urinating

"The last few days it's been really hard to urinate, even though my bladder seems very full."

Sounds like you may be under pressure—from your uterus. About 1 in 5 women have a tilted (aka retroverted) uterus, one that tilts toward the back instead of the front. When it refuses to right itself, a tilted uterus can press on the urethra, the tube leading from the bladder. The pressure of this ever-heavier load can make urination difficult. There may also be urinary leakage when the bladder becomes very overloaded.

In nearly all cases, the uterus shifts itself back into position by the end of the first trimester without any medical intervention. But if you're really uncomfortable now—or if you're finding it especially difficult to urinate—put in a call to your practitioner. He or she might be able to manipulate your uterus by hand to move it off the urethra so you can pee easily again. Most of the time that works. In the unlikely event that it doesn't, catheterization (removing the urine through a tube) may become necessary.

One other possibility if you're having trouble urinating (and another good reason to put in that call to your practitioner): a urinary tract infection. See page 498 for more.

Mood Swings

"I know I should feel happy about my pregnancy—and sometimes I am. But other times, I feel so weepy and sad."

They're up—and they're down. The very normal mood swings of pregnancy can take your emotions places they've never gone before, both to exhilarating highs and depressing lows. Moods that can have you over-the-moon one moment, down-in-the-dumps the next—and weeping inexplicably over insurance commercials. Can you blame it on your hormones? You bet. These swings may be more pronounced in the first trimester (when hormonal havoc is at its peak) and, in general, in women who ordinarily suffer from marked emotional ups and downs before their periods (it's sort of like PMS pumped up). Feelings of ambivalence about the pregnancy once it's confirmed, which are common even when a pregnancy is planned, may exaggerate the swings still more. Not to mention all those changes you're experiencing (the physical ones, the emotional ones, the logistical ones, the relationship ones—all of which can overwhelm your moods).

Mood swings tend to moderate somewhat after the first trimester, once hormone levels calm down a little—and once you've adjusted to some of those pregnancy changes (you'll never adjust to all of them). In the meantime, though there's no sure way to hop off that emotional roller coaster, there are several ways to minimize the mood mayhem:

- Keep your blood sugar up. What does blood sugar have to do with moods? A lot. Dips in blood sugar—caused by long stretches between meals—can lead to mood crashes. Yet another compelling reason to ditch your usual three-meals-a-day (or fewer) eating routine and switch to the Six-Meal Solution (see page 91). Give complex carbs and protein starring roles in your mini meals for the longest lasting blood sugar—and mood—highs.

- Keep sugar and caffeine down. That candy bar, that doughnut, that Coke will give your blood sugar a quick spike—followed soon after by a downward spiral that can take your mood down with it. Caffeine can have the same effect, adding to mood instability. So limit both, for happier results.

- Eat well. In general, eating well will help you feel your best emotionally (as well as physically), so follow the Pregnancy Diet as best you can. Getting plenty of omega-3 fatty acids in your diet (through walnuts, fish, and enriched eggs, to name a few) may also help with mood moderating (and they're also super important for your baby's brain development).

- Get a move on. The more you move, the better your mood. That's because exercise releases feel-good endorphins, which can send your spirits soaring. With your practitioner's guidance, build exercise into your day—every day.

- Get a groove on. If you're in the mood for love (and if you're not too busy puking), making love can turn that frown upside down by releasing happy hormones. It can also bring you closer to your partner at a time when your relationship may be facing new challenges. If sex isn't in the cards, just taking the time for intimacy of any kind (cuddling, pillow talk, handholding on the sofa) can help boost your mood.

- Light up your life. Research has shown that sunlight can actually lighten your moods. When the sun's shining, try catching some daily rays (just don't forget to apply sunscreen first).

- Talk about it. Worried? Anxious? Feeling unsettled? Feeling unsure? Pregnancy is a time of many mixed emotions, which play themselves out in mood swings. Venting some of those feelings—to your spouse (who's probably feeling plenty of the same things), to friends who can relate, to other expectant moms on online pregnancy message boards (check out the ones on whattoexpect.com)—can help you feel better, or at least help you see that what you're feeling is normal.

- Rest up. Fatigue can exacerbate normal pregnancy mood swings, so make sure you're getting enough sleep (but not too much, since that can actually increase fatigue and emotional instability).

- Learn to relax. Stress can definitely take your moods down, so find ways of moderating it or coping with it better. See page 142 for tips.

If there's one person in your life who's more affected—and bewildered—by your mood swings than you are, it's your spouse. It'll help for him to understand why you're acting the way you are these days (that surges of pregnancy hormones are holding your emotions hostage), but it'll also help for him to know exactly how he can help you. So tell him what you need (more help around the house? a night out at your favorite restaurant?) and what you don't need (hearing that your rear's looking a little wide; his leaving a trail of socks and underwear down the hallway) right now, what makes you feel better and what makes you feel worse. And be specific: Even the most loving spouse isn't a mind reader. See Chapter 19 for more on coping strategies for fathers-to-be.

Depression

"I expected some mood swings with pregnancy, but I'm not just a little down— I'm depressed all the time."

Every pregnant woman has her ups and downs, and that's normal. But if your lows are consistent or frequent, you may be among the 10 to 15 percent of pregnant women who battle mild to moderate depression during pregnancy. Here are some of the factors that can put an expectant mom at risk for such depression:

■ A personal or family history of mood disorder

■ Financial or marital stress

■ Lack of emotional support from and communication with the baby's father

■ Hospitalization or bed rest because of pregnancy complications

■ Anxiety about her own health, especially if she has a chronic medical condition or has previously experienced complications or illness during pregnancy

■ Anxiety about her baby's health, especially if there is a personal or family history of miscarriage, birth defects, or other problems

The most common symptoms of true depression, in addition to feeling sad, empty, and emotionally lethargic, include sleep disturbances (you get too much or too little); changed eating habits (not eating at all or eating continually); prolonged or unusual fatigue and/or excessive agitation or restlessness; extended loss of interest in work, play, and other activities or pleasures; reduced ability to concentrate and focus; exaggerated mood swings; and even self-destructive thoughts. There may also be unexplained aches and pains. If that sounds like what you're experiencing, start by trying those tips for dealing with mood swings in the previous question.

If the symptoms continue for longer than two weeks, speak to your practitioner about your depression (he or she may want to test you for a thyroid condition since that can trigger depression) or ask for a referral to a therapist who can offer supportive psychotherapy. Getting the right help is important. Depression can keep you from taking optimum care of yourself and your baby, now and after delivery. In fact, depression during pregnancy can increase risks for complications—much as depression can adversely affect your health when you're not pregnant. Deciding whether antidepressant medication will be part of the treatment plan will require sitting down with your practitioner (and therapist) to weigh possible risks against possible benefits (see page 518 for a discussion of antidepressants during pregnancy).

Panic Attacks

Pregnancy can be a time of high anxiety, especially for those who are expecting for the first time (and consequently don't know what to expect). And a certain amount of worry is normal, and probably unavoidable. But what about when that worry turns to panic?

If you've had panic attacks in the past, you're probably all too aware of the symptoms (and most women who have panic attacks during pregnancy have had them before). They're characterized by intense fear or discomfort accompanied by an accelerated heart rate, sweating, trembling, shortness of breath, feeling of choking, chest pain, nausea or abdominal distress, dizziness, numbness or tingling, or chills or hot flashes that appear seemingly out of the blue. They can be incredibly unsettling, of course, particularly when they strike for the first time. But happily, though they definitely affect you, there is no reason to believe that panic attacks affect the development of your baby in any way.

Still, if you do experience such an attack, tell your practitioner. Therapy is always the first choice during pregnancy (and other times, too). But if medications are necessary to ensure your well-being (and your baby's—if anxiety is keeping you from eating or sleeping or otherwise taking care of your precious cargo), your practitioner, together with a qualified therapist, can work with you to decide which medication offers the most benefits for the fewest risks (and how low a dose you can take and still derive those benefits). If you've been on a medication for panic attacks, anxiety, or depression prepregnancy, a change or an adjustment of dose might be necessary, too.

While medication is one solution to extreme anxiety, it certainly isn't the only one. There are many nondrug alternatives that can be used instead of or in conjunction with traditional therapy. These include eating well and regularly (including plenty of omega-3 fatty acids in your diet may be especially helpful); avoiding sugar and caffeine (caffeine, in particular, can trigger anxiety); getting regular exercise; and learning meditation and other relaxation techniques (prenatal yoga can be incredibly calming). Talking your anxieties over with other expectant moms can also provide enormous relief.

Consult your practitioner, too, before turning to any alternative treatments. Over-the-counter supplements, such as SAM-e and St. John's wort, touted for their mood-elevating properties, have not been studied enough to consider them safe for use in pregnancy. But other CAM therapies (see page 85) might help, and bright light therapy (which increases levels of the mood-regulating hormone serotonin in the brain) cuts depressive symptoms during pregnancy in half. Eating foods rich in omega-3 fatty acids lowers the risk of depression during pregnancy and possibly during the postpartum period as well. You can also ask your practitioner about taking a pregnancy-safe omega-3 supplement.

Being depressed during pregnancy does put you at somewhat greater risk of postpartum depression. The good news is that getting the right treatment during pregnancy—and/or right after delivery—can help prevent postpartum depression. Ask your practitioner about this.

Weight Gain During Pregnancy

Put two pregnant women together anywhere—in a doctor's waiting room, on an elevator, at a business meeting—and the questions are certain to start flying. "When are you due?" "Have you felt the baby kicking yet?" "Have you been feeling sick?" And perhaps the most commonly posed of all: "How much weight have you gained?"

Everybody expects to gain weight while they're pregnant (and after spending half a lifetime dieting, lots of women actually look forward to it). And, in fact, gaining the right amount of weight is vital when you're growing a baby. But what is the right amount of weight? How much is too much? How much is too little? How fast should you gain it all? And will you be able to lose it all once your baby's delivered? (Answer: yes—if you gain the right amount of weight at the right rate on the right type of foods.)

How Much Should You Gain?

If there were ever a legitimate reason to pile on the pounds, pregnancy is it. After all, when you grow a baby, you've got to do some growing, too. But piling on too many pounds can spell problems for you, your baby, and your pregnancy. Ditto if you pile on too few pounds.

What's the perfect pregnancy weight gain formula? Actually, since every pregnant woman—and every pregnant body—is different, that formula can vary a lot. Just how many pounds you should aim on adding dur-

ing your 40 weeks of baby growing will depend on how many pounds you were packing before you became pregnant.

Your practitioner will recommend the weight gain target that's right for you and your pregnancy situation (and that's the guideline to follow, no matter what you read here). Generally, weight gain recommendations are based on your prepregnancy BMI (a measurement of body fat calculated by multiplying your weight in pounds by 703, then dividing by your height in inches squared; see *What to Expect: Eating Well When You're Expecting* for a chart). If your BMI is average (between 18.5 and 26), you'll probably be advised to gain between 25 and 35 pounds, the standard recommendation for the average-weight pregnant woman. If you start out pregnancy overweight (BMI between 26 and 29), your goal will be somewhat scaled back—to somewhere between 15 and 25 pounds. If you're obese (with a BMI greater than 29), you'll likely be told to tally a total of between 11 and 20 pounds, or perhaps even less than that. Super skinny (with a BMI of less than 18.5)? Chances are your target will be higher than average—upward of 28 to 40 pounds. For moms providing room and board for more than one, extra babies require extra pounds (see page 407).

It's one thing to set an ideal weight gain goal; it's another thing to get there. That's because ideals aren't always completely compatible with reality. Piling on the right number of pounds isn't just about piling the right amount of food on your plate. There are other factors at work, too. Your metabolism, your genes, your level of activity, your pregnancy symptoms (the heartburn and nausea that make eating too much like hard work; those cravings for high-calorie foods that make gaining too much too easy)—all play a role in helping you (or keeping you from) packing on the perfect pregnancy poundage. With that in mind, keep an eye on the scale to ensure that you're reaching your weight gain target.

At What Rate Should You Gain?

Slow and steady doesn't only win the race—it's a winner when it comes to pregnancy weight gain, too. A gradual weight gain is best for your body and your baby's body. In fact, the rate at which weight is gained is as important as the total number of pounds you gain. That's because your baby needs a steady supply of nutrients and calories during his or her stay in your womb—

deliveries that come in fits and spurts won't cut it once your little one starts doing some significant growing (as will happen during the second and third trimesters). A well-paced weight gain will also do your body good, allowing it to gradually adjust to the increased poundage (and the physical strains that come with it). Gradual gain also allows for gradual skin stretching (think fewer stretch marks). Need more convincing? Pounds put on at a slow and steady rate will come off more easily when the time comes (after you've delivered and you're anxious to get back to your prepregnancy shape).

Does steady mean spreading out those 30 pounds or so evenly over 40 weeks? No—even if that were a possible plan, it wouldn't be the best one. During the first trimester, your baby is only the size of a few poppy seeds, which means that eating for two doesn't require extra eating at all, and only a minimum of weight gain. A good goal for trimester 1 is between 2 and 4

Why More (or Less) Weight Gain Isn't More

What do you have to lose by gaining too much weight when you're expecting? Packing on too many pounds can present a variety of problems in your pregnancy. More padding can make assessing and measuring your baby more difficult, and added pounds can add to pregnancy discomforts (from backache and varicose veins to fatigue and heartburn). Gaining too much weight can also increase your risk of preterm labor, of developing gestational diabetes or hypertension, of ending up with an oversize baby that may be too large to deliver vaginally, of postcesarean complications, of a host of problems for your newborn, and of having

more trouble with breastfeeding. Not surprisingly, too, those extra pounds may be extra hard to shed postpartum—and, in fact, many women who gain too much weight during pregnancy end up never shedding them all.

Gaining too little weight can also be a losing proposition during pregnancy, and in some cases it can be more dangerous than gaining too much. Babies whose mothers gain under 20 pounds are more likely to be premature, small for their gestational age, and to suffer growth restriction in the uterus. (The exception: very overweight women, who can safely gain less than 20 pounds under close medical supervision.)

Breakdown of Your Weight Gain

(All weights are approximate)

Baby	7½ pounds
Placenta	1½ pounds
Amniotic fluid	2 pounds
Uterine enlargement	2 pounds
Maternal breast tissue	2 pounds
Maternal blood volume	4 pounds
Fluids in maternal tissue	4 pounds
Maternal fat stores	7 pounds
Total average	**30 pounds overall weight gain**

month when ever-tighter abdominal quarters can make finding room for food a struggle.

How closely will you be able to follow this rate of gain formula? Realistically, not that closely. There will be weeks when your appetite will rule and your self-control will waver, and it'll be a rocky road (by the half-gallon) to your weight gain total. And there will be weeks when eating will seem too much of an effort (especially when tummy troubles send whatever you eat right back up). Not to worry or stress over the scale. As long as your overall gain is on target and your rate averages out to that model formula (a half pound one week, 2 pounds the next, 1 the following, and so on), you're right on track.

So for best weight gain results, keep your eye on the scale, since what you don't know can throw your weight gain way off target. Weigh yourself (at the same time of day, wearing the same amount of clothes, on the same scale) once a week (more often and you'll drive yourself crazy with day-to-day fluid fluctuations). If once a week is too much (because you're scale-phobic),

pounds—though many women don't end up gaining any at all or even losing a few (thanks to nausea and vomiting), and some gain somewhat more (often because their queasiness is comforted only by starchy, high-calorie foods), and that's fine, too. For those who start slowly, it should be easy to play weight gain catch-up during the next six months (especially once food starts tasting and smelling good again); for those who begin gangbusters, watching the scale a little more closely in the second and third trimester will keep their total close to target.

During the second trimester, your baby starts to grow in earnest—and so should you. Your weight gain should pick up to an average rate of about 1 to 1½ pounds per week during months 4 through 6 (totaling 12 to 14 pounds). During your final trimester, baby's weight gain will pick up steam, but yours may start to taper off to about a pound a week (for a net gain of about 8 to 10 pounds). Some women find their weight holding steady—or even dropping a pound or two—during the ninth

Weight Gain Red Flags

If you gain more than 3 pounds in any one week in the second trimester, or if you gain more than 2 pounds in any week in the third trimester, especially if it doesn't seem to be related to overeating or excessive intake of sodium, check with your practitioner. Check, too, if you gain no weight for more than two weeks in a row during the fourth to eighth months.

twice a month should do the trick. Waiting until your monthly prenatal is fine, too—though keep in mind that a lot can happen in a month (as in 10 pounds) or not happen (as in no pounds), making it harder for you to stay on track.

If you find that your weight gain has strayed significantly from what you and your practitioner planned (for instance, you gained 14 pounds in the first trimester instead of 3 or 4, or you packed on 20 pounds in the second instead of 12), take action to see that the gain gets back on a sensible track, but don't try to stop it in its tracks. Dieting to lose weight is never appropriate when you're pregnant, and neither is using appetite-suppressing drinks or pills (these can actually be very dangerous). Instead, with your practitioner's help, readjust your goal to include the excess you've already gained and to accommodate the weight you still have to gain.

The
Third
Month

Approximately 9 to 13 Weeks

A S YOU ENTER THE LAST MONTH of your first trimester (great!), many of those early pregnancy symptoms are probably still going strong (not so great!). Which means it's probably hard to tell whether you're exhausted because of first-trimester fatigue—or because you woke up three times last night to go the bathroom (it's likely a little of both). But chin up, if you have the strength to lift it. There are better days ahead. If morning sickness has had you—and your appetite— down, there's a less queasy day soon to dawn. As energy levels pick up, you'll soon have more get-up-and-go—and as urinary urges ease, you may have to get up and go less often. Even better, you may hear the amazing sound of your baby's heartbeat at this month's checkup, which might make all those uncomfortable symptoms seem much more worthwhile.

Your Baby This Month

Week 9 Your baby (who has officially graduated now from embryo to fetus) has grown to approximately 1 inch in length, about the size of a medium green olive. His or her head is continuing to develop and take on more baby-like proportions. This week, tiny muscles are starting to form. This will allow your fetus to move his or her arms and legs, though it'll be at least another month before you'll be able to feel those little punches and kicks.

While it's way too early to feel anything, it's not too early to hear something (possibly). The glorious sound of your baby's heartbeat might be audible via a Doppler device at your practitioner's office. Take a listen—it's sure to make your heart beat a little faster.

Your Baby, Month 3

istics by now, with hands and feet in the front of the body, ears nearly in their final shape (if not final location), open nasal passages on the tip of the nose, a tongue and palate in the mouth, and visible nipples.

Week 10 At nearly 1½ inches long (about the size of a prune), your baby is growing by leaps and bounds. And in gearing up for those first leaps and bounds (and baby steps), bones and cartilage are forming—and small indentations on the legs are developing into knees and ankles. Even more unbelievably for someone the size of a prune, the elbows on baby's arms are already working. Tiny buds of baby teeth are forming under the gums. Further down, the stomach is producing digestive juices, the kidneys are producing larger quantities of urine, and, if your baby's a boy, his testes are producing testosterone (boys will be boys—even this early on!).

Week 11 Your baby is just over 2 inches long now and weighs about a third of an ounce. His or her body is straightening out and the torso is lengthening. Hair follicles are forming, and fingernail and toenail beds are beginning to develop (nails will actually start to grow within the next few weeks). Those nails are forming on individual fingers and toes, having separated recently from the webbed hands and feet of just a few weeks ago. And though you can't tell baby's gender by looking yet (even with an ultrasound), ovaries are developing if it's a girl. What you would be able to see, if your womb had a view, is that your fetus has distinct human character-

Week 12 Your baby has more than doubled in size during the past three weeks, weighing in now at ½ ounce and measuring (crown to rump) about 2½ inches. About the size of a large fresh plum, your baby's body is hard at work in the development department. Though most of his or her systems are fully formed, there's still plenty of maturing to do. The digestive system is beginning to practice contraction movements (so your baby will be able to eat), the bone marrow is making white blood cells (so your baby will be able to fight off all those germs passed around the playgroup), and the pituitary gland at the base of the brain has started producing hormones (so your baby will one day be able to make babies of his or her own).

Week 13 As your first trimester comes to a close, your fetus (who seems to be working its way through the produce section) has reached the size of a peach, about 3 inches long. Your baby's head is now about half the size of his or her crown to rump length, but that cute little body is picking up steam and will continue growing overtime (at birth, your baby will be one-quarter head, three-quarters body). Meanwhile, your baby's intestines, which have been growing inside the umbilical cord, are now starting their trek to their permanent position in your baby's abdomen. Also developing this week: your baby's vocal cords (the better to cry with . . . soon!).

What You May Be Feeling

As always, remember that every pregnancy and every woman is different. You may experience all of these symptoms at one time or another, or only a few of them. Some may have continued from last month; others may be new. Still others may be hardly noticed because you've become so used to them. You may also have other, less common, symptoms. Here's what you might experience this month:

Physically

- Fatigue, lack of energy, sleepiness
- Frequent urination

A Look Inside

This month, your uterus is a little bigger than a grapefruit and your waist may start to thicken. By the end of the month, your uterus can be felt right above your pubic bone in the lower abdomen.

- Nausea, with or without vomiting
- Excess saliva
- Constipation
- Heartburn, indigestion, flatulence, bloating
- Food aversions and cravings
- Increasing appetite, especially if morning sickness is easing
- Breast changes: fullness, heaviness, tenderness, tingling; darkening of the areolas (the pigmented area around your nipples); lubrication glands in the areolas becoming prominent, like large goose bumps; expanding network of bluish lines under your skin
- Visible veins on your abdomen, legs, and elsewhere, as your blood supply pumps up
- Slight increase in vaginal discharge
- Occasional headaches
- Occasional faintness or dizziness
- A little more rounding of your belly; your clothes feeling a little snugger

Emotionally

- Continued emotional ups and downs, which may include mood swings, irritability, irrationality, weepiness
- Misgivings, fear, joy, elation—any or all
- A new sense of calm
- Still, a sense of unreality about the pregnancy ("Is there really a baby in there?")

What You Can Expect at This Month's Checkup

This month, you can expect your practitioner to check the following, though there may be variations depending on your particular needs and your practitioner's style of practice:

- Weight and blood pressure

- Urine, for sugar and protein

- Fetal heartbeat

- Size of uterus, by external palpation (feeling from the outside), to see how it correlates to due date

- Height of fundus (the top of the uterus)

- Hands and feet for swelling, and legs for varicose veins

- Questions or problems you want to discuss—have a list ready

What You May Be Wondering About

Constipation

"I've been terribly constipated for the past few weeks. Is this common?"

Irregularity—that bloated, gassy, clogged-up feeling—is a very regular pregnancy complaint. And there are good reasons why. For one, the high levels of progesterone circulating in your expectant system cause the smooth muscles of the large bowel to relax, making them sluggish—and allowing food to hang around longer in the digestive tract. The upside: There's added time for nutrients to be absorbed into your bloodstream, allowing more of them to reach your baby. The downside: You end up with what amounts to a waste-product traffic jam, with nothing going anywhere anytime soon. Another reason for the clogged-up works: Your growing uterus puts pressure on the bowel, cramping its normal activity. So much for the process of elimination, at least as you once knew it.

But you don't have to accept constipation as inevitable just because you're pregnant. Try these measures to com-

bat your colon congestion (and head off hemorrhoids, a common companion of constipation):

Fight back with fiber. You—and your colon—need about 25 to 35 grams of fiber daily. No need to actually keep count. Just focus on fiber-rich selections such as fresh fruit and vegetables (raw or lightly cooked, with skin left on when possible); whole-grain cereals and bread; legumes (beans and peas); and dried or freeze-dried fruit. Going for the green can also help get things going—look for it not only in the form of green vegetables, but in the juicy, sweet kiwi, a tiny fruit that packs a potent laxative effect. If you've never been a big fiber fan, add these foods to your diet gradually or you may find your digestive tract protesting loudly. (But since flatulence is a common complaint of pregnancy as well as a frequent, but usually temporary, side effect of a newly fiber-infused diet, you may find your digestive tract protesting for a while anyway.)

Really plugged up? You can try adding some wheat bran or psyllium

Another Reason for Being Tired, Moody, and Constipated

Have you been tired, moody, and constipated lately? Welcome to the pregnancy club. Surging gestational hormones, of course, trigger those pesky symptoms in most pregnant women. However, a shortage of another hormone, thyroxine, can mimic these common pregnancy complaints, as well as many others—weight gain, skin problems of all kinds, muscle aches and cramps, a decrease in libido, memory loss, and swelling—especially of the hands and feet. (Another common symptom, an increased sensitivity to cold, is more clear-cut during pregnancy, since expectant moms tend to be warmer rather than chillier.) Consequently, hypothyroidism (a deficiency of the thyroid hormone due to an underactive thyroid gland) may be easy for physicians to miss in an expectant mom. Yet the condition, which affects 1 in 50 women, can have an adverse effect on pregnancy (also wreaking havoc in the postpartum period; see page 460), so proper diagnosis and treatment are vital.

Hyperthyroidism (when too much thyroid hormone is produced by an overactive gland) is seen less often in pregnancy, but it can also cause complications if left untreated. Symptoms of hyperthyroidism—many of which may also be hard to distinguish from pregnancy symptoms—include fatigue, insomnia, irritability, warm skin and sensitivity to heat, rapid heartbeat, and weight loss (or trouble gaining weight).

If you have ever been diagnosed with any thyroid problems in the past (even if they have since cleared up) or if you currently take medication for a thyroid condition, be sure to let your practitioner know. Because the body's need for thyroid hormone fluctuates during pregnancy, it's possible you may need medication again or need your dose adjusted (see page 531).

If you have never been diagnosed with a thyroid condition, but you're experiencing some or all of the symptoms of hypo- or hyperthyroidism (and especially if you have a family history of thyroid disease), check with your doctor. A simple blood test can determine whether you have a thyroid problem.

---

to your diet, starting with a sprinkle and working your way up, as needed. Don't overdo these fiber powerhouses, though; as they move speedily through your system, they can carry away important nutrients before they've had the chance to be absorbed.

Resist the refined. While high-fiber foods can keep things moving, refined foods can clog things up. So steer clear of the refiner things in life, such as white bread (and other baked goods) and white rice.

Drown your opponent. Constipation doesn't stand a chance against an ample fluid intake. Most fluids—particularly water and fruit and vegetable juices—are effective in softening stool and keeping food moving along the digestive tract. Another time-honored way to get things moving: Turn to warm liquids, including that spa staple, hot water and lemon. They'll help stimulate peristalsis, those intestinal contractions that help you go. Truly tough cases may benefit from that geriatric favorite, prune juice.

When you gotta go, go. Holding in bowel movements regularly can weaken muscles that control them and lead to constipation. Timing can help avoid this problem. For example, have your high-fiber breakfast a little earlier than usual, so it will have a chance to kick in before you leave the house—instead of when you're in the car stuck in traffic.

Don't max out at mealtime. Big meals can overtax your digestive tract, leading to more congestion. Opt for six mini meals a day over three large ones—you'll also experience less gas and bloating.

Check your supplements and medications. Ironically, many of the supplements that do a pregnant body good (prenatal vitamins, calcium, and iron supplements) can also contribute to constipation. Ditto every pregnant woman's best buddy, antacids. So talk to your practitioner about possible alternatives or adjustments in dosages or, in the case of supplements, switching to a slow-release formula. Also ask your practitioner about magnesium supplements that may help fight constipation.

Get some bacteria. Probiotics (aka "good bacteria") may stimulate the intestinal bacteria to break down food better, aiding the digestive tract in its efforts to keep things moving. Enjoy probiotics in yogurt and yogurt drinks that contain active cultures. You can also ask your practitioner to recommend a probiotic supplement—in powder form, it can be easily added to smoothies (and it has no taste of its own).

Get some exercise. An active body encourages active bowels, so fit a brisk walk of about half an hour into your daily routine (some people find even a 10-minute walk works); supplement it with any exercise you enjoy that is safe during pregnancy (see page 224).

If your efforts don't seem to be productive, consult with your practitioner. He or she may prescribe a bulk-forming stool softener for occasional use. Don't use any laxative (including herbal remedies or castor oil) unless your practitioner specifically recommends it.

Lack of Constipation

"All my pregnant friends seem to have problems with constipation. I don't—in fact, I've remained very regular. Is my system working right?"

From the sound of things, your system couldn't be working better. Chances are your digestive efficiency is attributable to your lifestyle—one you've been enjoying for a long while or one you've adopted since you learned you were expecting. Stepped-up consumption of fiber-rich foods and fluids, along with regular exercise, are bound to counteract the natural digestive slowdown of pregnancy and keep things moving smoothly. If this dietary style is new to you, the productivity of your digestive tract may decrease a little (and flatulence, which often temporarily accompanies such dietary changes, may ease up) as your system gets used to the rough stuff, but you will probably continue to be "regular."

Diarrhea

"I'm not at all constipated. In fact, for the last couple of weeks I've had loose stools—almost diarrhea. Is this normal?"

When it comes to pregnancy symptoms, normal is often what's normal for you. And in your case, more frequent, looser stools may be just that. Every body reacts differently to pregnancy hormones—yours may be reacting by stepping up, not slowing down, on production of bowel movements. It's also possible that this increased bowel activity is due to a positive change in your diet and exercise habits.

You can try cutting back on bowel-stimulating foods, such as dried fruits, and adding bulking foods (such as bananas) until your stool becomes more firm. To compensate for the fluids you're losing through loose stools, make sure you're drinking enough.

If your stools are very frequent (more than three a day) or watery, bloody, or mucousy, check with your practitioner; this kind of diarrhea could require prompt intervention during pregnancy.

Gas

"I'm very bloated and I'm passing gas all the time. Will it be like this the whole pregnancy?"

Are you passing gas like a college frat boy (make that *more* than a college frat boy)? Sorry, guys, but nobody does gas like a pregnant woman. Fortunately, while the same can't be said for those who work and live within hearing and sniffing distance of you, your baby is oblivious and impervious to your digestive distress. Snug and safe in a uterine cocoon that's protected on all sides by impact-absorbing amniotic fluid, he or she is probably soothed by the bubbling and gurgling of your gastric Muzak.

Baby won't be happy, though, if bloating—which often worsens late in the day and, yes, generally persists throughout pregnancy—prevents you from eating regularly and well. To cut down on the sounds and smells from down under and to make sure your nutritional intake doesn't suffer on account of your intestinal outtakes, take the following measures:

Stay regular. Constipation is a common cause of gas and bloating. See the tips on page 173.

Graze, don't gorge. Large meals just add to that bloated feeling. They also overload your digestive system, which isn't at its most efficient anyway in pregnancy. Instead of those two or three supersize squares, nibble on six mini meals.

Don't gulp. When you rush through meals or eat on the fly, you're bound to swallow as much air as food. This captured air forms painful pockets of gas in your gut, which will seek release the only way they know how.

Keep calm. Particularly during meals. Tension and anxiety can cause you to swallow air, which can give you a full tank of gas. Taking a few deep breaths before meals may help relax you.

Steer clear of gas producers. Your tummy will tell you what they are—they vary from person to person. Common offenders include onions, cabbage, fried foods, rich sauces, sugary sweets, carbonated beverages, and, of course, the notorious beans.

Don't be quick to pop. Ask your practitioner before popping your usual anti-gas medications (some are safe, others are not recommended) or any remedy, over-the-counter or herbal. Sipping a little chamomile tea, however, may safely soothe all kinds of pregnancy-induced indigestion. Ditto for hot water with lemon, which can cut through gas as well as any medication.

Headaches

"I find that I'm getting a lot more headaches than ever before. Can I take something for them?"

That women are more susceptible to headaches during the time they're

What's a Corpus Luteum Cyst?

If your practitioner has told you that you have a corpus luteum cyst, your first question will probably be—what is it? Well, here's all you need to know. Every month of your reproductive life, a small yellowish body of cells forms after you ovulate. Called a corpus luteum (literally "yellow body"), it occupies the space in the follicle formerly occupied by the egg. The corpus luteum produces progesterone and some estrogen, and it is programmed by nature to disintegrate in about 14 days. When it does, diminishing hormone levels trigger your period. When you become pregnant, the corpus luteum hangs around instead of disintegrating, continuing to grow and produce enough hormones to nourish and support your baby-to-be until the placenta takes over. In most pregnancies, the corpus luteum starts to shrink about six or seven weeks after the last menstrual period and stops functioning altogether at about 10 weeks, when its work of providing board for the baby is done. But in about 10 percent of pregnancies, the corpus luteum doesn't regress when it's supposed to. Instead, it develops into a corpus luteum cyst.

So now that you know what a corpus luteum cyst is, you're probably wondering—how will it affect my pregnancy? The answer: probably not at all. The cyst is usually nothing to worry about—or do anything about. Chances are it will go away by itself in the second trimester. But just to be sure, your practitioner will keep an eye on your cyst's size and condition regularly via ultrasound (which means you get extra peeks at your baby).

supposed to stay away from certain pain relievers is one of the ironies of pregnancy. It's an irony you'll have to live with, but it's not necessarily one you'll have to suffer with—at least, not too much. Prevention, teamed with the right remedies (medicinal and non), can offer relief from the normal recurrent headaches of pregnancy.

The best route to headache relief depends on the cause or causes. Pregnancy headaches are most commonly the result of hormonal changes (which are responsible for the increased frequency and severity of many types of headaches, including sinus headaches), fatigue, tension, hunger, physical or emotional stress, or any combination of these.

There are plenty of ways around a headache (and some surprisingly effective ones don't come in capsule form). In many cases you'll be able to fit the probable cause with the possible cure:

Relax. Pregnancy can be a time of high anxiety, with tension headaches a common result. Some women find relief through meditation and yoga (which also makes a fabulous pregnancy exercise). You can take a class, turn to a DVD or CD, read a book on these or other relaxation techniques, or try the one on page 142.

Of course, relaxation exercises don't work for everyone; some women find that they step up tension instead of easing it. If that sounds like you, lying down in a dark, quiet room or stretching out on the sofa or with your feet up on your desk for 10 or 15 minutes may be a better foil for tension and tension headaches.

Get enough rest. Pregnancy can also be a time of extreme fatigue, particularly in the first and last trimesters, and often for the full nine months for women who work long hours at a job and/or have other children to care for. Sleep can be elusive once the belly starts swelling ("How will I ever get comfortable?") and the mind starts racing ("How will I ever get everything done before the baby comes?"), which compounds fatigue. Making a conscious effort to get more rest, day and night, can help keep headaches at bay. But be careful not to sleep too much—excess sleep can also give you a headache, as can sleeping with the covers over your head.

Eat regularly. To avoid hunger headaches triggered by low blood sugar, be sure not to run on empty. Carry high-energy snacks (such as soy chips, granola bars, dried fruit and nuts) with you in your bag, stash them in the glove compartment of your car and in your office desk drawer, and always keep a supply on hand at home.

Seek some peace and quiet. Noise can give you a headache, especially if you're extra sound-sensitive. Make it a point to avoid noisy locales (the mall, loud parties, restaurants with bad acoustics). If your job is extra noisy, talk to your boss about taking steps to reduce the excess noise—or even ask for a transfer to a quieter area, if possible. At home, lower the volume on the telephone's ringer, the TV, and the radio.

Don't get stuffy. An overheated room or unventilated space can give anyone a headache—but especially an expectant mom, who's overheated to start with. So try not to get stuffy, but when you can't avoid it (it's two days before Christmas and you have to brave that jam-packed mall—or you work there), step out for a stroll and a breath of fresh air when you can. Dress in layers when you know you're going somewhere stuffy, and keep comfortable (and hopefully, headache free) by removing layers as needed. Stuck inside? Try to crack a window, at least.

Switch lighting. Take the time to examine your surroundings, particularly the lighting around you, in a whole new . . . well, light. Some women find that a windowless work space lit by fluorescent bulbs can trigger headaches. Switching to incandescent lighting and/or a room with windows may help. If that's not practical, take outdoor breaks when you can.

Try alternatives. Some complementary and alternative medical approaches—including acupuncture, acupressure, biofeedback, and massage—can bring headache relief (see page 85).

Go hot and cold. For relief of sinus headaches, apply hot and cold compresses to the aching area, alternating 30 seconds of each for a total of 10 minutes, four times a day. For tension headaches, try ice applied to the back of the neck for 20 minutes while you close your eyes and relax. (Use an ordinary ice pack or a special neck pillow that holds a gel-based cold pack.)

Straighten up. Slouching or looking down to read or do other close work (knitting baby booties?) for long stretches of time can also trigger an aching head, so watch your posture.

Take two. Haven't got time for the pain? Acetaminophen (Tylenol) usually brings quick relief and is considered safe for pregnancy use (skip the ibuprofen and aspirin). Check with your practitioner for the right dosage and headache protocol. And don't take any pain medication (over-the-counter, prescription, or herbal) without your practitioner's okay.

If an unexplained headache persists for more than a few hours, returns very often, is the result of fever, or is accompanied by visual disturbances or puffiness of the hands and face, notify your practitioner.

"I suffer from migraine headaches. I heard they're more common in pregnancy. Is this true?"

Some women find their migraines strike more frequently during pregnancy; luckier ones find they are less frequent. It isn't known why this should be true, or even why some people have recurrent migraines and others never have a single one.

If you've had migraines in the past, discuss with your physician which migraine medications are safe to take during pregnancy so you'll be prepared for dealing with these killer headaches should they strike while you're expecting. Think prevention, too. If you know what brings on an attack, you can try to avoid the culprit. Stress is a common one, as are chocolate, cheese, and coffee. Try to determine what, if anything, can stave off a full-blown attack once the warning signs appear. You may be helped by one or more of the following: splashing your face with cold water or applying a cold cloth or ice pack; avoiding noise, light, and odors by lying down in a darkened room for two or three hours, eyes covered (napping, meditating, or listening to music, but not reading or watching TV); or trying CAM techniques such as biofeedback or acupuncture (see page 85).

Stretch Marks

"I'm afraid I'm going to get stretch marks. Can they be prevented?"

Nobody likes stretch marks, especially come skin-baring season. Still, they're not easy to escape when you're expecting. The majority of pregnant women develop these pink or reddish (sometimes purplish), slightly indented, sometimes itchy streaks on their breasts, hips, and/or abdomen sometime during pregnancy.

As their name implies, stretch marks are caused by tiny tears in the supporting layers of tissue under your skin as it becomes stretched to its limit. Expectant mothers who have good elastic skin tone (because they inherited it and/or earned it through years of excellent nutrition and exercise) may slip through several pregnancies without a single telltale mark. And actually, your mother may be your best crystal ball when it comes to predicting whether you'll end up with stretch marks or not; if she sailed through her pregnancies with smooth skin intact, odds are you will, too. If stretch marks struck her, they'll likely strike you, too.

You might be able to minimize, if not prevent, stretch marks by keeping weight gain steady, gradual, and moderate (the faster skin stretches, the more likely the stretching is to leave its mark). Promoting elasticity in your skin by nourishing it with a good diet (especially those vitamin C foods) may also help. And though no topical preparation has been proven to prevent stretch marks from zigzagging their way across your skin, there's no harm in applying moisturizers, such as cocoa butter. Even without the scientific proof to back them up, some women swear they work—and if nothing else, they'll prevent the dryness and itching associated with pregnancy-stretched skin. An added plus: It may be fun for your spouse to rub them on your tummy (and baby will enjoy the massage, too).

If you do develop stretch marks (frequently referred to as the red badge of motherhood), you can console yourself

Body Art for Two?

Heading off to The House of Ink for a "hot mama" tattoo? Think before you ink. While the ink itself won't enter your bloodstream, there is a risk of infection any time you get stuck with a needle, and why take that risk when you've got a baby on board?

Something else to ponder before getting a tattoo for two. What looks symmetrical on your pregnant skin might become lopsided or distorted after you regain your prepregnancy shape. So keep your skin free of any new marks for now, and wait until after you've weaned your baby to express yourself through body art.

If you already have a tattoo, no problem—just sit back and watch it stretch. And don't worry about that lower back tattoo and how it might affect the epidural you were hoping for come labor day. As long as the tattoo ink is fully dried and the wound healed, sticking that epidural needle through it won't be risky.

What about using henna to decorate your body during pregnancy? Since henna is plant based—and temporary—it's probably safe to use during pregnancy. Still, it's wise to follow certain caveats: Make sure the henna artist uses natural henna (it stains the skin reddish brown), not the kind that contains the potentially irritating chemical paraphenylendiamine (which stains black), and check the artist's references (read: no fair doing it at a street fair). To be extra-cautious (always the best way to be), ask your practitioner before using henna.

Keep in mind, too, that pregnant skin is often extra-sensitive skin, so there's a chance you'll have an allergic reaction to the henna, even if you've had it applied before without incident. To test your reaction to it, place a small amount of henna on a patch of skin and wait 24 hours to make sure no irritation appears.

---

with the knowledge that they will gradually fade to a silvery sheen some months after delivery. You can also discuss with a dermatologist the possibility of reducing their visibility postpartum with laser therapy or Retin-A. In the meantime, wear them with pride.

First-Trimester Weight Gain

"I'm nearing the end of the first trimester and I'm surprised that I didn't gain any weight yet."

Many women have trouble putting on an ounce in the early weeks—some even lose a few pounds, usually courtesy of morning sickness,

and others, because they started out overweight, don't need to gain any this early on. Fortunately, nature has your baby's back, offering protection even if you're too queasy or food-averse to eat. Tiny fetuses have tiny nutritional needs, which means that your lack of weight gain now won't have any effect on your baby. Not so, however, once you enter the second trimester. As your baby gets bigger and your baby-making factory picks up steam, calories and nutrients will be more and more in demand—and you'll need to begin playing weight gain catch-up, piling the pounds on at a steady pace.

So definitely don't worry, but do start eating (hopefully any morning sickness will ease up soon). And from the fourth month on, start watching your weight to make sure it begins to move upward at the appropriate rate (see page 167). If you continue to have trouble gaining weight, try packing more of a nutritional wallop with the calories you take in, through efficient eating (see page 91). Try, too, to eat a little more food each day, by not skipping meals and by adding more frequent snacks. If you can't eat a lot at one sitting (which isn't so good for pregnancy digestion anyway), graze on six small meals daily instead of three big squares. Save salads and soups and fill-you-up beverages for after your main course to avoid putting a damper on your appetite. Enjoy foods high in good fats (nuts, seeds, avocados, olive oil). But don't try to add pounds by adding lots of junk food to your diet. That kind of weight gain is more likely to round out your hips and thighs than your baby.

"I'm 12 weeks pregnant and I was shocked to find out that I'd already gained 13 pounds. What should I do now?"

First of all, don't panic. Lots of women have that "oops" moment—when they step on the scale at the end of their first trimester and discover they've gained 8, 10, a dozen pounds, or more in three short months. Sometimes it's because they've taken "eating for two" just a tad too literally (you are eating for two, but one of you is really, really small), relishing sweet release from a lifetime of dieting. Sometimes it's because they've found that comfort from queasiness can come in high-calorie packages (ice cream, pasta, burgers, or just bread by the loaf). Either way, all is not lost if you've gained a little too much in the first trimester. True, you can't turn back the scales—or apply the first three months' gain neatly to the next six. Your baby needs a steady supply of nutrients (espe-

cially in the second and third trimester, when he or she will be growing over-time), so cutting way back on calories now isn't a smart plan. But you can aim to keep your gain on target for the rest of your pregnancy—to slow it down, without putting the brakes on it alto-gether—by watching the scale (and what you eat) more carefully.

Check with your practitioner and work out a safe and sensible weight gain goal for the next two trimesters. Even if you stay in the pound-a-week club through month 8 (most women find their weight gain slows or stops in the ninth month), you won't end up more than a couple of pounds over 35 pounds, the outside limit for recommended weight gain. Check out the Pregnancy Diet (Chapter 5) to find out how to eat healthily for two without ending up looking like two (of you). Gaining effi-ciently, on the highest-quality foods pos-sible, will not only accomplish that goal but make the weight you do gain easier to shed in the postpartum period.

Boys Will Be Boys

Hungry, Mom? As you close in on your second trimes-ter, you'll likely notice that your appetite (which you may have lost somewhere around week 6 or so) is starting to make a comeback. But if you're bellying up to the refrigera-tor with the regularity of a teenage boy, you may be expecting one (or, at least, a male fetus on his way to becoming a teenage boy). Research shows that moms-to-be carrying boys tend to eat more than moms expecting girls—which could explain why boys tend to be heavier at birth than girls. Food (and more food) for thought!

Showing Early

"Why am I already showing if I'm only in my first trimester?"

Have lots more to show for your first trimester than you expected? Because every belly's different, some stay flat far into the second trimester while others seem to pop before the home pregnancy test is dry. An early bump can be disconcerting ("If I'm this big *now,* what will I look like in a few months?"), but it can also be welcome, tangible proof that there's actually a baby in there.

Several possibilities might explain why you're showing so early:

- Small build. If you're slender to begin with, your growing uterus may have nowhere to hide, causing a bulge even when it's still relatively little.

- Less muscle tone. A pregnant woman with loose abdominal muscles is more likely to produce a pronounced pooch faster than a mom-to-be with a taut and toned torso. That's why second timers tend to show earlier—their abdominal muscles have already been stretched.

- Overeating. If you've been eating for two (but forgetting that one of those two is only prune-sized right now), your belly might be sporting more fat than baby. If you've gained more than 4 or 5 pounds by this point, that could explain your prematurely protruding tummy.

- Wrong dates. A sooner-than-expected show time could be the result of a miscalculated conception date.

- Bloating. Excess gas and bloating could be behind that supersize stomach of yours. So could bowel distention if you've been going long stretches between movements.

- More than one on board. Some women who sport an impressive bump in their first trimester later discover they're having twins. But before you start doubling up the layette, keep in mind that most women whose bellies balloon early turn out to be carrying just one baby. A relatively round belly in the first trimester is not generally considered a reliable sign that an expectant mother is carrying multiples (see next question).

Carrying Multiples?

"How will my doctor know if I'm carrying twins or not?"

Have a hunch that there's more than one baby on board? There are plenty of clues you can look for when trying to determine whether or not you're toting twins:

A large-for-date uterus. The size of the uterus, not of the abdomen, is what counts in the diagnosis of multiples. If your uterus seems to be growing more rapidly than expected for your due date, a multiple pregnancy might be suspected. A big belly alone doesn't count.

Exaggerated pregnancy symptoms. When carrying twins, the typical troubles of pregnancy (morning sickness, indigestion, and so on) can be doubled, or at least seem that way. But all of these can also be exaggerated in a one-fetus pregnancy.

Predisposition. Several factors make a woman more likely to have nonidentical, or fraternal, twins. These include nonidentical twins in the mother's family, advanced age (women over 35 more frequently release more than one egg at a time), the use of fertility drugs to stimulate ovulation, and in vitro fertilization. Some evidence indicates that identical twins might also be genetically influenced (something in your egg or your spouse's sperm could cause a fertilized egg to split).

As for your practitioner, he or she might try to listen for two (or more) distinctly separate heartbeats, but it's not an exact science (the heartbeat of a single fetus may be heard at several locations), so twins aren't often diagnosed this way. The best diagnostic tool for detecting multiples is an early ultrasound. In virtually every case (except in the rare instance where one camera-shy fetus remains stubbornly hidden behind the other), this technique accurately diagnoses a multiple pregnancy. If you are carrying twins (or more), see Chapter 16.

Baby's Heartbeat

"My friend heard her baby's heartbeat at 10 weeks. I'm a week ahead of her, and my doctor hasn't picked up my baby's yet."

Hearing the first lub-dub of your baby's heartbeat is definitely music to every mom-to-be's (and dad-to-be's) ears. Even if you've already seen your little one's steady drumbeat on an early ultrasound, there's nothing like hearing it through the Doppler (a handheld ultrasound device that amplifies the sound with the help of a special jelly on the belly) in your practitioner's office.

Even though a heartbeat can be heard as early as the 10th or 12th week with a Doppler, not all expectant moms get to feast their ears on this fetal symphony that early. Your baby's position may be the cause of the inaudible heartbeat, or maybe the location of the placenta (or extra fat padding your belly) is muffling the sound. A slightly miscalculated due date may also explain why you're not hearing your baby's beat yet. By your 14th week, the miraculous sound of your baby's heartbeat is certain to be available for your listening pleasure. If it isn't, or if you are very anxious, your practitioner will likely do

At-Home Dopplers

Tempted to buy one of those inexpensive prenatal "heart listeners" so you can stay tuned in to your baby's heartbeat between practitioner visits? Being able to monitor your baby's heart rate can be loads of fun and may even help you have a better night's sleep if you're a stresser by nature. But listen to this: Though these devices are considered safe to use, they're not as sophisticated as the one your practitioner uses—and most aren't nearly sensitive enough to pick up fetal heart tones until after the fifth month of pregnancy. Use one before then, and you'll likely be met with silence instead of a steady beat, which can increase worry unnecessarily

instead of putting it to rest. Even later on in pregnancy, at-home Dopplers can't always pick up what you're looking for (baby's position or a bad angle on the device can easily throw off an at-home Doppler). The readings might not be accurate, either—or might be different enough from the ones you're used to getting at your checkups to prompt undue concern. So do try this at home, if you like (though you should get your practitioner's okay before placing your order, especially because the FDA requires a prescription for them). Just keep in mind that you get what you pay for, and you might get somewhat less than you bargained for.

The Heart of the Matter

Is it a boy or a girl, and can your baby's heart rate give you a clue? While old wives—and some practitioners—have been telling tales for ages (a heart rate of above 140 promises a girl, one under 140 delivers a boy), studies show no correlation between fetal heart rate and gender. It may be fun to make predictions based on your baby's heart rate (you'll be right 50 percent of the time, after all), but you might not want to make nursery color choices based on it.

an ultrasound, which will see a heartbeat that, for some reason, was difficult to hear with the Doppler.

When you do get to hear the heartbeat, listen carefully. Your normal heart rate is usually under 100 beats per minute, but your baby's will be around 110 to 160 beats per minute during early pregnancy and average between 120 and 160 beats per minute by midpregnancy. Don't compare fetal heartbeats with your pregnant friends, though—every baby beats to his or her own drummer, and normal fetal heart rates vary a lot.

Starting at about 18 to 20 weeks, the heartbeat can be heard without Doppler amplification, using a regular stethoscope.

Sexual Desire

"All of my pregnant friends say that they had an increased sex drive early in pregnancy. How come I feel so unsexy?"

Pregnancy is a time of change in many aspects of your life, not the least of them sexual. Hormones, which, as you've undoubtedly noticed, play a role in every physical and emotional high and low, also play an important role in sexuality. But those hormones hit every woman differently, turning up the heat for some and throwing ice water on others. Some women who have never had either an orgasm or much of a taste for sex suddenly experience both for the first time when they're expecting. Other women, accustomed to having a voracious appetite for sex and to being easily orgasmic, suddenly find that they're completely lacking in desire and are difficult to arouse. And even if your hormones have pushed your passion turn-on button, pregnancy symptoms (that nausea, that fatigue, those painfully tender breasts) can stand between you and a good time. These changes in sexuality can be disconcerting, guilt-provoking, wonderful, or a confusing combination of all three. And they are all perfectly normal.

Most important is recognizing that your sexual feelings during pregnancy—and your partner's as well—may be more erratic than erotic; you may feel sexy one day and not the next. Mutual understanding and open communication will see you through, as will a sense of humor. And remember (and remind your partner) that many women who've lost that loving feeling in the first trimester get it back in the second, in spades, so don't be surprised if a very warm front moves into your bedroom soon. Until then, you might want to try the tips on the next page to help heat things up.

"Ever since I became pregnant, I'm turned on all the time and I can't get enough of sex. Is this normal?"

Feeling a little hot under the collar (and under those very snug jeans)? Is your turn-on switch always on? Lucky you. While some women find their sex lives coming to a screeching halt in the first trimester (what with all those early pregnancy symptoms kicking their libidos out the bedroom door), others—like you—find they just can't get enough of a good thing. You can thank those extra hormones surging through your body these days, as well as the increase in blood flow to your pelvic region (which can make your genitals feel wonderfully engorged and ever-tingly), for turning up the sexual thermostat. On top (so to speak) of that are the new curves you're sprouting and the bigger-than-life breasts you're likely sporting, all of which can make you feel like one sexy mama. Plus, it might be the first time in your sexual life that you're able to make love when the mood moves you—without having to spoil the moment while you run to the bathroom for your diaphragm or calculate your fertility with an ovulation predictor. This happy state of sensual affairs may be most pronounced during the first trimester, when hormonal havoc is at its height, or it can continue right up until delivery day.

Since your increased sexual appetite is perfectly normal (as is a lack of sexual desire), don't worry or feel guilty about it. And don't be surprised or concerned if your orgasms are more frequent or more intense than ever (and if you're having orgasms for the first time, that's even more reason to celebrate). As long as your practitioner has green-lighted lovemaking in all its forms (and that's usually the case), seize the moment and your partner. Explore different positions before that belly of yours makes many of them a physical impossibility. And most of all, enjoy that cozy twosome while you can (and before that libido of yours takes its very likely postpartum nosedive).

"I'm interested in sex all the time, but my husband's never in the mood these days. I'm starting to take it personally."

What's putting your man off his favorite feed now that there's a bun in the oven? There are several possible explanations. One could be fear—of hurting you or hurting the baby (even though he can't). Another could be the weirdness factor of making love "in front of" the baby—or the nagging thought that the baby can see or feel his penis when it's inside you (which, by the way, is giving himself way too much credit). Maybe he's having a tricky time getting used to the changes in your body or adjusting to the idea that you're about to become somebody's mother. Or maybe he's just so focused on becoming a father that being a lover has taken a back seat. There might even be a physical trigger: Expectant and new fathers often experience a drop in testosterone and a surge in female hormones that can give their libidos a cold shower.

No matter what's causing your husband to run for cover every time he spies you with "that look," don't take it personally. But also don't resign yourself to a nine-month dry spell. Instead, initiate some frank pillow talk. Tell him how you're feeling (all revved up and no place to go), and find out what's going on in his head (which can explain what's not going on below his belt). Have him read the section on sex starting on page 255, as well as Chapter 19, which will reassure him that sex is perfectly safe in a normal pregnancy and that babies are completely oblivious to parental goings-on and gettings-it-on (and completely out of reach, even for the particularly gifted dad). Be understanding and patient if he has baggage he needs to unpack before you hit the sack again. Honest, open communication will allow the two of you to come to a meeting of the minds—and hopefully, a meeting of the bodies.

And don't just passively wait for love (and him) to land in your lap. Turn up his heat with some naughty lingerie that accentuates all your new (and dangerous) curves, add some mood lighting and music, and offer up a massage (complete with scented oils). If that just makes him feel more uncomfortable (and more pressured to perform), take the opposite tack. Cozy up on the sofa for some cuddling instead. Perhaps when the pressure's off, he might feel inspired to jump on the jumping-you bandwagon.

Cramp After Orgasm

"I get a cramp in my abdomen after orgasm. Is that normal, or does it mean something's wrong?"

Not to worry—and not to stop enjoying sex, either. Cramping (sometimes accompanied by lower backache)—both during and after orgasm—is common and harmless during a low-risk pregnancy. Its cause can be physical: a combination of the normal increased blood flow to the pelvic area during pregnancy, the equally normal congestion of the sexual organs during arousal and orgasm, and the normal contractions of the uterus following orgasm. Or it can be psychological: a result of the common, but unfounded, fear of hurting the baby during sex. Or it can be a combination of physical and psychological factors, since the mind-body connection is so strong when it comes to sex.

In other words, that cramping isn't a sign that you're hurting your baby while you're enjoying yourself. In fact, unless your practitioner has advised you otherwise, it's perfectly safe to mix the pleasure of sex and the business of making a baby. If the cramps bother you, ask your partner for a gentle low back rub. It may relieve not only the cramps but any tension that might be triggering them. Some women also experience leg cramps after they have sex; see page 271 for tips on relieving those.

ALL ABOUT
Pregnant on the Job

If you're pregnant, you've already got your work cut out for you. Add a full-time job to the full-time job of baby making, and your workload doubles. Juggling it all—practitioner visits with client meetings, trips to the bathroom with trips to the mailroom, morning sickness with business lunches, telling your best friend in accounting (who'll be excited for you) with telling your boss (who might not be), staying healthy and comfortable with staying motivated and successful, preparing for baby's arrival with preparing for maternity leave—can be a 9-to-5 challenge that keeps you working overtime. Here's some help for the pregnant and employed.

When to Tell the Boss

Wondering when to belly up to your boss's desk to spill the pregnancy beans? There's no universally perfect time (though it's a sure bet you should do it before that bump gets noticeably big). A lot will depend on how family friendly (or unfriendly) your workplace is. Still more will depend on your feelings (the physical and emotional). Here are some factors to consider:

The Pregnant Worker's Rights

There is much room for improvement in the U.S. workplace when it comes to families and their needs. Though individual policies vary from company to company, here's what federal law recognizes:

- The Pregnancy Discrimination Act of 1978. This act prohibits discrimination based on pregnancy, childbirth, or related medical conditions. Under this law, employers must treat you as they would treat any employee with a medical disability. However, it does not protect you if you end up not being able to do the job you were hired to do.

    It is considered discriminatory—and illegal—to pass up a woman for a promotion or a job or fire her solely on the basis of her pregnancy. But this kind of discrimination, like all kinds of discrimination, can be difficult to prove. Complaints of pregnancy discrimination can be reported to the U.S. Equal Employment Opportunity Commission (EEOC), (800) 669-4000; eeoc.gov.

- The Family and Medical Leave Act (FMLA) of 1993. All public agencies and private-sector companies that employ at least 50 workers within a 75-mile radius of each other are subject to regulation under this act. If you have worked for such a company for at least a year (and at least 1,250 hours during the year),

you are entitled to take up to 12 weeks of unpaid leave during your pregnancy and for a child's (or other member of your family's) illness each year that you are employed. Barring unforeseen complications or early delivery, you must notify your employer of your leave 30 days in advance. During your leave, you must continue to collect all benefits (including health insurance), and when you return, you must be restored to an equivalent position with equal pay and benefits. Keep in mind, too, that you can use FMLA for weeks during your pregnancy if you're not feeling well. (In some cases, companies may be able to exclude from FMLA women who are considered key employees—those the company can't do without for 12 weeks and who are in the top 10 percent compensation bracket.) The Wage and Hour Division of the U.S. Department of Labor can offer information on FMLA. For more help, contact them at (800) 827-5335; or go online to dol.gov.

- State and local laws. Some state and local laws offer additional protection against pregnancy discrimination. A very small handful of states and some larger companies also offer "temporary disability insurance," which allows for partial wages during time off for medical disabilities, including pregnancy.

How you're feeling and whether you're showing. If morning sickness has you spending more time hovering over the toilet than sitting at your desk; if first-trimester fatigue has you barely able to lift your head off your pillow in the morning; or if you're already packing a paunch that's too big to blame on your breakfast, you probably won't be able to keep your secret long. In that case, telling sooner makes more sense than waiting until your boss (and everyone else in the office) has come to his or her own conclusions. If, on the other hand, you're feeling fine and still zipping your pants up with ease, you may be able to hold off on the announcement until later.

What kind of work you do. If you work under conditions or with substances that could be harmful to your pregnancy or your baby, you'll need to make your announcement—and ask for a transfer or change of duties, if at all feasible—as soon as possible.

How work is going. A woman announcing her pregnancy at work may unfortunately—and unfairly—raise many red flags, including, "Will she still have the stamina to produce while pregnant?" and "Will her mind be on work or on her baby?" and "Will she leave us in the lurch?" You may head off some of those concerns by making your announcement just after finishing a report, scoring a deal, ringing up record sales, coming up with a great idea, or otherwise proving that you can be both pregnant and productive.

Whether reviews are coming up. If you're afraid your announcement might influence the results of an upcoming performance or salary review, wait until the results are in before sharing your news. Keep in mind that proving you've been passed up for a promotion or raise based solely on the fact that you're expecting (and that you'll soon be a worker and a mother, not necessarily in that order) may be difficult.

Whether you work in a gossip mill. If gossip is one of your company's chief products, be especially wary. Should word of mouth of your pregnancy reach your boss's ears before your announcement does, you'll have trust issues to deal with in addition to the pregnancy-related ones. Make sure that your boss is the first

to know—or, at least, that those you tell first can be trusted not to squeal.

What the family-friendliness quotient is. Try to gauge your employer's attitude toward pregnancy and family if you're not sure what it is. Ask other women who have walked in your soon-to-be-swollen footsteps before, if there are any (but keep inquiries discreet). Check the policies on maternity leave in your copy of the employee handbook that's been gathering dust on your desk. Or set up a confidential meeting with someone in human resources or the person in charge of benefits. If the company has had a history of being supportive of mothers and mothers-to-be, you may be inclined to make the announcement sooner. Either way, you'll have a better sense of what you'll be facing.

Making the Announcement

Once you've decided when to make your announcement, you can take some steps to ensure that it's well received:

Prepare yourself. Before you break the news, do your research. Learn everything you need to know about your employer's maternity-leave policies. Some companies offer paid leave, others unpaid. Still others allow you to use sick days or vacation days as part of your leave.

Know your rights. Pregnant women—and parents in general—have fewer rights in the United States than in most every other industrialized country. Still, some baby steps have been made on behalf of expectant workers on the federal level through the Pregnancy Discrimination Act and the Family and Medical Leave Act (see box, page 187) and on the state level (many states have

The Juggling Act

Even if you don't have any kids at home yet, staying on the job while you're expecting will require that you practice the fine art of juggling work and family (or, at least, a family-to-be). Especially during the first trimester and the last, when the symptoms of pregnancy may be dragging you down and the distractions of pregnancy may be competing for your attention, this juggling act may be exhausting, and sometimes overwhelming—in other words, good preparation for the years of working and parenting you may have ahead of you. These tips won't make working simultaneously at those two jobs easier, but they may help make your working life work more smoothly with your making-a-baby life:

- Schedule smart. Make appointments for checkups, ultrasounds, blood tests, glucose tolerance tests, and other procedures before your workday begins (you may be too tired afterward) or during your lunch break. If you need to leave work in the middle of the day, explain to your boss that you have a doctor's appointment, and keep a log of these visits (just in case anyone accuses you of slacking off). If necessary, request a note from your practitioner verifying your appointment, and give this to your employer or someone in your human resources department.

- Remember not to forget. If your brain cells seem to be dropping like flies, you can blame your hormones—and start taking precautions so your pregnancy-impaired memory doesn't get you into workplace hot water. To ensure that you don't forget that meeting, that lunch date, those calls that had to be made by noon: Make lists, write yourself reminders (Post-its are a pregnant worker's best friend), and keep your cell phone or tablet handy (if you can remember where you put it).

- Know your limits and stop before you reach them. This isn't the time to volunteer to take on extra projects or extra hours unless it's absolutely necessary. Focus on what needs to be done—and realistically can be done—without wearing yourself out. To avoid feeling overwhelmed, complete one task at a time.

- Just say "yes." If colleagues offer to help out when you're not feeling well, don't hesitate to take them up on their kindness (maybe you can return the favor someday). And attention all expectant micromanagers: If there was ever a time to learn how to delegate, this would be it.

- Recharge as needed. When you find yourself emotionally overwhelmed, and you will (a stuck stapler can start the tears flowing when you're pregnant), take a brief walk, a bathroom break, or some relaxation breaths to clear your head. Or indulge in a private moment of mom-to-be madness—you deserve it.

- Speak up. Not only are you only human, but you're human and pregnant. Which means you can't do it all and do it all well—especially if you feel crappy, as you will sometimes feel. If you can barely lift your head off your pillow (or leave the bathroom for more than five minutes) and you've got a pile of stuff on your desk or a major deadline looming, don't panic. Tell your boss you need extra time or extra help. And don't beat yourself up—or let anyone else beat you up. You're not lazy or incompetent, you're pregnant.

equal employment opportunity laws that protect against pregnancy discrimination). Many other big steps have been taken voluntarily by forward-thinking, family-friendly companies. Become familiar with what the law says you're entitled to, so you'll know what you can and probably can't ask for.

Put together a plan. Efficiency is always appreciated on the job, and being prepared invariably impresses people. So before you go in to make your announcement, prepare a detailed plan that includes how long you plan to stay on the job (barring any unforeseen medical problems), how long your maternity leave will be, how you plan to finish up business before you leave, and how you propose that any unfinished business be handled by others. If you would like to return part-time at first, propose that now. Writing up your plan will ensure you won't forget the details, plus it'll score you extra efficiency points.

Set aside the time. Don't try to tell your boss the news when you're in a taxi on the way to a meeting or when he or she's got one foot out the door Friday night. Make an appointment to meet, so no one will be rushed or distracted. Try to make it on a day and at a time that is usually less stressful at your office. Postpone the meeting if things suddenly take a turn for the tense.

Accentuate the positive. Don't start your announcement with apologies or misgivings. Instead, let your boss know that you are not only happy about your pregnancy but confident in your ability and committed in your plan to mix work and family.

Be flexible (but not spineless). Have your plan in place, and open it up to discussion. Then be ready to compromise (make sure there is room for negotiation built into your plan) but not to back

down completely. Come up with a realistic bottom line and stick with it.

Set it in writing. Once you've worked out the details of your pregnancy protocol and your maternity leave, confirm it in writing so there won't be any confusion or misunderstanding later (as in "I never said that . . .").

Never underestimate the power of parents. If your company is not as family friendly as you'd like, consider joining forces to petition for better parental perks. Realize, however, that you and other parents may be met with hostility by childless employees; as family policies become more generous, resentment tends to build among those who can't take advantage of them. Making sure that similar allowances are made for employees who must take time off to care for sick spouses or parents may help unite, rather than divide, the company.

Staying Comfortable on the Job

Between nausea and fatigue, backaches and headaches, puffy ankles and a leaky bladder, it's hard for any expectant mom to have a completely comfortable day. Put her at a desk or on her swollen feet or at a job that requires bending or lifting and you've got a recipe for even more pregnancy discomfort. To stay as comfortable as possible on the job when you're expecting, try these tips:

- Dress for success and comfort. Avoid tight, restrictive clothing, socks or knee-highs that cut off circulation, as well as heels that are too high or too flat (wide 2-inch heels are best). Wearing support hose designed for pregnancy will help ward off or minimize a variety of symptoms, from

Carpal Tunnel Syndrome

If you spend your day (and maybe your nights, too) tap-tap-tapping on a keyboard, you may already be familiar with the symptoms of carpal tunnel syndrome (CTS). A well-known worker's malady, CTS causes pain, tingling, and numbness in the hands and most often strikes those who spend a lot of time doing repetitive tasks (typing, punching numbers, working a Blackberry). What you might not know, however, is that CTS affects the majority of pregnant women. Even moms-to-be who never touch a computer keyboard are prone to it, thanks to swollen tissue in the body that presses on nerves. The good news is that carpal tunnel syndrome is not dangerous—just uncomfortable, especially on the job. Even better, you can try a number of remedies until you see the light at the end of the carpal tunnel:

- Raise your office chair so your wrists are straight and your hands are lower than your elbows as you type.

- Switch to a wrist-friendly ergonomic keyboard (one that has a wrist rest) as well as a mouse that offers wrist support.

- Wear a wrist brace while typing.

- Take frequent breaks from the computer.

- Use a speakerphone or headset if you're on the phone a lot.

- In the evenings, soak your hands in cool water to reduce any swelling.

- Ask your practitioner about other possible remedies, including vitamin B_6 supplements, acupuncture, or pain relievers.

swelling to varicose veins, and may be especially important if you're spending a lot of the day on your feet.

- Watch the weather—inside you. No matter the climate in your city (or your office), when you're pregnant, the forecast is for wildly swinging body temperatures. Sweating one minute and chilly the next, you'll want to favor the layered look—and have a layer ready for every possible condition. Thinking of bundling up in a wool turtleneck to brave a 12°F day? Don't do it unless you've got a lightweight layer underneath that you can strip down to when a hormone-driven heat wave starts burning inside. And even if you're usually toasty in just a tee, stash a sweater in your drawer or locker. Your body temp goes both ways fast these days.

- Stay off your feet—at least as much as possible. If your job demands that you stand for long stretches, take sitting or walking breaks. If possible, keep one foot on a low stool, knee bent, while you stand, to take some of the pressure off your back. Switch feet regularly. Flex them periodically, too.

- Put your feet up. Find a box, a wastebasket, or another sturdy object on which to discreetly rest your weary feet under your desk.

- Take a break. Often. Stand up and walk around if you've been sitting; sit down with your feet up if you've been standing. If there's a spare sofa and a slot in your schedule, lie down for a few minutes. Do some stretching exercises, especially for your back, legs, and neck. At least once (or even twice) every hour, do this 30-second stretch:

Raise your arms above your head, clasp your fingers, palms up, and reach up. Next, place your hands on a desk or table, step back a bit, and stretch out your back. Sit down and rotate your feet in both directions. If you can bend over and touch your toes—even from a seated position—go for it to release the tension in your neck and shoulders.

- Adjust your chair. Back hurt? Slip on a lumbar cushion for extra support. Bottom sore? Slide a soft pillow onto your seat. If your chair reclines, consider setting it back a few notches to create more (and more!) space between your belly and your desk.

- Hang out by the water cooler. Not for the latest gossip (though that certainly can be a perk) but for frequent refills of your cup. Or keep a refillable water bottle at your desk. Drinking at least 64 ounces of water a day can keep many troublesome pregnancy symptoms at bay, including excessive swelling, and may help prevent a UTI.

- Don't hold it in. Emptying your bladder as needed (but at least every two hours) also helps prevent UTIs. A good strategy: Plan to pee every hour or so, whether you need to or not. You'll feel better overall if you avoid getting to the bursting point. (Now's not the time to have to sprint to the bathroom.)

- Take time for your tummy. Every expectant mom's job description includes feeding her baby regularly, no matter what else is on her workday agenda. So plan accordingly—making room in even your busiest days for three meals, plus at least two snacks (or five to six mini meals). Scheduling meetings as working meals (and trying to have some say about what's served) may help. So will keeping a supply of nutritious snacks in your desk and your purse, as well as in the office fridge, if there is one. Rediscover brown bags—they're not particularly glam, but they can keep you and baby fed when time's not on your side.

- Keep an eye on the scale. Make sure job stress—or erratic eating—isn't keeping you from gaining enough or is contributing to excess weight gain (as it can for stress eaters, especially if they work near a vending machine or another easy junk food outlet).

- Pack a toothbrush. If you're suffering from morning sickness, brushing your teeth can protect them between bouts of vomiting—plus it helps freshen up your breath when it most needs freshening. Mouthwash will also be a welcome addition to the breath-freshening team, and it can help dry out a mouth that's full of excess saliva (which is common in the first trimester and can be extra embarrassing at work).

- Lift with care. Do any necessary lifting properly, to avoid strain on the back (see page 237).

- Watch what you breathe. Stay out of smoke-filled areas; not only is smoke bad for you and your baby, it can also increase fatigue.

- Take an occasional chill pill. Too much stress isn't good for you or your baby. So try to use breaks to relax as fully as you can: Bring an iPod so you can listen to music; close your eyes and meditate or indulge in some daydreaming; do some soothing stretches; take a five-minute stroll around the building.

- Listen to your body. Slow down your pace if you're feeling tired; go home early if you're exhausted (and can leave).

Staying Safe on the Job

Most jobs are completely compatible with the job of feeding and caring for an unborn baby, which is very good news to the millions of expectant mothers who must manage to work full time at both occupations. Still, some jobs are obviously safer and better suited to pregnant women than others. Most on-the-job problems can be avoided with the right precautions or a modification of duties (check with your practitioner for other workplace recommendations in your case):

Office work. Anyone with a desk job knows the pain of stiff necks, aching backs, and headaches, all of which can make a pregnant woman feel more uncomfortable than she already is. No harm done to baby—but a lot of wear and tear on your achy expectant body. If you spend a lot of time sitting, be sure to stand up, stretch, and walk away from your desk frequently. Stretch your arms,

Quiet, Please

By about 24 weeks, your baby's outer, middle, and inner ear are well developed. By 27 to 30 weeks, your baby's ear is mature enough to start to respond to the sounds that filter through to him or her. The sounds, of course, are muffled—and not just by the physical barrier of amniotic fluid and your own body. In his or her fluid-filled home, a baby's eardrum and middle ear can't do their normal job of amplifying sounds. So even sounds that are quite loud to you won't be for the baby.

Still, since noise is one of the most prevalent of all occupational hazards and has long been known to cause hearing loss in those (adults) exposed to it regularly, you might want to play it safe when it comes to excessive noise during pregnancy. That's because studies suggest that *prolonged* and *repeated* exposure to very loud noise raises the odds of a baby suffering some hearing loss, especially at lower frequencies. Such prolonged noise exposure—say, an eight-hour-a-day shift in an industrial workplace, where the sound level is more than 90 or 100 decibels (about the same as standing next to a loud lawn mower or a chain saw)—can also

increase the risk of premature delivery and low-birthweight babies. Extremely intense sound, 150 or 155 decibels (ever stand right next to a screaming jet engine?), can cause similar problems for the baby. Generally, it's safest to avoid more than eight hours of continuous exposure to noises louder than 85 or 90 decibels (such as a lawn mower or truck traffic) and more than two hours a day of exposure to noise louder than 100 decibels (such as that from a chain saw, pneumatic drill, or snowmobile).

More research needs to be done, but in the meantime, expectant mothers who work in an extremely noisy environment—such as a club where loud music is played, in a subway, or in a factory where protective hearing devices are required (you can't put these devices on your fetus)—or who are exposed to heavy vibrations on the job should play it safe and seek a temporary transfer or a new job. And try to avoid prolonged exposure to very loud noises in your everyday life: Listen to the concert from the middle of the amphitheater, or better yet, head back to the lawn seats; turn down the volume in your car; and wear headphones instead of blasting the music while you're vacuuming.

neck, and shoulders while sitting in your chair, put your feet up to reduce swelling (your boss may not appreciate your tootsies on the desk, so rest your feet on a low stool or box instead), and support your back with a cushion.

What about computer safety? Luckily, computer monitors are not a hazard to pregnant women, and neither are laptops. More worrisome is the multitude of physical discomforts, including wrist and arm strain, dizziness, and headaches, that can result from too much time spent in front of the computer. For fewer aches and pains, use a height-adjustable chair with a backrest that supports your lower back. Adjust the monitor to a comfortable height; the top should be level with your eyes and about an arm's length away from you. Use an ergonomic keyboard, designed to reduce the risk of carpal tunnel syndrome (see box, page 191), if possible, and/or a wrist rest. When you put your hands on the keyboard, they should be lower than your elbows and your forearms should be parallel to the floor.

Health care work. Staying healthy is every health care professional's top on-the-job priority, but it ranks even higher when you're staying healthy for two. Among the potential risks you'll need to protect yourself and your baby from are exposure to chemicals (such as ethylene oxide and formaldehyde) used for sterilization of equipment; to some anticancer drugs; to infections, such as hepatitis B and AIDS; and to ionizing radiation (such as that used in diagnosis or treatment of disease). Most technicians working with low-dose diagnostic X-rays are not exposed to dangerous levels of radiation. It is recommended, however, that women of childbearing age working with higher-dose radiation wear a special device that keeps track of daily exposure, to ensure that cumulative annual exposure does not exceed safe levels.

Depending on the particular risk you are exposed to, you might want to either take safety precautions as recommended by NIOSH (see box) or switch to safer work for now.

Manufacturing work. If you have a factory or manufacturing job that has you operating heavy or dangerous machinery, talk to your boss about a change of duties while you're pregnant. You can also contact the machinery's manufacturer (ask for the corporate medical director) for more information about the product's safety. How safe conditions are in a factory depends on what's being

---

Getting All the Facts

By law, you have the right to know what chemicals you are exposed to on the job; your employer is obliged to tell you. The Occupational Safety and Health Administration (OSHA) is the regulatory body that monitors those laws. Contact them for more information on your rights regarding workplace safety: (800) 321-OSHA—(800) 321-6742; osha .gov. Further information on workplace hazards can also be obtained by contacting the National Institute for Occupational Safety and Health (NIOSH), Clearinghouse for Occupational Safety and Health Information, (800) CDC-INFO—(800) 232-4636; cdc.gov/niosh/topics/repro.

If your job does expose you to hazards, either ask to be transferred temporarily to a safer post or, finances and company policy permitting, begin your maternity leave early.

made in it and, to a certain extent, on how responsible and responsive the people who run it are. OSHA lists a number of substances that a pregnant woman should avoid on the job. Where proper safety protocols are implemented, exposure to such toxins can be avoided. Your union or other labor organization may be able to help you determine if you are properly protected. You can also get useful information from NIOSH or OSHA (see box, facing page).

Physically strenuous work. Work that involves heavy lifting, physical exertion, long hours, rotating shifts, or continuous standing may somewhat increase a woman's risk for preterm delivery. If you have such a job, you should request a transfer, by 20 to 28 weeks, to a less strenuous position until after delivery and postpartum recovery. (See page 196 for recommendations on how long it is safe for you to stay at various strenuous jobs during your pregnancy.)

Emotionally stressful work. The extreme stress in some workplaces seems to take its toll on workers in general and on pregnant women in particular. So it makes sense to cut down on the stress in your life as much as possible, especially now. One obvious way to do that is to switch to a job that is less stressful or take early maternity leave. But these approaches aren't feasible for everyone; if the job is critical financially or professionally, you may find yourself even more stressed if you leave it.

You might, instead, consider ways of reducing stress, including meditation and deep breathing, regular exercise (to release those feel-good endorphins), and having more fun (seeing a movie instead of working until 10 P.M.). Talking to your employer, explaining that overtime, overwork, and general stress could affect your pregnancy, may help, too. Explain that being allowed to set your

own pace at work may make your pregnancy more comfortable (this kind of stress seems to increase the risk of backaches and other painful pregnancy side effects) and help you do a better job. If you're self-employed, cutting back may be even tougher (you're probably your own most demanding boss), but it's something you'd be wise to consider.

Other work. Teachers and social workers who deal with young children may come into contact with infections that can potentially affect pregnancy, such as chicken pox, fifth disease, and CMV. Animal handlers, meat cutters, and meat inspectors may be exposed to toxoplasmosis (but some may well have developed immunity already, in which case their babies would not be at risk). If you work where infection is a risk, be sure you're immunized as needed and take appropriate precautions, such as washing hands frequently and thoroughly, wearing protective gloves, a mask, and so on.

Flight attendants or pilots may be at a slightly higher risk for miscarriage or preterm labor (though studies are inconclusive) due to exposure to radiation from the sun during high-altitude flights, and they might want to consider switching to shorter routes (they're usually flown at lower altitudes and require less standing time) or to ground work during pregnancy.

Artists, photographers, chemists, cosmeticians, dry cleaners, those in the leather industry, agricultural and horticultural workers, and others may be exposed to a variety of possibly hazardous chemicals in the course of work, so be sure to wear gloves and other protective gear. If you work with any suspect substances, take appropriate precautions, which in some cases may mean avoiding the part of the job that involves the use of chemicals.

Staying on the Job

Planning to work until that first contraction hits? Many women successfully mix business with baby making right through the ninth month, without compromising the well-being of either occupation. Still, some jobs are better suited to pregnant women during the long haul (so to speak) than other jobs. And chances are, the decision of whether you'll continue to work until delivery will have at least something to do with the kind of work you're involved in. If you have a desk job, you can probably plan to go straight from the office to the birthing room. A sedentary job that isn't particularly stressful may actually be less of a strain on both you and baby than staying at home with a vacuum cleaner and mop, trying to tidy up the nest for your new arrival. And some walking—an hour or two daily, on the job or off—is not only harmless but beneficial (assuming you aren't carrying heavy loads as you go).

Jobs that are strenuous, very stressful, and/or involve a great deal of standing, however, may be another, somewhat controversial, matter. One study found that women who were on their feet 65 hours a week didn't seem to have any more pregnancy complications than women who worked many fewer and usually less stressful hours. Other studies, however, suggest that steady strenuous or stressful activity or long hours of standing after the 28th week—particularly if the expectant mother also has other children to care for at home—may increase the risk of certain complications, including premature labor, high blood pressure, and a low-birthweight baby.

Should women who stand on the job—salespeople, chefs and other restaurant workers, police officers, doctors, nurses, and so on—work past the 28th week? Most practitioners give the green light to work longer if a woman feels fine and her pregnancy is progressing normally. Standing on the job all the way to term, however, may not be a good idea, less because of the theoretical risk to the pregnancy than the real risk that such pregnancy discomforts as backache, varicose veins, and hemorrhoids will be aggravated.

It's probably a good idea to take early leave, if possible, from a job that requires frequent shift changes (which can upset appetite and sleep routines, and worsen fatigue); one that seems to exacerbate any pregnancy problems, such as headache, backache, or fatigue; or one that increases the risk of falls or other accidental injuries. But the bottom line: Every pregnancy, every woman, and every job is different. Together with your practitioner, you can make the decision that's right for your situation.

Changing Jobs

With all the changes going on in your life (like your growing belly and the ever-expanding responsibilities that come with it), it may seem counterintuitive to want to add another to your list. But there are dozens of valid reasons why an expectant mom might consider a job change. Maybe your employer isn't family friendly and you're concerned about balancing career and motherhood when you return from maternity leave. Maybe the commute is too long, the hours inflexible, or the grind all-consuming. It could be that you're bored or not fulfilled (and, hey—change is in the air anyway, so why not make the most of it?). Or perhaps you're worried that your current workplace might be hazardous to you and your developing baby. Whatever your reason, here are some things to consider before you make a job move:

■ Looking for work takes time, energy, and focus, three things you may be lacking these days as you concentrate on having a healthy pregnancy. Typically, you'll be asked to come in for several interviews and meetings before an offer is made (and if you're already suffering from pregnancy forgetfulness, forming the kind of sentences that make a good impression may be challenging). Starting a new job also demands a great deal of concentration (all eyes are on you, so you have to be extra careful not to make mistakes), and you should be certain you have the stamina and commitment to take these steps.

- Before you jump ship, you'll need to be sure the new job you're seeking out is really all it's cracked up to be (in your mind, at least). Does the company you're smitten with offer twice as much vacation time but charge double for health insurance? Do they allow people to work from home yet expect them to be on call morning, noon, and night? Are the salaries far higher and, likewise, the travel demands? Keep in mind that what looks like a great job now may not be so great when you're juggling it with new-baby care (your home life will be a lot more complicated, so you might not want your workplace life to be). Also bear in mind that companies often offer fewer paid short-term disability days or pay a lower percentage of your salary during leave if you have been employed for less than one year.

- By law, your potential employer has no right to ask whether you're pregnant (if it isn't already obvious), nor can he or she deny you an offer in light of the news. Still, some companies simply can't bring you on and let you leave so quickly. And not all employers appreciate what they consider to be a bait-and-switch strategy (you tell them you want to work there, then after you begin, you tell them you'll be

Unfair Treatment at Work

Think you're being treated unfairly on the job because of your pregnancy? Don't just sit there, do something. Let someone you trust—your supervisor, someone in human resources—know how you feel. If that doesn't fix the problem, see if there is a procedure for employees to follow in the case of pregnancy discrimination (you can probably find it in your employee handbook, if there is one). If that still doesn't work, contact the U.S. Equal Employment Opportunity Commission (eeoc.gov) to find your local office. They'll be able to help you determine if you have a legitimate complaint.

Remember to keep records of everything that'll bolster your claim (copies of e-mails, letters, a diary of events). This paper trail will also be helpful in case you ever need to contact an attorney.

out on maternity leave). So though it may be smart in the short run to keep your pregnancy a secret as you interview, it may damage your relationship with the company in the end. On the other hand, sometimes it's better to secure the offer first and then discuss the future once you know the company wants to hire you—but before you accept the position.

What if you started a new job before you found out you were pregnant? Be up front about what happened, and then get down to the business of doing your job to the best of your expectant ability. Just make sure you know your rights about job security should the situation take a negative turn.

The
Fourth
Month

Approximately 14 to 17 Weeks

F INALLY, THE BEGINNING OF THE second trimester—which, for many pregnant women, is the most comfortable of the three. And with the arrival of this momentous milestone (one down, two to go!) come some welcome changes. For one, most of the more pesky early pregnancy symptoms may be gradually easing up or even disappearing. That queasy cloud may be lifting (which means that food may actually smell and taste good for the first time in

a long time). Your energy level should be picking up (which means you'll finally be able pick yourself up off the sofa), and your visits to the bathroom should be dropping off. And though your breasts will likely still be super-size, they're less likely to be super-tender. Another change for the better: By the end of this month, the bulge in your lower abdomen may be looking less like the remains of a large lunch and more like the beginnings of a pregnant belly.

Your Baby This Month

Week 14 Beginning in the second trimester, fetuses (like the children they'll eventually become) start growing at different paces, some faster than oth-

ers, some more slowly. Despite the differences in growth rates, all babies in utero follow the same developmental path. This week, that path is leading your baby—who is about the size of your clenched fist—toward a straighter position as the neck is getting longer and the head more erect. And on top of that cute little head, your baby might actually be sprouting some hair.

Your Baby, Month 4

Eyebrow hair is also filling in about now, as is body hair, called lanugo. Don't worry, it's not permanent. This downy coating of hair is there to keep your baby warm for now—like a furry blanket. As baby fat accumulates later on in your pregnancy, most of that hair will be shed—though some babies, especially those born early, still have a temporary fuzzy coating at delivery.

Week 15 Your baby, who measures 4½ inches this week and weighs around 2 to 3 ounces, is about the size of a navel orange. Looking more and more like the baby you're picturing in your dreams, his or her ears are positioned properly on the sides of the head (they used to be in the neck), and the eyes are moving from the side of the head to the front of the face. By now your baby has the coordination, strength, and smarts to wiggle his or her fingers and toes and even suck a thumb. But that's not all your baby can do now. He or she can also breathe (or at least make breathing movements), suck, and swallow—all in preparation for the big debut and life outside the womb. And though it's unlikely that you'll be feeling any movements from your little one this week, your baby is certainly getting a workout—kicking, flexing, and moving those arms and legs.

Week 16 With a whopping weight of anywhere from 3 to 5 ounces and a length (crown to rump) of 4 to 5 inches, your baby is growing up fast. Muscles are getting stronger (you'll start to feel

movement in a few weeks), especially the back muscles, enabling your little one to straighten out even more. Your baby-to-be is looking more and more adorable, with a face that has eyes (complete with eyebrows and eyelashes) and ears in the right spots. What's more, those eyes are finally working! Yes, it's true: Your baby's eyes are making small side-to-side movements and can even perceive some light, though the eyelids are still sealed. Your baby is also becoming more sensitive to touch. In fact, he or she will even squirm if you poke your belly (though you probably won't be able to feel those squirms just yet).

Week 17 Take a look at your hand. Your baby is about palm-size now, with a crown-to-rump length of 5 inches and an approximate weight of 5 (or more) ounces. Body fat is beginning to form (baby's fat, that is, though yours is probably forming pretty quickly these days, too), but your little one is still quite skinny, with skin that is practically translucent. This week, your baby is all about practice, practice, practice in preparation for birth. One important skill your baby is sharpening now: sucking and swallowing—to get ready for that first (and second . . . and third) suckle at breast or bottle. Your baby's heart rate is regulated by the brain (no more spontaneous beats) and clocks in at 140 to 150 beats per minute (roughly twice your own heart rate).

More Baby

For week-by-week pics of your baby's amazing development, go to whattoexpect.com.

What You May Be Feeling

As always, remember that every woman and every pregnancy is different. You may experience all of these symptoms at one time or another, or only a few of them. Some may have continued from last month; others may be new. Still others may be hardly noticed because you've become so used to them. You may also have other, less common, symptoms. Here's what you might experience this month:

Physically

- Fatigue

- Decreasing urinary frequency

- An end to, or a decrease in, nausea and vomiting (for a few women, morning sickness will continue; for a very few, it is just beginning)

- Constipation

- Heartburn, indigestion, flatulence, bloating

- Continued breast enlargement, but usually decreased tenderness

- Occasional headaches

- Occasional faintness or dizziness, particularly with sudden change of position

- Nasal congestion and occasional nosebleeds; ear stuffiness

- Sensitive gums that may bleed when you brush

- Increased appetite

- Mild swelling of ankles and feet, and occasionally of hands and face

- Varicose veins of legs and/or hemorrhoids

- Slight increase in vaginal discharge

- Fetal movement near the end of the month (but usually not this early, unless this is your second or subsequent pregnancy)

Emotionally

- Mood swings, which may include irritability, irrationality, inexplicable weepiness

A Look Inside

Your uterus, now about the size of a small melon, has grown large enough to rise out of the pelvic cavity and by the end of the month, you'll be able to feel the top of it around 2 inches below your belly button (if you don't know what you're feeling for, ask your practitioner for some pointers at your next visit). If you haven't done so already, you'll probably begin to outgrow your regular clothes.

- Excitement and/or apprehension— if you have started to feel and look pregnant at last

- Frustration at being "in between"— your regular wardrobe doesn't fit anymore, but you're not looking pregnant enough for maternity clothes

- A feeling you're not quite together— you're scattered, forgetful, drop things, have trouble concentrating

What You Can Expect at This Month's Checkup

This month, you can expect your practitioner to check the following, though there may be variations depending on your particular needs and on your practitioner's style of practice:

- Weight and blood pressure

- Urine, for sugar and protein

- Fetal heartbeat

- Size of uterus, by external palpation (feeling from the outside)

- Height of fundus (top of the uterus)

- Hands and feet for swelling, and legs for varicose veins

- Symptoms you've been experiencing, especially unusual ones

- Questions or problems you want to discuss—have a list ready

What You May Be Wondering About

Dental Problems

"My mouth has suddenly become a disaster area. My gums bleed every time I brush, and I think I have a cavity. Is it safe to have dental work done?"

Smile—you're pregnant! But with so much of your attention centered on your belly during pregnancy, it's easy to overlook your mouth—until it starts screaming for equal time, as frequently happens during pregnancy. For starters, pregnancy hormones aren't kind to your gums—which, like your other mucous membranes, become swollen, inflamed, and tend to bleed easily. Those same hormones also make the gums more sus-

ceptible to plaque and bacteria, which can soon make matters worse in some women, possibly leading to gingivitis (inflammation of the gums) and even tooth decay.

To keep your mouth happy—and your smile safe—while you're growing a baby:

- Floss and brush regularly, and use toothpaste with fluoride for cavity protection. Brushing your tongue while you're at it will also help combat bacteria while keeping your breath fresher.

- Ask your dentist to recommend a rinse to reduce bacteria and plaque, protecting your gums and your teeth.

A Gum Alert

If it's not one thing in pregnancy, it's another. If you notice a nodule on the side of your gum that bleeds when you brush, get it checked out. It's most likely a canker sore or something called a pyogenic granuloma (also known by the ominous-sounding term "pregnancy tumor," despite the fact that it's perfectly harmless). More of a nuisance than anything else, such nodules usually regress on their own after delivery, but if it becomes very annoying before that, it can be removed by a doctor or dentist.

- When you can't brush after eating, chew a stick of sugarless gum (the action of chewing increases the amount of saliva, which rinses the teeth—and if the gum's sweetened with xylitol, chewing can actually help prevent decay). Or nibble on a chunk of hard cheese (it decreases the acidity in your mouth, and it's the acid that causes tooth decay).

- Watch what you eat, particularly between meals. Save sweets (particularly sticky ones) for times when you can brush soon after. Consume plenty of foods high in vitamin C, which strengthens gums, reducing the possibility of bleeding. Also be sure to fill your calcium requirements daily.

Pearly White Wisdom

Wondering if you can use teeth-whitening products while you're pregnant? Check out page 147 for the latest facts.

Calcium is needed throughout life to keep teeth strong and healthy.

- Whether or not you're experiencing dental discomfort, be sure to make an appointment with your dentist at least once during the nine months for a checkup and cleaning, preferably earlier than later. The cleaning is important to remove plaque, which can not only increase the risk of cavities but also make your gum problems worse (though hold off on any sealants until after pregnancy). Visit the periodontist if you've had gum problems in the past.

If you suspect a cavity or other tooth or gum trouble, make an appointment with your dentist or periodontist. Untreated gingivitis can develop into a more serious gum condition, periodontitis, which is associated with a variety of pregnancy complications. Decay that isn't cleaned up or other tooth issues that aren't tended to can also become a source of infection (and infection isn't good for you or your baby).

What happens if major dental work becomes necessary during pregnancy? Luckily, in most dental procedures, a local anesthetic will suffice, and that's safe. A low dose of nitrous oxide (laughing gas) is also safe to use after the first trimester, but more serious sedation should be avoided during pregnancy. In some cases, it may be necessary to take an antibiotic before or after major dental work; check with your practitioner.

Breathlessness

"Sometimes I feel a little breathless. Is this normal?"

Take a deep breath (if you can!) and relax. Mild breathlessness is normal, and many pregnant women experience it beginning in the second trimester.

Expecting X-Rays?

Routine dental X-rays (and other routine X-rays or CT scans) are usually postponed until after delivery, just to be on the extra-safe side. But if putting off dental (or other) X-rays during pregnancy just isn't a good idea (the risk of having one is outweighed by the risk of not having one), most practitioners will green-light the procedure. That's because the risks of X-rays during pregnancy are really very low and can be easily made even lower. Dental X-rays are targeted to your mouth, of course, which means the rays are directed far away from your uterus. What's more, a typical diagnostic X-ray of any kind rarely delivers more radiation than you'd get from spending a few days in the sun at the beach. Harm to a fetus, however, only occurs at very high doses, doses you're extremely unlikely to ever be exposed to. Still, if you do need an X-ray during pregnancy, keep the following guidelines in mind:

- Always inform the doctor ordering the X-ray and the technician performing it that you're pregnant, even if you're pretty sure they know.

- Have any necessary X-ray done in a licensed facility with well-trained technicians.

- The X-ray equipment should, when possible, be directed so that only the minimum area necessary is exposed to radiation. A lead apron should be used to shield your uterus and a thyroid collar should protect your neck.

- Follow the technician's directions precisely, being especially careful not to move while he or she is taking the picture, so retakes won't be needed.

Most important, if you had an X-ray before you found out you were pregnant, don't worry.

And, once again, you can blame your pregnancy hormones. Here's why: Those hormones stimulate the respiratory center to increase the frequency and depth of your breaths, giving you that out-of-breath feeling after nothing more strenuous than a trip to the bathroom. They also swell the capillaries in the body—including those of the respiratory tract—and relax the muscles of the lungs and bronchial tubes, making those breaths seem even harder to catch. Your uterus will also likely contribute to your breathlessness as pregnancy progresses, pushing up against your diaphragm as it grows, crowding your lungs and making it more difficult for them to expand fully.

Fortunately, though the mild breathlessness you're experiencing may make you feel uncomfortable, it doesn't affect your baby—who's kept well stocked with oxygen through the placenta. But if you're having a very hard time breathing, if your lips or fingertips seem to be turning bluish, or if you have chest pain and a rapid pulse, call your practitioner right away.

Nasal Stuffiness and Nosebleeds

"My nose has been stuffed up a lot, and sometimes it bleeds for no apparent reason. Is it pregnancy related?"

Your belly's not the only thing that's starting to swell these days. Thanks to the high levels of estrogen and progesterone circulating in your body, which bring with them increased blood flow, the mucous membranes of your nose start to swell, too, and soften (much as the cervix does in preparation for childbirth). Those membranes also produce more mucus than ever, with the intention of keeping infections and germs at bay. What's not so swell is the result—which your nose undoubtedly already knows: congestion, and possibly even nosebleeds. Also not so swell: The stuffiness may only get worse as your pregnancy progresses. You may develop postnasal drip, too, which in turn can occasionally cause coughing or gagging at night (as if you didn't have enough other things keeping you up—or enough gagging going on).

You can safely try saline sprays or nasal strips, especially if the congestion takes a turn for the truly uncomfortable. A humidifier in your room may also help overcome the dryness associated with any congestion. Medications or antihistamine nasal sprays are usually not prescribed during pregnancy, but do ask your practitioner what he or she recommends (some practitioners okay decongestants or steroid nasal sprays after the first trimester).

Taking an extra 250 mg of vitamin C (with your practitioner's okay), plus eating plenty of vitamin C–rich foods, may help strengthen your capillaries and reduce the chance of bleeding. Sometimes a nosebleed will follow overly energetic nose blowing, so easy does it.

To stem a nosebleed, sit or stand leaning slightly forward, rather than lying down or leaning backward. Using your thumb and forefinger, pinch the area just above your nostrils and below the bridge of your nose, and hold for five minutes; repeat if the bleeding contin-

ues. If the bleeding isn't controlled after three tries, or if the bleeding is frequent and heavy, call your practitioner.

Snoring

"My husband tells me that I've been snoring lately. Why is this happening?"

Snoring can disrupt a good night's sleep, for both the snorer and her bedmate, but it's usually not something to lose sleep over when you're expecting. Your nocturnal nasal symphony may simply be triggered by normal pregnancy stuffiness, in which case sleeping with a humidifier (or a nasal strip) on and with your head well elevated may help. Extra weight can also contribute to snoring, so make sure you aren't gaining too much.

Rarely, snoring can signal an elevated risk for gestational diabetes, or a sign of sleep apnea, a condition in which breathing stops briefly during sleep. Since you're breathing for two, it's probably a good idea to mention your snoring to your practitioner at your next visit.

Snooze or Lose?

Are pregnancy hormones—or that growing belly—getting between you and a good night's sleep? Sleep problems are common in pregnancy, and while insomnia may be good preparation for the sleepless nights that lie ahead once your baby arrives, you're likely eager to catch some expectant z's. Before turning to over-the-counter (or prescribed) sleep aids, however, talk to your practitioner. He or she may have other suggestions to help summon the sandman. You can also read the tips on page 265 to help with your insomnia.

Allergies

"My allergies seem to have gotten worse since my pregnancy began. My nose is runny all the time."

Expectant noses are stuffy noses, so it's possible that you're mistaking the normal (though uncomfortable) congestion of pregnancy for allergies. But it's also possible that pregnancy has aggravated your allergies. Though some lucky expectant allergy sufferers (about a third) find a temporary respite from their symptoms during pregnancy, the less lucky (also about a third) find their symptoms get worse, and the rest (that final third) find their symptoms stay about the same. Since it sounds like you're among the less lucky, you're probably itching (and tearing and sneezing) for relief. But before you join the rest of the other allergy sufferers in the antihistamine aisle at the drugstore, check with your practitioner to see what you can safely pull off the shelf or have filled at the pharmacy. Some antihistamines and other medications are safe for use in pregnancy; others, which may or may not include your usual over-the-counter or prescription medication, may not be (though don't worry about any that you took before you knew you were pregnant).

Allergy shots are considered safe for pregnant women who have been on the receiving end of them for a while before they conceived. Most allergists say it's not a good idea to start allergy shots during pregnancy because they may cause unexpected reactions.

In general, however, the best approach to dealing with allergies in pregnancy is prevention—which can be worth a pound of tissues this season. Steering clear of what causes your allergies may also reduce the risk that your baby will develop allergies to those triggers.

No Peanuts for Your Little Peanut?

It's as American as the sandwich bread it's spread on—plus it makes a convenient and wholesome snack—but is peanut butter safe for the little peanut you're feeding in utero? It's long been known that moms (and much less so, dads) who have or have had allergies may pass allergic tendencies—though not necessarily the specific allergies—to their unborn child. Some research suggests that *allergic* mothers who eat highly allergenic foods (such as peanuts and dairy products) while they're nursing may be more likely to pass on allergies to those foods in their offspring. The good news for expectant peanut butter lovers (and those who like to wash their PB&J down with a glass of milk) is that the research on this connection during pregnancy has been inconclusive thus far. Still, if you have ever suffered from allergies, speak to your practitioner and an allergist about whether you should think about restricting your diet while you're pregnant and/or breastfeeding. If not, there's no need to skip the Skippy.

To ease the sneeze, try these tips:

- If pollens or other outdoor allergens trouble you, stay indoors in an air-conditioned and air-filtered environment as much as you can during your susceptible season. When you come indoors, wash your hands and face and change clothes to remove pollen. Outdoors, wear large curved sunglasses to keep pollens from floating into your eyes.

- If dust is a culprit, make sure someone else does the dusting and sweeping (how's that for a good excuse to get out of housecleaning?). A vacuum cleaner (especially one with a HEPA filter), a damp mop, or a damp cloth-covered broom kicks up less dust than an ordinary broom, and a microfiber cloth will do better than a traditional feather duster. Stay away from musty places like attics and libraries full of old books.

- If you're allergic to certain foods, stay away from them, even if they're good foods for pregnancy. Check out the Pregnancy Diet (Chapter 5) for substitutes.

- If animals bring on allergy attacks, let friends know of the problem in advance so that they can rid a room of both pets and their dander before you visit. And of course, if your own pet is suddenly triggering an allergic response, try to keep one or more areas in your home (particularly your bedroom) pet free.

- Tobacco smoke allergy is easier to control these days, since there are fewer smokers around, and fewer places where they can smoke. To ease your allergy, as well as for the benefit of your baby, avoid exposure to cigarette, pipe, and cigar smoke.

Vaginal Discharge

"I've noticed a slight vaginal discharge that's thin and whitish. Does this mean I have an infection?"

A thin, milky, mild-smelling discharge (known in the obstetrics business as leukorrhea) is normal throughout pregnancy. Its purpose is noble: to protect the birth canal from infection and maintain a healthy balance of bacteria in the vagina. Unfortunately, in achieving its noble purpose, leukorrhea can make a mess of your underwear. Because it increases until term and may become quite heavy, some women are more comfortable wearing panty liners during the last months of pregnancy. Don't use tampons, which could introduce unwanted germs into the vagina.

Though it might offend your esthetic sensibilities (and possibly your partner's, during oral sex), and make you feel a little icky and sticky on occasion, this discharge is nothing to worry about. Keeping yourself clean, fresh, and dry will help, of course, but do not douche. Douching upsets the normal balance of microorganisms in the vagina and can lead to bacterial vaginosis (BV; see page 500). For information on vaginal infection and its symptoms, see page 499.

Elevated Blood Pressure

"My blood pressure was up a little bit at my last visit. Should I be worried?"

R elax. Worrying about your blood pressure will only send the readings higher. Besides, a slight increase at one visit is probably nothing to worry about. Maybe you were stressed because you were caught in traffic on the way to your appointment or because you had a pile of papers to finish back at work. Maybe you were just nervous—you were afraid you'd gained too much weight or not enough, or you had some strange symptoms to report, or you were anxious to hear the baby's heartbeat. Or maybe medical settings just make you edgy, giving you what is known as "white coat hypertension." An hour later, when you were relaxed, your pressure might very well have been perfectly normal. To make sure anxiety doesn't do a number on those numbers again, try to do some relaxation exercises (see page 142) while you're waiting for your next appointment—and, especially, while your blood pressure's being taken (think happy baby thoughts).

Even if your blood pressure remains slightly elevated at your next reading, such transient high blood pressure (which about 1 to 2 percent of women develop during pregnancy) is perfectly harmless and disappears after delivery (so you can still relax).

Most expectant mothers will see a slight drop in blood pressure readings during the second trimester as blood volume increases and the body starts working long hours to get that baby-making factory up to speed. But when you hit the third trimester, it usually begins to rise a bit. If it rises too much (if systolic pressure—the upper number—is 140 or more or the diastolic pressure—the lower number—is over 90) and stays up for at least two readings, your practitioner will monitor you more closely. That's because if such mildly elevated blood pressure is also accompanied by protein in the urine, swelling of the hands, ankles, and face, and/or sudden weight gain, it may turn out to be preeclampsia; see page 548.

Sugar in the Urine

"At my last office visit, the doctor said that there was sugar in my urine, but that it wasn't anything to worry about. Isn't it a sign of diabetes?"

Take your doctor's advice—don't stress. Your body is probably doing just what it's supposed to do: making sure that fetus of yours, which depends on you for its fuel supply, is getting enough glucose (sugar).

The hormone insulin regulates the level of glucose in your blood and

---

Get Your Flu Shots

The Centers for Disease Control and Prevention recommends that every woman who will be pregnant during flu season (generally October through April) be given the flu shot. The shot will not affect your baby and is unlikely to cause you any side effects. (The worst that can happen is you'll develop a mild fever and feel more tired than usual for a few days.) Ask if you can get the thimerosal-free (or reduced) vaccine, if available. Pregnant women should not get FluMist, the nasal spray flu vaccine. FluMist, unlike the flu shot, is made from live flu virus and could actually give you a mild case of the flu.

---

ensures that enough is taken in by your body cells for nourishment. Pregnancy triggers anti-insulin mechanisms to make sure enough sugar remains circulating in your bloodstream to nourish your fetus. It's a perfect idea that doesn't always work perfectly. Sometimes the anti-insulin effect is so strong that it leaves more than enough sugar in the blood to meet the needs of both mother and child—more than can be handled by the kidneys. The excess is "spilled" into the urine. Thus "sugar in the urine" is not uncommon in pregnancy, especially in the second trimester, when the anti-insulin effect increases. In fact, roughly half of all pregnant women show some sugar in the urine at some point in their pregnancies.

In most women, the body responds to an increase in blood sugar with an increased production of insulin, which usually eliminates the excess sugar by the next office visit. This may well be the case with you. But some women, especially those who are diabetic or have tendencies toward diabetes (because of a family history or because of their age or weight), may be unable to produce enough insulin at one time to handle the increase in blood sugar, or they may be unable to use the insulin they do produce efficiently. Either way, these women continue to show high levels of sugar in both blood and urine. In those who were not previously diabetic, this is known as gestational diabetes (see page 546).

You—like every pregnant woman—will be given a glucose screening test around the 28th week to check for gestational diabetes (those at higher risk may be screened earlier). Until then, don't give the sugar in your urine another thought.

Anemia

"A friend of mine became anemic during pregnancy—is that common?"

Iron-deficiency anemia is common during pregnancy—but it's also incredibly easy to prevent. And when it comes to prevention, your practitioner has your back. You were already tested for anemia at your first prenatal visit, though it's unlikely you were low on iron then. That's because iron stores are quickly replenished once those monthly periods stop.

As your pregnancy progresses and you hit the halfway mark (around 20 weeks, coming right up), your blood volume expands significantly and the amount of iron needed for producing red blood cells dramatically increases, depleting those stores once again. Fortunately, filling those stores up again—and effectively preventing anemia—is as easy as taking a daily iron

supplement (in addition to your prenatal vitamin), which your practitioner may prescribe starting midway through pregnancy. You should also pump up your diet by eating foods loaded with iron (though dietary sources, such as the ones listed on page 100, may not do the job alone, they provide a great backup for your supplement). For extra absorption, chase your iron down with vitamin C–rich foods (your morning OJ instead of your morning java, which will actually reduce the amount of iron absorbed).

Symptoms of Anemia

Pregnant women with mild iron deficiency rarely have symptoms. But as oxygen-carrying red blood cells are further depleted, an anemic mother-to-be becomes pale, extremely weak, easily tired or breathless, and might even experience fainting spells. This may be one of the few instances where fetal nutritional needs are met before Mom's, since babies are rarely iron deficient at birth.

Though all pregnant women are susceptible to iron-deficiency anemia, certain groups are at particularly high risk: those who have had several babies in quick succession, those who have been vomiting a lot or eating little because of morning sickness, and those who came to pregnancy undernourished (possibly because of an eating disorder) and/or have been eating poorly since they conceived. Daily iron supplementation, as prescribed by your practitioner, should prevent (or relieve) anemia.

Fetal Movement

"I haven't felt the baby moving yet; could something be wrong? Or could I just not be recognizing the kicking?"

Forget that positive pregnancy test, the early ultrasound, that expanding belly, or even the lub-dub of a baby's heartbeat. Nothing says you're pregnant like fetal movement.

That is, when you finally feel it. And you're sure you felt it. However, few expectant moms, particularly first timers, feel the first kick—or even the first flutter—in the fourth month. Though the embryo begins to make spontaneous movements by the seventh week, these movements, made by very tiny arms and legs, don't become apparent to mom until much later. That first momentous sensation of life, or "quickening," can occur anywhere between the 14th and 26th weeks, but generally closer to the average of the 18th to 22nd week. Variations on that average are common. A woman who's had a baby before is likely to recognize movement earlier (both because she knows what to expect and because her uterine and abdominal muscles are more lax, making it easier to feel a kick) than one who is expecting her first child. A very slender woman may notice very early, weak movements, whereas a woman who's sporting lots of padding on her belly may not be aware of movements until much later, when they've become more vigorous. The position of the placenta can also play a role: If it's facing front (an anterior placenta), it can muffle the movements and make the wait for those kicks weeks longer.

Sometimes, fetal movements aren't noticed when expected because of a miscalculated due date. Other times, mom doesn't recognize the movement when she feels it—or mistakes it for gas or other digestive gurgles.

So what do early movements feel like? They're almost as hard to describe as they are to recognize. Maybe it'll feel like a flutter (sort of like the "butterflies" you can get when you're nervous). Or a twitch. Or a nudge. Or even like the growling of hunger pangs. Maybe it'll feel like a bubble bursting—or that upside-down, inside-out sensation you get on a roller coaster. No matter what it feels like, it's bound to put a smile on your face—at least once you figure out for sure what it is.

Body Image

"I've always watched my weight—and now when I look in the mirror or step on a scale, I get so depressed. I look so fat."

When you've watched your weight your whole life, watching the numbers on the scale creep up can be unnerving—and maybe a little depressing, too. But it shouldn't be. If there's one place where thin is never in, it's in pregnancy. You're supposed to gain weight when you're pregnant. And there's an important difference between pounds added for self-indulgent reasons (just too many midnight dates with Ben and Jerry) and pounds gained for the best and most beautiful of reasons: your child and its support system growing inside you.

In the eyes of many beholders, a pregnant woman isn't just beautiful inside but outside as well. Many women and most spouses (and others who ogle) consider the rounded pregnant silhouette the most lovely—and sensuous—of feminine shapes. So instead of longing for the thin old days (you'll have them back soon enough), try getting on board with your expectant body. Embrace those new curves (which will become even more fun to embrace as they grow). Celebrate your new shape. Relish being rounder. Enjoy the pounds

A Pregnant Pose

If you've been dodging the camera lately ("no need to put yet another 10 pounds on me!"), consider striking a pregnant pose. Even if you may prefer to forget what you look like pregnant, your child-to-be will definitely relish seeing his or her first "baby" pictures one day—and so will you, eventually. To preserve your pregnant progress for posterity, have someone take a photo of your profile each month. Dress in something form-fitting (or belly-baring) for more dramatic documentation of your silhouette, and compile your photos in a pregnancy album or post them in an online photo gallery for easy sharing with family and friends, alongside the ultrasound shot, if you have one.

you pack on, instead of dreading them. As long as you're eating well and not exceeding the recommended guidelines for pregnancy weight gain, there's no reason to feel "fat"—just pregnant. The added inches you're seeing are all legitimate by-products of pregnancy and will disappear soon enough after the baby is born.

If you are exceeding the guidelines, feeling depressed about it won't keep you from getting fatter (and, if you're a typical estrogen producer, will only send you to the freezer for that vat of mint chocolate chip more often), but taking a good look at your eating habits might. Remember, the idea isn't to stop the weight gain (that's unsafe during pregnancy)—only to slow it down to the right rate if it's adding up a little too quickly. Instead of cutting back on the Pregnancy Diet requirements, just become more efficient in filling them

(a smoothie made with yogurt to fill a Calcium serving instead of a pint of ice cream).

Watching your weight gain isn't the only way to give your appearance an edge. Exercise will definitely help, too, by ensuring that the weight you do gain ends up in all the right places (more belly, less hips and thighs). Another workout plus: It'll give you a mood lift (it's hard to feel depressed when you've got an exercise-induced endorphin high going).

Being maternity fashion-forward can also help you make friends with your mirror. Instead of trying to squeeze into your civilian wardrobe (nothing flattering about the muffin-top look, especially when buttons keep popping), choose from the vast selection of creative maternity styles that accentuate the pregnant shape, rather than trying to hide it. You'll like your mirror image better, too, if you get a hairstyle that's slimming, pamper your complexion, and experiment with new makeup routines (the right techniques can take pounds off your pregnancy-rounded face; see page 149).

Maternity Clothes

"I can't squeeze into my jeans anymore, but I dread buying maternity clothes."

There's never been a more styling time to be pregnant. Gone are the days when pregnancy wardrobes were limited to tentlike muumuus intended to hide the expectant shape under yards and yards of polyester. Not only are today's maternity clothes a lot more fashion-forward and practical to wear, but they're designed to hug (and highlight) your beautiful baby-filled belly. Visit a nearby maternity store (or shop one online) and you'll likely be filled with excitement, instead of dread.

Looking Slim When You're Bulking Up

Big is beautiful when you're expecting, but that doesn't mean you can't try some tricks of the trim. With the right fashion choices, you can highlight your belly while slimming your overall silhouette. Here's how to show in all the right places:

Think black. And navy blue, chocolate brown, or charcoal. Dark colors are slimming, minimizing body bulk and giving you an overall trimmer appearance, even if you're wearing a T-shirt and yoga pants.

Think monotone. One color fits all—or at least looks slimmer. Sticking to a single hue (or to one color with slight variations) from top to bottom will make you look longer and leaner. A two-tone look, however, will create a break in your figure, causing the eye to stop right at the color change (and possibly right where your hips start spreading).

Think vertical. It's the oldest trick in the fashion book, but for good reason—it works. As you widen, choose clothes with vertical lines (which create height and give you a leaner look) instead of horizontal lines (which widen you even further). Look for clothes with vertical stripes, vertical zippers, vertical stitching, and vertical rows of buttons.

Focus on the pluses. Like those probably plus-size breasts of yours (there's never been a better time to spotlight your cleavage). And minimize attention to the spots that you might be less inclined to want to show off, such as those swollen ankles (keep them under pants or comfortable boots, or wear slimming black tights).

Stay fit. With your clothes, that is. While you'll definitely want clothes that have room to grow in the bust and the belly, look for tops—shirts, sweaters, jackets, and dresses—that fit you well in the shoulders (probably the only part of your body that won't be widening). Hanging shoulders will give you a sloppy (and bulky) look. And though clinging can be slimming, watch out for clothes that are so clingy they appear too tight, like you've outgrown them (which you probably have). The overstuffed sausage look is never in style, after all.

Here are some tips to consider when making your purchases:

- You still have a long way to grow. So don't set off on a whirlwind spending spree on the first day you can't button your jeans. Maternity clothes can be costly, especially when you consider the relatively short period of time they can be worn. So buy as you grow, and then buy only as much as you need (once you've checked what you can use that's already in your closet, you may end up needing a lot less than you'd figured). Though the pregnancy pillows available in try-on rooms in maternity stores can give a good indication of how things will fit later, they can't predict how you will carry (high, low, big, small) and which outfits will end up being the most comfortable when you crave comfort most.

- You're not limited to maternity clothes. If it fits, wear it, even if it isn't from the maternity department. Buying non-maternity clothing for maternity use (or using items you already own) is, of course, the best way of avoiding throwing away a fortune on clothes you'll only wear briefly. And depending on what the stores are showing in a particular season, anywhere from a few to many of the fashions on the regular racks may be suitable for pregnant shapes (though you may need to size up). Still, be wary of spending a lot on such purchases. Though you may love the clothes now, you may love them considerably less after you've worn them throughout your pregnancy. Plus, if you've bought them on the big side, they may not fit once you've shed your baby fat.

- You've got it, so flaunt it. Bellies are out of the closet—and out from under those polyester pup tents. Most maternity clothes celebrate the pregnant belly, with clingy fabrics and snug-fitting styles. And that's something to celebrate, since belly-accentuating maternity wear actually slims your silhouette down. Another great option: low-cut jeans and pants that can be worn under your belly. A low rise is also elongating (and what expectant mom couldn't use a little elongating?).

- Don't overlook those accessories the public never sees. A well-fitting, supportive bra should be your bosom buddy during pregnancy, especially as that bosom expands . . . and expands. Skip the sale racks and put yourself in the hands of an experienced fitter at a well-stocked lingerie department or shop. With any luck, she will be able to tell you approximately how much extra room and support you need and which kind of bra will provide it. But don't stock up. Buy just a couple (one to wear and one to wash), and then go back for another fitting when you start growing out of them.

  Special maternity underwear isn't usually necessary, but if you do decide to go that route, you'll probably be relieved to find that it's a lot sexier than it used to be (good-bye granny panties, hello thongs and bikinis). You can also opt for regular bikini panties—bought in a larger-than-usual size if you need the room—worn under your belly. Buy them in favorite colors and/or sexy fabrics to give your spirits a lift (but make sure the crotches are cotton).

- Dip into your partner's drawers. It's all there for the taking (though it's probably a good idea to ask first): oversize T-shirts and regular shirts that look great over pants or leggings, sweatpants that accommodate more inches than yours do, running shorts that will keep up with your waistline for at least a couple more months, belts with the few extra notches you need. Keep in mind, though, that by the sixth month (possibly a lot sooner), no matter how big your man is, you're likely to outgrow him and his clothes.

- Both a borrower and a lender be. Accept all offers of used maternity clothes, as long as they fit. In a pinch, any extra dress, skirt, or pair of jeans may do—you can make any borrowed item more "yours" with accessories (a fabulous scarf or a flashy pair of sneakers, for example). When your term is over, offer to lend those maternity outfits you bought and can't or don't want to wear postpartum to newly pregnant friends; between you and your friends, you'll be getting your money's worth from your maternity clothes.

- Cool is hot. Hot stuff (fabrics that don't breathe, such as nylon and other synthetics) isn't so hot when you're pregnant. Because your metabolic rate is higher than usual, making you warmer, you'll feel more comfortable in cottons. You'll also be less likely to get heat rash (a common complaint among the pregnant set). Knee-highs or thigh-highs will also be more comfortable than pantyhose, but avoid those that have a narrow constrictive band at the top. Light colors, mesh weaves, and looser fits will also help you keep your cool in warm weather. When the weather turns cold, dressing in layers is ideal, since you can selectively peel off as you heat up or when you go indoors.

Pre-Baby Jitters

"Now that my abdomen is swelling, the fact that I'm really pregnant has finally sunk in. Even though we planned this pregnancy, we suddenly feel scared."

Sounds like you've got a little case of the pre-baby jitters—which, you'll be relieved to hear, many parents-to-be come down with at some point in their pregnancies. Even the most eager of expectant couples may find themselves with second thoughts once pregnancy starts to become a reality—and that isn't so surprising when you think about it. After all, a little person you haven't even met yet is already turning your lives upside down, making unexpected demands on you, both physically and emotionally. Every aspect of your lifestyle—from how you spend your evenings and your money to what you eat and drink to how often (and how) you make love—may already be changing, with plenty more changes on the postpartum horizon.

Not only is the prenatal ambivalence you're confronting completely understandable and extremely common, it's really pretty healthy. Facing it now gives you a chance to work out these feelings—and adjust to these major life changes—before baby arrives. The best way to do this is to talk it all out, both with each other and with friends who've already made the transition to parenthood (and will be able to offer you a reassuring perspective).

Without a doubt, becoming a parent is a life-changing experience—in other words, your life will never be the same. But as any parent will tell you—and as you'll soon find out for yourselves—it's a life-changing experience that's likely to bring a change for the better. Or even more likely, the best.

Unwanted Advice

"Now that it's obvious I'm expecting, everyone—from my mother-in-law to strangers on the elevator—has advice for me. It drives me crazy."

There's just something about a bulging belly that brings out the so-called expert in everyone, and that brings down social barriers that usually keep strangers minding their own business. Take your morning jog around the park and someone is sure to chide, "You shouldn't be running in your condition!" Lug home two bags of groceries from the supermarket and you're bound to hear, "Do you think you ought to be carrying that?" Double dip at the ice cream parlor, and expect the fingers to start wagging: "That baby fat's not going to be easy to lose, honey."

Between the pregnancy police, the gratuitous advice-givers, and all those inevitable predictions about the sex of the baby, what's an expectant mother to do? First of all, keep in mind that most of what you hear is probably nonsense. Old wives' tales that do have foundation in fact have been scientifically substantiated and have become part of standard medical practice. Those that do not might still be tightly woven into pregnancy mythology but can be confidently dismissed. Those recommendations that leave you with a nagging doubt ("What if they're right?") are best checked out with your doctor, midwife, or childbirth educator.

Whether it's possibly plausible or obviously ridiculous, however, don't let unwanted advice get you going—who needs the added stress anyway? Instead, keep your sense of humor handy and take one of two approaches: Politely inform the well-meaning stranger, friend, or relative that you have a trusted practitioner who counsels you on your pregnancy and that, even though you appreciate the thought, you can't accept advice from anyone else. Or, just as politely, smile, say thank you, and go on your way, letting their comments go in one ear and out the other—without making any stops in between.

But no matter how you choose to handle unwanted advice, you might also want to get used to it. If there's anyone who attracts a crowd of advice-givers faster than a woman with a belly, it's a woman with a new baby.

Unwanted Belly Touching

"Now that my pregnant belly is showing, friends, colleagues, even strangers come up to me and touch it—without even asking. I'm uncomfortable with that."

They're round, they're cute, and they're filled with something even cuter. Let's face it, pregnant bellies just scream out to be touched. Still, touching a pregnant belly may be an irresistible impulse, but it's also an inappropriate one—particularly without the owner's permission.

Some women don't mind being the center of so much touching attention; others actually enjoy it. But if all this uninvited rubbing is rubbing you the wrong way, don't hesitate to say so. You can do this bluntly (though politely): "I know you find my belly tempting to touch, but I'd really rather you didn't."

Or a playful "No touching, please—the baby's sleeping!" can discourage those uninvited advances. Or you can try a little belly turning, rubbing the rubber right back (patting someone's potbelly might make him or her think twice next time before reaching out and touching another pregnant belly without permission). Or make your statement without saying a word: Cross your arms protectively over your belly, or take the rubber's hand off your midsection and place it somewhere else (like on his or her own belly).

Forgetfulness

"Last week I left the house without my wallet; this morning I completely forgot an important business meeting. I can't focus on anything, and I'm beginning to think I'm losing my mind."

You're in good (forgetful) company. Many pregnant women begin to feel that as they're gaining pounds, they're losing brain cells. Even women who pride themselves on their organizational skills, their capacity to cope with complicated issues, and their ability to maintain their composure suddenly find themselves forgetting appointments, having trouble concentrating, and losing their cool (along with their wallets and cell phones). And it's not in their heads—it's in their brains. Researchers have found that a woman's brain-cell volume actually decreases during pregnancy (which could explain why you won't remember what you just read about in that last paragraph). And—for reasons unknown—women pregnant with girls are more forgetful, on average, than those carrying boys (who would have guessed?). Fortunately, the pregnancy brain fog (similar to what many women experience premenstrually, only thicker) is only temporary.

Your brain will plump back up a few months after delivery.

Like numerous other symptoms, forgetfulness is caused by the hormonal changes of pregnancy. Sleep deprivation can also play a role (the less you sleep, the less you remember), as can the fact that you're constantly zapped of energy—energy your brain needs to stay focused. Also contributing to your scatterbrained self: the mother-to-be mind overload that's keeping all brain circuits busy contemplating nursery colors and negotiating baby names.

Feeling stressed about this intellectual fogginess will only make it worse (stress also compounds forgetfulness). Recognizing that it is normal (and not imagined), even accepting it with a sense of humor, may help to ease it—or, at least, make you feel better about it. Realistically, it might just not be possible to be as efficient as you were before you took on the added job of baby making. Keeping written checklists at home and at work can help contain the mental chaos. So can recording everything you need to remember on a mobile device— that is, if you can remember where you put it last. Set electronic reminders of important dates and appointments, and tap into the What to Expect Pregnancy Tracker, too (yes, there's an app for that). Strategically placed Post-its (one on the front door to remind you to take your keys so you don't lock yourself out, for instance) can also help keep you on track.

Although ginkgo biloba has been touted for its memory-boosting properties, it is not considered safe for use during pregnancy, so you'll have to forget about using this and any other herbal preparation in your battle against pregnancy-induced forgetfulness.

And you might as well get used to working at a little below peak efficiency. The fog may well continue after your baby's arrival (due to fatigue, not hormones) and perhaps may not lift completely until baby (and you) start sleeping through the night.

ALL ABOUT

Exercise During Pregnancy

You're aching and you can't sleep and your back is killing you and your ankles are swelling and you're constipated and bloated and you're passing more gas than a busload of high school football players. In other words, you're pregnant. Now if only there were something you could do that might minimize the aches and pains and unpleasant side effects of pregnancy.

Actually, there is, and it'll take just minutes (make that 30 minutes) a day: exercise. Thought pregnancy was a time to take it easy? Not anymore. Lucky for you (or unlucky, if you're a member of the couch potato club), the official advice of ACOG reads like a personal trainer's pep talk: Women with normal pregnancies should get 30 minutes or more a day of moderate exercise on most (if not all) days.

More women than ever are taking that advice, making fitness a part of their daily—or almost daily—routine. And barring any red light from your practitioner, you can, too. It doesn't matter whether you started out as an iron woman in peak physical condition or a sofa slacker who hasn't laced up sneakers since your last high school gym class (except as a fashion statement). There are plenty of health perks to exercising for two.

The Benefits of Exercise

So what's in it for you? Regular exercise can help:

- Your stamina. It seems paradoxical, but sometimes getting too much rest can actually make you feel more tired. A little exercise can go a long way

when it comes to giving your energy level the boost it needs.

- Your sleep. Many pregnant women have a hard time falling asleep (not to mention staying asleep), but those who exercise consistently often sleep better and wake up feeling more rested.

- Your health. Exercise may prevent gestational diabetes, a growing problem among pregnant women.

- Your mood. Exercise causes your brain to release endorphins, those feel-good chemicals that give you a

Working in Workouts

Your mission when it comes to exercise during pregnancy, should you choose to accept it (and there are lots of reasons why you should), is to work your way up to 30 minutes of some sort of activity a day. And if that sounds daunting, keep in mind that three 10-minute walks sprinkled throughout the day are just as beneficial as 30 minutes on the treadmill. And even non-exercise activity—like 15 minutes of vacuuming and 15 minutes of light yard work—counts toward your daily goal. (See, it's not as hard as it sounds.)

Still not convinced that you have the time? To make your mission possible, try thinking of exercise as part of your day—like brushing your teeth and going to work—and build it into your routine (that's how it becomes routine, after all).

If there's no place in your schedule to block out gym time, just incorporate exercise into your daily activities: Get off the bus two stops from the office, and walk the rest of the way. Park your car in a faraway spot at the mall instead of cruising for the closest (and while you're at the mall, take a few extra laps

around—those count, too). Take a brisk walk to the deli instead of ordering in your sandwich. Use the stairs instead of the elevator. Walk up the escalator instead of going along for the ride. Visit the ladies' room at the far end of your office instead of the one across the hall.

Have the time but lack the motivation? Find it in a pregnancy exercise class (the camaraderie will help cheer you on) or by exercising with a friend (form a lunchtime walking club or hit the hiking trails with your buds on Saturdays before your weekly brunch). Just plain bored with your workouts? Switch it up—try pregnancy yoga if you're tired (literally) of running, or swimming (or water aerobics) if the stationary cycle is getting you nowhere. Find your exercise excitement in a pregnancy DVD workout.

Sure, there'll be days (especially in those fatigue-prone first and third trimesters), when you're too pooped to lift your legs off the coffee table, never mind actually do leg lifts. But there's never been a better time, or better reasons, to get yourself moving.

natural high—improving your mood, diminishing stress and anxiety.

- Your back. A strong set of abs is the best defense against back pain, which plagues many pregnant women. But even exercise that's not directly targeting the tummy can also relieve back pain and pressure.

- Your (tense) muscles. Stretching does your body good—especially a pregnant body, which is more prone to muscle cramps in the legs (and elsewhere). Stretching can help you uncover little pockets of tension, warding off sore muscles. Plus you can do it anywhere, anytime—even if you spend most of your day sitting down—and you don't even have to break a sweat.

- Your bowels. An active body encourages active bowels. Even a 10-minute stroll helps get things going.

- Your labor. Though exercise during pregnancy can't guarantee that you'll race through childbirth, moms who exercise tend to have shorter labors and are less likely to need labor and delivery interventions (including C-sections).

- Your postpartum recovery. The more fit you stay during pregnancy, the faster you'll recover physically after childbirth (and the sooner you'll be zipping up those prepregnancy jeans again).

What's in it for baby? Plenty. Researchers theorize that changes in heart rate and oxygen levels in exercising moms-to-be stimulate their babies. Babies are also stimulated by the sounds and vibrations they experience in the womb during workouts. Exercise regularly during pregnancy, and your baby might end up being:

Can You Kegel?

If you do only one exercise during your pregnancy, make it this one. Kegels help strengthen your pelvic floor (the muscle group that controls the flow of urine and the contraction of the vagina and anal sphincter). One of the many benefits of doing your Kegels is they prevent urinary incontinence, a pretty common complaint late in pregnancy and during postpartum—as well as fecal incontinence, which, though less common, can be even more uncomfortable and embarrassing. They can also tone your pelvic floor in preparation for labor and delivery—and possibly help you avoid an episiotomy or a tear. Finally, flexing your pelvic muscles through Kegels can improve sexual satisfaction postpartum, when those muscles will need some tightening up. For more about Kegels and instructions on how to flex those amazing muscles, see page 295.

- More fit. Babies of moms who exercise during pregnancy are born at healthier weights, are better able to weather labor and delivery (they're less stressed by it), and recover from the stresses of birth more quickly.

- Smarter. Believe it or not, research shows that babies of moms who exercise throughout pregnancy score higher, on average, on general intelligence tests by age 5 (meaning that your workout may boost both your muscle power and baby's brain power!).

- Easier. Babies of pregnant exercisers tend to sleep through the night sooner, are less prone to colic, and are better able to soothe themselves.

Exercise Smarts

Exercising with a baby on board? Remember to use your exercise smarts:

- Drink before you exercise. To avoid becoming dehydrated, have a drink before your workout—even if you're not thirsty (waiting until you're thirsty means you've waited too long). End your workout with a drink, also, to replenish the fluids you lost through sweat.

- Bring on the snacks. A light but sustaining before-workout snack will help keep your energy up. Follow up with a light snack, too, especially if you've burned a lot of calories.

- Stay cool. Any exercise or environment that raises a pregnant woman's temperature more than 1.5 degrees should be avoided (it causes blood to be shunted away from the uterus to the skin as the body attempts to cool off). So stay out of saunas, steam rooms, or hot tubs, and don't exercise outdoors in very hot or humid weather or indoors in a stuffy, overheated room (no Bikram yoga). If you generally walk outdoors, try an air-conditioned mall instead when the temperature soars.

- Dress for exercise success. Play it cool by wearing loose, breathable, stretchable clothes. Choose a bra that provides plenty of support for your larger-than-life breasts but that doesn't pinch once you get moving (a sports bra can be a great addition to your maternity wardrobe).

- Put your feet first. If your sneakers are showing their age, replace them now to minimize your chances of injury or falls. And make sure you choose workout shoes that are designed for the sport you're pursuing.

- Select the right surface. Indoors, a wood floor or a tightly carpeted sur-

Exercising the Right Way When You're Expecting

Not only does your pregnant body not fit into your regular workout clothes anymore, it also may not fit into your regular workout routine. Now that you're exercising for two, you'll need to make doubly sure you're exercising the right way. Here are some pointers, whether you're a gym junkie or a Sunday stroller:

The starting line is the practitioner's office. Before you lace up your sneaks and hit the aerobics class, make a pit stop at your practitioner's office for the green light. It's highly likely you'll get it—most women do. But if you have any medical or pregnancy complications, your practitioner may limit your exercise program, nix it entirely, or—if you have gestational diabetes—even encourage you to be a little more active. Be sure you're clear about what exercise programs are appropriate for you and whether your normal fitness routine (if you have one) is safe to continue when you're expecting. If you're in good health, your practitioner will likely encourage you to stick with your regular routine as long as you feel up to it, with certain modifications (especially if your regular routine includes pregnancy-taboo sports, like ice hockey).

face is better than tile or concrete for your workouts. (If the surface is slippery, don't exercise in socks or footed tights.) Outdoors, soft running tracks and grassy or dirt trails are better than hard-surfaced roads or sidewalks; level surfaces are better than uneven ones.

- Stay off the slopes. Because your growing abdomen will affect your sense of balance, ACOG suggests women in the latter part of pregnancy avoid sports that come with a higher risk of falling or abdominal injury. These include gymnastics, downhill skiing, ice-skating, vigorous racquet sports (play doubles instead of singles), and horseback riding, as well as cycling and contact sports such as ice hockey, soccer, or basketball (see page 224 for more).

- Stay on the level. Unless you're living at high altitudes, avoid any activity that takes you up more than 6,000 feet. On the flip(per) side, scuba diving, which poses a risk of decompression sickness for your baby, is also off-limits, so you'll have to wait until you're no longer carrying a passenger to take your next dive.

- Stay off your back. After the fourth month, don't exercise flat on your back. The weight of your enlarging uterus could compress major blood vessels, restricting circulation.

- Avoid risky moves. Pointing, or extending, your toes—at any time in pregnancy—could lead to cramping in your calves. Flex your feet instead, turning them up toward your face. Full sit-ups or double leg lifts pull on the abdomen, so they're probably not a good idea when you've got a baby on board. Also avoid any activity that requires "bridging" (bending over backward) or other contortions, or that involves deep flexion or extension of joints (such as deep knee bends), jumping, bouncing, sudden changes in direction, or jerky motions.

Respect your body as it changes. Expect your routines to change as your body does. You'll need to modify your workouts as your sense of balance shifts, and you'll probably also have to slow down to avoid taking a spill (especially once you can no longer see your feet). Also expect workouts to seem different, even if you've been doing a particular routine for years. If you're a walker, for example, you'll feel more pressure on your hips and knees as your pregnancy progresses and as your joints and ligaments loosen. You'll also have to accommodate your pregnant body by avoiding any exercise that requires you to lie flat on your back or stand without moving (like some yoga and tai chi poses do) after the first trimester. Both can restrict your blood flow.

Start slow. If you're new at this, start slowly. It's tempting to start off with a bang, running 3 miles the first morning or working out twice the first afternoon. But such enthusiastic beginnings usually lead not to fitness but to sore muscles, sagging resolve—and abrupt endings. Start the first day with 10 minutes of warm-ups followed by 5 minutes of a more strenuous workout (but stop sooner if you begin to tire) and a 5-minute cool-down. After a few days, if your body has adjusted well, increase the period of strenuous activity by about 5 minutes until you are

Thirty Minutes Plus?

Is more (exercise) more—or less? That depends. If you're really ambitious (or just really fit), and you've been green-lighted by your practitioner (based on your fitness level), it's safe to work out for up to an hour or even more, as long as you listen to your body. Moms-to-be tend to fatigue sooner than they used to, and tired bodies are more apt to injure themselves. Plus, overexertion could lead to other problems (dehydration, for one, if you don't take in enough fluids; for another, lack of oxygen to the baby if you're short of breath for long periods). Burning more calories during your marathon sessions also means you'll need to take in more, so be sure to compensate appropriately (the best part of a workout, wouldn't you say?).

up to 30 minutes or more, if you feel comfortable.

Of course, if you're already a gym rat, remember that while pregnancy is a great time to maintain your fitness level, it's not a time to increase it (you can set new personal bests after baby is on the scene).

Get off to a slow start every time you start. Warm-ups can be tedious when you're eager to get your workout started—and over with. But as every athlete knows, they're an essential part of any exercise program. They ensure that the heart and circulation aren't taxed suddenly and reduce the chances of injury to muscles and joints, which are more vulnerable when cold—and particularly during pregnancy. So walk before you run; swim slowly or jog in place in the pool before you start your laps.

Finish as slowly as you start. Collapse may seem like the logical conclusion to a workout, but it isn't physiologically sound. Stopping abruptly traps blood in the muscles, reducing blood supply to other parts of your body and to your baby. Dizziness, faintness, extra heartbeats, or nausea may result. So finish your exercise with exercise: about 5 minutes of walking after running, easy paddling after a vigorous swim, light stretching exercises after almost any activity. Top off your cool-down with a few minutes of relaxation. You can help avoid dizziness (and a possible fall) if you get up slowly when you've been exercising on the floor.

Watch the clock. Too little exercise won't be effective; too much can be debilitating. A full workout, from warm-up to cool-down, can take anywhere from 30 minutes to an hour. But keep the level of exertion mild to moderate.

Divide and conquer your workout. Can't find time in your day for a 30-minute workout? Divide your exercise schedule into two, three, or even four shorter ones. Not only will any combo that adds up to 30 minutes do the trick, this can tone muscles more effectively.

Keep it up. Exercising erratically (four times one week and none the next) won't get you in shape. Exercising regularly (three or four times a week, every week) will. If you're too tired for a strenuous workout, don't push yourself, but do try to do the warm-ups so that your muscles will stay limber and your discipline won't dissolve. Many women find they feel better if they do some exercise—if not necessarily their full workout—every day.

Compensate for the calories you burn. Perhaps the most fun part of a pregnancy exercise program is the extra eating you'll have to do. You'll have to

Shoulder and Leg Stretches

▲ **Shoulder stretch.** To ease tension in your shoulders (especially good if you spend a lot of time at the computer), try this simple move: Stand with your feet shoulder-width apart and knees slightly bent. Bring your left arm out in front of you at chest height and bend it slightly. Take your right hand, place it on your left elbow, and then gently pull your left elbow toward your right shoulder as you exhale. Hold the stretch for 5 to 10 seconds, then switch sides.

▲ **Standing leg stretch.** Give your legs a much-needed break with this easy stretch: Stand and hold on to a countertop, the back of a heavy chair, or another sturdy object for support. Bend your right knee and bring your right foot back and up toward your buttocks. Grasp your foot with your right hand and bring your heel toward your buttocks while extending your thigh backward from the hip joint. Keep your back straight and hold the stretch for 10 to 30 seconds. Repeat with the left leg.

consume about 150 to 200 additional calories for every half hour of moderate exercising. If you believe you're consuming enough calories but you still are not gaining weight, you may be exercising too much.

Replace the fluids you use up. For every half hour of moderate activity, you will need at least a full glass of extra liquid to compensate for fluids lost through perspiration. You will need more in warm weather, or whenever you're sweating a lot: Drink before, during, and after exercising—but no more than 16 ounces at a time. It's a good idea to start your fluid intake 30 to 45 minutes before your planned workout.

Choose the right group. If you prefer a group approach to exercise, take an exercise class that is specifically designed for pregnant women (ask for the instructor's credentials before enrolling). For some women, classes are better than solo exercising (particularly when self-discipline is lacking) and provide support and feedback. The best programs maintain moderate intensity, meet at least three times weekly, individualize to each woman's capabilities, and have a network of medical and exercise specialists available for questions.

Make it fun. Any workout, group or otherwise, should be an experience you look forward to rather than dread, one you think of as fun, not as torture. If you choose something you like doing, it'll be easier to stick with—particularly on days when you have no energy, feel the size of an SUV, or both. Some women find it helpful to pick a workout with a social component, from a prenatal yoga class to a romantic after-dinner walk. Exercising with a mate or a pal, incidentally, increases the odds of sticking with a program. So instead of meeting a friend for a coffee and scone, meet for a walk.

Do everything in moderation. Never exercise to the point of exhaustion, especially when you're pregnant. (Even if you're a trained athlete, don't exercise to your fullest capacity, whether it exhausts you or not.) There are several ways of checking to see whether you're overdoing it. First, if it feels good, it's probably

Dromedary Droop

A great way to relieve back pressure (your constant companion these days) is to get down on your hands and knees and relax your back, keeping your head straight and making sure your neck is lined up with your spine. Then arch your back—you'll feel your abs and buttocks tighten. Let your head gently droop down. Slowly return to your original position. Repeat several times—and do several times a day if you can, especially if you're standing or sitting a lot on the job.

Neck Relaxer

This exercise will ease tension in your neck. Sit up straight in a supportive chair. Close your eyes and breathe deeply, then gently tilt your head to one side and let it slowly drop toward your shoulder. Don't raise your shoulder to meet your head, and don't force your head down. Hold for 3 to 6 seconds, then switch sides. Repeat three or four times. Gently bring your head forward, letting your chin relax into your chest. Roll your cheek to the right toward your shoulder (again, don't force the motion, and don't move your shoulder toward your head) and hold for 3 to 6 seconds. Switch sides and repeat. Do three or four sets per day.

okay. If there's any pain or strain, it's not. A little perspiration is fine; a drenching sweat is a sign to slow down. So is being unable to carry on a conversation as you go. Work hard enough so you feel yourself breathing more heavily, but never be so out of breath that you aren't able to talk, sing, or whistle while you work(out). Needing a nap after completing a workout means you've worked too hard. You should feel exhilarated, not drained, after exercising.

Know when to stop. Your body will signal when it's time by saying, "Hey, I'm tired." Take the hint right away, and throw in the towel. More serious signals suggest a call to your practitioner: pain anywhere (hip, back, pelvis, chest, head, and so on); a cramp or stitch that doesn't go away when you stop exercising; uterine contractions and chest pain; lightheadedness or dizziness; very rapid heartbeat; severe breathlessness; difficulty walking or loss of muscle control; sudden headache; increased swelling of

your hands, feet, ankles, or face; amniotic fluid leakage or vaginal bleeding; or, after the 28th week, a slowing down or total absence of fetal movement. In the second and third trimesters, you may notice a gradual decrease in your performance and efficiency. This is normal and another signal to take it easier.

Taper off in the last trimester. Most women find that they need to slack off somewhat in the third trimester, particularly during the ninth month, when stretching routines and brisk walking or water workouts will probably provide enough exercise. If you feel up to sticking with a more vigorous program (and you're in excellent athletic shape), your practitioner may green-light your usual exercise agenda right up until delivery, but definitely ask first.

Even when you're not working out . . . don't just sit there. Sitting for an extended period without a break causes blood to pool in your leg veins, can cause your feet to swell, and could lead to other problems. If your work entails a lot of sitting, or if you watch TV for hours at a time or travel long distances frequently, be sure to break up every hour or so of sitting with 5 or 10 minutes of walking. And while at your seat, periodically do some exercises that enhance circulation, such as taking a few deep breaths, extending your lower legs, flexing your feet, and wiggling your toes. Also try contracting the muscles in your abdomen and buttocks (a sort of sitting pelvic tilt). If your hands tend to swell, periodically stretch your arms above your head, opening and closing your fists several times as you do.

Choosing the Right Pregnancy Exercise

While it's true that pregnancy isn't the time to learn to water-ski or enter a horse-jumping competition, you will still be able to enjoy most fitness activities—and use many of the machines at the gym (with a few caveats). You can select, too, from the growing number of exercise programs specifically designed for expecting moms (pregnancy water aerobics and prenatal yoga classes, for example). But be sure to ask your practitioner about what's okay and what's not when it comes to choosing an exercise program or sport. You'll probably find that most of the activities that are off-limits when you're expecting are ones you'd probably have a hard time doing well anyway once you have a basketball-size belly (like competitive basketball . . . or football or scuba diving or downhill racing or mountain biking). Here are the do's and don'ts of pregnancy workouts:

Walking. Just about anyone can do it—and do it just about anywhere, anytime.

Pelvic Tilt

This simple routine can help improve your posture, strengthen your abs, reduce back pain, and help prepare you for labor. To do a pelvic tilt, stand with your back against a wall and relax your spine. As you inhale, press the small of your back against the wall. Exhale; then repeat several times. For a variation that also helps reduce the pain of sciatica, try rocking your pelvis back and forth—keeping your back straight—while either kneeling on all fours or standing up. Do pelvic tilts regularly (take a 5-minute pelvic-tilt break several times during your workday).

Biceps Curl

Start by selecting light weights (3- or 5-pound weights if you're a beginner, and never lift more than 12-pound weights). Stand with your legs shoulder-width apart, making sure not to lock your knees. Keep your elbows in and your chest up. Slowly raise both weights toward your shoulders by bending your elbows and keeping your arms in front of you (remember to breathe), stopping when your forearms are perpendicular to the floor and the weights are facing the ceiling. Lower slowly and repeat. Try to do 8 to 10 repetitions, but take breaks if needed and don't overdo it. You'll feel a burn in your muscles, but never strain or start holding your breath.

There's no easier exercise to fit into your busy schedule than walking (don't forget, all the walking you do counts, even if it's walking two blocks to the market or 10 minutes while the dog does its business). And you can continue to fit it in right up until delivery day (and even on delivery day if you're anxious to get those contractions moving along). Best of all, there's no equipment necessary—and no gym membership or classes to pay for, either. All you need is a supportive pair of sneakers and comfortable, breathable clothes. If you're just beginning a walking routine, go slowly at first (start out at a stroll before you move on to a brisk pace). Need some time for yourself? Walking alone can give you that quiet moment you crave. But if you'd rather have company along for the walk, stroll with your partner, friends, or colleagues. You can even start a walking club (in the morning with neighbors or at lunchtime with coworkers). Weather's not cooperative? Do the mall walk.

Jogging. Experienced runners can stay on track during pregnancy—but you may want to limit your distances and stick to level terrain or use a treadmill (if you weren't a runner prepregnancy, stick to walking for now). Keep in mind that loosening ligaments and joints during pregnancy can make running harder

Leg Lifts

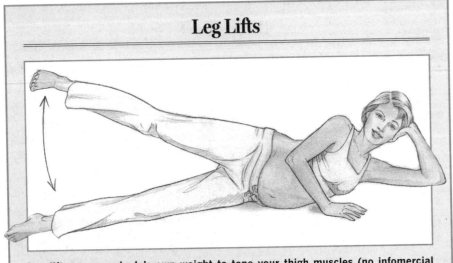

Leg lifts use your body's own weight to tone your thigh muscles (no infomercial equipment necessary). Simply lie on your left side with your shoulders, hips, and knees lined up straight. Support yourself by holding your head with your left arm and placing your right arm on the floor in front of you. Then slowly lift your right leg as high as you comfortably can (remember to breathe). Do 10 repetitions, then switch sides and repeat.

on your knees and also make you more prone to injury—yet another reason not to overdo it.

Exercise machines. Treadmills, ellipticals, and stair-climbers are all fine during pregnancy. Adjust the machines' speed, incline, and tension to a level that's comfortable for you (starting out slowly if you're a novice). During your last trimester, though, you may find a machine workout too strenuous. You may also have to be more conscious of avoiding stumbles on the machine when you're no longer able to see your feet.

Aerobics. Experienced athletes in good shape can continue dance and aerobic workouts during pregnancy. Tone down the intensity level, and never exert yourself to the point of exhaustion. If you're a beginner, choose low-impact aerobics or consider the water version, which is uniquely suited to the pregnant set.

Step routines. As long as you're already in good shape and have experience doing step routines, it's usually fine to continue them during much of your pregnancy. Just remember that your joints are more prone to injury when you're pregnant, so stretch out well beforehand and don't overexert yourself. And, of course, don't step on something too high off the ground. As your abdomen expands, avoid any activities that require careful balance.

Kickboxing. Kickboxing takes a great deal of grace and speed—two things pregnant women don't typically possess. Many pregnant kickboxers find they can't kick as high or move as quickly, but if you're still comfortable getting your exercise from getting your kicks, and you have plenty of experience (no novices now), it's okay to continue while you're expecting. Just be sure to avoid any movements that you have difficulty with or cause you to strain. Make sure you keep a safe distance from other kickboxers (you don't want to be kicked in the belly by accident) by leaving two leg lengths of space between you and those around you. Be sure, too, that everyone in the class knows you're pregnant, or look for pregnancy-specific classes (where everyone around you is pregnant—and far away).

Swimming and water workouts. You might not feel like slipping into a teeny bikini right now, but consider this: In the water, you weigh just a tenth of what you do on land (how often do you have the chance to be close to weightless these days?), making water workouts the perfect choice for a pregnant woman. Working out in the water boosts your strength and flexibility but is gentle on your joints—plus there's much less risk of overheating (unless the pool is overheated). What's more, many pregnant women report that water workouts help ease swelling in their legs and feet and relieve sciatic pain. Most gyms with a pool offer water aerobics, and many have classes specifically designed for expectant moms. Just be careful when walking on slippery poolsides, and don't dive. And stick to workouts in chlorinated pools.

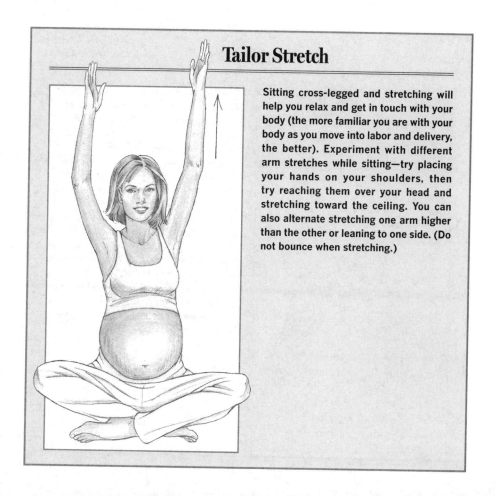

Tailor Stretch

Sitting cross-legged and stretching will help you relax and get in touch with your body (the more familiar you are with your body as you move into labor and delivery, the better). Experiment with different arm stretches while sitting—try placing your hands on your shoulders, then try reaching them over your head and stretching toward the ceiling. You can also alternate stretching one arm higher than the other or leaning to one side. (Do not bounce when stretching.)

Outdoor sports (hiking, skating, bicycling, skiing). Pregnancy isn't the time to take up a new sport—especially one that challenges your balance—but experienced athletes should be able to continue these activities (with their practitioner's approval and some precautions). When hiking, be sure to avoid uneven terrain (especially later on in pregnancy when it won't be easy to see that rock in your path), high altitudes, and slippery conditions (and of course, rock climbing is out). When biking, be extra careful—wear a helmet; don't ride on wet pavement, winding paths, or bumpy surfaces (falling is never a good idea but especially not when you're pregnant);

and don't lean forward into racing posture (it can tax your lower back, plus this isn't the time for racing; slow and steady should win all your races now). As for ice-skating, you can give it a whirl (and a figure eight) early in pregnancy if you're experienced and careful—later on, you'll probably face balance issues, so stop as soon as you get more bulky than graceful. Ditto for in-line skating and horseback riding. Avoid downhill skiing or snowboarding altogether, even if you've got years of double black diamonds under your belt; the risk of a serious fall is too great (after all, even pros take the occasional tumble). Cross-country skiing and snowshoeing are okay

Hip Flexors

The hip flexor muscles are what allow you to lift your knees and bend at the waist. Stretching these muscles periodically will help keep you limber and make it easier for you to spread your legs when it's time for the baby to exit (not to mention during sex). To flex your flexors, stand at the bottom of a flight of stairs as though you were about to climb them. (Hang on to the railing with one hand for support if you need to.) Place one foot on the first or second stair up (whatever you can comfortably reach) and bend your knee. Keep your other leg behind you, knee straight, foot flat on the floor. Lean into your bent leg, keeping your back straight. You'll feel the stretch in your straight leg. Switch legs and repeat.

Squats

This exercise strengthens and tones your thighs and is particularly useful for women who plan to deliver in the squatting position. To begin, stand with your feet shoulder-width apart. Keeping your back straight, bend at the knees and slowly lower yourself as close to the ground as you comfortably can, keeping your feet flat on the floor. If you can't, try moving your feet farther apart. Hold the squat for 10 to 30 seconds, then slowly come back to a standing position. Repeat five times. (Note: Squats are fine, but avoid lunges and deep knee bends because your joints will be more prone to injury.)

for the experienced during pregnancy, but you'll have to be extra careful to avoid falling. And, of course, no matter what activity's taking you outdoors (or to the indoor rink), make sure you don't work out to the point of exhaustion.

Weight training. Using weights can increase your muscle tone, but it's important to avoid heavy weights or those that require grunting or breath holding, which may compromise blood flow to the uterus. Use light weights with multiple repetitions instead.

Yoga. Yoga encourages relaxation, focus, and paying attention to your breathing—so it's just about perfect for pregnancy (and great preparation for childbirth, as well as for parenting). It also increases oxygenation (bringing more oxygen to the baby) and increases flexibility, mak-

ing pregnancy—and delivery—easier. Select a class that's specifically tailored to expectant women or ask your instructor how to modify poses so that they're safe for you. For instance, you won't be able to exercise on your back after the fourth month, and your center of gravity changes with pregnancy, so you'll have to adjust your favorite poses accordingly. One important caveat: Avoid Bikram yoga. It's done in a hot room (one that's generally 90°F to 100°F), and you need to pass on any exercises that heat you up too much.

Pilates. Pilates is similar to yoga in that it's a low- to no-impact discipline that improves your flexibility, strength, and muscle tone. The focus is on strengthening your core, which will improve your posture and ease backaches. Look for

Waist Twists

If you've been sitting for a while or just feel generally tensed up or uncomfortable, try this easy circulation-boosting move. Stand up and place your feet shoulder-width apart. Twist gently from the waist, slowly turning from side to side. Keep your back straight and let your arms swing freely. Can't get up? You can even do this exercise while you're sitting.

a class specifically tailored to pregnant women, or let your instructor know that you're expecting so you can avoid pregnancy-inappropriate moves (including those that overstretch).

Tai chi. An ancient form of meditative exercises, tai chi's basic slow movements allow even the stiffest person

Exercise in Bed

Have you been sent to bed (rest)? Not only will continuing to flex your muscles (in a modified way) be possible, it'll be extra important. See page 571 for more.

the opportunity to relax and strengthen the body without the risk of injury. If you're comfortable with it and have plenty of experience, it's fine to continue tai chi when you're expecting. Look for pregnancy-specific classes, or only do moves that you can easily complete—take care with the balancing poses.

Breathing. Believe it or not, you even get exercise credit for breathing—at least, if you do it right. Deep breathing is relaxing, improves body awareness, and allows for better oxygen intake than the shallow chest breaths most people take. Here's how to do it: Sit up straight and place your hands on your belly. Feel it rise and fall as you inhale (through your nose, unless it's too stuffy) and exhale (out your mouth). Concentrate on your breathing by counting: As you inhale, count to 4; as you exhale, count to 6. Try taking a few minutes each day to focus on breathing deeply.

If You Don't Exercise

Exercising during pregnancy can certainly do the average pregnant body good. But sitting it out (whether by choice or on practitioner's orders) and getting most of your exercise from opening and closing your car door won't hurt, either. In fact, if you're abstaining from exercise on practitioner's orders, you're helping your baby and yourself. Your practitioner will almost certainly restrict exercise if you have a history of miscarriages or of premature labor, or if you

have an incompetent cervix, bleeding or persistent spotting in the second or third trimester, heart disease, or a diagnosis of placenta previa or preeclampsia. Your activity may also be limited if you're expecting multiples; have high blood pressure, thyroid disease, anemia or other blood disorders, or a fetus that isn't thriving; are seriously over- or underweight; or have had an extremely sedentary lifestyle up until now. A history of precipitous (very brief) labor or of a fetus that didn't thrive in a previous pregnancy might also be a reason for a red light (or at least a yellow one) on exercise. In some cases, arm-only exercises or water workouts designed for pregnancy may be okayed when other exercises are taboo. Check with your practitioner for your pregnancy exercise protocol.

Chest Stretches

Pregnancy changes your posture and center of gravity, and it causes you to make a number of new and strange bodily adjustments—many of which can lead to aches and pains. Gently stretching your chest muscles will help you feel more comfortable while improving your circulation. Here's how: With your arms bent and at shoulder level, grasp both sides of a doorway. Lean forward, feeling the stretch in your chest. Hold this position for 10 to 20 seconds and release; do five reps.

The
Fifth
Month

Approximately 18 to 22 Weeks

HAT WAS ONCE COMPLETELY abstract is fast becoming palpable, literally. Chances are that sometime this month or the beginning of the next, you will feel your baby's movements for the first time. That miraculous sensation, along with the serious rounding of your belly, will finally make the pregnancy feel more like a reality. Though your baby is far from ready to make a personal appearance in the nursery, it's really nice to know for sure there's actually someone in there.

Your Baby This Month

Week 18 At 5½ inches long and about 5 ounces in weight (as much as that chicken breast you're having for dinner, but a lot cuter), your baby is filling out nicely and getting large enough that you might even be feeling those twists, rolls, kicks, and punches he or she is perfecting. Another set of skills your baby is mastering now is yawning and hiccuping (you might even begin to feel those hiccups soon!). And your one-of-a-kind baby is truly one of a kind now, complete with unique fingerprints on his or her fingertips and toes.

Week 19 This week your baby is hitting the growth charts at 6 inches long and a full half pound in weight. What fruit is it this week? Your baby's about the size of a large mango. A mango dipped in greasy cheese, actually. Vernix caseosa—a greasy white protective substance (it resembles cheese)—now covers your baby's sensitive skin, protecting it from the surrounding amniotic fluid. Without that protection, your baby would look very wrinkled at birth. The coating sheds as delivery approaches, but some babies born early are still covered with vernix at delivery.

Week 20 You've got a baby the size of a small cantaloupe in your melon-size belly this week, about 10 ounces and 6½ inches (crown to rump). Your ultrasound this month

Your Baby, Month 5

should be able to detect—if you want to know—whether your baby is a boy or a girl. And oh boy—or oh girl—has that baby been busy. If you're having a girl, her uterus is fully formed, her ovaries are holding about 7 million primitive eggs (though at birth, the number of eggs will be closer to 2 million), and her vaginal canal is starting to develop. If you're having a boy, his testicles have begun their descent from the abdomen. In a few months, they'll drop into the scrotum (which is still under construction). Luckily for your baby, he or she still has plenty of room in your womb, which means there's plenty of space for twisting, turning, kicking, punching, and even an occasional somersault. If you haven't felt these acrobatics yet, you almost certainly will in the coming weeks.

Week 21 How big is baby this week? About 7 inches in length (think large banana) and almost 11 ounces in weight. And talking about bananas, you might want to eat some this week if you'd like your baby to have a taste for them. Some carrots, too. That's because amniotic fluid differs from day to day depending on what you've eaten (hot chili one day, sweet banana another), and now that your baby is swallowing amniotic fluid each day (for hydration, nutrition, and also to get practice swal-

lowing and digesting), he or she will be getting a taste of—and a taste for—whatever's on your menu. Here's another baby update: Arms and legs are finally in proportion, neurons are now connected between the brain and muscles, and cartilage throughout the body is turning to bone. Which means that when your baby makes his or her moves (which you're probably feeling by now), they're much more coordinated—no more jerky twitches.

Week 22 Forget about ounces, baby. This week, we're talking a whopping weight of 1 pound and a length of nearly 8 inches, about the size of a small doll. But your doll is a living one—with developing senses, including touch, sight, hearing, and taste. What's your baby touching? He or she may grab onto the umbilical cord (there's not much else to hang onto in there) and practice the strong grip that will soon be clutching your fingers (and pulling on your hair). What's your baby seeing? Though it's dark in the uterine cocoon—and even with fused eyelids—fetuses this age can perceive light and dark. If you shine a flashlight over your belly, you might feel your baby react, perhaps trying to turn away from the "bright" light. What's your baby hearing? The sound of your voice and that of your partner, your heart beating, the whoosh-whoosh of your blood circulating through your body, those gastric gurgles produced by your stomach and intestines, the dog barking, sirens, a loud TV. And what's your baby tasting? Pretty much everything you're tasting (so pass the salad).

What You May Be Feeling

As always, remember that every pregnancy and every woman is different. You may experience all of these symptoms at one time or another, or only a few of them. Some may have continued from last month; others may be new. Still others may be hardly noticed because you've become so used to them. You may also have other, less common, symptoms. Here's what you might experience this month:

Physically

- More energy

- Fetal movement (probably by the end of the month)

- Increasing vaginal discharge

- Achiness in the lower abdomen and along the sides (from stretching of the ligaments supporting the uterus)

- Constipation

- Heartburn, indigestion, flatulence, bloating

- Occasional headaches, faintness, or dizziness

- Backache

- Nasal congestion and occasional nosebleeds; ear stuffiness

- Sensitive gums that may bleed when you brush

- Hearty appetite

- Leg cramps

- Mild swelling of ankles and feet, and occasionally of hands and face

- Varicose veins of legs and/or hemorrhoids

- Skin color changes on abdomen and/or face

- A protruding navel

- Faster pulse (heart rate)

- Easier—or more difficult—orgasm

Emotionally

- A growing sense of reality about the pregnancy

- Fewer mood swings, though you'll likely still be weepy and irritable occasionally

- Continued absentmindedness

A Look Inside

You're halfway through your pregnancy now—and the top of your uterus will hit your belly button sometime around the 20th week. By the end of this month, your uterus will be about an inch above your belly button. By this point, there is no hiding the fact that you're pregnant.

What You Can Expect at This Month's Checkup

Yet another checkup, and by this time you probably know the drill. This month, you can expect your practitioner to check the following, though there may be variations depending on your particular needs and your practitioner's style of practice:

- Weight and blood pressure

- Urine, for sugar and protein

- Fetal heartbeat

- Size and shape of uterus, by external palpation (feeling from the outside)

- Height of fundus (top of uterus)

- Feet and hands for swelling, and legs for varicose veins

- Symptoms you have been experiencing, especially unusual ones

- Questions or problems you want to discuss—have a list ready

What You May Be Wondering About

Heating Up

"I feel hot and sweaty all the time these days, even when everybody else is cool. What's that about?"

Feeling like hot stuff these days? You can thank your hormones (as always), increased blood flow to the skin, and a hopped-up pregnancy metabolism for that perpetually damp feeling. Throw in a particularly warm climate or the hottest summer on record (or even just an over-heated office in the middle of winter), and the heat is on—big time. Luckily, there are plenty of ways to stay comfortable when the temperature—outdoors, indoors, or inside of you—is soaring. To stay cool while you're heating for two:

- Wear loose, light clothing in breathable fabrics, such as cotton, and dress in layers so you can peel them off as you heat up.

- Avoid exercising outside in the heat of the day; take your power walks before breakfast or after dinner

instead, or attend exercise classes in an air-conditioned fitness center. Always quit before you feel overheated.

- Stay out of the sun as much as possible, particularly on very hot days.

- Take a tepid bath or shower to cool off. Or go for a swim, if that's practical—it's the one exercise that's almost sure not to overheat you.

- Seek out AC. Fans alone won't help you keep your cool when the temperature is over 90°F, so if you have no air-conditioning at home, spend time at the movies, a museum, a pal's house, or a mall.

- Be a thermostat hog. Commandeer the temperature control at home so you're always comfortable. Let your partner add a sweater or a blanket if he's chilly.

- Drink, drink, drink. Staying hydrated will help keep you from feeling weak and dizzy when you heat up. Down at least eight 8-ounce glasses of water a day, more if you're exercising and/or perspiring a lot.

- A sprinkle of powder can help absorb some moisture (plus help to prevent heat rash).

On the plus side, while you'll be sweating more—you'll be smelling less. That's because the production of apocrine perspiration (the stinkier kind produced by glands under the arms and breasts and in the genital area) actually slows down when you're expecting.

Dizziness

"I feel dizzy when I get up from a sitting or lying-down position. And yesterday I nearly fainted while I was shopping. Am I okay?"

Feeling a little dizzy can definitely be disconcerting when you're pregnant (especially because you might already be having a hard enough time staying on your feet), but it isn't dangerous. In fact, it's a pretty common—and almost always a normal—symptom of pregnancy. Here's why:

- In the first trimester, dizziness may occur because there's not yet an adequate blood supply to fill your rapidly expanding circulatory system; in the second trimester, it may be caused by the pressure of your expanding uterus on your blood vessels.

- Throughout your pregnancy, high levels of your old friend progesterone cause your blood vessels to relax and widen, increasing the flow of blood to your baby (good for baby) but slowing the return of blood to you (not so good for mom). Less blood flow to you means lower blood pressure and reduced blood flow to your brain, which can contribute to that light-headed, dizzy feeling.

- Getting up too quickly, which results in a sudden blood pressure drop, can trigger an especially light-headed moment. The cure for that kind of dizziness is simple: Just get up very gradually. Jumping up in a hurry to answer the phone is likely to land you right back on the sofa.

- You might also feel dizzy when your blood sugar is low—something expectant moms are particularly prone to. To avoid those blood sugar dips, get some protein and complex carbs at every meal (the combo helps maintain even blood sugar levels) and eat more frequently (choosing the minimeal approach or snacking in between meals). Carry a bag of trail mix, a piece of fruit, a granola bar, or some soy chips in your bag for quick blood sugar lifts.

When Too Much Is Too Much

Feel breathless or exhausted when you're jogging? What about when you're doing heavy cleaning—does the vacuum suddenly feel as if it weighs a ton? Stop before you drop. Exerting yourself to the point of exhaustion is never a good idea. During pregnancy it's a particularly bad one, because overwork takes its toll not only on you but on your baby as well. Instead of marathon activity sessions, pace yourself. Work or exercise a bit, rest a bit. Ultimately, the work, or the workout, gets done, and you won't feel drained afterward. If occasionally something doesn't get done, consider it good training for the days when the demands of parenthood will often keep you from finishing what you started.

- Dizziness can be a sign of dehydration, so be sure you're getting your full quota of fluids—at least 8 cups a day, more if you've been sweating.

- A dizzy spell can also be triggered by indoor stuffiness—in an overheated or crowded store (which might explain why you felt faint while you were shopping), office, or bus—especially if you're overdressed. In that case, getting some fresh air by stepping outside or opening a window may bring relief. Taking off your coat and loosening your clothes—especially around the neck and waist—should help, too.

If you feel dizzy or faint, lie down on your left side—with your legs elevated, if you can—or sit with your head lowered between your knees. Take deep breaths, and loosen any tight clothing (like that button on your jeans you struggled to close in the first place). As soon as you feel a little better, get something to eat and drink.

Tell your practitioner about the dizzy spells at your next visit. Actual fainting is rare, but if you do faint, there is no need for concern—it won't affect your baby. But do call right away (once you come to, of course).

Backache

"I'm having a lot of back pain. I'm afraid I won't be able to stand up at all by the ninth month."

The aches and discomforts of pregnancy aren't designed to make you miserable, though that's often the upshot. They're the side effects of the preparations your body is making for that momentous moment when your baby is born. Backache is no exception. During pregnancy, the usually stable joints of the pelvis begin to loosen up to allow easier (hopefully) passage for the

baby at delivery. This, along with your oversize abdomen, throws your body off balance. To compensate, you tend to bring your shoulders back and arch your neck. Standing with your belly thrust forward—to be sure that no one who passes fails to notice you're pregnant—compounds the problem. The result: a deeply curved lower back, strained back muscles, and pain.

Even pain with a purpose hurts. But without defeating the purpose, you can conquer (or at least subdue) the pain. The following should help:

- Sit smart. Sitting puts more stress on your spine than almost any other activity, so it pays to do it right. At home and at work, make sure the chairs you use most provide good support, preferably with a straight back, arms, and a firm cushion. A chair back that reclines slightly can also help take the pressure off. Use a footrest to elevate your feet slightly (see illustration on page 239), and don't cross your legs, which can cause your pelvis to tilt forward, exacerbating those strained back muscles.

- Sitting for long periods can be as bad for your back as sitting the wrong way. Try not to sit for more than an hour without taking a walking and stretching break; setting a half-hour limit would be even better.

- Try not to stand too long, either. If you work on your feet, keep one foot on a low stool to take some pressure off your lower back. When you're standing on a hard-surfaced floor—in the kitchen while cooking or washing dishes, for example—put a small skid-proof rug underfoot to ease the pressure.

- Avoid lifting heavy loads, but if you must, do it slowly. Stabilize yourself by assuming a wide stance; bend at the knees, not at the waist; and lift with your arms and legs, not your back (see illustration below.) If you have to carry a heavy load of groceries, divide them between two shopping bags and carry one in each arm rather than carrying it all in front of you.

- Try to keep weight gain within the recommended parameters (see page 166). Excess pounds will only add to the load your back is struggling under.

- Wear the right shoes. Extremely high heels are a pain for your back—as are very flat ones. Experts recommend a chunky 2-inch heel to keep your body in proper alignment. You might also consider orthotics, orthopedic shoe inserts designed for muscle support.

- A comfortable sleeping position aided by a body pillow (one that's at least 5 feet long) will help minimize aches and pains when you're awake. When getting out of bed in the morning, swing your legs over the side of the bed to the floor rather than twisting to get up.

- Consider a crisscross support sling designed specifically for a pregnant figure, which will help take the burden of your belly's weight off your lower back.

- No reaching for the stars—or the crackers on the top shelf. Use a low, stable step stool to get items from high places and you'll avoid additional strain.

- Alternate cold and heat to temporarily relieve sore back muscles. Use an ice pack for 15 minutes, followed by a heating pad for 15 minutes. Wrap both cold pack and heating pad in a towel or cloth.

Bend at the knees when you lift

- Take a warm (but not hot) bath. Or turn the shower head to pulsating and enjoy the back massage.

- Rub your back the right way. Treat yourself to a therapeutic massage (with a massage therapist who knows you're pregnant and is trained in the art of prenatal massage).

- Learn to relax. Many back problems are aggravated by stress. If you think yours might be, try some relaxation exercises when pain strikes. Also follow the suggestions beginning on page 141 for dealing with stress in your life.

- Do simple exercises that strengthen your abdominal muscles, such as the Dromedary Droop (page 222) and the Pelvic Tilt (page 224). Or sit on an exercise ball and rock back and forth (or lie back on it to ease back—and hip—discomfort). Join a pregnancy yoga or water gymnastics class, or consider water therapy if you can find a medically (and pregnancy) savvy water therapist.

- If pain is significant, ask your practitioner about physical therapists or alternative medicine specialists (such as acupuncturists or those who specialize in biofeedback), who might be able to help.

Sit comfortably

Abdominal Aches

"What are those aches and pains I've been getting on the lower sides of my abdomen?"

What you're probably feeling is the pregnancy equivalent of growing pains: the stretching of muscles and ligaments supporting your enlarging uterus. Technically, it's known as round ligament pain (though when it's tugging at your sides, do you really care what the pros call it?), and most expectant moms experience it. But there's a wide variety of ways to experience it. The pain may be crampy, sharp and stabbing, or achy, and it may be more noticeable when you're getting up from bed or from a chair, or when you cough. It can be brief, or it may last for several hours. And it's completely normal. As long as it is occasional and fleeting, and there are no other symptoms accompanying it (such as fever, chills, bleeding, or lightheadedness), this kind of pain is absolutely nothing to be concerned about.

Kicking up your feet (though not literally) and resting in a comfortable position should bring some relief. Of course, mention the pain—like all pains—to your practitioner at your next visit so you can be reassured that this is just another normal, if annoying, part of pregnancy.

The New Skin You're In

If you haven't already noticed, pregnancy impacts just about every inch of your body—from head (that forgetfulness!) to toes (those expanding feet!) and everything in between (breasts, belly!). So it's not surprising that your skin is also showing the effects of pregnancy. Here are some changes you may expect when it comes to your expectant skin:

Linea nigra. Sporting a zipper down the center of your burgeoning belly? Just as those pregnancy hormones caused the hyperpigmentation, or darkening, of the areolas, they are now responsible for the darkening of the linea alba, the white line you probably never noticed that runs between your belly button and your pubic area. During pregnancy, it's renamed the linea nigra, or black line, and may be more noticeable in dark-skinned women than in those who are fair-skinned. It usually starts to appear during the second trimester and most often will begin to fade a few months after delivery (though it may never go away entirely). Interested in a round of "guess-the-sex-of-my-baby"? According to an old wives' tale, if the linea nigra runs only up to the belly button, you're having a girl. If it runs past the navel up to the xiphoid process (near your ribs), it's a boy.

Mask of pregnancy (chloasma). Around 50 to 75 percent of expectant mothers, particularly those with darker complexions, develop discolorations—in a masklike configuration or a confetti-like appearance—on foreheads, noses, and cheeks. The patches are dark in light-skinned women and light in dark-skinned women. Not a fan of the blotchy look? Never fear. Chloasma will fade within a few months after delivery; if it doesn't (or if you'd like to speed up its postpartum retreat), a dermatologist can prescribe a bleaching cream (if you aren't nursing) or recommend another treatment (such as a laser or a peel). Because those treatments are no-no's for now, bring on the concealer and foundation in the meantime (see page 149).

Other skin hyperpigmentation. Many women also find that freckles and moles become darker and more noticeable and that darkening of the skin occurs in high-friction areas, such as between the thighs. All this hyperpigmentation should fade after delivery. Sun can intensify the discoloration, so use a sunscreen with an SPF of 15 or more on all exposed skin and avoid spending long hours in the sun (even with sunscreen on). A hat that completely shades your face and long sleeves to protect your arms (if you can take the heat) can also help.

Red palms and soles. It's your hormones at work again (plus an increase

Foot Growth

"My shoes are all beginning to feel uncomfortably tight. Could my feet be growing, too?"

The belly isn't the only part of the pregnant body that's prone to expansion. If you're like many expectant women, you'll discover that your feet are growing, too. Good news if you're looking to revamp your entire shoe collection; not so good if you've just indulged in a pricey pair or two.

What causes your feet to go through a growth spurt? While some expansion in blood flow), and this time they're causing red, itchy palms (and sometimes soles of the feet) in more than two thirds of white and one third of nonwhite pregnant women. There's no specific treatment, but some women find relief by soaking their hands and/or feet in cold water or applying an ice bag for a few minutes a couple of times a day. Steer clear of anything that heats up your hands and feet (such as taking hot baths, washing dishes, wearing wool gloves), because that can make the condition worse. Also, stay away from potential irritants, such as harsh soaps or scented lotions. The dishpan look will disappear soon after delivery.

Bluish, blotchy legs. Due to stepped-up estrogen production, many expectant women experience this kind of transitory, mottled discoloration on their legs (and sometimes their arms) when they're chilly. It's harmless and will disappear postpartum.

Skin tags. A skin tag, which is essentially a tiny piece of excess skin, is another benign skin problem common in pregnant women and often found in high-friction areas, such as under the arms. Skin tags frequently develop in the second and third trimesters and may regress after delivery. If they don't, your physician can easily remove them.

Heat rash. Though heat rashes are usually associated with babies, pregnant women get them, too. Caused by the combination of an already overheated pregnant body, dampness from excessive perspiration, and the friction of skin rubbing against itself or against clothing (as it tends to do when there's more skin to rub), heat rash can be irritating. It is most common in the crease between and beneath the breasts, in the crease where the bulge of the lower abdomen rubs against the top of the pubic area, and on the inner thighs. (The pregnancy beauty bonuses just keep on coming, don't they?) A cool, damp compress can take some of the heat out of your heat rash. Patting on some powder after your shower and trying to keep as cool as possible will help minimize discomfort and recurrence. A dab of calamine lotion can also be soothing and is safe to use, but before you apply any medicated lotions, check with your practitioner. If any rash or irritation lasts longer than a couple of days, ask your practitioner about next steps.

Irritated skin rashes. Often, rashes are triggered by pregnancy-sensitive skin reacting to a product you've used prepregnancy without a reaction. Switching to a gentler product often relieves these contact rashes, but still do let your practitioner know about any persistent rash.

But wait, there's more. Believe it or not, there are a host of other skin changes you might experience. For information on stretch marks, see page 179; itchy pimples, see page 288; dry or oily skins, see pages 158–59; spider veins, see page 156.

can be attributed to the normal fluid retention and swelling of pregnancy (or to new fat in your feet if your weight gain has been substantial or quick), there's another reason, too. Relaxin, the pregnancy hormone that loosens the ligaments and joints around your pelvis so your baby can fit through, doesn't discriminate between the ligaments you'd want loosened up (like those pelvic ones) and those you'd rather it just leave alone (like those in your feet). The result: When the ligaments in the feet are loosened, the bones under them tend to spread slightly, resulting, for many women, in a half or whole shoe-size increase. Though the joints will tighten back up again after delivery, it's possible that your feet will be permanently larger.

In the meantime, try the tips for reducing excessive swelling (see page 286) if that seems to be your problem, and get a couple of pairs of shoes that fit you comfortably now and will meet your "growing" needs (so you won't end up barefoot and pregnant). When shoe shopping, put comfort before style— even if it's just this once. Look for shoes with heels that are no more than 2 inches high and have both nonskid soles and plenty of space for your feet to spread out (shop for them at the end of the day when your feet are the most swollen). The shoes should be made from a material that will allow your swollen, sweaty dogs to breathe (nothing synthetic).

Are your feet and legs achy, especially at the end of the day? Shoes and orthotic inserts specially designed to correct the distorted center of pregnancy gravity not only can make your feet more comfortable but can reduce back and leg pain as well. Getting off your feet periodically during the day can (obviously) help with swelling and pain, as can elevating (and periodically flexing) your feet when you get the chance. You can also try slipping on elasticized slippers while you're at home; wearing them for several hours a day may not make a great fashion statement, but it can ease fatigue and achiness.

Fast-Growing Hair and Nails

"It seems to me that my hair and nails have never grown so fast before."

Though it may seem as if pregnancy hormones only team up to make you miserable during your nine months (constipation, heartburn, and nausea come to mind), those same hormones are actually responsible for a substantial pregnancy perk: nails that grow faster than you can manicure them and hair that grows before you can secure appointments with your stylist (and if you're really lucky, hair that is thicker and more lustrous). Those pregnancy hormones trigger a surge in circulation and a boost in metabolism that nourish hair and nail cells, making them healthier than ever before.

Of course, every perk has its price. That extra nourishment can, unfortunately, have less than happy effects, too: It can cause hair to grow in places you would rather it didn't (and probably didn't know it could, at least on a woman). Facial areas (lips, chin, and cheeks) are most commonly plagued with this pregnancy-induced hairiness, but arms, legs, chest, back, and belly can be affected, too. (To read about which hair removal treatments are safe during pregnancy, see page 145). And though your nails might be long, they can also turn dry and brittle.

Do keep in mind that these hair and nail changes are only temporary. Your good-hair-day run ends with delivery— when the normal daily hair loss that's suppressed during pregnancy (thus the thicker hair) resumes with a vengeance. And your nails will likely go back to their slower growth schedule postpartum, too (probably not such a bad thing—you'll want to keep your nails short anyway with a new baby around).

Vision

"My eyesight seems to be getting worse since I got pregnant. And my contact lenses don't seem to fit anymore. Am I imagining it?"

Nope, you're not seeing things— that is, you're not seeing things as well as you were prepregnancy. The eyes are just another of the seemingly unrelated body parts that can fall prey to pregnancy hormones. Not only can your vision seem less sharp, but your contact lenses, if you wear them, may suddenly no longer feel comfortable. Eye dryness, which is caused by a hormone-induced decrease in tear production, may be at least partially to blame for irritation and discomfort. If that's not enough, fluid increases that change the eye lenses' shape can actually cause some pregnant women to become more near- or farsighted. Your vision should clear up and your eyes return to normal after delivery (so don't bother to get a new prescription unless the change is so pronounced that you really can't see well anymore).

Now isn't the time to consider corrective laser eye surgery. Though the procedure wouldn't harm the baby, it could overcorrect your vision and take longer to heal, possibly requiring a second corrective surgery later on (plus the eyedrops used aren't recommended for pregnant women). Ophthalmologists recommend avoiding the surgery during pregnancy, in the six months preconception, and for at least six months postpartum (and if you're nursing, six months postweaning).

Though a slight deterioration in visual acuity is not unusual in pregnancy, other symptoms do warrant a call to your practitioner. If you experience blurring or dimming vision or often see spots or floaters, or have double vision that persists for more than two or three hours, don't wait to see if it passes; call your practitioner at once. Briefly seeing spots after you have been standing for a while or when you get up suddenly from a sitting position is fairly common and nothing to worry about, though you should report it at your next visit.

Fetal Movement Patterns

"I felt little movements every day last week, but I haven't felt anything at all today. What's wrong?"

Feeling your baby twist, wriggle, punch, kick, and hiccup is simply one of pregnancy's biggest thrills (it sure beats heartburn and puffy feet). There may be no better proof that a brand-new—and impressively energetic—life is developing within you. But fetal movements can also drive a mom-to-be to distraction with questions and doubts: Is my baby moving enough? Too much? Moving at all? One minute you're sure those were kicks you were feeling, the next you're second-guessing yourself (maybe it was just gas?). One day you feel your baby's twists and turns nonstop. The next day your little athlete seems to have been benched, and you barely feel a thing.

Not to worry. At this stage of pregnancy, concerns about your baby's movements—while understandable—are usually unnecessary. The frequency of noticeable movements at this point varies a great deal, and patterns of movement are erratic at best. Though your baby is almost certainly on the move much of the time, you probably won't be feeling it consistently until he or she is packing a more powerful punch. Some of those dance moves may be missed because of the fetal position (facing and kicking inward, for instance, instead of outward). Or because of your own activity—when you're walking or moving about a lot, your fetus may be rocked to sleep; or it may be awake, but you may be too busy to notice its movements. It's also possible that you're sleeping right through your baby's most active period; for many babies that's in the middle of the night. (Even at this stage, babies are most likely to act up when their moms are lying down.)

One way to prompt fetal movement if you haven't noticed any all day is to lie down for an hour or two in the evening, preferably after a glass of milk, orange juice, or other snack. The combination of your inactivity and the jolt of food energy may be able to get your fetus going. If that doesn't work, try again in a few hours, but don't worry. Many moms-to-be find they don't notice movement for a day or two at a time, or even three or four days, this early on. If you're still worried, call your practitioner for reassurance.

After the 28th week, fetal movements become more consistent, and it's a good idea to get into the habit of checking on your baby's activity daily (see page 289).

Second-Trimester Ultrasound

"I already had one ultrasound early in pregnancy. Now I'm in my second trimester and am scheduled for another ultrasound. What's the reason for the second one?"

These days it's pretty much routine for women in the second trimester to be scheduled for a level 2 ultrasound, no matter how normally their pregnancies are proceeding and no matter how many ultrasounds they've already had. Practitioners have found that a second trimester ultrasound is a great way to see how a baby is developing and to offer reassurance that everything is going exactly the way it should be. On the plus side for parents, it's fun to get a sneak peek at your baby—and with today's 3-D and 4-D technology (if you spring for the upgrade from 2-D) that sneak peek is more lifelike than ever before.

What's more, you get to leave with a great souvenir—a photo or digital video that you can share with your friends and family. It can also give you the 4-1-1 on baby's sex (on a want-to-know basis, of course; see next question).

The more detailed level 2 sonogram (also called an anatomy scan), typically performed between 18 and 22 weeks, gives your practitioner additional valuable information about what's going on in that belly of yours. For example, it can measure the size of your baby and check out all the major organs. It can determine the amount of amniotic fluid to make sure there's just the right amount, and evaluate the location of your placenta. In short, this second-trimester ultrasound—besides being fun to watch—will give you and your practitioner a clear picture (literally) of the overall health of your baby and your pregnancy.

If you're concerned about the upcoming picture show (and what those grainy images reveal), talk to your practitioner about what he or she is looking for. Chances are you'll come away enlightened (and relieved).

A Picture That Lasts a Lifetime

Now that you've got your baby's first portrait, courtesy of your second-trimester ultrasound exam, you'll want to preserve it forever—right? To make sure that precious picture doesn't get damaged (or fade), scan it into your computer and save it on your hard drive or onto a CD. Or scan it into a photo website and have it printed out on acid-free paper with real photo ink. That way your memories won't fade with, well, your memory.

Baby's First Mall Portrait

Want a womb with a view? Ultrasound is a window into the wonderful world of your womb, and to get a sneak peek into that world, you often don't have to go farther than your local mall. But is it safe to take that peek inside your tummy on the way to Sears?

The FDA hasn't yet established rules for these storefront prenatal photography studios, but it does warn against having ultrasounds for fun (instead of for medical reasons), since the three-dimensional imaging machines they use are much higher powered than the typical ultrasound machines at your doctor's office. What's more, many medical professionals fear that nervous moms-to-be will come away wrongly convinced there's something wrong with their babies, or, worse, that the less-trained wand wavers will miss real problems that a pro would detect.

If you're still intrigued by the idea, check with your practitioner before you leap (or in this case heave yourself) onto the exam table at the mall. If you decide to go ahead with this kind of elective sonography, do so wisely: Limit your visits to one or two, with each ultrasound no more than 15 minutes in length. And bring your wallet. The image may be priceless, but some studios charge a hefty price for that suitable-for-framing photo, CD, and DVD of your baby-to-be.

"I'm going for my 20-week ultrasound, and we're not sure whether to find out the baby's sex or not."

This is one pregnancy decision only a mom and dad can make—and there's no right or wrong when it comes to making it. Some parents opt to know for practical reasons: It makes layette shopping, nursery painting, and name selection (only one to pick!) a lot simpler. Others opt to know because they simply can't stand the suspense. But many parents still prefer the guessing game, and they decide to find out the old-fashioned way—when baby's lower half finally makes its way out into the world. The choice is yours.

If you do decide to find out now, keep in mind that determining the sex of a baby through ultrasound is not an exact science (unlike amniocentesis, which determines the sex of the baby through chromosomal analysis). Very occasionally, parents are told by the sonographer that they're expecting a girl only to hear at delivery, "It's a boy!" (or vice versa). So if you do choose to find out your baby's gender when you go for your ultrasound, remember that it's only a guess, however educated it may be.

Placenta Position

"The doctor said my ultrasound showed that the placenta was down near the cervix. She said that it was too early to worry about it, but of course I started worrying."

Think your baby is the only thing moving around in your uterus? Think again. Like a fetus, a placenta can move around during pregnancy. It doesn't actually pick up and relocate, but it does appear to migrate upward as the lower segment of the uterus stretches and grows. Though an estimated 10 percent of placentas are in the lower segment in the second trimester (and an even larger percentage before 14 weeks), the vast majority move into the upper segment by the time delivery nears. If this doesn't happen and the placenta remains low in the uterus, partially or completely covering the cervix (the mouth of the uterus), a diagnosis of "placenta previa" is made. This complication occurs in very few full-term pregnancies (about 1 in 200). In other words, your doctor is right. It's too early to worry—and statistically speaking, the chances are slim that you'll ever have to worry.

"During my ultrasound, the technician told me I have an anterior placenta. What does that mean?"

It means your baby is taking a backseat to the placenta. Usually, a fertilized egg situates itself in the posterior uterus—the part closest to your spine, which is where the placenta eventually develops. Sometimes, though, the egg implants on the opposite side of the uterus, closest to your belly button. When the placenta develops, it grows on the front (or anterior) side of your uterus, with the baby behind it. And that, apparently, is what happened in your case.

Happily, your baby doesn't care which side of the uterus he or she is lying on, and where the placenta is located certainly makes no difference to his or her development. The downside for you is that you might be less able to feel (and later see) your baby's early kicks and punches because the placenta will serve as a cushion between your baby and your tummy (which could lead to unnecessary worrying). For the same reason, your doctor or midwife may find it a bit harder to hear fetal heart sounds (and it could make amniocentesis a little more challenging). But despite those slight inconveniences—which are nothing to be concerned about—an anterior placenta is inconsequential. What's more, it's very likely that the placenta will move into a more posterior position later on (as anterior placentas commonly do).

Sleeping Position

"I've always slept on my stomach. Now I'm afraid to. And I just can't seem to get comfortable any other way."

Unfortunately, two common favorite sleeping positions—on the belly and on the back—are not the best (and certainly not the most comfortable) choices during pregnancy. The belly position, for obvious reasons: As your stomach grows, it's like sleeping on a watermelon. The back position, though more comfortable, rests the entire weight of your pregnant uterus on your back, your intestines, and major blood vessels. This pressure can aggravate backaches and hemorrhoids, make digestion less efficient, interfere with optimum circulation, and possibly cause hypotension, or low blood pressure, which can make you dizzy.

Sleeping on your side

Carrying Baby, Fifth Month

Here are just three of the very different ways that a woman may carry near the end of her fifth month. The variations on these are endless. Depending on your size, your shape, the amount of weight you've gained, and the position of your uterus, you may be carrying higher, lower, bigger, smaller, wider, or more compactly.

This doesn't mean you have to sleep standing up. Curling up or stretching out on your side—preferably the left side, though either side is fine—with one leg crossed over the other and with a pillow between them (see illustration, facing page), is ideal for both you and your fetus. It not only allows maximum flow of blood and nutrients to the placenta but also enhances efficient kidney function, which means better elimination of waste products and fluids and less swelling (edema) of ankles, feet, and hands.

Very few people, however, manage to stay in one position through the night. Don't worry (repeat: do not worry) if you wake up and find yourself on your back or abdomen. No harm done (repeat: no harm done); just turn back to your side. You may feel uncomfortable for a few nights, but your body will soon adjust to the new position. A body pillow that's at least 5 feet long or a wedge-shaped pillow can offer support, making side sleeping much more comfortable and staying on your side much easier.

If you don't have either of these, you can improvise with any extra pillows, placing them against your body in different positions until you find that perfect combination for catching z's.

Class Womb?

"I have a friend who insists that taking her unborn baby to concerts will make him a music lover, and another one whose husband reads to her tummy every night to give their baby a love of literature. Should I be trying to stimulate my baby, too?"

All parents want only the best for their children—or in this case, for their children-to-be. But it's important to keep some perspective before switching on the Beethoven and reciting the Shakespeare.

While it's true the fetus's ability to hear is well developed by the end of the second trimester, there is no proof that an in utero concerto or a lesson in the great classics gives the baby a head start in education (or on a musical or literary career). Promoting an educational or cultural agenda this early can also come with a potential downside—especially if it signals the start of extremely premature parental pushiness, and begins placing too much emphasis on achievement at a too-tender age (and before birth is definitely too tender an age). Fetuses (like the babies and children they'll become before you know it) develop—and later, learn—best at their own pace, no prodding necessary. There's also the theoretical risk that when parents attempt to turn the womb into a classroom, they may unwittingly disrupt the natural sleep patterns of their baby-to-be, actually hampering development instead of nurturing it (just as waking up a newborn for a game of name-this-letter might).

That said, there's nothing wrong—and a lot right—with providing a uterine environment that's rich in language and music, and much more important, about finding ways to get close to your little one long before you even have that first cuddle. Talking, reading, or singing to your baby while in the womb (no amplification necessary) won't guarantee a scholarship to Yale, but it will guarantee that your baby will know your voice at birth—and will give you both a head start on bonding.

Playing classical music now may increase the likelihood that your newborn will appreciate, and even be soothed by, these sounds later on (though it's been shown that exposure to music and literature has a much more significant effect once your baby is actually born than it does prenatally—so keep the sonatas handy once baby's arrived). And don't underestimate the power of touch. Since this sense also begins to develop in utero, stroking your belly now may also help strengthen the bond between you and your baby later.

So turn on the Mozart, bring on the Bach, pull out those dusty Shakespeare sonnets and read away to your belly if you like (and if you can do it without cracking up). Just make sure you're doing it all to get closer to your baby—not to get your baby closer to an Ivy League degree.

Of course, if you feel silly performing for your bloated belly, there's no reason to worry that your baby will miss out on getting to know you. He or she is getting used to the sound of your voice—and Dad's, too—every time you speak to each other or someone else. So enjoy making baby contact now, but definitely don't worry about early learning this early. As you'll discover, kids grow up all too soon anyway. There's no need to rush the process, particularly before birth.

Carrying Older Children

"I have a three-year-old who always wants to be carried. Is it okay to keep doing it at this point in pregnancy? It's definitely killing my back."

Carrying moderately heavy loads (even some 35 or 40 pounds of pre-schooler) is safe throughout pregnancy unless your practitioner has told you otherwise. What giving in to those choruses of "carry me" can end up doing to your back is another story—a probably painful one. Breaking her of the being-carried habit would definitely be a better strategy than continuing to break your back—so try making walking fun for her. Challenge her to mini races, or climb the stairs to a song. Don't forget to applaud her efforts when she does agree to walk on her own two feet instead of hailing the mommy taxi—and try to blame your back (not her sibling-to-be) for the slowdown in pick ups. Compensate, too, with plenty of holding and hugging from a sitting position. And because there will be times when she definitely won't take "walk" for an answer, save your back some strain by learning the proper way to lift her (see page 237).

Approaching Parenthood

"I keep wondering if I will be happy with this whole parenthood thing. I have no clue what it'll really be like."

Most people approach any major change in their lives—and there's no more major change than an upcoming birth—wondering whether it will be a change they'll be happy with. And it's always much more likely to be a happy change if you keep your expectations realistic.

So, if you have images of bringing a cooing, smiling, picture-perfect baby home from the hospital, you may want to read up on what newborns are really like. Not only won't your newborn be smiling or cooing for many weeks, he or she may hardly communicate with you at all, except to cry—and this will almost invariably be when you're sitting down to dinner or starting to get busy in bed, have to go to the bathroom, or are so tired you can't move.

And if your visions of parenthood consist of nothing but leisurely morning walks through the park, sunny days at the zoo, and hours coordinating a wardrobe of miniature, picture-perfect clothes, another reality check is probably in order. You'll have your share of walks in the park, but there will also be many mornings that turn into evenings before you and your baby have the chance to see the light of day; many sunny days that will be spent largely in the laundry room; very few tiny outfits that will escape unstained by spit-up, pureed bananas, and baby vitamins.

What you can expect realistically, however, are some of the most wondrous, miraculous experiences of your life. The fulfillment you will feel when cuddling a warm, sleeping bundle of baby (even if that cherub was howling moments before) is incomparable. That—along with that first toothless smile meant just for you—will be well worth all the sleepless nights, delayed dinners, mountains of laundry, and frustrated romance.

Happy? Just you wait, Mom.

Wearing a Seat Belt

"Is it safe to buckle my seat belt in the car? And is the air bag an issue when you're pregnant?"

There's no safer way for an expectant mother—and her unborn baby—to travel than buckled up. Plus, it's the law in most places. For maximum safety and minimum discomfort, fasten the belt below your belly, across your pelvis and upper thighs. Wear the shoulder harness over your shoulder (not under your arm), diagonally between your breasts and to the side of your belly. And don't worry that the pressure of an abrupt stop will hurt your baby; he or she is well cushioned by amniotic fluid and uterine muscle, among the world's best shock-absorbing materials.

As for air bags, it's safest to keep your distance. So if you're sitting in the passenger seat, set the seat as far back as you can (your legs will appreciate the stretching room, too). If you're driving, tilt the wheel up toward your chest, away from your tummy, and sit at least 10 inches from the steering wheel, if possible.

Travel

"Is it safe for me to go ahead and take the vacation we had planned for this month?"

Never again will it be so easy to vacation with your baby. Fast-forward to next year when you'll be lugging a car seat, diapers, toys, and child-proofing kits wherever you go, and you'll see why. And there's no better time for pregnant travel than the second trimester. After all, the fatigue, queasiness, and emotional extremes of the first trimester are behind you—but you're not yet at the point where your belly has a life of its own, making it hard enough to drag yourself around, never mind the luggage.

So don't have reservations about those reservations you've made. But before you pack your suitcase, do get the

go-ahead from your practitioner. Chances are your vacation plans will be green-lighted, since travel is rarely restricted during pregnancy unless there's an obstetrical or medical complication.

Once you've been cleared for takeoff, you'll only need to do a little planning to ensure a safe and pleasant expectant voyage, whether it's a quick business trip or a leisurely babymoon:

Time it right. When you're planning a pregnancy vacation, timing is everything. For long-distance travel, the second trimester is the clear winner. Far-flung travel during the first trimester, even in a low-risk pregnancy, can be pretty uncomfortable, especially if morning sickness, fatigue, and other early symptoms have hit hard. Likewise, roaming far from home isn't recommended in the last part of the last trimester for obvious reasons: Should you go into labor early, you'd be stranded far from your practitioner.

Choose a suitable destination. A hot, humid climate may be hard for you to handle because of your hopped-up metabolism; if you do choose such a locale, make sure that your hotel and transportation are air-conditioned

Buckling up for two

Jettisoning Jet Lag

Add jet lag to the normal fatigue of pregnancy and you're likely to want to end your trip before it begins. So it makes sense to try to minimize—if you can't completely eliminate—the physically draining effects of travel across time zones. Here's how:

Start switching time zones before you leave. Ease yourself into the time zone you're headed for by setting your watch—and your schedule—gradually back or forward. If you're heading east, start getting up a little earlier and going to bed a little earlier a few days before your departure. If you're heading west, go to bed a little later and get up a little later (if you can). On your plane ride, try to sleep if it's an appropriate sleeping time at your destination, or stay awake if it's not.

Live on local time. Once you arrive at your destination, start living on local time full-time. If you arrive at your Paris hotel room at 7 A.M., exhausted from an overnight flight, resist the urge to nap until noon. Instead, try to get a second wind going with a shower and a hearty breakfast, and then step out for a slow-paced day. Don't push yourself—take frequent breaks to sit down with your feet up—but do try hard to stay vertical. Lie down and you're sure to surrender to sleep. Dine, too, according to the local clock and not your internal one (snack if you're hungry, but hold off on a full meal until the clock strikes "eat"), and strive to stay awake until as close to your usual bedtime (local time) as possible. This should help you sleep through the local night. Avoid sleeping in, too, which could make going to bed at a normal time the next night more difficult. Ask for a wake-up call, even if you think you won't need it.

Seek out sun. Getting some sunlight will help you reset your biological clock, so be sure to spend some time outdoors on your first day at your new destination. If there's no sun to be found, at least spend some time outdoors. If you've gone west to east, the best sun to seek is morning sun; if you've gone east to west, get your daylight in the late afternoon.

Eat, drink, and be less jet-lagged. Anyone who travels frequently knows how dehydrating air travel can be. And dehydration can make jet lag symptoms more severe (not to mention put you at risk for pregnancy complications). So drink plenty of water on the plane, and continue drinking once you have arrived. Take time to eat regularly, too. Concentrate on foods that are high in long-term energy boosters, such as protein and complex carbohydrates, preferably eaten in combo. Getting some exercise (nothing strenuous; a walk in a park or a few laps in the hotel pool are just right) will also help you feel less fatigued.

Don't look for a miracle. Don't use any over-the-counter, prescription, or herbal preparation for jet lag (or any purpose) without your practitioner's approval.

Give it time. You should start to feel less tired and more in sync with the local schedule within a couple of days.

You may find sleep problems—and the fatigue that inevitably accompanies them—continue to plague you during the entire trip. But let's face it, that may have less to do with jet lag and more to do with the fact that you're carrying around a lot of extra baggage—the kind you can't ask a skycap or bellman to help you with.

252 NINE MONTHS AND COUNTING

Pregnant at a High Altitude

Women who are accustomed to breathing thinner air because they live at a high altitude are far less likely to encounter an altitude-induced problem in their pregnancies (hypertension, water retention, a somewhat smaller-than-average baby) than those who just moved there after a lifetime at sea level. For that reason, many practitioners suggest postponing a contemplated move or visit from low altitude to high until after delivery. And scaling Mount Rainier is definitely out for now.

If you must make a trip to a destination at a high altitude, try to ascend gradually, if possible (if you're driving, for example, try to go up 2,000 feet a day, rather than going up 8,000 feet all at once). To minimize the risk of developing acute mountain sickness (AMS), also plan on limiting exertion for a few days after your arrival, drink lots of fluids, eat frequent small meals instead of three large ones, avoid rich and heavy food, and seek sleeping accommodations, if feasible, at a somewhat lower altitude.

and that you stay hydrated and out of the sun. Travel to areas at high altitude (more than 7,000 feet above sea level) may be unsafe, because adjusting to the decrease in oxygen may be too taxing for both you and your baby. Other inappropriate destinations are developing regions of the world for which vaccinations would be necessary, since some vaccines may be hazardous during pregnancy (check with your practitioner). Not insignificantly, these same locales may be hotbeds of certain potentially dangerous infections for which there are no vaccines—another reason to avoid them when you're expecting. Not to mention the risk of food- and water-borne illnesses common in those parts.

Plan a trip that's relaxing. A single destination trumps a whirlwind tour that takes you to six cities in six days. A vacation for which you set the pace is a lot better than one where a group tour guide sets it for you. A few hours of sightseeing or shopping (or meetings) should be alternated with time spent with your feet up. You'll need to listen

to your pregnant body, which may have to set the agenda.

Insure yourself. Sign up for reliable travel insurance, in case a pregnancy complication should require you to change your plans and stick close to home. Consider medical evacuation insurance as well if you're traveling overseas, in case you need to return home quickly and under medical supervision. Medical travel insurance may also be useful if your regular insurance plan does not include foreign medical care. Check your policy ahead of time.

Pack a pregnancy survival kit. Make sure you take enough prenatal vitamins to last the trip; some healthy snacks; Sea-Bands if you're susceptible to motion sickness and a medication for traveler's stomach that's been recommended by your practitioner; comfortable shoes roomy enough to accommodate feet swelled by long hours of sightseeing or work; and sunscreen.

If you're traveling overseas, have the name of a local obstetrician handy, just in case. Contact the International

Association for Medical Assistance to Travelers (IAMAT) at (716) 754-4883 or at iamat.org, which can provide you with a directory of English-speaking physicians throughout the world. Some major hotel chains can also provide you with this kind of information. When you're overseas, if for any reason you find yourself in need of a doctor in a hurry and your hotel can't provide you with one, you can call the American embassy, an American military base, or the nearest teaching hospital. Or you can head for the hospital's emergency room. If you have medical travel insurance, you should have a number to call for help.

Take healthy eating habits with you. You may be on vacation, but your baby is working as hard as ever at growing and developing and has the same nutritional requirements as always. Order thoughtfully and you will be able to savor the local cuisine while also fulfilling your baby's requirements. Most important: Eat regularly and snack as needed. Don't skip breakfast or lunch to save up for a six-course dinner.

Eat selectively. In some regions, it may not be safe to eat raw unpeeled fruits or vegetables or salads. (Peel fruit yourself, washing the fruit first and your hands after peeling to avoid transferring germs to the fruit; bananas and oranges tend to be safer than other fruits because of their thick skins.) No matter where you roam, avoid cooked foods that are lukewarm or at room temperature, raw or undercooked meat, fish, and poultry, as well as unpasteurized or unrefrigerated dairy products and juice and food sold by street vendors, even if it's hot. For complete information on such restrictions, on other foreign health hazards, and on immunizations for travel, contact the Centers for Disease Control and Prevention's Traveler's Hotline at (877) FYI-TRIP (394-8747) or at wwwn

.cdc.gov/travel. Travel warnings are also available from the State Department at (202) 647-5225 or at travel.state.gov.

Don't drink the water (or even brush your teeth with it) unless you're certain it's safe. If the purity of the water is questionable at your destination, plan to use bottled water for drinking and brushing (and always make sure the seal on the bottle cap is intact when you open it). Avoid ice, too, unless you are certain it was made from bottled or boiled water.

Don't swim in the water, either. In some areas, lakes and oceans may be polluted.

Pregnant Women Are Delicious

If mosquitoes seem to love snacking on you more than ever now that you're pregnant, it's not just your imagination. Scientists have found that pregnant women attract twice as many mosquitoes as nonpregnant women do, possibly because those pesky bugs are fond of carbon dioxide and pregnant women tend to take more frequent breaths, thereby releasing more of this mosquito-friendly gas. Another reason why mosquitoes make a beeline for expectant mothers: They're heat-seeking, and expectant mothers generally have higher body temperatures, what with all that baby making going on. So if you live in or travel to an area where mosquitoes are a problem (especially if they pose a health risk), take proper precautions. You can avoid their bites by staying indoors in heavily mosquito-infested areas, by using tight-fitting screens on windows, and by using a non-DEET-based insect repellent.

Check with the CDC about the waters at your destination to be sure of safety before taking a dip. Any pool you swim in should be properly chlorinated (a whiff will usually clue you in).

Head off traveler's irregularity. Changes in schedule and diet can compound constipation problems. So make sure you get plenty of the three most effective constipation combaters: fiber, fluids, and exercise. It may also help to eat breakfast (or at least a morning snack) a little early so you'll have time to use the bathroom before you set out for the day.

When you've gotta go, go. Don't encourage a UTI or constipation by postponing trips to the bathroom. Go as soon as you feel the urge (and can find a rest room).

Get the support you need. Support hose, that is, particularly if you already suffer from varicose veins. But even if you only suspect you may be predisposed to them, consider wearing support hose when you'll be doing a lot of sitting (in cars, planes, or trains, for example) and when you'll be doing a lot of standing (in museums, in airport lines). They'll also help minimize swelling in your feet and ankles.

Don't be stationary while on the move. Sitting for long periods can restrict the circulation in your legs, so be sure to shift in your seat frequently, and stretch, flex, wiggle, and massage your legs often—and avoid crossing your legs. If possible, take your shoes off and elevate your feet a bit. Get up at least every hour or two to walk the aisles when you are on a plane or train. When traveling by car, don't go for more than two hours without stopping for a stretch and a stroll.

If you're traveling by plane. Check with the airline in advance to see if it has spe-

cial regulations concerning pregnant women (many airlines do). Arrange ahead of time for a seat in the bulkhead (preferably on the aisle, so you can get up and stretch or use the rest room as needed), or if seating is not reserved, ask for preboarding.

When booking your flight, ask whether any meal will be served or available for purchase. More and more often, the so-called friendly skies are also the go-hungry skies. If the pickings will be slim (half an ounce of snack mix) at best, bring along a meal of your own (a sandwich or salad, for instance). Even if you will be scoring a meal, keep in mind that it may be (a) tiny (b) inedible (c) a long time in coming due to flight delays, or (d) all of the above. Pack snacks accordingly: cheese sticks or wedges, raw vegetables, fresh fruit, trail mix, dry cereal, some healthy chips. And don't forget to drink plenty of bottled water (don't drink airplane tap water or water that you suspect might have originated in the airplane tap), milk, and juice to counter the dehydration caused by air travel. This tactic will also encourage trips to the bathroom, which will ensure your legs get stretched periodically.

Wear your seat belt comfortably fastened below your belly. If you're traveling to a different time zone, take jet lag (see box, page 251) into account. Rest up in advance, and plan on taking it easy for a few days once you arrive.

If you're traveling by car. Keep a bagful of nutritious snacks and a thermos of juice or milk handy for when hunger strikes. For long trips, be sure the seat you will occupy is comfortable; if it isn't, consider buying or borrowing a special cushion for back support, available in auto supply or speciality stores or online. A pillow for neck support may also add to your comfort. For car safety tips, see page 250.

If you're traveling by train. Check to be sure there's a dining car with a full menu. If not, bring adequate meals and snacks along. If you're traveling overnight, book a sleeper car, if you can. You don't want to start your trip exhausted.

Sex and the Pregnant Woman

Religious and medical miracles aside, every pregnancy starts with sex. So why does what probably got you here in the first place become so complicated now that you're here?

Whether you're having it more often or you're having it less often, whether you're enjoying it more or enjoying it less—or whether you're not doing it or enjoying it at all—chances are that making a baby has changed the way you make love. From sorting out what is and isn't safe in bed (or on the living room rug or on the kitchen counter) to figuring out which positions best accommodate your ever-bigger belly; from mismatched moods (you're turned on, he's turned off; he's turned on, you're turned off) to hormones gone wild (leaving your breasts more enticing than ever, yet too tender to touch), pregnancy sex is full of challenges on both sides of the bed. But not to worry. A little creativity, a good sense of humor, plenty of patience (and practice), and lots of love will conquer all when it comes to pregnancy lovemaking.

Sex Through the Trimesters

Down-up-down. While that might sound like a new sex position, it's actually a good description of the roller-coaster pattern most couples can expect their sex lives to follow during their nine months of pregnancy. In the first trimester, many women find that their libidos take a nosedive, plummeting promptly as soon as pregnancy hormones kick in. And that slowdown in sexual interest should come as no shocker. After all, fatigue, nausea, vomiting, and painfully tender nipples don't make great sex partners. But as with all things pregnancy, no two women are alike, which means no two libidos are alike, either. If you're lucky, you might actually find that the first trimester makes you hotter than ever, thanks to the happy side of hormonal changes: genitals that are ultrasensitive and ever-tingly, and breasts that are extra big and extra fun to touch (or have touched).

Interest often—though not always—picks up during the second trimester, when early pregnancy symptoms have subsided and there's more energy to put into lovemaking (and when less time in the bathroom leaves more time in the bedroom). Never had multiple orgasms before (or any orgasms)? This may be your lucky break—and your chance to get lucky again and again. That's because extra blood flow to the labia, clitoris, and vagina can make it easier to climax than ever before—and to have orgasms that are stronger and longer lasting, too. But again, nothing's a given during pregnancy. Some women actually lose that loving feeling in the second trimester—or never end up finding it at all during their nine months, and that's normal, too.

As delivery nears, libido usually wanes again, sometimes even more drastically than in the first trimester, for obvious reasons: First, your watermelon-size abdomen makes the target more difficult for your partner to reach, even with creative positioning; second, the aches and discomforts of advancing pregnancy can cool even the hottest passion; and third, late in the trimester it's hard to concentrate on anything but that eagerly and anxiously awaited event. Still, some couples manage to overcome those late-pregnancy obstacles and keep up the action until that first contraction.

What's Turning You On (or Off)?

With all the many physical changes you're undergoing during your nine months of pregnancy, it's no wonder desire and sexual pleasure are being affected, both positively and negatively. You'll have to learn to accommodate some of the negative effects so their interference in your sex life is minimal.

Nausea and vomiting. Morning sickness can certainly come between you and a good time. After all, it's hard to purr with pleasure when you're busy gagging up dinner. So use your time wisely. If your morning sickness rises with the sun, put after-dark hours to good use. If your evenings are queasy, hop on the morning love train. If morning sickness stays with you day and night, you and your spouse may just have to wait out its symptoms, which typically taper off by the end of the first trimester. Whatever you do, don't pressure yourself to feel sexy when you're feeling lousy; the result won't be satisfying for anyone.

Fatigue. It's hard to get busy when you barely have the energy to get undressed. Happily, the worst of pregnancy fatigue should pass by the fourth month (though exhaustion will probably return in the last trimester). Until then, make love while the sun shines (when the opportunity presents itself) instead of trying to force yourself to stay up for after-dinner romance. Cap off a weekend afternoon of lovemaking with a nap or the other way around. Have the kind of breakfast in bed that doesn't leave crumbs.

Your changing shape. Making love can be both awkward and uncomfortable when your bulging belly seems to loom as large and forbidding as a Himalayan mountain. As pregnancy progresses, the gymnastics required to scale that growing abdomen may not seem, to some couples, worth the effort. (But there are ways to manage that mountain; read on for more.) What's more, your fuller-than-ever figure may make you feel less sexy (though some women—and most partners—find that pregnant shape the most sensual of all female forms). If your body is a turnoff to you, try dressing it up in lacy lingerie or lighting your love nest with the flattering glow of candles. Also try to shed those negative body images by thinking: Big (in pregnancy) is beautiful.

Your engorged genitals. Increased blood flow to the pelvic area, caused by hormonal changes of pregnancy, can make some women more sexually responsive than ever. But it can also make sex less satisfying (especially later in pregnancy) if a residual fullness persists after orgasm, leaving you feeling as though you didn't quite make it. For your partner, too, the engorgement of your genitalia may increase pleasure (if he feels pleasantly and snugly caressed) or decrease it (if the fit is so tight he loses his erection).

Leakage of colostrum. Late in pregnancy, some women begin producing the pre-

The Ins and Outs of Sex During Pregnancy

Wondering what's safe and what's not when it comes to making love during pregnancy? Here's the lowdown:

Oral sex. Cunnilingus (oral stimulation of the female genitals) is as safe as it is potentially pleasurable throughout pregnancy, so don't hesitate to go for it (just make sure your partner doesn't forcefully blow air into your vagina). Fellatio (oral stimulation of the penis) is always safe during pregnancy (as is swallowing semen), and for some couples is a very satisfactory substitute when intercourse isn't permitted. It's wise to avoid oral sex if your partner has an STD.

Anal sex. Anal sex is probably safe during pregnancy, but proceed to the back door with caution. First, it probably won't be comfortable if you have hemorrhoids, an occupational hazard of pregnancy—and it can make them bleed (which can really spoil the moment). Second, you'll need to remember the same safety rule of anal sex whether you're pregnant or not, but be especially fastidious about following it now: Never go from anal to vaginal sex without cleaning up first. Doing so may introduce harmful bacteria into your vaginal canal, setting you up for infection and risk to the baby.

Masturbation. Unless orgasm is off-limits because of a high-risk pregnancy or premature labor, masturbating during pregnancy is perfectly safe—and a great way to release all that tension you're feeling.

Vibrators or dildos. As long as your practitioner has okayed vaginal penetration, dildos and vibrators are safe to use during pregnancy; after all, they're just mechanical versions of the real thing. But be sure anything you introduce into the vagina is clean before you use it, and be careful not to penetrate the vagina too deeply with it.

---

milk called colostrum, which can leak from the breasts during sexual stimulation and can be a little disconcerting (and messy) in the middle of foreplay. It's nothing to worry about, of course, but if it bothers you or your partner, concentrate on other parts of the body (like that possibly trigger-happy clitoris of yours!).

Breast tenderness. For some couples, pregnant breasts (full, firm, and possibly larger than life) are favorite toys that can't get enough play time. But for many, that early pregnancy swelling comes with a high price—painful tenderness—and along with it, a look-but-don't-touch policy. If your breasts are bringing you more pain than pleasure, make sure your partner gets the memo—and remind him that the tenderness will ease up by the end of the first trimester, at which point he'll be able to enjoy a hands-on approach.

Changes in vaginal secretions. Wet isn't always wild when you're expecting. Normal vaginal secretions increase during pregnancy and also change in consistency, odor, and taste. If you've always been on the dry or narrow side, that extra lubrication may make sex more enjoyable. But sometimes, too much of a good thing can make the vaginal canal so wet and slippery that it actually decreases sensation for both of you—and even makes it more difficult for your partner to keep his erection or reach orgasm. (A little extra foreplay for him may help him out in that department.) The heavier scent and taste of the secretions may also make oral sex off-putting. Massaging scented oils into the pubic area or the inner thighs (but not the vagina) may help.

Some expectant moms experience vaginal dryness during sex, even with all those extra secretions. Unscented water-based lubricants, such as K-Y or Astroglide, are safe to use as needed when you're having a dry spell.

Bleeding caused by the sensitivity of the cervix. The mouth of the uterus also becomes engorged during pregnancy—crisscrossed with many additional blood vessels to accommodate increased blood flow—and is much softer than before pregnancy. This means that deep penetration can occasionally cause spotting, particularly late in pregnancy when the cervix begins to ripen for delivery (but also at any time during pregnancy). This type of bleeding is usually nothing to be concerned about, though do mention it to your practitioner for extra reassurance.

There are also plenty of psychological hang-ups that can get between you, your partner, and full sexual enjoyment during pregnancy. These, too, can often be minimized.

Fear of hurting the fetus or causing a miscarriage. Stop worrying and start enjoying. In normal pregnancies, sex isn't harmful. Your baby is well cushioned and protected inside the amniotic sac and uterus, and your uterus is securely sealed off from the outside world by a mucous plug in the mouth of your cervix. Your practitioner will let you know if there's a reason why you shouldn't have sex during your pregnancy. Otherwise, go for it.

Fear that having an orgasm will stimulate miscarriage or early labor. Although

the uterus does contract following orgasm—and these contractions can be quite powerful in some women, lasting as long as half an hour after intercourse—such contractions are not a sign of labor and aren't harmful in a normal pregnancy. Again, if there's a reason why you should avoid orgasm while you're expecting (because you're at high risk for miscarriage or preterm labor, or have a placenta problem, for instance), your practitioner will let you know.

Fear that the fetus is "watching" or "aware." Not possible. Though your baby may enjoy the gentle rocking of uterine contractions during orgasm, he or she can't see what you're doing, has no clue what's happening, and will certainly have no memory of it. Fetal reactions (slowed movement during sex, then furious kicking and squirming and a speeded-up heartbeat after orgasm) are solely responses to uterine activity.

Fear of "hitting" the baby on the head. Though your partner may not want to admit it, no penis is big enough to hurt a fetus—or big enough to get close to it. Once again, the baby is well sealed off in a cozy uterine home. Even if your baby's head is engaged in your pelvis, deep penetration can't do any harm (though if it's uncomfortable, avoid it).

Fear that sex will cause infection. As long as your partner doesn't have a sexually transmittable disease and your cervix is not open, there is no danger of infection to either mother or fetus through intercourse. In the amniotic sac, the baby is safely sealed off from both semen and infectious organisms.

Anxiety over the coming attraction. Sure, you're both preoccupied and maybe a little (or a lot) stressed out. You might be experiencing mixed feelings, too, over your baby's imminent arrival. And it's

Sexercise

There's no better way to mix business with pleasure than performing Kegels during sex. These exercises tone the perineal area in preparation for childbirth, reducing the likelihood that you'll need an episiotomy, as well as minimizing the risk of a tear. Doing Kegels often will also speed postpartum recovery in the area. And though you can perform Kegels anywhere, anytime (see page 295 for how), doing them during intercourse can double the pleasure for you both. Exercise was never this much fun!

sometimes hard to have sexy thoughts when your mind's cluttered with worries about all those upcoming responsibilities and lifestyle changes, not to mention the financial and emotional cost of bringing up baby. Your best move? Talk about these feelings openly and often—and don't bring them to bed.

The changing relationship. Maybe you're having trouble adjusting to those impending changes in your family dynamic—the idea that you'll no longer be just lovers, or partners, but mother and father as well. Or you may be discovering that the new dimension in your relationship brings a new intimacy to lovemaking—and with it, a new excitement.

Resentment. Feelings of resentment—of your partner toward you, perhaps because he is jealous that you and the pregnancy have become the center of attention, or of you toward him because you feel you're doing all the heavy lifting for the baby you both want and will both

enjoy—can keep things chilly under the sheets. Such feelings are important to talk out, but again, do your chatting before you hit the sack.

Belief that sex later in pregnancy will cause labor to begin. It is true that the uterine contractions triggered by orgasm become stronger as pregnancy proceeds. But unless the cervix is ripe and ready, these contractions do not appear to bring on labor—as many hopeful and eager overdue couples can attest. In fact, studies show that couples who are sexually active during late pregnancy are more likely to carry to term.

Of course, psychological factors can also add to pregnancy sex pleasure (good news!). For one, some couples who worked hard at becoming pregnant may be happy to switch from procreational to recreational sex. Instead of being slaves to ovulation predictor kits, charts, calendars, and monthly anxiety, they can enjoy spontaneous sex for pleasure's sake. For another, many couples find that creating a baby brings them closer together than ever before, and they find the belly a symbol of that closeness—instead of an awkward obstacle.

When Sex May Be Limited

Since lovemaking has so much to offer you and your partner when you're expecting, it would be wonderful if every couple could take advantage of those perks throughout pregnancy. Alas, for some this isn't possible. In high-risk pregnancies, intercourse may be restricted at certain times or even for the full nine months. Or intercourse may be permitted without orgasm for the woman. Or foreplay may be allowed as long as penetration is avoided. Or penetration is permitted but only if a condom is used. Knowing precisely what is safe and when it's safe is essential, so ask for details if your practitioner instructs you to abstain. Find out why sex is off the table and whether that refers to intercourse, orgasm, or both, and whether the restrictions are temporary or apply for the entire pregnancy.

Sex will probably be restricted under the following, and possibly other, circumstances:

- If you are experiencing signs of preterm labor or, possibly, if you have a history of preterm labor

- If you've been diagnosed with incompetent cervix or placenta previa

- Possibly, if you are experiencing bleeding or if you have a history of miscarriages

If penetration is off-limits, but orgasm's allowed, consider mutual masturbation. If orgasm's taboo for you,

you might get pleasure out of pleasuring your partner this way (he certainly won't object). If intercourse has been okayed—but orgasm's prohibited—you could try making love without your reaching climax. Though this definitely won't be completely satisfying for you (and may be impossible if you climax easily), you'll still get some of the intimacy you're both craving while providing pleasure for your partner. If all lovemaking activities have been banned for the duration, try not to let that come between you as a couple. Focus on other ways of getting close—the romantic, G-rated kinds you might not have tapped into since early on in your relationship (like hand-holding, cuddling, and old-fashioned making out).

Enjoying It More, Even If You're Doing It Less

Good, lasting sexual relationships are rarely built in a day (or even a really hot night). They grow with practice, patience, understanding, and love. This is true, too, of an already established sexual relationship that undergoes the emotional and physical changes of pregnancy. Here are a few ways to "stay on top":

- Enjoy your sex life instead of analyzing it. Seize the moment as you seize each other. Don't focus on how frequently or infrequently you're having sex (quality is always more important than quantity, but especially when you're expecting) or compare prepregnancy sex with your sex life now (they're two different animals and, for that matter, so are both of you).

- Accentuate all the positives. Think of making love as good physical preparation for labor and delivery—especially true if you remember to do your Kegels during intercourse. (Not many

---

Getting Comfortable

When you're making love at this point in your pregnancy (and later on, too), position matters. Side-lying positions (front-to-front or front-to-back) are often most comfortable because they keep you off your back. Ditto woman on top (which allows you more control over penetration). Rear entry can work well, too. Man on top is fine for quickies (as long as he keeps his weight off you by supporting himself with his arms), but after the fourth month, it's not a good idea to spend too much time flat on your back.

athletes have this much fun in training.) Think of sex as relaxing—and relaxation is good for all involved (including baby). Think of the roundness of your pregnant body as sensual and sexy. Think of every embrace as a chance to get closer as a couple, not just a chance to get closer to closing the deal.

■ Get adventurous. The old positions don't fit anymore? Look at this as an opportunity to try something new (or a lot of somethings new). But give yourselves time to adjust to each position you try. You might even consider a "dry run"—trying out a new position fully clothed first, so that it'll be more familiar (and you'll be more successful) when you try it for real. See the box on the facing page for ideas.

■ Keep your expectations within reality's reach. Pregnant sex presents plenty of challenges, so cut yourself some slack in the sack. Though some women achieve orgasm for the first time during pregnancy, other women find the big "O" more elusive than ever. Your goal doesn't always have to be mutual

fireworks. Remind yourself that getting close is sometimes the best, and most satisfying, part of getting it on.

■ Don't forget the other kind of intercourse (talking, that is). Communication is the foundation of every relationship, particularly one that's going through life-changing adjustments. Discuss any problems you're facing as a couple openly instead of trying to sweep them under the bed (and instead of taking them to bed). If any problems seem too big to handle by yourselves, seek professional help. There was never a better time to work on your twosome than now that it's about to become a threesome.

Good, bad, or indifferent, remember, too, that every couple feels differently about sex during pregnancy, both physically and emotionally. The bottom line (whether you're on top, on bottom, side to side, or not doing it at all): What's normal, as is almost always the case when you're expecting, is what's normal for you and your partner. Embrace that, embrace each other—and try not to sweat the rest.

The
Sixth
Month

Approximately 23 to 27 Weeks

N O DOUBT ABOUT THOSE TUMMY moves these days: They're all baby, not gas (though you're probably still having plenty of that, too). And as those little arms and legs start to pack more of a punch, these baby calisthenics—and sometimes bouts of baby hiccups—will become visible from the outside and may even entertain those around you. This month marks the last of the second trimester, which means you're almost two thirds of the way there. Still, you've got a ways to go, and a ways to grow—as does baby, who's a relatively light load compared to what you'll be carrying around in a month or two. Take advantage—and while you can still see your feet (if not touch your toes), kick up your 2-inch heels a little.

Your Baby This Month

Week 23 A window into your womb would reveal that your baby's skin is a bit saggy, hanging loosely from his or her little body. That's because skin grows faster than fat develops, and there's not much fat to fill that skin out yet. But don't worry—the fat is about to start catching up. Beginning this week, your baby (who is around 8 inches long and just over a pound in weight) begins to pack on the pounds (which means you will, too!). In fact, by month's end, your baby will be double the weight he or she is now (fortunately, you won't be).

Once those fat deposits are made, your baby will be less transparent, too. Right now, the organs and bones can still be seen through the skin, which has a red hue thanks to the developing blood veins and arteries just underneath. But by month 8, no more see-through baby!

Your Baby, Month 6

Week 24 At a weight of 1½ pounds and a length of about 8½ inches, your baby has outgrown the fruit references and is now the size of a standard letter (but would take a lot more than a standard stamp to mail). Baby's weekly weight gain is now about 6 ounces—not quite as much as you're putting on, but getting a lot closer. Much of that weight is coming from accumulating baby fat, as well as from growing organs, bones, and muscle. By now, your baby's tiny face is almost fully formed, and achingly adorable—complete with a full set of eyelashes and eyebrows and a good sprinkling of hair on that head. Is your baby a brunette, a blond, or a redhead? Actually, right now, he or she's snow white, since there's no pigment in that hair just yet.

Week 25 Baby's growing by leaps and bounds (and inches and ounces), this week reaching 9 inches in length and more than 1½ pounds in weight. And there are exciting developments on the horizon, too. Capillaries are forming under the skin and filling with blood. By week's end, air sacs lined with capillaries will also develop in your baby's lungs, getting them ready for that first breath of fresh air. Mind you, those lungs aren't ready for prime-time breathing yet—and they have a lot of maturing left to do before they will be. Though they're already beginning to develop surfactant,

a substance that will help them expand after birth, your baby's lungs are still too undeveloped to sufficiently send oxygen to the bloodstream and release carbon dioxide from the blood (aka breathe). And talking about breathing, your baby's nostrils, which have been plugged up until now, are starting to open up this week. This enables your baby to begin taking practice "breaths." Your baby's vocal cords are functioning now, leading to occasional hiccups (which you'll certainly be feeling).

Week 26 Next time you're browsing through the meat department, pick up a 2-pound chuck roast. No, not for dinner—just so you can get a sense of how big your baby is this week. That's right—your baby now weighs a full 2 pounds and measures in at 9-plus inches long. Another momentous development this week: Your baby's eyes are beginning to open. The eyelids have been fused for the past few months (so the retina, the part of the eye that allows images to come into focus, could develop). The colored part of the eye (the iris) still doesn't have much pigmentation, so it's too early to start guessing your baby's eye color. Still, your baby is now able to see—though there's not much to see in the dark confines of his or her uterine home. But with the heightened sense of sight and hearing that your baby now possesses, you may notice an increase in activity when your baby sees a bright light or hears a loud noise. In fact, if a loud vibrating noise is brought close to your belly, your baby will respond by blinking and startling.

Week 27 Your baby graduates onto a new growth chart this week. No longer will he or she be measured crown to rump, but rather from head to toe. And this week that head-to-toe length is a full 15 inches (more than a foot long)! Your baby's weight is creeping up the charts as well, coming in at just over 2 pounds this week. And here's an interesting fetal factoid: Your baby has more taste buds now than he or she will have at birth (and beyond). Which means that not only is your baby able to taste the difference in the amniotic fluid when you eat different foods, he or she might even react to it. For instance, some babies respond to spicy foods by hiccupping. Or by kicking when they get that spicy kick.

What You May Be Feeling

As always, remember that every pregnancy and every woman is different. You may experience all of these symptoms at one time or another, or only a few of them. Some may have continued from last month; others may be new. Still others may be hardly noticed because you've become so used to them. You may also have other, less common, symptoms. Here's what you might experience this month:

Physically

- More definite fetal activity

- Continued vaginal discharge

- Achiness in the lower abdomen and along the sides (from stretching of ligaments supporting the uterus)

- Constipation

- Heartburn, indigestion, flatulence, bloating

- Occasional headaches, faintness, or dizziness

- Nasal congestion and occasional nosebleeds; ear stuffiness

- Sensitive gums that may bleed when you brush

- Hearty appetite

- Leg cramps

- Mild swelling of ankles and feet, and occasionally of hands and face

A Look Inside

At the beginning of this month, your uterus is around 1½ inches above your belly button. By the end of the month, your uterus has grown an inch higher and can be felt approximately 2½ inches above your belly button. Your uterus is the size of a basketball now, and you might even look like that's what you're carrying around in your belly.

- Varicose veins of the legs and/or hemorrhoids

- Itchy abdomen

- A protruding navel

- Backache

- Skin pigmentation changes on abdomen and/or face

- Stretch marks

- Enlarged breasts

Emotionally

- Fewer mood swings

- Continued absentmindedness

- Some boredom with the pregnancy ("Can't anyone think about anything else?")

- Some anxiety about the future

- Plenty of excitement about the future

What You Can Expect at This Month's Checkup

It will probably be business pretty much as usual at this month's checkup. As you end your second trimester, you can expect your practitioner to check the following, though there may be variations, depending on your particular needs and on your practitioner's style of practice:

- Weight and blood pressure

- Urine, for sugar and protein

- Fetal heartbeat

- Height of fundus (top of uterus)

- Size of uterus and position of fetus, by external palpation (feeling from the outside)

- Feet and hands for swelling, and legs for varicose veins

- Symptoms you may have been experiencing, especially unusual ones

- Questions and problems you want to discuss—have a list ready

What You May Be Wondering About

Trouble Sleeping

"I've never had a sleep problem in my life—until now. I can't seem to settle down at night."

Between midnight bathroom runs, a racing mind, cramping legs, heartburn that's keeping you upright, a hopped-up metabolism that's keeping the heat on even when it's off, and the impossibility of getting comfortable when you're sporting a basketball in your midsection, it's no wonder that you can't settle in for a good night's sleep. While this insomnia is definitely good preparation for the sleepless nights you'll encounter as a new parent, that doesn't mean you have to take it lying down. Try the following tips for summoning the sandman:

- Move your body during the day. A body that gets a workout by day will be sleepier at night. But don't exercise too close to bedtime, since the postexercise high could keep you from crashing when your head hits the pillow.

- Clear your mind. If you've been losing sleep over problems at work or at home, unload them on your spouse or a friend during the early evening so they don't weigh you down at bedtime. If no one's around to talk them over with, write your concerns down. Putting them on paper can be therapeutic, plus it may help you figure out some solutions. As bedtime approaches, put those worries aside, empty your head, and try thinking happy thoughts only.

- Take your (dinner)time. Instead of wolfing your dinner down (as hungry as you are by the time it's in front of you), serve up a leisurely approach to your evening meal. Eating slowly and calmly will take a bite out of nighttime heartburn and ideally keep you from tossing and turning when you turn out the light. And don't go straight from dinner to bed, because a full tummy can leave you too energized—and too uncomfortable—to sleep.

- Top off before you turn in. Too much food right before bed can interfere with sleep, but so can too little. To keep the midnight munchies from waking you, have a light snack as part of your bedtime routine. That old sleepy-time standard, a glass of warm milk, may be especially effective, probably because it reminds you of being tucked in with your teddy bear. You'll get a similar soporific effect by combining any light protein with some complex carbs, so nibble on fruit and cheese or yogurt and raisins, or dunk a muffin or some oatmeal cookies in your milk.

- Slow the flow. If frequent trips to the bathroom are standing between you and a good night's sleep, limit fluids after 6 P.M. (just make sure you get your daily quota of fluids before then). Drink if you're thirsty, but don't guzzle a 16-ounce bottle of water right before bedtime.

- Don't get buzzed. Avoid caffeine in all its forms in the afternoon and evening (its effects can keep you buzzing for up to six hours). Ditto for sugar (especially combined with caffeine, as in chocolate), which will give you an energy boost when you least want one and then leave your blood sugar levels wobbly during the night.

- Give yourself a bedtime routine. It's not just for kids. The relaxing repetition of the right bedtime rituals can help adults settle down for a good night's sleep, too. Easy does it, so focus on activities that slow you down after dinner, preferably practiced in a predictable order. Good options to consider adding to your routine: light reading (but nothing you can't put down) or television (though steer clear of anything that's violent or emotionally wrenching), soothing music, some stretching, serene yoga poses or relaxation exercises, a warm bath, a backrub, some lovemaking.

- Get comfy. There is no such thing as too many pillows when you're pregnant. Use them to prop you up, support you where you need it, or just cozy up to. The sooner in pregnancy you learn to sleep comfortably on your side, the easier it will be for you to do it later on. Be sure, too, that your mattress is comfortable and your bedroom isn't too hot or too cold.

- Get some air. It's hard to get sleepy when you're stuffy, especially when you're heating for two. So open a window in all but the coldest or hottest weather (when a fan or air-conditioning can help circulate the air). And don't sleep with the covers over your head. This will decrease the oxygen and increase the carbon dioxide you breathe in, which can cause headaches.

- Ask before you pop. While there are sleep aids that are safe for occasional pregnancy use, don't take any sleep aid (prescription, over-the-counter, or herbal) unless it's been prescribed by your practitioner. If your practitioner has recommended that you take a magnesium supplement (or a calcium-magnesium supplement) to combat constipation or leg cramps, it makes sense to take it before bed because magnesium has natural relaxing powers.

- Smell your way to sleep. A lavender-scented pillow that you tuck into bed with you or a dried lavender sachet slipped between the pillowcase and pillow can help relax you and bring on sleep faster.

- Save your bed for sleep (and sex). Don't invite activities you associate with being wide awake and possibly stressed (answering office e-mails on your laptop, paying bills) into your bed. Take care of business in other parts of your home, and reserve your bedroom for its more traditional purposes.

- Go to bed when you're tired. Climbing into bed before you're sleepy is a recipe for a restless night. Putting off your bedtime may, paradoxically, help you sleep better. But don't wait until you're overtired and less able to settle down.

- Avoid clock-watching. Judge whether you're getting enough sleep by how you feel, not by how many hours you stay in bed. Keep in mind that many people who believe they have sleep problems actually get more sleep than

they think—and as much as they need. You're getting enough rest if you're not chronically tired (beyond the normal fatigue of pregnancy). And speaking of clocks, if the sight of that glowing dial (and the hours ticking by) stresses you out, turn it so you can't see it.

- Don't just lie there. When sleep's eluding you—and you've run out of sheep to count—get up and do something relaxing (read, watch TV) until you feel sleepy.

- Don't lose sleep over losing sleep. Stressing about your lack of shut-eye will only make it harder to grab any. In fact, sometimes just letting go of that "will I ever fall asleep?" worry is all it takes to drop off into dreamland.

Save Time (in a Capsule)

Time flies when you're having babies—and raising them. Before it has a chance to fly away, preserve your pregnancy for posterity by making a time capsule. Years from now, your baby (who won't be a baby anymore) will get a kick out of seeing the way things were back in the day, before he or she arrived on the scene. Just take a box (or a capsule) and put in pictures of you (pregnant, of course), your spouse, any pets, and your house and car. Add ultrasound pictures, a menu from the restaurant that always delivers your cravings to the door, a current magazine and newspaper—and any other souvenirs of this expectant era you'd like to hold on to. No need to bury it—just seal it and put it away (don't forget where next time you move) until your baby's old enough to appreciate it.

Protruding Navel

"My belly button used to be a perfect 'innie.' Now it's sticking all the way out. Will it stay that way even after I deliver?"

Has your innie been outed? Is it poking straight through your clothes these days? Taking on a life of its own? Don't worry: There's nothing novel about navels that pop during pregnancy. Just about every belly button does at some point. As the swelling uterus pushes forward, even the deepest "innie" is sure to pop like a timer on a turkey (except, on most women, the navel "pops" well before baby's "done"). Your belly button should revert back to its regular position a few months after delivery, though it may bear the mommy mark: that stretched-out, lived-in look. Until then, you can look at the bright side of your protruding navel: It gives you a chance to clean out all the lint that's accumulated there since you were a kid. If you find that the outie look doesn't quite work with the clingy fashion statement you're trying to make, consider taping it down (you can use a Band-Aid, as long as it doesn't irritate, or specially designed belly button tape). But in the meantime, remember, it's just one more pregnancy badge of honor to wear proudly.

Baby Kicking

"Some days the baby is kicking all the time; other days he seems very quiet. Is this normal?"

Fetuses are only human. Just like us, they have "up" days, when they feel like kicking up their heels (and elbows and knees), and "down" days, when they'd rather lie back and take it easy. Most often, their activity is related to what you've been doing. Like babies out of the womb, fetuses are lulled by rocking. So when you're on the go all day, your baby is likely to be pacified by the rhythm of your routine, and you're likely not to notice much kicking—partly because baby's slowed down, partly because you're so busy. As soon as you slow down or relax, he or she is bound to start acting up (a pattern babies, unfortunately, tend to continue even after they're born). That's why you're more apt to feel fetal movement in bed at night or when you're resting during the day. Activity may also increase after you've had a meal or snack, perhaps in reaction to the surge of sugar in your blood. You may also notice increased fetal activity when you're excited or nervous—about to give a presentation, for example—possibly because the baby is stimulated by your adrenaline response.

Babies are actually most active between weeks 24 and 28, when they're small enough to belly dance, somersault, kickbox, and do a full aerobic step class in their roomy uterine home. But their movements are erratic and usually brief, so they aren't always felt by a busy mother-to-be, even though they are visible on ultrasound. Fetal activity usually becomes more organized and consistent, with more clearly defined periods of rest and activity, between weeks 28 and 32. It's definitely felt later and less emphatically when there's an anterior placenta getting in the way (see page 246).

Don't be tempted to compare baby movement notes with other pregnant women. Each fetus, like each newborn, has an individual pattern of activity and development. Some seem always active; others mostly quiet. The activity of some fetuses is so regular their moms could set their watches by it; in others there's no discernible activity pattern at all. As long as there is no radical slowdown or cessation of activity, all variations are normal.

Keeping track of your baby's kicks isn't necessary until week 28 (see page 289).

"Sometimes the baby kicks so hard it hurts."

As your baby matures in the uterus, he or she becomes stronger and stronger, and those once butterfly-like fetal movements pack more and more punch. Which is why you shouldn't be surprised if you get kicked in the ribs or poked in the abdomen or cervix with such force it hurts. When you seem to be under a particularly fierce attack, try changing your position. It may knock your little linebacker off balance and temporarily stem the assault.

"The baby seems to be kicking all over. Could I be carrying twins?"

At some point in her pregnancy, just about every woman begins to think that she's carrying either twins or a human octopus. That's because until a fetus grows out of room to move (usually at about 34 weeks), it's able to perform numerous acrobatics. So, while it may sometimes feel as if you're being pummeled by a dozen fists (or a litter), it's more likely to be two fists that really get around—along with tiny knees, elbows, and feet. (And if you did have a second passenger on board, you would have likely made that discovery during one of your ultrasounds.)

Itchy Belly

"My belly itches constantly. It's driving me crazy."

Join the club. Pregnant bellies are itchy bellies, and they can become progressively itchier as the months pass. That's because as your belly grows, the skin stretches rapidly, becoming increas-ingly moisture-deprived—leaving it itchy and uncomfortable. Try not to scratch, which will only make you itchier and could cause irritation. Moisturizer can temporarily curb the itching; apply a gentle one frequently and liberally. An anti-itching lotion (such as calamine) may provide more relief, as can an oat-meal bath. If you have an all-over itch that's not related to dry or sensitive skin, however, or develop a rash on your abdomen, check with your practitioner.

Clumsiness

"Lately I've been dropping everything I pick up. Why am I suddenly so clumsy?"

Like the extra inches on your belly, the extra thumbs on your hands and those two left feet you suddenly feel you're sporting are part of the pregnancy package. This real (and, unfortunately, plain for everyone to see) pregnancy-induced clumsiness is caused by the loosening of joints and ligaments and the retention of water, both of which can make your grasp on objects less firm and sure. Other factors include a lack of concentration as a result of pregnancy forgetfulness (see page 214) or a lack of dexterity as a result of carpal tunnel syndrome (see next question). And it certainly doesn't help matters that your growing belly has shifted your center of gravity, throwing your balance off-kilter. This uneasiness in balance—whether conscious or not—is most apparent when you're climbing a flight of stairs, walking on a slippery surface (something you really shouldn't be doing anyway), or carrying something heavy (ditto). Not being able to see past your belly to your feet (which, if it hasn't happened yet, definitely will) can also make tripping—over curbs, on steps, on the sneakers your spouse left in front of the bath-room door—a lot easier to do. Finally, pregnancy fatigue can keep you off your game (or knock you off your feet), making it easier to both trip and drop.

Most pregnancy clumsiness is just annoying. Repeatedly retrieving the car keys from the floor, for instance, is merely an ongoing pain in the neck (as well as a pain in the back if you don't remember to bend from the knees). Falls, however, can be a more serious matter, which is why "caution" should be your middle name when you're expecting.

If you're feeling like a bull in a china shop these days, you'll have to make some modifications to your daily activities. Definitely stay out of china shops (and keep your clumsy paws off the good china at home). Leave your favorite crystal on the shelf for the duration and let someone else load and unload the dishwasher, especially when the good stuff's involved. It'll also help to slow down, walk more deliberately and carefully (especially when there's ice or snow underfoot), use extra caution in the tub or shower, keep hallways and stairs clear of objects that might trip you up, refrain from standing on any chairs (no matter what you need to reach), and avoid pushing yourself (the more tired you are, the more clumsy you'll be). Most important, recognize your current limitations and your lack of coordination, and try to have a sense of humor about it.

Numbness in the Hands

"I keep waking up in the middle of the night because some of the fingers on my right hand are numb. Is that related to pregnancy?"

Feeling all atingle these days? Chances are it isn't romance or even excitement about the baby—it's the normal numbness and tingling in the fingers and toes that many women experience during pregnancy, probably the result of swelling tissues pressing on nerves. If the numbness and pain are confined to your thumb, index finger, middle finger, and half of your ring finger, you probably have carpal tunnel syndrome (CTS). Though this condition is most common in people who regularly perform tasks that require repetitive motions of the hand (such as piano playing or typing), it is also extremely common in pregnant women—even in those who don't do repetitive hand motions. That's because the carpal tunnel in the wrist, through which the nerve to the affected fingers runs, becomes swollen during pregnancy (as do so many other tissues in the body), with the resultant pressure causing numbness, tingling, burning, and pain. The symptoms can also affect the hand and wrist, and they can radiate up the arm.

Though the pain of CTS can strike at any time of day, you might feel yourself wrestling with wrist pain more at night. That's because fluids that accumulate in your lower extremities during the day are redistributed to the rest of your body (including your hands) when you're lying down. Sleeping on your hands can make the problem worse, so try elevating them on a separate pillow at bedtime. When numbness occurs, shaking your hands may relieve it. If that doesn't do the trick, and the numbness is interfering with your sleep, discuss the problem with your practitioner. Often wearing a wrist splint is helpful. Acupuncture can also bring relief.

The nonsteroidal anti-inflammatory drugs and steroids usually prescribed for CTS may not be recommended during pregnancy. Check with your practitioner. Luckily, when the regular swelling of pregnancy resolves once you've delivered, the carpal tunnel symptoms will diminish, too.

If you think the CTS is related to your work habits (or at-home computer use) as well as your pregnancy, see page 191.

Leg Cramps

"I have leg cramps at night that keep me awake."

Between your overloaded mind and your bulging belly, you probably have enough trouble catching those z's without leg cramps cramping your sleeping style. Unfortunately, these painful spasms that radiate up and down your calves and occur most often at night are very common among the expectant set in the second and third trimesters.

No one's quite sure what causes leg cramps. Various theories blame fatigue from carrying pregnancy weight, compression of the blood vessels in the legs, and possibly diet (an excess of phosphorus and a shortage of calcium or magnesium). You might as well blame hormones, too, since they seem to cause so many pregnancy aches and pains.

Whatever the cause, there are ways of both preventing and alleviating them:

- When a leg cramp strikes, be sure to straighten your leg and flex your ankle and toes slowly up toward your nose (don't point your toes). This should soon lessen the pain. Doing this several times with each leg before turning in at night may even help ward off the cramps.

- Stretching exercises can also help stop cramps before they strike. Before you head to bed, stand about 2 feet away from a wall and put your palms flat against it. Lean forward, keeping your heels on the floor. Hold the stretch for 10 seconds, then relax for 5. Try this three times. (See the illustration.)

- To ease the daily load on your legs, put your feet up as often as you can, alternate periods of activity with periods of rest, and wear support hose during the day. Flex your feet periodically.

- Try standing on a cold surface, which can sometimes stop a spasm.

- You can add massage or local heat for added relief, but don't massage or add heat if neither flexing nor cold helps the situation.

- Make sure you're drinking enough fluids—at least eight glasses a day.

Stretching Away Leg Cramps

When Something Just Doesn't Feel Right

Maybe it's a twinge of abdominal pain that feels too much like a cramp to ignore, a sudden change in your vaginal discharge, an aching in your lower back or in your pelvic floor—or maybe it's something so vague you can't even put your finger on it. Chances are it's just par for the pregnancy course, but to play it safe, check page 138 to see if a call to your practitioner is in order.

If you can't find your symptoms on the list, it's probably a good idea to call anyway. Reporting odd symptoms could help identify early signs of premature labor or other pregnancy complications, which could make a big difference in your pregnancy. Remember, you know your body better than anyone. Listen up when it's trying to tell you something.

■ Eat a well-balanced diet that includes plenty of calcium and magnesium.

Really bad cramps (like a charley horse) can cause muscle soreness that lasts a few days. That's nothing to worry about. But if the pain is severe and persists, contact your practitioner because there's a slight possibility that a blood clot may have developed in a vein, making medical treatment necessary (see page 563).

Hemorrhoids

"I'm dreading getting hemorrhoids—I've heard they're common during pregnancy. Is there anything I can do to prevent them?"

It's a big pain in the butt, but more than half of all pregnant women experience hemorrhoids. Just as the veins of the legs are more susceptible to varicosities at this time, so, too, are the veins of the rectum. Pressure from your enlarging uterus, plus increased blood flow to the pelvic area, can cause the veins in your rectal wall to swell, bulge, and itch (how's that for a pleasant thought?).

Constipation can aggravate, or even cause, hemorrhoids (also called piles because of the resemblance these swollen veins sometimes bear to a pile of grapes or marbles), so your best prevention is to avoid constipation in the first place (see page 173). Doing your Kegels (see page 295) can also ward off hemorrhoids by improving circulation to the area, as can taking the pressure off by sleeping on your side, not your back; avoiding long hours of standing or sitting; and not lingering on the toilet (keep this book and other reading material out of the bathroom so you aren't tempted to just sit and read). Sitting with your feet on a step stool may make that other stool easier to pass.

To soothe the sting of hemorrhoids, try witch hazel pads or ice packs. A warm bath might reduce discomfort, too. If sitting is a pain, use a doughnut-shaped pillow to ease pressure. Ask your practitioner before using any medication, topical or otherwise. But forget about your grandma's cure—downing a spoonful of mineral oil—which can carry valuable nutrients right out the back door.

Hemorrhoids can sometimes bleed, especially when you're bearing down during a bowel movement, though anal fissures (painful cracks in the skin of the anus caused by straining from constipation) can also be the cause of rectal bleeding. Rectal bleeding should always be evaluated by your physician, but hemorrhoids or fissures are probably the culprits. Hemorrhoids aren't dangerous (just uncomfortable) and usually go away after delivery—though they can also develop postpartum as a result of pushing during delivery.

Breast Lump

"I'm worried about a small tender lump on the side of my breast. What could it be?"

Though you're still months away from being able to nurse your baby, it sounds like your breasts are already gearing up. The result: a clogged milk duct. These red, tender-to-the-touch, hard lumps in the breast are very common even this early in pregnancy, especially in second and subsequent pregnancies. Warm compresses (or letting warm water run on it in the shower) and gentle massage will probably clear the duct up in a few days, just as it will during lactation. Some experts suggest that avoiding underwire bras also helps, but make sure you get ample support from the bra you do wear.

Keep in mind that monthly self-exams of your breasts shouldn't stop when you're pregnant. Though checking for lumps is trickier when you're expecting because of the changes in your breasts, it's still important to try. Show any lump to your practitioner at your next visit.

Childbirth Pain

"I'm eager to become a mother, but not so eager to experience childbirth. Mostly, I worry about the pain."

Almost every expectant mother eagerly awaits the birth of her child,

---

Bleeding in Mid- or Late Pregnancy

It's always unsettling to see pink or red on your underwear when you're expecting, but light or spotty bleeding in the second or third trimester is generally not a cause for concern. It's often the result of bruising to the increasingly sensitive cervix during an internal exam or sexual intercourse, or it is sometimes simply triggered by causes unknown and innocuous.

Still, let your practitioner know about any bleeding or spotting in case it's a sign something more serious is going on. If you're bleeding heavily or if the spotting is accompanied by pain or discomfort, give your practitioner a call right away. An ultrasound exam can often determine whether or not there's a problem.

---

but few look forward to labor and delivery—and far fewer still to the pain of labor and delivery. And many, like you, spend much of the months leading up to this momentous event obsessing about the pain. That's not surprising. For those who've never experienced significant discomfort (except maybe a toothache here, a pulled muscle there), the fear of labor pain—which is, after all, an unknown quantity of pain—is very real and very normal.

But it's important to keep in mind the following: Childbirth is a normal life process, which women have been experiencing as long as there have been women. Sure it comes with pain, but it's a pain with a positive purpose (though it won't necessarily feel positive when you're in it): to thin and open your cervix, and bring your baby into your arms. And it's also a pain with a built-in time limit. You might not believe it (especially somewhere around the 5-cm mark), but labor won't last forever. Not only that, but the pain of childbirth is a pain you don't even have to put up with at all. Pain medication is always just a request away, should you end up wanting it or needing it—or both.

So there's no point in dreading the pain (especially because you have the option of avoiding it, or at least, avoiding most of it), but there's a lot to be said for being prepared for it—and for preparing realistically and rationally, with eyes wide open to every option and every eventuality. Preparing now (both your body and mind—since both are involved in how you experience pain) should help reduce the anxiety you're feeling now and the amount of discomfort you'll feel once those contractions kick in.

Get educated. One reason earlier generations of women found labor so frightening was that they didn't understand what was happening to their bodies or why. They only knew that it hurt. Today, a good childbirth education class can reduce fear (and ultimately pain) by increasing knowledge, preparing women and their coaches, stage by stage and phase by phase, for labor and delivery. If you can't take a class or if you just don't want to, read up as much as you can on the subject of labor and delivery. What you don't know can worry you more than it has to. Taking classes makes sense, by the way, even if you're planning on having an epidural—or even if you have a cesarean delivery scheduled.

Get moving. You wouldn't consider running a marathon without the proper physical training. Neither should you consider signing up for labor (which is no less challenging an event) untrained. Work out with all the breathing, stretching, and toning-up exercises your practitioner and/or childbirth educator recommends, plus plenty of Kegels.

Team up. Whether you have your partner there to comfort you and feed you ice chips, a doula (see page 298) to mas-

---

Diagnosing Preeclampsia

Chances are you've heard of (or know) someone who developed preeclampsia (or pregnancy-induced hypertension) during pregnancy. But the reality is that it isn't that common, occurring in only 3 to 7 percent of pregnancies, even in its mildest form. And luckily, in women who are receiving regular prenatal care, preeclampsia can be diagnosed and treated early, preventing needless complications. Though routine office visits sometimes seem a waste of time in a healthy pregnancy ("I have to pee in a cup again?"), the earliest signs of preeclampsia can be picked up at such visits.

Early symptoms of preeclampsia include sudden weight gain apparently unrelated to overeating, severe swelling of the hands and face, unexplained headaches, pain in the stomach or the esophagus, all-over itching, and/or vision disturbances. If you experience any of these, call your practitioner. Otherwise, assuming you are getting regular medical care, there's no reason to worry about preeclampsia. See pages 524 and 548 for more information on and tips for dealing with high blood pressure and preeclampsia.

sage your back, or a friend to wipe your brow—or if you really like company, all three—a little support can go a long way in easing your fears. Even if you end up feeling more tense than chatty during labor, it will be comforting to know that you're not going it alone. And make sure your team is trained, too. Have your coach attend childbirth classes with you, or if that's not possible, suggest that he read the section on labor and delivery beginning on page 380, so that he'll know what to expect—and how best to help.

Have a plan—and a backup plan. Maybe you've already decided that an epidural has your name on it. Maybe you're hoping to breathe your way through those contractions—or use hypnosis or another CAM approach to pain management. Maybe you're waiting to make that decision until you see how much pain you're facing. Either way, think ahead, and then keep your mind open (because labor has a way of not always following plans). In the end, you'll need to do what's best for you and your baby (even if that's accepting pain relief when you were hoping to tough it out). Remember, you don't have to be a martyr to be a mother. This is one time when you can have the gain without the pain. In fact, sometimes pain relief's absolutely necessary to keep a laboring mom at her most effective. See page 301 for more on pain relief during labor and delivery.

Labor Inhibitions

"I'm afraid I'll do something embarrassing during labor."

That's because you're not in labor yet. Sure, the idea of screaming, cursing, or involuntarily emptying your bladder or bowel might seem embarrassing now—but during labor, embarrassment will be the furthest thing from your mind. Besides, nothing you can do or say during labor will shock your birth attendants, who've seen and heard it all before—and then some. So check your inhibitions when you check into the hospital or birthing center and feel free to do what comes naturally, as well as what makes you most comfortable. If you are ordinarily a vocal, emotive person, don't try to hold in your moans or hold back your grunts and groans—or even your ear-shattering screams. But if you're normally very soft-spoken or stoic and would prefer to whimper quietly into your pillow, don't feel obligated to out yell the woman next door.

Calling the Labor Shots

"I have pretty definite ideas of what I'd like to happen during labor and delivery. I don't like the idea of losing control of the situation."

If you're a take-charge kind of person, the thought of handing control of your labor and delivery over to the medical team can be a little unnerving. Of course you want the doctors, nurses, and midwives to take the best possible care of you and your baby. But you'd still like to call as many shots as possible (including whether or not you get those shots). And chances are you'll be able to, especially if you prepare thoroughly for labor and delivery at your childbirth preparation exercises, become familiar with the birth process, and develop an open and productive rapport with your practitioner, if you haven't already. Setting up a birth plan (see page 294), specifying what you would like to happen and not happen during a normal labor and delivery, also increases your control.

But with that said and done and written down, it's important to understand that you won't necessarily be able to call all the shots during labor, no matter how well prepared you are and no matter what type of practitioner you are laboring with. The best-laid plans of obstetrical patients and their practitioners can give way to a variety of unforeseeable circumstances, and it makes sense to prepare for that possibility, too. For instance, you'd planned to go through labor completely unmedicated, but an extremely long and trying active phase has sapped you of your strength. Or you'd hoped for an epidural, but your labor's going extremely quickly and the anesthesiologist doesn't arrive in time. Learning when it's necessary to relinquish the reins—and be flexible—is also in the best interest of you and your baby, and it is an important part of your childbirth education.

Hospital Tours

"I've always associated hospitals with sick people. How can I get more comfortable with the idea of giving birth in one?"

The labor and delivery floor is by far the happiest in the hospital. Still, if you don't know what to expect, you can arrive not only with contractions, but with apprehension. That's why the vast majority of hospitals and birthing centers encourage expectant couples to take advance tours of maternity facilities. Ask about such tours when you preregister, and look online, too. Some hospitals and birthing centers have websites that offer virtual tours. You can also stop in for an informal peek during visiting hours; even if the actual labor and delivery area is off-limits then, you'll be able to view postpartum rooms and take a good look at the nursery. Besides making you feel more comfortable about the surroundings where you'll be giving birth, this will give you the opportunity to check out what real newborns look like before you hold your own in your arms.

Chances are you'll be happily surprised by what you see when you pay your visit. Facilities vary from hospital to hospital and from birthing center to birthing center, but as competition for obstetrical patients increases, the range of amenities and services offered in many areas has become more and more impressive—less hospital, more hotel. Comfy birthing rooms are the rule, rather than the exception, in more and more hospitals (they've always been common at birthing centers staffed by midwives).

Childbirth Education

The countdown is on—and baby's just around the corner (give or take a few months). Of course you're eagerly awaiting the arrival of your little one. But are you just as eager for the arrival of labor and delivery? Could that be trepidation (make that panic) mixed in with that excited anticipation?

Relax. It's normal to be a little nervous about childbirth—or even a lot, especially if you're a first timer. Just about every parent-to-be is. But fortunately, there's a great way to ease jitters, to calm worries, and to feel less anxious and more confident when that first contraction strikes: by getting educated.

A little knowledge and a lot of preparation can go a long way in helping you feel more comfortable when you enter the birthing room. Reading all about childbirth can definitely give you an idea of what to expect (and you can start doing that on page 380), but a good childbirth education class can fill in even more blanks. So it's back to school, Mama (and Papa).

Benefits of Taking a Childbirth Class

What's in a childbirth education class for you and your coach? That depends, of course, on the course you take, the instructor who teaches it, and on your attitudes (as was true back in your school days, the more you put in, the more you tend to get out of a childbirth education class). No matter what, there's something in it for every soon-to-be-laboring team. Some potential benefits include:

- A chance to spend time with other expectant couples who are at the same stage of pregnancy as you are—to share experiences and tips; compare progress; trade tales of woes, worries, aches, and pains; and swap notes on baby gear, nursery gear, pediatricians, and child care. In other words, lots of expectant camaraderie and empathy. It's also a chance to make friends with other couples who, like you, will soon be parents (a definite plus if your current crowd of friends hasn't taken the baby plunge yet). Keep in touch with these classmates after delivery and you've got yourself a ready-to-go parent's group—and playgroup for the kids. Many classes hold "reunions" once everyone has delivered.

- A chance for dad to join in. So much of pregnancy revolves around mom, which can sometimes leave an expectant father feeling like he's on the outside looking in. Childbirth education classes are aimed at both parents and help to get dad feeling like the valued member of the baby team he is—particularly important if he hasn't been able to attend all the prenatal visits. Classes will also get dad up to speed on labor and delivery so that he can be a more effective coach when those contractions start coming. Best of all, perhaps, he'll be able to hang out with other guys who can relate—among other things, to those maternal mood swings he's been on the receiving end of and to nagging feelings of daddy self-doubt. Some courses include a special session for fathers only, which gives them the chance to open up about concerns they might otherwise not feel comfortable expressing.

- A chance to ask questions that come up between prenatal visits or that you don't feel comfortable asking your practitioner (or that you never seem to have the time to ask in the context of a hurried visit).

- A chance to learn all about it—labor and delivery, that is. Through lecture, discussion, models, and video, you'll get an inside peek at what childbirth's all about—from prelabor symptoms to crowning to cutting the cord. The more you know, the more comfortable you'll feel when it's actually happening to you.

- A chance to learn all about your pain relief options, from Demerol to an epidural to a spinal—even to CAM approaches.

- A chance to get hands-on instruction in breathing, relaxation, and other alternative approaches to pain relief and to get feedback from an expert as you learn. Mastering these coping strategies—and coaching techniques—may help you be more relaxed during labor and delivery, while somewhat decreasing your perception of pain. They'll also come in handy if you're planning on signing up for an epidural or other pain meds.

■ A chance to become familiar with the medical interventions sometimes used during childbirth, including fetal monitoring, IVs, vacuum extraction, and C-sections. You may not encounter any of the available interventions during your labor—or only one or two—but knowing about them ahead of time will make labor a little less intimidating.

■ A chance to have a relatively more enjoyable labor—and a relatively less stressful one—thanks to all of the above. Couples who've had childbirth preparation generally rate their childbirth experiences as more satisfying overall than those who haven't.

■ A chance to become empowered. Knowledge is always power, but it can be especially powerful when you're in labor. By eliminating the fear of the unknown (what you don't know, in this case, can definitely hurt your confidence), a childbirth education class can leave you feeling more in control, more empowered—ready to handle just about any labor scenario that nature throws your way.

Choosing a Childbirth Class

So you've decided to take a childbirth class. But where do you begin looking for one? And how do you choose?

In some communities, where childbirth class options are limited, the choice of which class to take is a rela-

tively simple one. In others, the variety of offerings can be overwhelming and confusing. Courses are run by hospitals, by private instructors, by practitioners through their offices. There are "early bird" prenatal classes, taken in the first or second trimester, which cover such pregnancy topics as nutrition, exercise, fetal development, and sex; and there are down-to-the-wire 6- to 10-week childbirth preparation classes, usually begun in the seventh or eighth month, which concentrate on labor, delivery, and postpartum mother and baby care. There are even weekend getaway classes.

If the pickings are slim, any childbirth class is probably better than none at all. If there is a selection of courses where you live, it may help to con-

Back To School

Besides studying up on childbirth techniques these days, there's another class you should consider signing up for now: infant CPR and first aid. Even though you don't actually have the baby yet, there's no better time to learn how to keep that little bundle you're about to deliver safe and sound. First, because you won't have to line up a babysitter to attend class now. And second—and more important—because you'll be able to bring baby home, secure in the knowledge that you have all the necessary know-how at your fingertips in case of an emergency. You can find a course by contacting the American Red Cross (redcross.org) or the American Heart Association (americanheart.org/cpr), or check with your local hospital.

sider the following when making your decision:

Who sponsors the class? A class that is run by, under the auspices of, or recommended by your practitioner often works out best. Also useful could be a class provided by the hospital or birthing center where you'll be delivering. If the laboring and delivering philosophy of your childbirth education teacher varies a lot from that of the person or staff who will be assisting you during labor and delivery, you're bound to run into contradictions and conflicts. If differences of opinion do arise, make sure you address them with your practitioner well before your delivery date.

What's the size of the class? Small is best. Five or six couples to a class is ideal; more than 10 or 12 may be too large. Not only can a teacher give more time and individual attention to couples in an intimate group—particularly important during the breathing and relaxation technique practice sessions—but the camaraderie in a small group tends to be stronger.

What's the curriculum like? To find out, ask for a course outline. A good course includes a discussion of cesarean delivery (recognizing that more than a quarter of the students may end up having one) and of medication (recognizing, too, that many will need or want it). It deals with the psychological and emotional as well as the technical aspects of childbirth.

How is the class taught? Are films of actual childbirths shown? Will you hear from mothers and fathers who've recently delivered? Will there be ample opportunity for parents-to-be to ask questions? Is enough time allowed during class for practicing the various techniques that are taught?

For Information on Pregnancy/Childbirth Classes

Ask your practitioner about classes in your area, or call the hospital where you plan to deliver. The following organizations can also give you referrals to local classes:

Lamaze International:
(800) 368-4404; lamaze.org

Bradley: The Bradley Method:
(800) 4-A-BIRTH (422-4784);
bradleybirth.com

International Childbirth Education Association:
(952) 854-8660; icea.org

Association of Labor Assistants and Childbirth Educators:
(617) 441-2500; alace.org

New Way Childbirth:
(864) 268-1402;
newwaychildbirth.com

The American Society of Clinical Hypnosis:
(630) 980-4740; asch.net

Society for Clinical and Experimental Hypnosis:
(617) 469-1981; sceh.us

Childbirth Education Options

Childbirth education classes in your area may be taught by nurses, nurse-midwives, or other certified professionals. Approaches may vary from class to class, even among those trained in the same programs. The most common classes include:

Lamaze. The Lamaze approach to childbirth education, pioneered by Dr. Fernand Lamaze in the 1950s, is probably the most widely used in the United States. Its foundation is the use of relaxation and breathing techniques by the laboring woman, along with continuous support from a spouse (or other coach) and trained nurse to allow the laboring woman to experience a more "natural" childbirth (remember, back in the 1950s, most delivering moms were put to sleep). According to the Lamaze philosophy, birth is normal, natural, and healthy, and a woman's confidence and ability to give birth naturally can be either enhanced or diminished by the level of support she receives from her care provider, as well as by the comfort of the birthing environment (which could be a birthing center or home as well as a hospital).

The goal of Lamaze training is active concentration based on relaxation and rhythmic breathing patterns. To help with concentration, women are encouraged to direct their attention to a focal point. Courses also cover comfortable labor and birthing positions; breathing, distraction, and massage techniques; communication skills; and other comfort measures, as well as information on the early postpartum period and breastfeeding. Though the Lamaze philosophy states that women have a right to give birth free from routine medical interventions, classes generally cover most common interventions (including pain relief) to prepare couples for any birthing scenario. A traditional Lamaze course consists of six 2- to 2½-hour sessions.

Bradley. This approach emphasizes deep abdominal breathing rather than panting. Bradley recommends that the laboring woman concentrate within herself and tune in to her own body to control the pain of the contractions, rather than relying on distractions. In Bradley classes, women learn to mimic their nighttime sleeping positions and breathing (which is deep and slow) for use during labor and to use relaxation techniques to make labor more comfortable.

According to the Bradley technique, during labor a woman needs darkness, quiet, physical comfort aided by pillows, and closed eyes. Bradley teachers acknowledge that labor hurts, and they stress acceptance of pain. Medication is reserved for complications and C-sections (which are discussed so parents can be prepared for any eventuality), and about 87 percent of Bradley graduates who have vaginal births go without it. The typical Bradley course runs 12 weeks, beginning in the fifth month, and most are taught by married couples. "Early bird" Bradley classes, which focus on matters prenatal, are available.

International Childbirth Education Association (ICEA) classes. These classes tend to be broader in scope, covering more of the many options available today to expectant parents in family-centered maternity care and newborn care. They also recognize the importance of freedom of choice, and so classes focus on a wide range of possibilities rather than on a single approach to childbirth. Teachers are certified through ICEA.

Hypnobirthing. Classes for individuals or groups that teach how to use hypnosis to reduce discomfort and pain (and in some highly suggestible women, to eliminate it entirely), achieve a deep state of relaxation, as well as improve mood and attitude during labor and childbirth, are becoming more available. Check with your practitioner or a national clinical hypnosis organization for names of licensed health professionals who teach hypnobirthing. (For more on hypnobirthing, see page 306.)

Other childbirth classes. The range is wide. Association of Labor Assistants and Childbirth Educators (ALACE) champions a woman's right to a natural or unmedicated birth when at all possible. Rather than try to teach expectant parents how to avoid labor and childbirth pain, classes provide coping tools to work with the discomfort. Childbirth Education Preparation (CEP) certifies nurses and practical nurses as childbirth educators who are trained to run classes that explain and teach the many options, including Lamaze and Bradley, available to expectant parents during labor. In addition, there are childbirth education classes designed to prepare parents to deliver in a particular hospital, and classes sponsored by medical groups, health maintenance organizations (HMOs), or other health care provider groups. In some areas, prenatal classes, which cover all aspects of pregnancy as well as childbirth, are also offered, usually beginning in the first trimester.

Home study. If you are on bed rest, live in a remote area, or for some other reason can't or don't want to attend a group class, you can look into the Lamaze program on video or DVD available from Lamaze International. There are also courses and childbirth education classes online that you can tap into.

Private classes. Not interested in being part of a crowd? You can even take private childbirth education classes that can be tailored to fit your schedule and your specific questions. While these classes allow for more flexibility and individualization, they will also cost more.

Weekend classes at resorts. These offer the same curriculum as typical classes,

Classes for Second Timers

Been there, done that? Pregnant with your second baby? Even seasoned pros stand to benefit from taking a childbirth education class. First of all, every labor and delivery is different, so what you experienced last time may not be what you can expect this time. Second, things change quickly in the delivery business, and they may have changed quite a bit, even if it's only been a couple of years since you were last on a birthing bed. There may be different childbirth options available than there were last time: Certain procedures that were routine may now be uncommon; certain procedures that were uncommon may now be routine. Taking another course may be especially useful if you'll be using a different hospital or birthing center. Chances are, however, that you won't have to sit in with the rookies. "Refresher" courses are available in most areas.

packed into a single weekend instead of spaced out over a series of weeks, and they are a nice choice for those who can—and would like to—get away. In addition to promoting camaraderie among expectant parents (especially rewarding if you don't have other pregnant friends to talk to at home), these weekends can promote romance, too—a nice plus for twosomes who are about to become threesomes. Plus, they're a great opportunity for some pre-baby pampering.

The
Seventh
Month

Approximately 28 to 31 Weeks

WELCOME TO YOUR THIRD— and final!—trimester. Believe it or not, you're two thirds of the way to the finish line, and just three months away from holding (and kissing, and cuddling) your prize. In this last stretch of pregnancy (definitely the biggest stretch, at least as far as your belly is concerned), you'll probably find the excitement and anticipation mounting—along with your pregnancy aches and pains, which tend to multiply as the load you're lugging gets heavier and heavier. Drawing near to the end of pregnancy also means you're closing in on labor and delivery, an event you'll begin planning for, preparing for, and getting educated about. Time to think about signing up for those classes, if you haven't already.

Your Baby This Month

Week 28 This week, your amazing baby has reached 2½ pounds and may be almost 16 inches long. Baby's skill of the week: blinking. Yes, along with the other tricks in a growing repertoire that already includes coughing, sucking, hiccupping, and taking practice breaths, your baby can now blink those sweet little eyes. Dreaming about your baby? Baby may be dreaming about you, too, courtesy of the REM (rapid eye movement) sleep he or she has started getting. But this little dreamer isn't ready for birth day just yet. Though his or her lungs are nearly fully mature by now (making it easier for your baby—and you—to breathe a little easier if he or she were born now), your baby still has a lot of growing to do.

Your Baby, Month 7

Week 29 Your baby can be as tall as 17 inches now and can weigh nearly 3 pounds. Though already coming pretty close (within 3 inches or so) of his or her ultimate birth length, baby still has lots to gain. In fact, over the next 11 weeks, your baby more than doubles—and may even come close to tripling—his or her weight. Much of that weight will come from the fat accumulating under his or her skin right now. And as your baby plumps up, the room in your womb will start to feel a little cramped, making it less likely that you'll feel hard kicks from your little one, and more likely that you'll be feeling jabs and pokes from elbows and knees.

Week 30 What's 17 inches long, just over 3 pounds in weight, and cute all over? It's your baby—and he or she is getting bigger by the day (in case you couldn't tell from the size of your belly). Also getting bigger daily is baby's brain, which is preparing for life outside the womb—and for a lifetime of learning. Starting this week, your baby's brain is starting to look like one, taking on those characteristic grooves and indentations. These wrinkles allow for future expansion of brain tissue that is crucial as your baby goes from helpless newborn to responsive infant to verbal toddler to curious preschooler and beyond. Your baby's bigger and better brain is also starting to take on tasks previously delegated to other parts of the body, like temperature regulation. Now that the brain is capable of turn-

ing up the heat (with the help of that growing supply of baby fat), your baby will start shedding lanugo, the downy, soft body hair that has been keeping him or her warm up to this point. Which means that by the time your baby is born, he or she probably won't be fuzzy wuzzy anymore.

Week 31 Though your baby still has 3 to 5 pounds more to gain before delivery, he or she is weighing in at an impressive 3-plus pounds this week. And at 18 inches long (give or take a couple because fetuses this age come in all sizes), your baby is quickly approaching his or her birth length. Also developing at an impressive clip these days: your baby's brain connections (baby has to make trillions of them). And he or she is able to put that complex web of brain connections to good use, too—already processing information, tracking light, and perceiving signals from all five senses. Your brainy baby is also a sleepy one, putting in longer stretches of snooze time, specifically in REM sleep—which is why you're probably noticing more defined patterns of awake (and kicking) and sleeping (quiet) times from your little one.

Baby Brain Food

Have you been feeding your baby's brain? Getting enough of those fabulous fats, the omega-3's, is more important than ever in the third trimester when your baby's brain development is being fast-tracked. See page 101 for all the good-fat facts.

What You May Be Feeling

As always, remember that every pregnancy and every woman is different. You may experience all of these symptoms at one time or another, or only a few of them. Some may have continued from last month, others may be new. Still others may hardly be noticed because you've become so used to them. You may also have other, less common, symptoms. Here's what you might experience this month:

A Look Inside

At the beginning of this month, your uterus is approximately 11 inches from the top of your pubic bone. By the end of the month, your baby's home has grown another inch in height and can be felt around 4½ inches above your belly button. You may think that there's no more room for your womb to grow (it seems to have already filled up your abdomen), but you still have 8 to 10 more weeks of expansion ahead of you!

Physically

- Stronger and more frequent fetal activity

- Increasing vaginal discharge

- Achiness in the lower abdomen or along the sides

- Constipation

- Heartburn, indigestion, flatulence, bloating

- Occasional headaches, faintness, or dizziness

- Nasal congestion and occasional nosebleeds; ear stuffiness

- Sensitive gums that may bleed when you brush

- Leg cramps

- Backache

- Mild swelling of ankles and feet, and occasionally of hands and face

- Varicose veins of the legs

- Hemorrhoids

- Itchy abdomen

- Protruding navel

- Stretch marks

- Shortness of breath

- Difficulty sleeping

- Scattered Braxton Hicks contractions, usually painless (the uterus hardens for a minute, then returns to normal)

- Clumsiness

- Enlarged breasts

- Colostrum, leaking from nipples (though this premilk substance may not appear until after delivery)

Emotionally

- Increasing excitement (the baby's coming soon!)

- Increasing apprehension (the baby's coming soon!)

- Continued absentmindedness

- Strange and vivid dreams

- Increased boredom and weariness with pregnancy or a sense of contentment and well-being, particularly if you're feeling great physically

What You Can Expect at This Month's Checkup

A couple of new items are on the agenda at this month's checkup, along with the old standards. As you enter your last trimester, you can expect your practitioner to check the following, though there may be variations depending on your particular needs and on your practitioner's style of practice:

- Weight and blood pressure

- Urine, for sugar and protein

- Fetal heartbeat

- Height of fundus (top of uterus)

- Size and position of fetus, by external palpation (feeling from the outside)

- Feet and hands for swelling, and legs for protruding varicose veins

- Glucose screening test

- Blood test for anemia

- Symptoms you have been experiencing, especially unusual ones

- Questions and problems you want to discuss—have a list ready

What You May Be Wondering About

Fatigue Revisited

"I was feeling really energetic for the last few months, and now I'm starting to drag again. Is this what I have to look forward to in the third trimester?"

Pregnancy is full of ups and downs—not only when it comes to moods (and libidos) but when it comes to energy levels. That trademark first-

trimester fatigue is often followed by a second-trimester energy high, making those typically comfortable middle months the ideal time to pursue just about any activity (Exercise! Sex! Travel! All three in one weekend!). But by the third trimester, many moms-to-be find themselves once again dragging—and eyeing the sofa longingly.

And that's not surprising. Though some women continue to sprint as they close in on the pregnancy finish line (remember, every pregnancy is different, even when it comes to energy levels), there are lots more good reasons why you might be lagging behind. The best reason can be found around your midsection. After all, you're carrying much more weight there (and other places) than you were earlier on—and carting those extra pounds can be exhausting. Another reason: These days, that extra bulk may be lying (literally) between you and a good night's sleep, leaving you less rested each morning. Your baby-overloaded mind (jam-packed with shopping lists, to-do lists, baby-name lists, questions-to-ask-the-doctor lists) may also be costing you z's—and energy. Add other, unrelated life responsibilities to the mix—a job, the care and feeding of other children, and so on—and the fatigue factors multiply exponentially.

But just because fatigue often comes with the third-trimester territory doesn't mean you have to resign yourself to three months of exhaustion—or relocate yourself to the sofa for the duration. As always, fatigue is a signal from your body, so pay attention. If you've been living life in the fast lane (too much baby prep, not enough rest), slow down the pace a bit. Cut back on any nonessential essentials (no fair calling them all essential), and start building some R&R into your daily schedule. Get some exercise, but make sure it's the right kind (a 30-minute walk may leave you energized, an hour run will have you running for the sofa), at the right time (not too close to bedtime, so it'll induce sleep, not prevent it). And since running on empty can bench you in a hurry, don't forget to fuel your energy levels. Keeping your blood sugar levels up with frequent healthy snacks (cheese and crackers, trail mix, a yogurt smoothie) will give those levels a longer lasting boost than caffeine or sugar. Most of all, remember that

third-trimester fatigue is nature's way of telling mothers-to-be to conserve their energy. You'll need every bit of strength you can save up now for labor, delivery, and, more important, what follows. For more energy-saving tips, revisit the ones on page 128.

If you do get the extra rest your body is calling for but you still feel consistently run-down, talk to your practitioner. Sometimes, extreme fatigue that doesn't ease up is triggered by third-trimester anemia (see page 208), which is why most practitioners repeat a routine blood test for it in the seventh month.

Swelling

"My ankles and feet seem to be swollen, especially at the end of the day. What's going on?"

Your belly's not the only thing that's swelling these days. That puff mama look often extends to the extremities, too. And although all that swelling's not so swell—especially as your shoes and watch get uncomfortably tight and your rings become harder and harder to pry off your fingers—mild swelling (aka edema) of the ankles, feet, and hands is completely normal, related to the necessary increase in body fluids in pregnancy. In fact, 75 percent of women develop such swelling at some point in their pregnancies, usually around this point (the other 25 percent never notice any at all, which is normal, too). As you've probably already noticed, the puffiness is likely to be more pronounced late in the day, in warm weather, or after spending too much time sitting or standing. In fact, you may find that much of the swelling disappears overnight or after several hours spent lying down (another good reason to get that rest).

Generally, this type of swelling means nothing more than a little discomfort—and a few fashion compromises if you can no longer squeeze your ankles into stylish shoes. Still, you'll want to find ways to deflate, if you can. To spell swell relief, keep these tips in mind:

- Stay off your feet and off your butt. If long periods of standing or sitting are part of your job description—at home or at the office—take periodic breaks. Have a seat if you've been standing, and get up if you've been sitting. Or for best results, take a brisk 5-minute walk to rev up your circulation (which should get those pooled fluids flowing).

- Put 'em up—your legs, that is. Elevate them when you're sitting. If anyone deserves to put her feet up, it's you.

- Get some rest on your side. If you're not already in the side-lying habit, time to try it now. Lying on your side helps keep your kidneys working at peak efficiency, enhancing waste elimination and reducing swelling.

- Choose comfort. Now's the time to make a comfort statement, not a fashion statement. Favor shoes that are accommodating (those slinky sling-backs don't fit now, anyway), and once home, switch to soft slippers.

- Move it. Keeping up your exercise routine (if your practitioner has green-lighted one) will actually keep down the swelling. Walking (you'll probably soon call it waddling) is swell for swollen feet since it'll keep the blood flowing instead of pooling. Swimming or water aerobics are even better because the water pressure pushes tissue fluid back into your veins; from there it goes into your kidneys, after which you'll be able to pee it out.

- Wash away that water weight. Though it sounds counterintuitive, it's true: The more water you drink, the less you'll retain. Drinking at least eight to ten 8-ounce glasses of liquid a day will help your system flush out waste products. Restricting fluid intake, on the other (puffy) hand, will *not* decrease swelling.

- Use salt to taste. It used to be believed that salt restriction would help keep the swelling down, but it is now known that limiting salt increases swelling. So salt to taste, but as with most everything, moderation is key.

- Get the support you need. Support hose may not be sexy, but they're very effective in relieving swelling. Several types are available for pregnancy wear, including full panty hose (with roomy tummy space) and knee- or thigh-highs (which are at least cooler to wear), though avoid those with tight elastic tops.

The good news about edema, besides that it's normal, is that it's temporary. You can look forward to your ankles deflating and your fingers depuffing soon after you give birth (though

Take Them Off, While You Can

Have your rings been getting snugger and snugger? Before they get too tight for comfort (and much too tight to remove), you might want to consider taking them off and putting them away for safekeeping until your fingers have slimmed down again. Having trouble prying them off already? Try taking them off in the morning and after cooling your hands down (the hotter they are, the puffier they'll be). Some liquid soap can make the rings slippery and easier to slide off, too.

some moms find it takes at least a few weeks, sometimes a month or more, for swelling to disappear completely). In the meantime, look on the bright side: Pretty soon your belly will be so big, you won't even be able to see how swollen your feet are.

If your swelling seems to be more than mild, talk to your practitioner. Excessive swelling can be one sign of preeclampsia, but when it is, it's accompanied by a variety of other symptoms (such as sudden excessive and unexplained weight gain, elevated blood pressure, and protein in the urine). If your blood pressure and urine are normal (they're checked at each prenatal visit), there's nothing to be concerned about. If, along with your swelling, you've suddenly and inexplicably gained a lot of weight in a short time, or if you're experiencing severe headaches or vision disturbances, call your practitioner and describe what's going on.

Strange Skin Bumps

"As if it's not bad enough that I have stretch marks, now I seem to have some kind of itchy bumps breaking out in them."

Cheer up. You have less than three months left until delivery, when you'll be able to bid a grateful good-bye to most of the unpleasant side effects of pregnancy—among them, these new eruptions. Until then, it may help to know that although they may be uncomfortable (and slightly unsightly), the bumps aren't dangerous to you or your baby. Known medically—and unpronounceably—as pruritic urticarial papules and plaques of pregnancy (try saying that fast three times), aka PUPPP, or PEP (polymorphic eruption of pregnancy), the condition generally disappears after delivery and doesn't recur in subsequent pregnancies. Though PUPPP most often

develops in abdominal stretch marks, it sometimes also appears on the thighs, buttocks, or arms of expectant moms. Show your rash to your practitioner, who may prescribe topical medication, an antihistamine, or a shot to ease any discomfort.

A variety of other skin conditions and rashes can develop during pregnancy (lucky you!), making you less than happy with the skin you're in. Though you should always show any rash that crops up to your practitioner, keep in mind that they're rarely cause for concern. See page 240 for more.

Lower Back and Leg Pain (Sciatica)

"I've been having pain on the side of my lower back, running right down my hip and leg. What's that about?"

Sounds like your baby's getting on your nerves—your sciatic nerve, that is. Toward the middle to end of your pregnancy, your baby begins to settle into the proper position for birth (a big positive). In doing that, however, his or her head—and the weight of your ever-enlarging uterus—may settle on the sciatic nerve in the lower part of your spine (a big negative). Such so-called sciatica can result in sharp, shooting pain, tingling, or numbness that starts in your buttocks or lower back and radiates down the back of either of your legs. Sciatica can be quite intense at times, and though it may pass if your baby shifts positions, it can also linger until you've delivered—and sometimes linger for a little while postpartum.

How can you get baby off your nerves and relieve the pain of sciatica? Try these tips:

- Take a seat. Getting off your feet can ease some of the leg and lower back pain associated with sciatica. Lying down can also relieve pressure—as long as you find the position that feels best.

- Warm it up. A warm heating pad applied on the spot where you feel the pain can help ease it, as can a long soak in a warm bath.

- Work it out. Pelvic tilts or just some stretches can take off some of the pressure.

- Get in the swim of things. Since swimming and water exercises aren't weight bearing, they are particularly good choices when you've got sciatic pain. Swimming stretches and strengthens the muscles in your back, providing relief for that searing pain.

- Seek an alternative. CAM therapies, such as acupuncture, chiropractic medicine, or therapeutic massage (always with a trained and licensed practitioner), might help relieve your sciatica.

If your pain is particularly bad, ask your practitioner if pain medications would be helpful in your case.

Restless Leg Syndrome

"As tired as I am at night, I can't seem to settle down because my legs feel so restless. I've tried all the tips for leg cramps, but they don't work. What else can I do?"

With so many other things coming between you and a good night's sleep in your last trimester, it hardly seems fair that your legs are, too. But for the 15 percent or so of pregnant women who experience restless leg syndrome (RLS)—yes, it's got a name—that's exactly what happens. The name captures it all—that restless, creeping, crawling, tingling feeling inside the foot

Count Your Kicks

From the 28th week on, it may be a good idea to test for fetal movements twice a day—once in the morning, when activity tends to be sparser, and once in the more active evening hours. Your practitioner may recommend a test, or you can use this one: Check the clock and start counting. Count movements of any kind (kicks, flutters, swishes, rolls). Stop counting when you reach 10, and note the time (if you like, you can use the fetal movement tracker in the *What to Expect Pregnancy Journal and Organizer*). Often, you will feel 10 movements within 10 minutes or so—sometimes it will take longer.

If you haven't counted 10 movements by the end of an hour, have some juice or a snack, walk a bit, even jiggle your belly a little; then lie down, relax, and continue counting. If two hours go by without 10 movements, call your practitioner. Though such an absence of activity doesn't necessarily mean something's wrong, it can occasionally be a red flag that needs quick evaluation.

The closer you are to your due date, the more important regular checking of fetal movements becomes.

and/or leg that keeps the rest of your body from settling down. It's most common at night, but it can also strike in the late afternoon or pretty much any time you're lying or sitting down.

Experts aren't certain what causes RLS in some pregnant women (though there does seem to be a genetic component to it), and they're even less sure of how to treat it. None of the tricks of the leg cramp trade—including rubbing or flexing—seem to bring relief.

Medications may not be a good option, either, because many of those currently used to treat RLS aren't safe for use during pregnancy (check with your practitioner).

It's possible that diet, stress, and other environmental factors may contribute to the problem, so it may help to keep track of what you eat, what you do, and how you feel each day so you can see what lifestyle habits, if any, bring on symptoms. Some women, for instance, find that eating carbohydrates late in the day can worsen RLS. It's also possible that iron-deficiency anemia may cause RLS, so it's worth asking your practitioner about testing to rule that out, as well as asking him or her for any other suggested treatments. Acupuncture may help some women, as can yoga, meditation, or other relaxation techniques. And, of course, it couldn't hurt to try the sleep tips on page 266. Unfortunately, however, some women continue to find relief—and sleep—elusive. If you are one of them, RLS is something you may just have to put up with until delivery. If you came into pregnancy with the condition, you may have to wait until after delivery (and possibly after weaning, if you're nursing) to resume any drug treatment you were using.

Fetal Hiccups

"I sometimes feel regular little spasms in my abdomen. Is this kicking, or a twitch, or what?"

Believe it or not, your baby's probably got hiccups, a phenomenon not uncommon among fetuses during the last half of pregnancy. Some get hiccups several times a day, every day. Others never get them at all. The same pattern may continue after birth.

But before you start holding your breath or trying other hiccup tricks, you should know that hiccups don't cause the same discomfort in babies—in or out of the uterus—as they do in adults, even when they last 20 minutes or more. So just relax and enjoy this little entertainment from within.

Accidental Falls

"I missed the curb today when I was out walking and fell belly first on the pavement. Could the fall have hurt the baby?"

Is pregnancy tripping you up? That's not surprising—after all, once you enter the third trimester, there are plenty of factors that can combine to literally put you head over heels. For one, your impaired sense of balance, which has been thrown off-kilter as your center of gravity keeps shifting forward, along with your belly. For another, your looser, less stable joints, which add to awkwardness and make you prone to minor falls, especially those belly flops. Also contributing to clumsiness are your tendency to tire easily, your predisposition to preoccupation and daydreaming, and the difficulty you may be having seeing past your belly to your feet—all of which makes those curbs and other stumbling blocks easy to miss.

But while a curbside spill may leave you with multiple scrapes and bruises (particularly on your ego, if it was a public flop), it's extremely rare for a fetus to suffer the consequences of its mother's clumsiness. Your baby is protected by one of the world's most sophisticated shock absorption systems, comprised of amniotic fluid, tough membranes, the elastic, muscular uterus, and the sturdy abdominal cavity, which is girded with muscles and bones. For it to be penetrated, and for your baby to be hurt, you'd have to sustain very serious injuries, the kind that would very likely land you in the hospital.

If you're concerned, however, do call your practitioner for extra reassurance.

Orgasm and Baby's Kicking

"After I have an orgasm, my baby usually stops kicking for about half an hour. Does that mean that sex isn't safe at this point in pregnancy?"

No matter what you do these days, your baby's along for the ride. And when it comes to lovemaking, the ride can make baby very sleepy. The rocking motion of sex and the rhythmic uterine contractions that follow orgasm often lull fetuses to dreamland. Some babies, on the other hand (because every baby's an individual), become more lively after their parents make love. Either reaction is normal and healthy, and it is in no way a sign that sex isn't safe. Nor, in case you're wondering, is it a sign that baby's in the know about what's going on between those sheets (baby's completely in the dark, literally).

In fact, unless your practitioner has prescribed otherwise, you can continue enjoying lovemaking—and orgasms—until delivery. And you might as well get that sex in while you can. Let's face it—it may be a while before it's this convenient to make love with your baby in the house again.

Dreams and Fantasies

"I've been having so many vivid dreams—day and night—about the baby that I'm beginning to think I'm losing my mind."

Been catching some pretty strange late shows along with your z's? Dreams—and daydreams and fantasies—from the horrifying (like the one about leaving the baby on the bus) to the heartwarming (snuggling chubby cheeks, pushing strollers through a sunny park), to the bizarre (giving birth to an alien baby with a tail or to a litter of puppies) are healthy, normal, and very, very common during pregnancy. And though they may make you feel as though you're losing your mind (was that really a giant salami that chased you around the parking lot of Babies "R" Us last night?), they're actually helping you stay sane. They're just one way that your subconscious works through your mind's overload of pre-baby anxieties, fears, hopes, and insecurities and comes to terms with the impending upheaval in your life—an outlet for the 1,001 conflicting emotions (from ambivalence to trepidation to overwhelming excitement and joy) you're feeling but may be uneasy expressing any other way. Think of it as therapy you can sleep through.

Hormones contribute, also, to your heavier-than-usual dream schedule (what don't they contribute to?). Plus, they can make your dreams much more vivid. The lighter sleep you've been getting also plays a part in your ability to recall your dreams—and recall them in high definition. Because you're waking up more often than you used to, whether to use the bathroom, kick off some blankets, or just toss, turn, and try to get comfortable, you have more opportunities to wake up in the middle of a REM dream cycle. With the dreams so fresh in your mind each time you awaken, you're able to remember them in greater—and sometimes unnerving—detail.

Here are some of the most commonly reported dream and fantasy themes during pregnancy. Some probably sound familiar.

- Oops! dreams. Dreaming about losing or misplacing things (from your car

Preparing Fido and Whiskers

Already a parent—to the kind of baby that has four legs, fur, and a tail? Concerned that your pet, who's used to ruling the roost (and curling up on your bed and your lap), will suffer from a bad (and possibly dangerous) case of sibling rivalry when you show up with a new baby? Taking steps now to prepare your dog or cat for when baby makes three (people, that is) is crucial. See *What to Expect the First Year* for tips and recommendations on preparing the family pet for baby's arrival.

keys to your baby); forgetting to feed the baby; missing a doctor's appointment; going out to shop and leaving baby home alone; being unprepared for the baby when he or she arrives can reveal the common fear that you're not up to being a mother.

- Ouch! dreams. Being attacked or hurt—by intruders, burglars, animals; or falling down the stairs after a push or a slip—may represent a sense of vulnerability.

- Help! dreams. Dreams of being enclosed or unable to escape—trapped in a tunnel, a car, a small room; drowning in a pool, a lake of snowy slush, a car wash—can signify the fear of being tied down by the expected new family member, of losing your once carefree life to a demanding newborn.

- Oh no! dreams. Dreams of gaining no weight or gaining a lot of weight overnight; overeating; eating or drinking the wrong things (a tray of sushi washed down with a pitcher of marti-

nis)—are common among those trying to stick to a dietary regimen.

- Ugh! dreams. Dreaming about becoming unattractive or repulsive to your spouse or about your spouse taking up with someone else—expresses the common fear that pregnancy will destroy your looks forever and make you unappealing to your partner.

- Sexual dreams. Dreams about sexual encounters—either positive or negative, pleasure or guilt provoking—may reflect the sexual confusion and ambivalence often experienced during pregnancy.

- Memory dreams. Dreaming of death and resurrection—lost parents or other relatives reappearing—may be the subconscious mind's way of linking old and new generations.

- Life with baby dreams. Dreaming about getting ready for the baby and loving and playing with the baby in a dream is practice parenting, a way that your subconscious bonds you with your baby before delivery.

- Imagining baby dreams. Dreaming about what your baby will be like can reveal a wide variety of concerns. Dreams about the baby being deformed, sick, or too large or too small express anxiety about its health. Fantasies about the infant having unusual skills (like talking or walking at birth) may indicate concern about the baby's intelligence and ambition for his or her future. Premonitions that the baby will be a boy or a girl could mean your heart's set on one or the other. So could dreams about the baby's hair or eye color or resemblance to one parent or the other. Nightmares of the baby being born fully grown could signify your fear of having to handle a tiny infant.

THE SEVENTH MONTH

293

- Labor dreams. Dreaming about labor pain—or lack of it—or about not being able to push the baby out may reflect your anxieties about labor.

Bottom line about your dreams and fantasies—don't lose any sleep over them. They're completely normal and as common among expectant moms as heartburn and stretch marks (just ask around and you'll get an interesting earful). Keep in mind, too, that you may not be the only one in your bed who's dreaming up a sometimes unsettling storm. Expectant dads may also have strange dreams and fantasies as they attempt to work out their conscious and subconscious anxieties about impending fatherhood (and it's not as easy for them to blame it on the hormones). Swapping dreams in the morning can be fun (can you top this one?) as well as therapeutic, making that transition into real-life parenthood easier—plus it can help bring you closer together. So dream on!

Handling It All

"I'm beginning to worry that I won't be able to manage my job, my house, my marriage—and the baby, too."

Here's the first thing you should know about doing it all: You can't do it all, do it all well, do it all well at the same time, and do it all well all the time. Every mom's super, but even the best among us are only human. Many new mothers have tried to don the cape—handling a full workload on the job; keeping the house spotless, the laundry basket empty, the refrigerator stocked, and home-cooked meals on the table; being a doting (read: sexy) partner and an exemplary parent; and leaping the occasional building at a single bound—but most have realized somewhere in midflight that something's gotta give.

Just how well you'll manage your new life will probably depend on how quickly you come to that realization. And there's no better time than now—before your latest (and cutest) life challenge arrives—to start.

First, you'll need to give some thought to what your priorities are so you can begin arranging them in order of importance (and not everything can make that top spot). If baby, spouse, and job are priorities, perhaps keeping the house clean will have to take a (messy) backseat. Maybe home-cooked will give way to home-delivered, at least some of the time, or the laundry basket will become someone else's responsibility. If you're thinking that full-time motherhood might have your name on it, and you can afford to stay home for a while, maybe you can put your career on hold temporarily. Or you might consider working part-time or job sharing with another mom, if you can swing it, or working from home, if possible.

Once you've settled on your priorities, you'll need to let go of your unrealistic expectations (you know, the ones your daydreams are filled with). Check in with experienced moms, and you'll get a reality check fast. As every mother finds out sooner or later—and you'll save yourself a lot of stress if you find out sooner—nobody's perfect. As much as you'll want to do everything right, you won't be able to—and there will be those days when it seems like you can't do anything right. Despite your best efforts, beds may go unmade and laundry unfolded, take-out may take over your dinner table, and getting "sexy" may mean finally getting around to washing your hair. Set your standards too high—even if you were able to meet them in your prepaenting days—and you'll set yourself up for a whole lot of unnecessary disappointment.

However you decide to rearrange your life, it will be easier if you don't have to go it alone. Beside most successful moms is a dad who not only shares equally in household chores but also is a full partner in parenting, in every department from diapering to bathing to cuddling. If dad's not available as much as you'd like (or isn't in the picture at all), then you are going to need to consider other sources of assistance: baby's grandparents or other relatives, child care or household help, baby-sitting co-ops, or child-care centers.

A Birth Plan

"A friend who recently delivered said she worked out a birth plan with her doctor before delivery. Should I?"

Decisions, decisions. Childbirth involves more decisions than ever

Some Cookies with That Birth Plan?

Once you've passed your approved birth plan on to your practitioner, it should become part of your chart and find its way to your delivery. But just in case it doesn't make it in time, you might want to print up several copies of the plan to bring along to the hospital or birthing center, just so there's no confusion about your preferences. Your coach or doula can make sure that each new shift (with any luck, you won't have to labor through too many of these) has a copy for reference. Some expectant parents have found that placing the birth plan in a small basket of goodies makes it even more welcome.

before, and expectant women and their partners are involved in making more of those decisions than ever before. But how can you and your practitioner keep track of all those decisions—from how you'll manage the pain to who'll catch your emerging baby? Enter the birth plan.

A birth plan is just that—a plan (or more aptly, a wish list). In it, pregnant women and their partners can offer up their best-case birthing scenario: how they'd ideally like labor and delivery to play out if all goes according to "plan." Besides listing those parental preferences, the typical birth plan factors in what's practical, what's feasible, and what the practitioner and hospital or birthing center find acceptable (not everything on a birth plan may fly medically, obstetrically, or policywise). It isn't a contract but a written understanding between a patient and her practitioner and/or hospital or birthing center. Not only can a good birth plan deliver a better birth experience, it can head off unrealistic expectations, minimize disappointment, and eliminate major conflict and miscommunication between a birthing woman and her birth attendants. Some practitioners routinely ask an expectant couple to fill out a birth plan; others are happy to oblige if one is requested. A birth plan is also a springboard for dialogue between patient and practitioner.

Some birth plans cover just the basics; others are extremely detailed (down to the birthing room music and lighting). And because every expectant woman is different—not only in what she'd like out of the birth experience but what she can likely expect, given her particular medical and obstetrical background—a birth plan should be individualized (so don't fill yours out based on your friend's). Some of the issues you may want to tackle in your

Your Main Squeeze

Your baby might not be ready for delivery yet, but it isn't too soon to start getting your body—and your pelvic floor muscles, in particular—geared up for the big day. Never thought much about your pelvic muscles—or maybe never even realized you had any? It's time to start paying attention. They're the muscles that support your uterus, bladder, and bowels, and they're designed to stretch so your baby can come out. They're also the muscles that keep your urine from leaking when you cough or laugh (a skill set you're only likely to appreciate when it's gone, as can happen with postpartum incontinence). These multitalented muscles can also make for a much more satisfying sexual experience.

Luckily, there are exercises that can easily work these miracle muscles, whipping them into shape with minimal time and minimal effort (no workout clothes necessary, no visit to a gym required, and you don't even have to break a sweat). Just 5 minutes of these amazing exercises, called Kegels, three times a day and you'll tone your way to a long list of both short- and long-term benefits. Toned pelvic floor muscles can ease a host of pregnancy and postpartum symptoms from hemorrhoids to urinary and fecal incontinence. They can help you prevent an episiotomy or even a tear during delivery. Plus doing your Kegels faithfully during pregnancy will help your vagina snap back more gracefully after your baby's grand exit.

Ready to Kegel? Here's how: Tense the muscles around your vagina and anus and hold (as you would if you were trying to stop the flow of urine), working up to 10 seconds. Slowly release and repeat; shoot for three sets of 20 daily. Keep in mind when you Kegel that all your focus should be on those pelvic muscles—and not any others. If you feel your stomach tensing or your thighs or buttocks contracting, your pelvics aren't getting their full workout. Make this exercise your main squeeze during pregnancy (doing them each time you stop at a traffic light, while you check your e-mail, in line at the ATM, while waiting for the cashier to ring up your groceries, or while working at your desk), and you'll reap the benefits of stronger pelvic floor muscles. Try doing them during sex, too—both you and your partner will feel the difference (now that's a workout you can get excited about!).

birth plan, should you decide to fill one out, are listed below. You can use it as a general guideline, then flesh it out as needed (you can refer to the appropriate pages before making your decisions). For a more detailed list and sample birth plan, see the *What to Expect Pregnancy Journal and Organizer.*

- How far into your labor you would like to remain at home and at what point you would prefer to go to the hospital or birthing center

- Eating and/or drinking during active labor (page 369)

- Being out of bed (walking around or sitting up) during labor

- Personalizing the atmosphere with music, lighting, items from home

- The use of a still camera or video camera

- The use of a mirror so you can see the birth

- The use of an IV (intravenous fluid administration; page 372)

- The use of pain medication and the type of pain medication (page 301)

- External fetal monitoring (continuous or intermittent); internal fetal monitoring (page 372)

- The use of oxytocin to induce or augment contractions (page 368)

- Delivery positions (page 376)

- Use of warm compresses and perineal massage (pages 352 and 375)

- Episiotomy (page 374)

- Vacuum extractor or forceps use (page 375)

- Cesarean delivery (page 398)

- The presence of significant others (besides your spouse) during labor and/or at delivery

- The presence of older children at delivery or immediately after

- Suctioning of the newborn; suctioning by the father

- Holding the baby immediately after birth; breastfeeding immediately

- Postponing cutting the cord, weighing the baby, and/or administering eye drops until after you and your baby greet each other

- Having the father help with the delivery and/or cut the cord

- Cord blood banking (page 330)

You may also want to include some postpartum items on your birth plan, such as:

- Your presence at the weighing of the baby, the pediatric exam, and baby's first bath

- Baby feeding in the hospital (whether it will be controlled by the nursery's schedule or your baby's hunger; whether supplementary bottles and pacifiers can be avoided if you're breastfeeding)

- Circumcision (see *What to Expect the First Year*)

- Rooming-in (page 431)

- Other children visiting with you and/or with the new baby

- Postpartum medication or treatments for you or your baby

- The length of the hospital stay, barring complications (page 430)

Of course, the most important feature of a good birth plan is flexibility. Since childbirth—like most forces of nature—is unpredictable, the best-laid plans don't always go, well, according to plan. Though chances are very good that your plan can be carried out just the way you drew it up, there's always the chance that it won't. There is no way to predict precisely how labor and delivery will progress (or not progress) until those contractions start coming, so a birth plan you design in advance may not end up being obstetrically or

Don't Hold It In

Making a habit of not urinating when you feel the need increases the risk that your inflamed bladder may irritate the uterus and set off contractions. Not going when you've got the urge could also lead to a UTI, another cause of preterm contractions. So don't hold it in. When you gotta go, go . . . promptly.

Lifesaving Screenings for Newborns

Most babies are born healthy and stay that way. But a very small percentage of infants are born apparently healthy and then suddenly sicken. Luckily, there are ways to screen for such metabolic disorders. Most babies born in the U.S. live in states that require screening for at least 21 life-threatening disorders—and there is an effort under way to push all 50 states to screen for 29 universally recommended diseases. These include phenylketonuria (PKU), congenital hypothyroidism, congenital adrenal hyperplasia, biotinidase deficiency, maple syrup urine disease, galactosemia, homocystinuria, and sickle cell anemia.

If your state doesn't offer at least the core group of these tests, you can request that a private lab arrange testing. The lab will use blood that's collected in the hospital during your baby's routine heel stick (when drops of blood are drawn from

baby's heel after a quick stick with a needle).

In the very unlikely event your baby screens positive for any of the disorders, your baby's pediatrician and a genetic specialist can verify the results and begin treatment, if necessary (there is a high rate of false positives, so any positive result should be followed up by retesting). Early diagnosis and intervention can make a tremendous difference in the prognosis. For more information on private lab screening and newborn screening in general, contact Baylor University Medical Center: (800) 4BAYLOR (422-9567); baylorhealth.com/medicalspecialties/ metabolic/newbornscreening.htm; or Pediatrix Screening: (954) 384-0175; pediatrixscreening.com.

To find out if your state screens for the 29 conditions that the March of Dimes recommends, go to genes-r-us .uthscsa.edu/.

---

medically wise, and it may have to be adjusted at the last minute. After all, there's no greater priority than your well-being and your baby's—and if your birth plan doesn't end up being consistent with that priority, it'll have to take a backseat. A change of mind (yours) can also prompt a change of plan (you were dead set against having an epidural, but somewhere around 4 cm, you become dead set on having one).

Bottom line: Birth plans, though by no means necessary (you can definitely decide to go with the flow when it comes to childbirth, and you'll give birth with or without one), are a great option, one that more and more expectant parents are taking advantage of. To find out more, and to figure out whether a birth

plan is right for you, talk it over with your practitioner at your next visit.

Glucose Screening Test

"My practitioner says I need to take a glucose screening test to check for gestational diabetes. Why would I need it, and what does the test involve?"

Don't feel too picked on. Almost all practitioners screen for gestational diabetes in almost all patients at about 24 to 28 weeks (though those at higher risk for gestational diabetes, including older or obese mothers or those with a family history of diabetes, are screened earlier in their pregnancies and more

Doulas: Best Medicine for Labor?

Think three's a crowd? For many couples, not when it comes to labor and delivery. More and more are opting to share their birth experience with a doula, a woman trained as a labor companion. And for good reason. Studies have shown that women supported by doulas are much less likely to require cesarean deliveries, induction, and pain relief. Births attended by doulas may also be shorter, with a lower rate of complications.

Doula is a term that comes from ancient Greece, where it was used to describe the most important female servant in the household, the one who probably helped mom out the most during childbirth. What exactly can a doula do for you and your birth experience? That depends on the doula you choose, at what point in your pregnancy you hire her, and what your preferences are. Some doulas become involved well before that first contraction strikes, helping with the design of a birth plan and easing prelabor jitters. Many, on request, come to the house to help a couple through early labor. Once at the hospital or birthing center, the doula takes on a variety of responsibilities, again depending on your needs and wishes. Typically, her primary role is as a continuous source of comfort, encouragement, and support (both emotional and physical) during labor. She'll serve as a soothing voice of experience (especially valuable if you're first-timers), help with relaxation techniques and breathing exercises, offer advice on labor positions, and do her share of massage, hand holding, pillow plumping, and bed adjusting. A doula can also act as a mediator and an advocate, ready to speak for you as needed, to translate medical terms and explain procedures, and to generally run interference with hospital personnel. She won't take the place of your coach (and a good doula won't make him feel like she's taking his place, either) or the nurse on duty; instead, she will augment their support and services (especially important if the nurse assigned to you has several other patients in labor at the same time or if labor is long and nurses come and go as shifts change). She will also likely be the only person (besides the coach)

often). So chances are the test your practitioner ordered is just routine.

And it's simple, too, especially if you have a sweet tooth. You'll be asked to drink a very sweet glucose drink, which usually tastes like flat orange soda, one hour before having some blood drawn; you don't have to be fasting when you do this. Most women chugalug the stuff with no problem and no side effects; a few, especially those who don't have a taste for sweet liquids, feel a little queasy afterward.

If the blood work comes back with elevated numbers, which suggests the possibility that you might not be producing enough insulin to process the extra glucose in your system, the next level of test—the glucose tolerance test—is ordered. This fasting three-hour test, which involves a higher-concentration glucose drink, is used to diagnose gestational diabetes.

Gestational diabetes occurs in about 4 to 7 percent of expectant mothers, which makes it one of the most common pregnancy complications. Fortunately, it's also one of the most easily managed. When blood sugar is closely controlled through diet, exercise, and, if necessary,